A HISTORY OF EUROPE
H.G.Koenigsberger & Asa Briggs

Medieval Europe 400–1500   H. G. **Koenigsberger**

Early Modern Europe 1500–1789   H. G. **Koenigsberger**

Modern Europe 1789–1980   Asa **Briggs**

Frontispiece (overleaf) Durham Cathedral.
Built mainly between 1093 and 1130, the cathedral is one of the largest
medieval buildings in Europe, 400 ft (c. 120 m) in length. Since the
vast majority of people at the time lived in small cottages, the visual
and psychological impact of buildings such as this must have been
even greater than it is now. Durham was certainly meant to represent
the might and magnificence of the new Norman monarchy and its
Church in the north of England. (For a view of the interior see Plate
3.9.)

A HISTORY OF EUROPE
H.G. Koenigsberger & Asa Briggs

MEDIEVAL EUROPE 400-1500

H.G. KOENIGSBERGER

Longman

Longman Group Limited
Longman House, Burnt Mill, Harlow
Essex CM20 2JE, England
and Associated Companies throughout the world

*Published in the United States of America
by Longman Inc., New York*

First published 1987
Seventh impression 1994

British Library Cataloguing in Publication Data
Koenigsberger, H. G.
  Medieval Europe 400–1500. — (History of Europe)
  1. Europe — History — 476-1492
  I. Title   II. Series
  940.1   D117

ISBN 0-582-49403-6 PPR

Library of Congress Cataloging-in-Publication Data
Koenigsberger, H. G. (Helmut Georg)
  Medieval Europe, 400–1500.
  (History of Europe)
  Includes index.
  1. Europe — History — 476–1492. 2. Middle Ages —
History. I. Title II. Series: Koenigsberger, H. G.
(Helmut Georg). History of Europe.
D117.K62 1986   940.1   87-6459

ISBN 0-582-49403-6

Set in Linotron 202 10/12pt Palatino
Produced by Longman Singapore Publishers Pte Ltd
Printed in Singapore

Contents

List of maps

List of plates

Acknowledgements

We would like to thank Professor Theodore K. Rabb for having, in a somewhat different context, first proposed that we write this *History* and for his continued encouragement of this enterprise. We would also like to thank Professor Averil Cameron, Dr Dorothy Koenigsberger and Dr Janet Nelson for having read drafts of individual chapters and made valuable suggestions.

For their specific permission to reproduce plates in the text, we are grateful to the following: Ashmolean Museum, Oxford (5.4); Bibliothèque Nationale, Paris (5.8); BBC Hulton Picture Library (5.3); The British Library (2.9, 5.5); John R. Freeman and Co. (Photographers) Ltd (3.3a & b, 4.8); V. Gipenreiter (3.5); Sonia Halliday Photographs (1.6); Robert Harding Picture Library Ltd (1.4); Hirmer Verlag München (2.5); A. F. Kersting (frontispiece, 2.3, 3.2, 3.9); Dr J. Kollmann (5.6); Lauros-Giraudon (2.2, 3.4, 3.8, 4.7, 5.1); MAS, Barcelona (2.7, 3.7, 4.6); Middle East Photographic Archive Ltd (2.6); C. Osborne (2.6); The Pierpont Morgan Library (2.1); J. Powell, Rome (1.2); Ronald Sheridan's Photo-Library (1.3); Scala/Firenze (1.1, 3.1, 3.10, 4.2, 4.3, 4.5, 6.1, 6.2, 6.3, 6.4, 6.5, 6.6, 6.9); University Museum of National Antiquities, Oslo, Norway (2.4); and the Württembergische Landesbibliothek, Stuttgart (5.7). We have unsuccessfully attempted to trace the copyright owners of plates 1.5, 2.8, 3.6, 4.1, 4.4, 5.2, 6.7 and 6.8 and would appreciate any information that would enable us to do so.

To Dorothy

Introduction

The beginnings of European history

European history began in the fifth century with the collapse of the western half of the Roman Empire under the attacks of the 'barbarian' Germanic tribes. In the succeeding one thousand six hundred years the fragments left by this catastrophic event expanded into a new cultural entity which covered the whole European continent, established itself in the American and Australian continents and, in one form or another, came to dominate the rest of the world.

The basic problem

It seems to be a fundamental characteristic of organized human societies that the stronger will tend to dominate and exploit the weaker, and that the strongest will try to establish empires as large as geographical and human circumstances will allow. The old, meta-historical beliefs of Christian theologians in a succession of empires therefore had a basis in human experience, even if we are now disinclined to accept the orderliness and providential nature which the theologians ascribed to this succession. The basic problem of the history of Europe is therefore not, why the Europeans should have wished to dominate other people, but why, how, and under what circumstances the Europeans developed the qualities and abilities: firstly, to defend themselves successfully, for over a thousand years, from the attacks of their powerful and often more highly organized neighbours; secondly, to impose their rule and much of their value system on non-

European societies; and thirdly, how far this process has actually succeeded or been reversed, and what problems have arisen for our contemporary world in the process.

To answer these questions it is not necessary to postulate an overall law of historical development, which we do not think exists. Nor do we propose to pass judgement on the sixteen hundred years of European history or on the Europeans as a human group compared with others. We will try, however, to show the existence of certain regularities in the development of human societies and we are quite willing to pass value judgements on specific European cultural achievements and moral judgements on the actions of individuals and groups. To do this we shall use criteria which are necessarily derived from the European cultural experience.

Europe, its neighbours and the rest of the world

Clearly, the history of Europe is comprehensible only if it is constantly seen in its relation to Europe's neighbours. For over a thousand years, after the end of the Roman Empire in the west, Europe was on the defensive: against the Muslim Arabs along its Mediterranean frontier in the south, against the seafaring Norsemen from Scandinavia in the north and west, and against successive attacks of different Asiatic peoples in the east, from the Huns, in the fifth century, to the Avars, Magyars, Mongols and, eventually and most persistently, the Turks. In spite of great losses, the defence of the core of Latin Europe held. The Huns and Avars were defeated and absorbed. The Vikings and Magyars were christianized and assimilated. But of the two major efforts of the Middle Ages to reconquer territory lost to the Muslims only one succeeded, the reconquest of the Iberian peninsula (Spain and Portugal) and the reconquest of the large Mediterranean island of Sicily. The other attempt, the crusades which were meant to reconquer Jerusalem and establish Christian states on the shores of the eastern Mediterranean, ended in failure. This failure was the more disastrous for Christian Europe because the Latin Christians, in one of their crusades, dealt a mortal blow to the surviving part of the old Roman Empire by conquering Constantinople (Byzantium). With this previously most effective barrier against Islam on Europe's south-eastern flank broken, the Ottoman Turks were able to sweep through Asia Minor, conquer

Constantinople for themselves and soon the whole Balkan peninsula. As late as 1683 Vienna had to fight for its life against a Turkish siege. Only in the course of the eighteenth, nineteenth and twentieth centuries did Christian Europe succeed in recovering most of the Balkans from the Turks, but not Constantinople and Asia Minor. By that time, the Christian aspect of the reconquest was no longer a major motive force, and Turkey itself was gradually becoming assimilated to Europe. Other divisions became more significant.

From the fifteenth century, however, and while still on the defensive against Islam in the Mediterranean and the Balkans, the Europeans successfully broke out of their besieged fortress-continent by sailing to America and around Africa to southern and eastern Asia. In the following four centuries they settled the American continent, discovered and settled Australia, conquered huge empires in India, Indochina and Indonesia, reconquered what remained of the Mongol empire in southern and eastern Russia, colonized the steppes of northern Asia (Siberia) from the Urals to the Pacific Ocean, and divided the whole of Africa between a handful of European states. Without actual conquest or settlement, they forced their trade on the Chinese Empire and persuaded the Japanese to open their country to western trade and technology.

The political definition of Europe

This unprecedentedly successful imperial expansion took place while Europe itself remained divided into mutually hostile states. The political division of Europe was the direct result of the erection of a number of tribally dominated Germanic successor states on the ruins of the western half of the Roman Empire in the fifth century. Several of these successor states disappeared again, and it took half a millennium before the political map of Europe became relatively stable and began to show some resemblance to Europe's modern political divisions. But the fact of political division has remained, and attempts to reverse it have always failed. Thus, as the Europeans carried their flags over the globe, they carried with them their own political enmities.

From a global point of view, these enmities were rather parochial; but up to the Second World War (1939–45) they still determined world politics. In the course of the twentieth century,

3

however, the centre of gravity of European global power has shifted outwards, from the European continent and its old imperial monarchies, Spain, France, Great Britain and Germany, to greater Russia (the U.S.S.R.) and to North America (the U.S.A.). These are bigger, more populous states, with greater natural resources, but still strongly influenced by Europe. From the middle of the twentieth century, the Europeans have had to abandon the direct political control of those parts of the world they had not actually settled. Strong Asian and African movements, which have accepted European technology and some, but not all, European ideologies and value systems, have since been attempting to break the European/American economic predominance and indirect political influence on their continents. There have been successes and failures.

European economic and social development

Like all settled agricultural societies, European society consisted originally of a great mass of peasants who produced food and of a small élite, with varied and advanced skills, who controlled most available property, especially land, and dominated the food producers. Economic advance, i.e. the production of more food and other goods and the raising of the standard of living of the whole population, or at least of some part of it, would depend on the acquisition of more resources, especially again of land, and on a greater and more efficient division of labour. Both methods were used in the course of European history. Since, in the long run, the supply of land was limited, the decisive motor for improvement was, as Adam Smith had clearly seen in the eighteenth century, the increasing division of labour. To understand the economic and social dynamism of Europe it is therefore necessary to study the history of the élites and of the professionalisation of the mass of the population. Technical and technological improvements and inventions were an important part of this dynamism. They were never absent, even in the Middle Ages. Gradually the number of inventions and innovations increased until they became self-generating in what came to be called an 'industrial revolution,' or rather in a series of 'industrial revolutions' which have transformed practically every aspect of our physical and social life and many of our most basic ways of thinking and feeling.

Cultural dynamism

It is unlikely that the European elite would have been as dynamically effective in economic life as it has been if its attitudes in other fields had not also been dynamic. Elites have existed in all highly organized civilizations. By definition, they were all effective within their own traditions. But not all have been equally dynamic. Here is the connection with the problem which we raised at the beginning of this Introduction: what made the Europeans behave in the way they did? what was this way? and what advantages did it give them over other societies? It is important to stress once more that the question is *not*: why was European civilization better than any other civilization? There is no way that such a better, or not so good, could be measured.

Educated Europeans during the Middle Ages, however, did think in just such terms, and many of them think in such terms now. In the Middle Ages they saw their own civilization as vastly inferior to a past civilization, that of the Greeks and Romans, and, they strained all their endeavours therefore, to recapture this golden age. They had a most powerful motivation for striving to attain always greater excellence in all cultural fields; for these were the fields in which most information about the ancients had survived, either in a directly visual form, in their monuments, or in a readable form, in their literature and laws. At certain times these endeavours to recapture the world of the ancients were more intense than at others. The intense periods were the 'renaissances' of European cultural life. They fitted in with the counterpoint, the mutual stimulus in a multicentred society, of regionalism and 'internationalism', a concept of a later period.

The multicentred nature of European civilisation was not only geographical and linguistic but also had an intellectual and emotional dimension. The division of Church and state produced a clash of claims and a division of loyalties. Both proved to be creative and stimulating, although also highly uncomfortable, for those caught up in them. Who had the greater claims on men's loyalties, the spiritual or the secular power? No outright victory, no annihilation of one power by the other was desired or even conceivable in the Middle Ages. Both powers were therefore driven to justify their claims rationally. Rational thinking is valued in all highly organized societies. But here was a stimulus to rational argument which did not exist in other societies. Inevitably, it came to colour all forms of creative thinking.

In the early modern period the dualism between Church and state was gradually transformed into an even more fundamental dualism, between religious and secular ways of thinking. This dualism, too, proved to be enormously dynamic; for it allowed music, art, the natural sciences, and political ideas to emancipate themselves from their medieval positions as 'handmaidens of theology' and to stake claims for a more and more absolute rational and emotional commitment of their practitioners.

The consequences for European society were enormous and help to explain both its continued dynamism and the feelings of mingled admiration and repulsion with which European values have been regarded by non-European societies. This is shown most dramatically in the development of political thought. Like all other aspects of human life, people in the Middle Ages had seen political thought as a part of moral and religious thought. From the time of Machiavelli onwards, at the beginning of the sixteenth century, purely rational and secular arguments began to push moral and religious arguments more and more into the background. But for a long time this was still a matter largely for princes, their advisers and philosophers. From the latter part of the eighteenth century, however, and especially with the writings of Rousseau, political thought began to acquire a secular and popular spirituality by arousing secular emotions which were as strong as religious emotions had been. Here was the source of political ideology. From the French Revolution to our own time, ideology has proved to be a most powerful, and again a very dynamic, element, not only in European but also in world history. For the most powerful ideologies have shown themselves to be almost infinitely flexible and adaptable to local traditions and, in some modern societies, they have shown a startling ability to fuse with more conventional religious emotions – a development which would not have surprised our medieval ancestors. Ideologies have also manifested themselves in a range of new institutions, including the political party.

The limits of rationalism

While rationalism, the systematic application of reason to the analysis and solution of human problems, has proved a most creative element in the European tradition, history has also shown its limitations. As the Greek dramatist Euripides (*c.* 484–406 BC) showed in his play *The Bacchae*, human beings who ignore the irrational, emotional side of their nature will produce tragedy, for themselves and for others. From the second half of the eighteenth century, the Romantic movement in European culture sought to use non-rational and deeply emotive forces in order to create new artistic, literary and musical expression. The Romantics painted, wrote or composed many of the most splendid works of the European genius. In politics, too, their aims were essentially humane. But the Romantic attack on rationalism also brought many of the darker human emotions to the surface: tribalism and sectional loyalties, intolerance and the exultation of violence. These emotions have never been far below the surface of European or any other human society. In a quite fundamental way the history of all societies has always been the story of the attempts by human beings to find a workable balance between reason, tradition and emotions. It is still our problem.

Present trends and prospects

Many historians of Europe have been interested since the eighteenth century in predicting future trends and prospects, some in hope, others in fear. There have been general theories both of progress and of decline, but there have also been more modest empirical studies involving limited projections, particularly during the last twenty-five years. Present themes which lend themselves to various kinds of prediction include demography, a perennial theme; the role of immigrant populations, among them immigrants from very different cultures; unemployment, not least youth unemployment, which has increased dramatically since the early 1970s; the structure and dynamics of industry, once the foundation of Europe's prosperity; agriculture, still the key to the budgets of the European Economic Community; and changing patterns of work and leisure, influenced by social aspirations as well as by technological changes.

In the light of the development of the European Economic Community, based originally on a Treaty, the Treaty of Rome, signed in Europe's oldest capital, an increasing number of historians are seeking to rewirte the more recent history of Europe in European rather than in national terms. Since 1989 this has become even more urgent; for the communist regimes of eastern Europe have collapsed or, as in the Soviet Union, have been fundamentally modified. The two parts of Germany have been united and most of the states of Europe west of the Soviet Union are now aspiring to join the renamed European Community. At the time of writing this passage, in 1991, the movement towards some form of European unity is certainly strong. At the same time, problems of nationality, localism and ethnicity remain powerful, putting a question mark over the future of the political structure of Europe and over its relations with the Soviet Union and the United States of America.

A history of Europe, written in the 1980s, can have no ending. The last three decades have all had their own distinctive identity, the last dominated by economic issues. The relationship between what has happened in one country and in another still raises basic questions about the parts and the whole. These are volumes, therefore, which raise questions rather than supply answers, which open up history to debate rather than close the record. Few, if any, questions are finally answered. That has usually been one of the most prominent features in the study of European history.

Chapter 1

The End of the Ancient World and the Beginning of the Middle Ages, 400–700

The Roman Empire in AD 400

About the year 400 John, bishop of Constantinople, called Chrysostom or 'of the golden mouth' because of the eloquence of his preaching, looked with satisfaction on the world around him. 'Now these vast spaces the sun shines upon,' he wrote, 'from the Tigris to the Isles of Britain, the whole of Africa, Egypt and Palestine and whatever is subject to the Roman Empire lives in peace. You know the world is untroubled and of wars we hear only rumours.'

History has a way of making the prophecies of intelligent men look foolish. Indeed, many of St John Chrysostom's contemporaries, especially those living in the western part of the Roman Empire, did not share his optimism. Nevertheless, no one as yet foresaw the collapse of the whole of the western part of the Empire. Even now it remains at least doubtful whether by AD 400 this collapse had already become inevitable.

There was a number of perfectly good reasons for optimism. The terrible civil wars of the third century had been ended and effective government had been re-established by the emperors Diocletian and Constantine. The fourth century was a period of considerable economic vitality. The rapid growth of Constantinople shows this very clearly; for, unlike Rome which had grown as a centre of administration and hence economically mainly as a centre of consumption, the new capital on the Bosphorus developed also as a trading and manufacturing city. In order to assure the supply of labour after the great losses of population in the plagues of the third century, the emperors had issued laws

requiring sons to follow the occupations of their fathers, whether as civil servants, soldiers, craftsmen or peasants. Modern historians have often condemned these laws, but they were not universally effective and they did not altogether prevent social mobility. The army, in particular, was a ladder for the socially ambitious and even a peasant could rise in it to the highest ranks. One, Justin, became emperor.

Even more impressive than the economic recovery of the fourth century was the recovery of morale. Christianity, for centuries the religion of only small groups, had rapidly outclassed all its rivals. More and more of the literary, philosophical and artistic talents of the citizens of the Roman Empire were channelled into the service of Christianity and Christianity, in its turn, acted as a powerful challenge and stimulus to men's creative abilities. Constantinople became the essentially Christian capital of the Empire, without any of Rome's memories and traditions of a pagan past.

Christianity was an oriental, i.e. non-Graeco-Roman religion. There were other oriental traditions, too, dormant for centuries under the cloak of hellenistic civilization, which were beginning to re-assert themselves along the shores of the eastern Mediterranean. Most important of these was the belief in the divinity of the emperor whose subjects threw themselves on the ground before his statues and icons. For them Christian and Roman became synonymous terms. The monks and hermits and the holy men sitting on their pillars provided ordinary people with a link with the emperor; for the emperor would listen to the holy men's interventions and admonitions. This link provided a strong bond of loyalty for the subjects of the eastern part of the Roman Empire and it was one of its greatest strengths. But in the long run it turned out to be a very brittle loyalty when Egyptians and Syrians quarrelled with their emperor over the precise nature of their

Plate 1.1 Equestrian statue of the Roman Emperor Marcus Aurelius (AD 161–80), Capitol Hill, Rome.
The medieval mind was haunted and challenged by the visible survivals of the vanished might of Rome. This magnificent second-century statue was restored and placed on the Capitol by Michelangelo in the sixteenth century, but had been known for many years beforehand. Not until the time of Donatello, at the very end of our period, was a sculptor again able to attempt the formidable task of casting a large bronze equestrian statue (see Plate 6.5).

11

Christian beliefs. In 400, however, no one could know this.

The west was different. Here pagan traditions were still strong, and it was among the pagan senatorial class of Rome that traditional Roman ideology was revived. *Roma aeterna*, eternal Rome, the holy city, the centre and high point of all civilization – this was a constant theme in the literature of the time. Later, in a Christianized version, this theme was to dominate the literary, artistic, religious and even political sensibilities of western Europeans for more than a thousand years. More immediately, it played its part in the progressive Romanization of the western provinces of the Empire. The Celtic and Basque languages disappeared from most of Gaul and Spain, and eventually survived only in the remote mountain areas of the Pyrenees and Brittany. They were replaced by a low Latin which, as linguists tell us, was soon to develop the basic linguistic characteristics of medieval French and Spanish, just as was happening with Italian in Italy.

The calm at the end of the emperor Theodosius' reign and the uncontested succession of his two minor sons, Arcadius in the east and Honorius in the west (395) – this calm which had been the basis of St John Chrysostom's optimism – was deceptive. Many thoughtful men at the time were aware of impending crisis. The danger from the German barbarians in the north and from the Persians in the east had not passed away. So far they had always been defeated. But would this always be possible in the future?

The resources of the Roman Empire

The most fundamental and also the most urgent problem facing the Roman Empire was that of military defence. But successful military defence depended on the resources of the Empire, on the organization and, hence, effective use of these resources, and finally on the ability and the will of the Roman leadership and of the Roman people to use their resources. How much freedom of choice did they have?

The Roman Empire was a world of cities, Mediterranean ports or towns situated on rivers or estuaries close to the sea. They formed a vast free-trade area, linked by seafaring and by a stable and universally accepted gold coinage. In the cities was concentrated most of the visible wealth of the Empire, its splendid temples and theatres, its palaces, aqueducts and public baths, its market places and the forums with their triumphal arches and rows of Corinthian columns. The technology of the ancient world had reached highly advanced levels in certain fields, especially in building and civil engineering, but also in the manufacture of fine textiles and all sorts of metal implements, tools and weapons. These technical achievements, however, were in 400 already centuries old and there is no evidence that the Roman world was moving in the direction of further technological advance.

The reasons for this failure are neither obvious nor simple; but the very formulation of this problem in this form is modern. Educated Romans of the fifth century would not have thought of it as a failure. They were certainly not averse to the comforts which technology could give them, such as warm baths or central heating; but the concept of increasing wealth by technological inventions that would enhance or even replace human labour by the use of machines – such a concept did not and indeed could not yet exist. There is no evidence that educated Romans thought about such problems at all. Since they were educated they belonged to the class of *possessores*, the property owners, even if they were relatively poor. Life for them was reasonably comfortable within the existing state of technology and with the services provided by domestic slaves. Perhaps more important still, acceptable social and intellectual ambitions did not include technical investigations or the attainment of personal success through the use of technology. Men became lawyers or politicians and administrators. If they did not wish to pursue such practical careers there was the whole rich world of Greek and Latin literature to entertain them. The schools and universities taught these subjects, as well as philosophy and some theoretical science but, apart from medicine, little applied science and certainly no technology. The rise of Christianity accentuated this tendency, for now many of the most brilliant minds of the age became fascinated with theology. How firmly Roman intellectual traditions were set along these lines is shown by the history of Byzantium: for another millennium this brilliant, sophisticated and enormously vital society continued to live without major technological changes except in the art of war; and even there, the Byzantines took over most of their military inventions from their enemies.

In these circumstances, industrial (i.e. handicraft) production could provide only a relatively small part of the gross national

13

product, the effective wealth of the Empire. By far the larger part was, and could only be, supplied by agriculture. Through the experience of several millennia, Mediterranean farmers had learnt to use different types of soil to best advantage. Yields of wheat, of which alone we have a very few figures, do not of course compare well with the most advanced modern standards, but not badly with those of underdeveloped countries. But, just as in the case of manufactures, agricultural techniques in 400 had hardly changed since the days of the Roman Republic. The most modern agricultural handbook of the period, by Palladius, does little more than repeat the advice given by Pliny and other writers of the early Empire. Total output could therefore only be increased by extending the area under cultivation. But here, too, the limits had been reached. Some areas, such as Syria and North Africa, were indeed better cultivated than at any later time before the mid-twentieth century. But Mediterranean agricultural techniques were not easily adapted to the heavier soils and the colder and wetter climate of western and central Europe. In consequence, the provinces beyond the Alps remained sparsely settled and inefficiently cultivated. There seems to have been a serious lack of manpower. Little is known of the growth or decline of population during this period, but the third century had certainly experienced great losses, through war and epidemics, and it is at least doubtful whether these losses had been made fully good in the more peaceful fourth century.

The Romans were well aware of the importance of agriculture. The upper classes invested most of their wealth in land and drew the greater part of their income from it. Even the revenues of the cities and their officials were derived from land rather than from trade. The Christian churches lived on rents and offerings, usually the first fruits of the harvests. Most important of all, the state had come to rely for its revenues on taxes imposed on the country population, the surplus of the labour of millions of peasants beyond the needs of their own and their families' subsistence. Put into modern terms, the basic problem of the Roman Empire was that of the distribution of the relatively small surplus of a geographically huge but static economy. There were three sets of claims on this surplus, those of the upper classes for their private consumption, those of military defence, and those of the imperial courts and the civil service. All of them were increasing.

The *possessores*

The *possessores*, the property owners who lived on agricultural rents, contributed little to economic production. It is impossible to know how large this class was, and its size in relation to the total population was different in different provinces. But even if this class was relatively small, perhaps 10 per cent of the total population, its total numbers would still have been quite large. Among the *possessores* there was a quite small number of the very rich, the senatorial class. In the west they were probably even fewer and richer than in the east. Some families had huge estates scattered all over Italy, Africa and Spain. These rich families were not altogether without a social conscience. Those who still lived in the large cities competed with each other in spending money on bread and circuses for the poor. In this way Rome itself could still survive with a largely unproductive population of well over half a million.

But more and more rich men moved out of the slums and unhealthy cities into the country where they built themselves splendid and luxurious villas. Life could still be sweet here, even with the evil-smelling barbarians, as Sidonius Appolinaris characterized them, already at the gates. In his letters this cultured aristocrat has left us a vivid description of the life of the very rich in southern Gaul in the mid-fifth century:

> On the southwest side are the baths, hugging the base of a wooded cliff, and when along the ridge the branches of light wood are lopped, they slide almost of themselves in falling heaps into the mouth of the furnace. At this point there stands the hot bath, and this is of the same size as the anointing room which adjoins it, except that it has a semi-circular end with a roomy bathing-tub, in which part a supply of hot water meanders sobbingly through a labyrinth of leaden pipes that pierce the wall. Within the heated chamber there is full day and such an abundance of enclosed light as forces all modest persons to feel themselves something more than naked. . . . The inner face of the walls is content with the plain whiteness of polished concrete. Here no disgraceful tale is exposed by the nude beauty of painted figures, for though such a tale may be a glory to art it dishonours the artist.[1]

There were large work rooms and cool dining rooms with mosaic

15

Plate 1.2   The classical tradition of naturalism: farmer milking a goat. Mosaic from the Great Palace, Constantinople.
There was nothing unusual in having this humble, everyday scene depicted on the floor of a palace. The art of making mosaics, i.e. covering floors, walls or ceilings with tesserae – small pieces of coloured stone, tile, glass or some other hard material – was at least a thousand years old at the time and was very popular in Mediterranean villas.

floors and with splendid views on colonnades and gardens and a lakeside harbour.

A certain Christian prudery has evidently begun to affect the sensibilities of a Roman gentleman. Greek and Roman tradition, although not without some puritan streaks, had in general accepted the sexuality of men and women as natural. Christianity, developing Jewish and other oriental traditions, virtually equated sin with sexuality, anathematized homosexuality and disapproved of the naked male and female bodies. From the fourth century it became normal that at least bishops, though not yet the rest of the clergy, should be celibate. Monks and hermits in the eastern part of the Empire inveighed against the iniquities of baths and, by an apparently logical extension, also of washing and personal cleanliness. This latter attitude, at least, was not yet acceptable to Roman aristocrats, as Sidonius' description of his baths makes clear.

Late in life Sidonius became bishop of Clermont-Ferrand (470) and distinguished himself by organizing the defence of that city against the Visigoths. And yet, like many of his class, he urged co-operation between Romans and Goths. It was an attitude compounded both of a genuine conviction of the benefit to the public of such a course and of more narrow class interests. Sidonius judged correctly that the Roman aristocrats would be able to keep their social position and at least some of their estates if they co-operated with the barbarians. When the Empire failed as a shield against the barbarians the Roman aristocracy lost the will to support it further and, once lost, this will could never be recreated. Self-interest and the now developing new links of loyalty came to bind the landowning class to the regional political structures of the barbarian successor states. Only another successful conquest, such as the Romans had initially achieved during the great expansion of the Republic, could have reversed aristocratic loyalties once again. The history of Europe in the next fifteen hundred years is, at least in one of its most important aspects, the history of the attempts and failures to achieve just such a conquest.

An important part of the economically unproductive class of the *possessores* was the clergy. With the increasing Christianization of the population of the Empire, the number of the clergy and the wealth of the Christian churches also increased. Was this development a growing burden on the limited productive resources of the Empire? It seems at least likely, even though the Church redistributed some of its wealth in the form of alms.

The army

The sums swallowed up by the defence of the Empire had been increasing steadily for more than a century. Diocletian and his immediate successors had doubled the size of the army so that at the beginning of the fifth century it numbered about half a million men. Given the population of the Empire (possibly 50 million) and its very long and vulnerable frontiers, this was not an excessively large number. But to the pay and provisioning of the soldiers had to be added the military supplies from the elaborate system of government factories and the building and upkeep of the famous Roman roads, together with the horses and vehicles for all overland transport and the building of fortifications. Yet the greatest problem was to find enough recruits. The larger part of the army had to do garrison duty on the northern frontiers. That was not an inviting prospect for young men from the Mediterranean countries. At the same time it was not easy to recruit men locally at the frontiers; for it was precisely in these areas of the Empire that population was sparse and, in consequence, the great landowners of these parts were most unwilling to see their precious labour force recruited into the imperial legions.

Since the imperial government neither would nor could coerce the landowners, it fell back on the expedient of recruiting into the army the very barbarians against whom the Empire had to be defended. Historians have usually condemned this policy, but it is not easy to see what else the emperors could have done. In the nineteenth and twentieth centuries the French and the British trained considerable numbers of Africans and Indians for their colonial armies. They served loyally and it was not this policy which caused the dissolution of the French and British empires after the Second World War. The barbarians on the Roman frontiers were not a monolithic force. They were quite used to fighting each other and many were perfectly willing to fight for the emperor, especially as this often involved the attractive offer of pay in the form of land inside the Empire. As long as their numbers were not large and as long as they were settled in small groups dispersed over large areas, the barbarians would eventually be Romanized and absorbed. But these conditions were precisely what the emperors did not manage to maintain. By the beginning of the fifth century an alarmingly large part of the Roman army had come to consist of barbarian units and even the highest military offices were sometimes filled by barbarians. During the minority of Honorius (395–408), the effective control of the western half of the Empire was in the hands of a Romanized Vandal, Stilicho, who held the title of *magister militum*, or commander-in-chief.

Stilicho successfully defended Italy from two Gothic invasions. The Roman aristocracy, however, hated him and accused him of collusion with the invaders. True or not, the Roman troops

murdered Stilicho's officers and he himse
career shows the political and psychological
policy of employing barbarians in the defer
does not show, however, that it was necessa

The civil service and the social conseque.
Roman system of taxation

By modern standards, the Roman civil service ..as remarkably
small, probably not much more than 30,000 for the whole vast
Empire. This fact alone should warn us not to think of the later
Roman Empire in terms of a modern totalitarian state. Nevertheless, the civil service had greatly increased since the time of the
early Empire and this not only because the reforms of Diocletian
had extended government supervision over economic and social
life but also because the Roman bureaucracy, like every other
bureaucracy, had the tendency to extend its powers and create
new jobs even when they were not really needed. Even so, there
were not really enough civil servants to provide the citizens of
the Empire with an equitable administration, especially of taxes,
and their numbers in themselves were hardly an excessive burden
on the economy. They were, however, a great burden on the
finances of the imperial government which could not afford to
pay them reasonable salaries. The officials would make up for
their low pay by blackmailing the public which needed their
services, especially in the law courts. This was naturally much
resented. But by far the greatest burden on the common people
was that of imperial taxation.

Governments will always try to tax the greatest sources of
wealth within the state, and in the Roman Empire this was the
land and those who cultivated it. But governments do not
necessarily tax those best able to bear the burden. The imperial
civil servants fixed the amounts due from each district, but left
the detailed assessment to the local authorities. Even when there
was no collusion between the imperial and the local authorities,
and there often was, the tax burden was almost invariably shuf-
fled off onto the peasants, while the rich found innumerable legal
loopholes to escape it. The emperors knew quite well what was
happening and from time to time granted tax relief to certain
cities or provinces which had been devastated by war or suffered
some other disaster. But this relief did not always work out as

nded to. 'What else have the reliefs that were granted e cities achieved,' wrote Salvian, a priest of Marseilles, in middle of the fifth century, 'but to give immunity to the wealthy and burden the poor even more?'[2] From the latter part of the fourth century onwards taxation rose steeply. Such few actual figures as we have suggest that in Egypt the rate of taxation on average land was a third of the total crop. In Italy it was more than two-thirds.

Our literary evidence confirms the crushing burden of taxes on the country population. St John Chrysostom has left graphic descriptions of the exploitation and misery of the *humiliores*, the common people. Salvian's invectives against the tax collectors and landlords of Gaul have become famous: the only reason men oppressed by the tax collectors do not go over to the barbarians is that they would lose even 'the tiny remnants of their fortunes'. Hence 'they surrender themselves to rich men's hands and put themselves completely under their power and jurisdiction . . . they make over almost all their estates to their patrons before they can procure their favour; and so the children may lose their inheritance that fathers may gain protection'.

Salvian was a moralist with a strong social conscience. His picture may, at times, be overdrawn. But the process he describes was real enough. Large estates were sometimes still worked by slaves, especially in Italy. They did not work in gangs, as on the West Indian and American plantations in the eighteenth and nineteenth centuries. They were usually settled on plots of land from which they obtained their own subsistence and which they could pass on to their children, or else they acted as bailiffs or agents of the owners. (The vast majority of slaves in the later Roman Empire were domestic slaves. All citizens with any social pretensions at all would try to have at least one or two, somewhat as Victorian middle-class households would try to keep at least one housemaid. Rich men had hundreds of slaves.) In so far as they were not cultivated by slaves, most large estates were rented out in small parcels to cultivators who performed labour services, paid rents and, of course, taxes. What Salvian describes is the process by which free peasants made over the ownership of their small properties to a rich man, the patron, but continued to farm them for rent and services. They and their children thus effectively lost their freedom although they were not legally regarded as slaves. The patron, in return, would promise them protection from powerful and rapacious neighbours and, above all, from the worst extortions of the tax collectors.

Thus the great landowners made the inhabitants of whole areas dependent. They acquired and enforced rights over local markets. They employed potters, smiths, weavers, bakers and other craftsmen in order, as the agricultural writer Palladius innocently said, to save the peasants the bother of going to town. The great estates, therefore, tended to become self-contained economic units and, at the same time, their owners were effectively interposing themselves between the state and a large section of its subjects. Here, as has rightly been remarked, was one of the prototypes of the later development of feudalism. What was still missing was the later military aspect and the rather specific feudal relationship of personal loyalty.

The problem of loyalty in the Roman Empire was complex and we know little about it. But it is significant that in the fifth century the peasants in large areas of Gaul and Spain rebelled against both their Roman and Gothic landlords. For these peasants, as Salvian tells us, 'being pillaged, distressed and murdered by cruel and unjust judges after they had lost the privilege of Roman liberty', had evidently also lost all feelings of loyalty, whether to the Empire or to their local lords. In all, the common people of the Roman Empire, while appreciating the *pax romana*, the peace which the Empire claimed to bestow but so often failed to maintain, seem to have felt little sense of loyalty to its institutions and were rarely prepared, nor often encouraged by their social superiors, to fight in the Empire's defence.

Theories of the fall of the Roman Empire in the west

By the beginning of the fifth century the Roman Empire was clearly living beyond its resources. the increasing demands of the army and the civil service, the increasing number of unproductive and privileged groups, from the senators with their hordes of personal slaves to the clergy and the monks, the need to feed large and economically parasitical cities – all this put a growing burden on the limited productive capacity of the Empire. This in turn accounts for the social stresses of the time, the depression of a free peasantry into servile status and the social rebellions of

21

men driven beyond the limits of endurance. All this undoubtedly weakened the capacity of the Empire to defend itself against outside attack. But is it sufficient to account for the fall of the Roman Empire in the west?

It does not seem so. Most of the problems we have just described affected the eastern part of the Empire as much as the western, or almost as much. Yet the eastern part of the Empire did not collapse. It is essential to hang on to this indisputable fact. The great landed estates were perhaps not quite as vast in the east as in the west; there were probably more free peasants in the east; there were also more old-established cities with old civic traditions and with urban 'middle classes' who showed greater economic vitality than those of the west. But the extent of these differences is not fully agreed on by historians and it seems doubtful whether, by themselves, they can explain the different histories of the eastern and western parts of the Roman empire. On the contrary, the experience of the east would suggest that, at the beginning of the fifth century, the Empire was facing a severe economic, social and military crisis, but that it was by no means doomed.

All the other single causes which have been advanced to explain the fall of the Roman Empire are inadequate for the same reasons. There have been many of these theories. There are the moral ones, that contrast the supposed decadence of the Romans with the supposedly untainted virility of the German barbarians. In the converse of this theory it is argued that Christianity weakened the ancient Roman virtues and was thus responsible for the fall. The notion that Roman decadence was the result of the mixing of races belongs to the same category of moral reasons and also to that of pseudo-scientific ones. In this latter category must be classed the theory of the inevitable spread of epidemics through a politically and economically unified Mediterranean basin and also the rather different argument of a change in climate which supposedly ruined Mediterranean agriculture.

All these theories are either improbable or largely speculative, quite apart from their tainted origins in narrowly Christian, anti-Christian, or national and racial preconceptions. But, most important, they all apply to the whole Roman Empire and therefore cannot explain why it was only the western half that fell. This catastrophe can only be explained by looking at actual events, as well as at underlying causes. These events were precipitated by the peoples outside the Empire.

The German barbarians

The Romans knew the German barbarians well. (The term barbarian is here used in the technical sense in which it was used at the time, meaning outsiders or foreigners; it did, however, also have its modern connotation of uncivilized.) They had been their northern neighbours for more than five hundred years. At times they had tried to break into the Empire and some of these invasions had been serious affairs; but every time the frontiers had eventually been restored. More often, and for long periods of time, they had lived peacefully enough or had indulged their love of fighting by turning on each other. For the Romans such inter-tribal fighting had the further advantage of providing the Empire with a much-prized commodity, slaves. Nevertheless, no Roman general or provincial governor could ever forget that the Germans were always dangerous neighbours.

Most of the German tribes had long since ceased to be nomads. They farmed land, however primitively, and traded with the Romans across the frontier. The Visigoths who lived north of the lower Danube and about whom we are better informed than about most of the other German tribes, were no longer the classless society of free and equal warriors described by Tacitus in the first century. The Visigoths had a class whom the Romans called *optimates*, rich men who held effective political power, even though they had not yet developed an elaborate state machinery. Family, clan and tribe still provided the basic social and political organization. Only very few were literate. The Gothic monk Ulfilas (died *c.* 381) who translated the bible into Gothic had effectively to invent his alphabet. Before that, the Germans had used runes, a script of which the letters were derived from the Greek and Etruscan alphabets. Runes were used mainly for the writing of magical formulas. Christianity had made little progress among the Germans. Only few individuals had been converted and, as yet, none of the big tribes outside the frontiers of the Empire.

The relatively balanced situation between the Roman Empire and the German tribes was suddenly upset in 376. In that year the Huns destroyed the Ostrogothic kingdom in southern Russia. The Huns were a nomadic people who had recently emerged from the Asian steppe. Their previous history and wanderings and the reasons for their westward march are still obscure. As true nomads, driving their cattle and sheep and living in primitive wagons or tents, they left no writings or inscriptions for the historian and no artefacts for the archaeologist. Their standard of living was desperately low; but they were superb horsemen and ferocious fighters, and they had in their composite bow, made of horn and wood, a weapon that was perhaps more powerful than the famous English longbow of the fourteenth and fifteenth centuries. Their extraordinary mobility, their superior fire power, their unpredictable tactics, their savagery (remarked on even by the unsqueamish Germans) and not least their frighteningly ugly appearance – all this inspired terror and loathing, among both Romans and Germans.

After the collapse of the Ostrogoths, the Visigoths, to the south-west, tried unsuccessfully to fight off the Huns. But, outmanoeuvred and defeated, the whole tribe decided to seek refuge south of the Danube, inside the Roman Empire. In the autumn of 376 the Roman authorities permitted them to do so.

For the first time a whole tribe of barbarians had been admitted into the Empire. Contemporaries spoke of 200,000 Visigoths, though modern historians think 70,000 a more likely number. In general the German tribes numbered between 25,000 and 90,000 persons, of whom perhaps a fifth would have been effective fighters. Inevitably, there was friction between the Goths and their reluctant Roman hosts. Soon friction flared into open hostilities. Over-confidence and tactical mistakes led the emperor Valens to defeat and death in the battle of Adrianople (378).

For a moment the very existence of the Empire seemed at stake. To St Ambrose, archbishop of Milan, it seemed that the end of the world had come. But Valens' successor, Theodosius I, re-established the military situation in the Balkans. In the first years of the fifth century the imperial government built the triple walls on the landward side of the Golden Horn which were to make Constantinople impregnable for the next 800 years.

The division of the Roman Empire

Since the reign of Diocletian, at the end of the third century, the Roman Empire had been ruled by a college of emperors, mostly two, but sometimes more. This was not originally intended as a division of the Empire but rather as an effective means of dealing with the burdens of administration and defence of such a huge area. Thus general decrees by either emperor were regarded as valid law in both the eastern and the western parts. Yet we know from the experience of our own century that administrative boundaries which are made for political convenience have a habit of becoming permanent. Vested interests will create new patterns of political thinking and loyalty and they will tend to emphasize originally slight cultural differences.

In the Roman Empire, although the administrative division was not drawn along the linguistic frontier between Greek and Latin, these languages gradually came not only to dominate their two halves of the Empire but even to exclude each other. It was similar with the ecclesiastical division. Bishoprics in the east which acknowledged the authority of the patriarch of Constantinople; and those in the west which acknowledged the authority of the pope, the bishop of Rome, gradually came to be points of friction, rather than bridges between the churches in the eastern and in the western halves of the Empire. Immediately most important, however, was the financial division. The western emperor, with a revenue barely half that of his eastern colleague, had to defend the enormous frontier that stretched from Hadrian's Wall in northern Britain to the middle Danube. On some occasions the eastern emperors, so far from giving help, deliberately deflected their own problems to the west.

The first sack of Rome

To get rid of the Visigoths in Greece and Epirus, the government in Constantinople appointed their king, Alaric, imperial commander in Illyricum, roughly the modern Yugoslavia (397). By 401 the Goths had exhausted that province and moved on to Italy. Stilicho, commander-in-chief for the western government, which had moved from Rome to the strategically more advantageous Ravenna, held the Visigoths in check for almost a decade. But to do so he had to recall the legions from the Rhine frontier – temporarily, it was hoped. On New Year's Eve 406, the German tribes of the Vandals, Alans and Sueves crossed the frozen Rhine into Gaul. Like the Visigoths, thirty years earlier, they had been pushed by the westward march of the Huns from their territories in (modern) Hungary and Austria. Once the

25

Rhine frontier had been breached, there was no further tenable line of defence in the west. The plundering and marauding tribes moved south and west without meeting serious resistance. 'The whole of Gaul is smoking like an enormous funeral pyre', wrote a despairing contemporary. In 408 and 409 the German tribes crossed the Pyrenees into Spain and were then followed into Gaul by Franks and Burgundians. Britain, from which the Roman legions had also been withdrawn, was conquered rather more slowly by Angles, Saxons and Jutes, Germanic tribes from the North Sea coastal areas.

After Stilicho's fall, in 408, the imperial government in Ravenna was no longer able to hold off Alaric. Negotiations to settle the Visigoths in Italy failed, and on 24 August 410, Alaric captured and sacked Rome.

The political effects of the fall of Rome were relatively slight. Alaric died in 412 and his successor, Athaulf, led his starving tribe from an exhausted Italy into south-western Gaul. The moral effects of the fall of Rome were, however, enormous; for had not Rome been unconquered for a thousand years? 'When the brightest light was extinguished,' exclaimed St Jerome, then an old man, living in Bethlehem, 'when the whole world perished in one city, then I was dumb with silence.' For the last time serious doubts were voiced by traditional Romans about the new Christian god who had so signally failed to save the eternal city. It was after 410 that there was a real crisis of morale in the west.

Nevertheless, it was to take another sixty-six years until the last emperor in the west was deposed. The German tribes, pushed by the Huns and attracted by the wealth of the Mediterranean world – its wheaten bread and its wine, its fine textiles and its gold – invaded the Empire for the possession of land and subjects, rather than to destroy its political and cultural unity. They concluded more than a hundred different treaties with the imperial governments and they continued to fight each other in imperial service or even without imperial prompting. Athaulf is said to have wished to transform Romania into Gothia; but since his Goths were too undisciplined he had decided to become the restorer of the Roman world. The imperial government in the west was not sympathetic to such ideas. Although hampered by court factions, rebellious provincial governors, lack of resources and often sheer incompetence, it could still win considerable military and diplomatic successes. In the thirties and forties of the

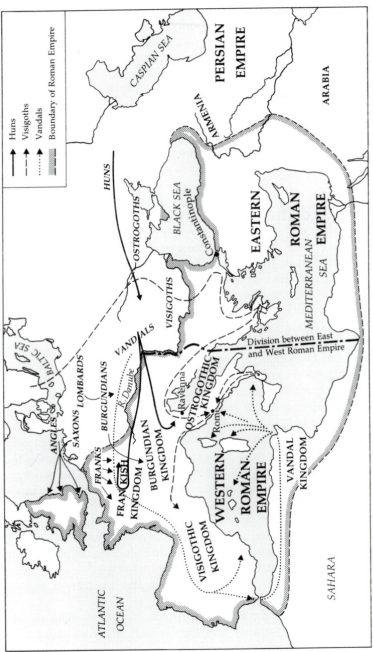

Map 1.1 The Roman Empire AD 400, showing the direction of fifth-century barbarian invasions.

fifth century, the western commander-in-chief, Aëtius, was a virtuoso in the game of using different groups of Germans and even the Huns in defence of imperial authority. In one such encounter, Aëtius and his Hunnic allies destroyed the kingdom of the Burgundians on the upper Rhine in 436. The memories of this catastrophic event were transformed into the most famous of the Germanic sagas of the Middle Ages, the Nibelung Song (see Ch. 4).

In the end, Aëtius was playing a losing game. To pay for it, taxes had to be continually increased and, as province after province was lost, the burden on the remainder became intolerable.

Attila and the empire of the Huns

The Huns were desperately dangerous allies for the Romans. Their conquest of the Ostrogoths and other German tribes north of the Danube had supplied the Huns with sufficient food to concentrate their scattered forces and form a federation of clans and tribes under one king. So great was the terror the Huns inspired, despite their relatively small numbers, that their kings could compel the obedience of men from the Caucasus to the Baltic, and blackmail the emperor in Constantinople into paying huge tributes in gold. 'Instead of herding cattle they had now learned the more profitable business of herding men', writes a modern historian of the Huns.[3]

In 450 the Hunnic king Attila decided to march against his old enemies, the Visigoths in south-western Gaul. A characteristically frivolous court intrigue at Ravenna seemed to promise him at the same time the hand of an imperial princess and, so he believed, half the western Empire as her inheritance. This was too much even for his old friend Aëtius. In 451 the now allied Roman and Gothic armies defeated Attila in the Battle of the Catalaunian fields, in Champagne. At the time the battle was hailed as a turning point in the fight against the dreadful Huns; but already in the following year Attila invaded Italy. Only plague in his army and his sudden death, in 453, saved the west from further devastation.

Terrible as were the Hunnish invasions to those who experienced them, it is unlikely that the Huns themselves could have overthrown the Empire and replaced Roman rule by their own.

For all their bravery and considerable shrewdness in dealing with the Romans, they were at too primitive a stage of civilization. Moreover, once they had moved west of the Carpathian mountains, and even more definitely after they had moved west and south of the river Danube, they had lost the vast grazing grounds of the Eurasian steppe. Without these grazing grounds they could not keep their large number of horses. It has been estimated that they needed up to ten horses for each armed rider in order to assure their typical nomad tactics of mobility and surprise for large numbers of horsemen. At the battle of the Catalaunian fields they had already moved so far away from the steppe that they were unable to use their traditional tactics. Once inside the Roman Empire, the rule of the Huns was based on little more than terror and the personal renown of a successful leader and his henchmen. This renown did not survive Attila's death and the quarrels of his sons. All later invasions of Europe by Asiatic nomads, such as those of the Avars in the sixth and seventh centuries, by the Magyars (Hungarians) in the ninth and tenth, and by the Mongols in the thirteenth century were to run up against the same insoluble problems once they had advanced beyond the steppe east of the Carpathians. Their raids into the more densely settled regions of Europe could still be terrible; but they could no longer think of permanent conquests. The contrast with the Arab invasions of the Roman world in the seventh and eighth centuries could not be more striking (see Ch. 2).

The German kingdoms in the Roman Empire

The historical significance of the Huns, who now virtually disappear from history, lies in having pushed the German tribes into the Roman Empire. For the Germans had come to stay. Athaulf might think of himself as the restorer of Romania; other German leaders might still recognize the authority of the emperor, rejoice in Roman titles and settle in Roman provinces by treaty as *foederati*, allies. In Gaul and Spain and, later, in Italy they would share the great estates with their Roman owners and exploit their peasants in the best Roman manner; for unlike the Huns, the Germans were not nomads but basically farmers. But in fact, where they settled they simply ignored the authority of

29

the imperial government. The Vandals, driven by the Visigoths out of Spain, invaded North Africa (429). Ten years later they had conquered Carthage, and the emperor had to recognize their independence. More serious still than the loss of Africa, the 'granary of the Mediterranean', was the piracy of the Vandals. The *Codex Theodosianus* of 438, a compilation of laws ordered by the emperor Theodosius II, set the death penalty on instructing the barbarians in ship-building. It was a wise law; but there was no one to enforce it. In 455 a Vandal fleet sailed to the mouth of the Tiber. The Vandals sacked Rome and carried off a former empress and her daughters to Africa.

There was no mistaking the difference between the Romans and the Germans, and nowhere was this difference more evident than in religion. As long as the Germans lived beyond the frontiers of the Empire, the Romans had done little to convert them to Christianity. Once they had broken into the Empire, however, they were quite rapidly converted and always by other Germans. We know very little of the details of these conversions or of the reasons for their rapid success. Was it that the Germans, having once settled on Roman land and in a clearly superior civilization, found their tribal organization breaking down and with it the belief in their old tribal gods? Was it at the same time an attempt to preserve their racial or ethnic identity which made them choose to accept Arianism, a Christian heresy, rather than the orthodox Christianity of the vast majority of the citizens of the Empire? (see pp. 53–4). However this may be, the fact of Arianism was an added, sometimes even the most important, reason for the Romans' dislike of the Germans and for the Germans' aloofness from the Romans. Arianism added to the effective independence of the German kingdoms within the Empire; but at the same time it allowed the Catholic Church in the west to survive unhampered by the new political authorities – a development of enormous importance for the future.

The end of the Roman Empire in the west

In 454 the emperor Valentinian III murdered his brilliant but wilful general, Aëtius. The emperor was himself assassinated in the following year. The next twenty years were a period of political confusion. No fewer than eight emperors were set up and deposed, either by the Roman senatorial aristocracy or at the instigation of the eastern emperor. On 23 August 476, the German troops in Italy who now formed the greater part of the Roman army elected their general, Odoacer, as king and deposed the last western emperor, Romulus Augustulus. His government had refused the soldiers' demand for a third of the land which was what the Roman 'allies' in Gaul had been given.

This was the end of the Roman Empire in the west. Theoretically, the eastern emperor Zeno now reigned again over the whole Empire. In practice, Odoacer had become the independent ruler of Italy, hated by the Roman aristocracy and unrecognized by Constantinople.

The Ostrogoths in Italy

Zeno was in no position to reconquer Italy, but he did have his revenge on Odoacer. The Ostrogoths, defeated and tyrannized by the Huns, had, like the Visigoths, eventually moved into the Balkan provinces of the Empire. In 488 Zeno persuaded their leader, Theodoric, to march from Moesia (modern Serbia) into Italy. It was an astute move on the emperor's part; for whoever won in Italy, the Eastern Empire at least would be rid of the last complete tribe of barbarians still within its provinces.

By 493 the Ostrogoths controlled Italy and Odoacer was dead, murdered it was said by Theodoric himself. In theory Theodoric was the emperor's representative and enjoyed the title of *patricius*. In practice he was as independent as the other barbarian rulers.

The Roman Empire in the east: Justinian

The Ostrogothic invasion of Italy freed the eastern part of the Roman Empire from the last of the barbarian tribes which had broken into its territory during the fifth century. Now, in the sixth century, Graeco-Roman civilization showed its continued vitality and, just as in the fourth century, the military and administrative organization of the Empire proved to be still admirably flexible and effective in meeting new challenges. The great cities of Alexandria and Antioch, of Caesarea and Jerusalem had not lost their wealth. Their merchants continued to send their ships across

31

Plate 1.3 The Empress Theodora and attendants: mosaic from the church of San Vitale, Ravenna.
The church was built to mark Justinian's reconquest of Ravenna, the former capital of the western half of the Roman Empire, from the Ostrogoths. The mosaics on the walls of the chancel (the eastern end of the church) are perhaps the finest surviving Byzantine mosaics in Europe. Their predominantly blue, green and gold tesserae are not set to form a smooth surface but at irregular angles, to catch the light. The result is a shimmering brilliance. The figure of Justinian's formidable empress combines imperial and religious symbolism. On her cloak are represented the gifts of the Magi.

the Mediterranean and down the Red Sea to East Africa, Ceylon and beyond. The Byzantine, i.e. Roman gold coin, the solidus with the emperor's image stamped upon it, circulated throughout the whole known world, from Ireland to China. Caravans crossed the whole Asian land mass along innumerable staging points. One of them secretly brought silk worms from China to the Mediterranean, and soon a native silk industry began to flourish on the island of Cyprus and in other parts of the Empire. For the rich city dwellers, life had not greatly changed from what it had been for centuries. Young men still received a classical, as well as a Christian, education in the urban academies and universities. The Christian Church, protected and favoured by the state for the last three centuries, displayed its wealth in hundreds of churches adorned with rich hangings, sculptures and mosaics.

But it was Constantinople itself which was now becoming the greatest and richest of the imperial cities. Warned by the fate of Rome in 410, the emperors built a huge system of multiple walls and towers around Constantinople, protecting both its landward and seaward sides. Until 1204, when the crusaders treacherously attacked and conquered the city, these walls withstood all assaults. As earlier in Rome, so now in Constantinople the emperors had to take account of the urban politics of the huge capital city. Bread and circuses, i.e. publicly funded support and entertainment for the mass of the poorer population, were still essential. In the hippodrome, the huge stadium for horse and chariot races and for animal fights, the fans were organized as 'greens' and 'blues'. They had the characteristics of both supporters of teams and politico-religious mass parties. Usually they fought each other, but in 532 they combined in riots against the government. For days they terrorized the city and the emperor Justinian's advisers urged him to flee. But Justinian's wife, Theodora, encouraged him to stand firm, and his general, Belisarius, with his professional soldiers put a bloody end to the anarchy.

These riots were Justinian's last internal crisis. From then on he ruled the Empire as effectively and more autocratically than any of his predecessors and often with the advice of the empress Theodora. He controlled the imperial bureaucracy and imposed taxes at will. As supreme legislator and judge he ordered the codification of imperial law, the famous *corpus iuris civilis*. Of its three parts the *Codex Justinianus* contained all imperial edicts since the time of the emperor Hadrian (AD 117–38) up to AD 533. Later edicts were added as *novellae*. It was this part of the *corpus* which emphasized the absolute legislative powers of the emperor. The second part, the Digest or *pandectae*, contained the writings and judgements, in fifty books, of Roman jurists which served as precedents in civil and criminal cases. The third part, the Institutions, was a shortened version of the other two parts, a kind

33

of textbook for the study of law. Perhaps no other non-religious text has had such a wide and long-lasting influence in European history as the *corpus iuris civilis*. It provided a comprehensive and rational system of law and of legal training for the remaining centuries of the eastern Roman Empire. Still more important was its history in the west. It served as the model for canon law, the ecclesiastical law of the Roman Catholic Church. From the twelfth century it also gradually became the dominant influence in western law courts and law schools, eventually superseding most of traditional law on the Continent. Through Roman law, Justinian's autocracy became the intellectual basis of the absolutism of the western monarchies of the sixteenth, seventeenth and eighteenth centuries. Even where, as in England, Roman law did not displace the common law, the development of systematic and rational jurisprudence, the science and philosophy of law, would probably have been unthinkable without the model of the *corpus iuris civilis*.

The visual expression of the greatness of the emperor and of the Christian Church, of which the emperor was the effective head, was the rebuilding of the church of the Hagia Sophia (Holy Wisdom) which had been burnt down in the 532 riots. Justinian brought the most distinguished architects, mathematicians and craftsmen from the whole Empire to the capital. There they built the biggest and most splendid church of Christendom. Even now, its huge, shallow dome still dominates the skyline of Istanbul (the present, Turkish name for Constantinople). Procopius of Caesarea, Justinian's court historian, has left us a description, in the rhetorical style of his day, of the dazzling interior of the Hagia Sophia. He gives at the same time a good idea of the religious sensibilities of sixth-century Byzantium.

> It abounds exceedingly in sunlight and in the reflection of the sun's rays from the marble. Indeed one might say that its exterior is not illuminated from without by the sun, but that the radiance comes into being within it, such an abundance of light bathes the shrine. . . . The whole ceiling is overlaid with pure gold which adds glory to the beauty, yet the light reflected from the stones prevails, shining out in rivalry with the gold. . . . But who would fittingly describe the galleries of the women's side, or enumerate the many colonnades and the colonnaded aisles by which the church is surrounded? Or who could recount the beauty of the columns and the stones with which the church is adorned? One

Plate 1.4 Constantinople: Hagia Sophia.
The huge central dome is surrounded by smaller, subsidiary domes.
The four slender towers (minarets) were added when the Hagia Sophia
became a mosque, after the Turkish conquest of Constantinople in
1453.

might imagine that one had come across a meadow with its
flowers in full bloom. For one would surely marvel at the purple
of some, the green tint of others and at those on which the
crimson glows and those from which the white flashes, and again
at those which nature, like some painter, varies with the most
contrasting colours. And whenever anyone enters this church to
pray, he understands at once that it is not by any human power
or skill, but by the influence of God, that this work has been so
finely turned. And so his mind is lifted up towards God and
exalted, feeling that He cannot be far away but must especially
love to dwell in this place which He has chosen.[4]

Majesty and splendour, softened by beauty, light and God's love
– this was the message of the emperor who saw himself as God's

35

representative on earth. It goes far to explain the long survival of the eastern Roman Empire.

The reconquest of the western Mediterranean

At Justinian's court it seemed as if the greatest days of the Christian Roman Empire had returned. The time had clearly come to reassert imperial authority in those western provinces in which it had been lost in practice but whose loss had never been acknowledged in law. Justinian, himself a Latin speaker, prepared his ground carefully. In Syria and in the Balkans he built a chain of fortresses. Smaller satellite and buffer states on the frontiers were kept in line by an elaborate and expensive system of embassies, bribes and subsidies. With Persia, the only power which the emperor ever acknowledged as having equal status, he concluded an 'eternal peace'. In time, Byzantine methods of diplomacy were to be imitated by all the major European states.

But such developments were in the future. In the sixth century the barbarian kingdoms in the west were disunited, with only intermittent diplomatic contact with each other and unwilling and unable to make a common front against the emperor. Justinian's first move fulfilled all expectations. In a brilliant short campaign, Belisarius defeated the Vandals in North Africa and brought their king in triumph to Constantinople. It was a most convincing demonstration of the continued military superiority of the Roman army and of the effectiveness of the Roman navy when given sufficient resources and when well led. Justinian's propaganda stressed his divine mission as the restorer of the Roman Empire 'up to the two oceans' and of the true Christian faith against the heretical barbarians. There is no reason to doubt that, for all his sophistication and opportunism, the emperor himself believed in this role.

In 536 Belisarius landed in Sicily. After four years of hard campaigning against the Ostrogoths he had taken Rome and Ravenna and had sent another barbarian king to Constantinople. Then Justinian's fortunes turned. King Khusro I of Persia broke the 'eternal peace' and his armies captured and sacked Antioch. Justinian had to concentrate his forces against the deadly danger from the east. The Goths seized this opportunity and recovered large parts of Italy. Not until 552 was Justinian able to raise an army large enough finally to defeat the Ostrogoths and re-establish imperial rule over the whole of Italy. About the same time Byzantine armies and naval squadrons reconquered the great western Mediterranean islands and the southern coast of Spain from the Visigoths. Nearly the whole of the Mediterranean coast-line was now again under Roman control.

With hindsight, historians have accused Justinian of over-extending the resources of his empire in useless conquests instead of concentrating them on his eastern provinces and thus safe-guarding them from the disasters that were to befall them. In the 530s, however, such considerations were not at all obvious. Slavs and Bulgars, raiding the Balkan provinces in as yet small groups, did not seem to be a danger comparable to the large, compact and well-led German tribes; and these, after all, were being success-fully defeated. The Persian danger was certainly taken seriously in Constantinople; but it had been contained before by a mixture of military and diplomatic means, and there was no reason to think that this could not be done again. After Belisarius' very economical victory in Africa, no one could foresee either that Byzantium would become involved in a chronic and costly guer-illa war with the Berber tribes in North Africa (just as was to happen to later imperial powers in that area, the Umayyad Caliphate of Córdoba, the Ottoman Turks in the sixteenth century and the French in the nineteenth and twentieth). Nor did it seem likely that the reconquest of Italy would take two decades and shatter the still considerable prosperity of that country. Above all, no one could have foreseen the devastations of the plague which broke out between 541 and 543 and which swept through the Mediterranean countries in several recurring deadly waves until the 1570s.

However hard pressed they were in the east and in the Balkans, Justinian and his successors were never prepared to give up the reconquered provinces voluntarily. They held southern Spain against the Visigoths until 629 and North Africa until the Arab invasions of 670. Carthage fell only in 698. In Italy the crisis came earlier. In 568 the Lombards or Langobards, a German tribe settled for some time between the rivers Danube and Theiss, moved south-west into Italy. Like the German invaders of previous generations they were both attracted by the wealth of

Italy, even though now much diminished, and pushed by a more primitive and even more ferocious Asiatic people, the Avars. Unlike the Ostrogoths, the Lombards did not come as Roman allies. The Byzantines, at first too disheartened to fight, later rallied. Controlling the sea, they managed to hold on to Ravenna, Genoa, Rome and most of southern Italy and Sicily. These areas and cities they defended with extraordinary skill and tenacity. Venice and Rome with central Italy eventually became independent, Venice as a republic and Rome as the 'patrimony' of the bishops of Rome, the popes. As late as the ninth century, the Byzantines defended Sicily for over forty years against the attacks of the north African Saracens. Syracuse, their last stronghold, fell in 879. Only in the middle of the eleventh century did they lose Calabria and Apulia to the Normans.

Justinian's *recuperatio imperii*, his reconquest of parts of the western Roman Empire, may or may not have been a mistaken policy of romantic nostalgia; its results cannot be regarded as short-lived. They preserved a Greek-Byzantine presence in Italy for over 500 years, and this presence, apart from the immediate experience of generations of imperial subjects in Italy, had a great indirect influence on the development of the papacy, on that of the western concept of the Holy Roman Empire and on the whole western conception of the classical tradition.

Byzantium and Persia

It was not in the western and central Mediterranean that the Empire had to face its most deadly danger. In the years after Justinian's death, in 565, the Danube frontier became vulnerable again, as it had been in the fifth century. This time it was not Germanic but Slavonic speaking peoples who filtered into the Balkan provinces of the Empire. The system of fortresses Justinian had built, a defence in depth, was a strategically brilliant conception. Yet to be effective this system also needed a mobile army. But such an army was precisely what Justinian's successors could not afford because their resources were overstretched in the wars against the Lombards and the Persians. The Slavs and the Bulgars (a Turkish people who came to adopt a Slavonic language) were driven, like the Lombards, across the Roman frontiers by the Avars. They by-passed the fortresses and penetrated into

Dalmatia and Macedonia. From the 580s they began to settle as far south as Greece.

The crisis for Byzantium came when this pressure from the north coincided with renewed pressure from the east. Persia had been ruled by the Sasanian dynasty since the first half of the third century. Its civilization was older and even more varied than that of the Roman Empire. The Iranian ruling classes were Zoroastrians, believers in a mainly monotheistic religion originating in the sixth century BC. But Manichaeans (believers in a dualism of good and evil forces dominating the world), Nestorian Christians (followers of a fifth-century patriarch of Constantinople whose beliefs had been declared heretical) and Jews were all left to practise their religions. In Constantinople Justinian attempted to censor what the Jews should be allowed to read – just as he was censoring what his Christian subjects should read. In Ctesiphon, the Persian capital on the river Tigris, Jewish rabbis were freely compiling the Babylonian Talmud, the compendium of Jewish laws and customs, second in authority only to the bible itself. It would become the final authority on the law for all orthodox Jewish communities. Byzantine architects had helped to build the great royal palace of the Sasanians at Ctesiphon. Byzantine models served the Persian government for the imposition of a land tax. King Khusro II's wife was a Nestorian Christian. This cosmopolitan society, a bridge between the Mediterranean world and India, could well appeal for sympathy to the civilized urban populations of Syria and Egypt. There was no necessary culture clash with the Byzantine Empire. It was the political ambitions and fears of two essentially militaristic political structures which made the clash between the Byzantine and the Persian empires inevitable.

For the old Persian aristocracy of the arid Iranian plateau lived for war, just as they had done since the days of Darius and Xerxes for the previous thousand years. In the sixth century AD they had come through the hard school of defending their northern frontiers against the Avars. Khusro II (590–628) dreamed of restoring old imperial glories, just as Justinian had done; only his reached back even further. Using the murder of the Byzantine emperor Maurice in 602 as both a pretext and an opportunity, he threw his armies against the Empire. It was the most formidable Persian offensive the eastern Roman Empire had yet experienced. Antioch fell to the Persians in 611, Damascus and Tarsus, birthplace of the apostle St Paul, in 613, Jerusalem a year later. It seemed like Alexander the Great's conquests in reverse, the final revenge of the Persians against the Greeks. From 617 to 626 Persian generals – Khusro, unlike Alexander, did not command his armies himself – faced Constantinople across the Bosphorus, while in 626 the Avars, now allied to the Persians, besieged the city on the landward side. But the great fortifications of the capital held. Its citizens, unlike those of Syria and Egypt, fought fanatically to keep out the invaders and the Byzantine navy managed to keep control of the sea. Eventually, the Avars and Persians had to retreat. The emperor Heraclius outflanked the Persians from the north and, in 627, annihilated their army on the Tigris. Khusro was murdered by his own soldiers. The Byzantines reoccupied Syria, Palestine and Egypt. The Holy Cross, robbed by the Persians from Jerusalem, was restored to the Holy Sepulchre. In a legend which spread rapidly throughout Christendom, Emperor Heraclius had fought the war, as a kind of crusader before the letter, precisely for this pious purpose.

The Byzantine Empire appeared as gloriously triumphant as ever. In fact, it was the Persian war, a war for which Byzantium was not primarily responsible, rather than Justinian's Gothic wars, which shattered the prosperity and military power of the East Roman Empire. It also shattered that of the Persian Empire, and it demonstrated the unwillingness of the Syrians and Egyptians to defend themselves against military attack from whichever quarter. The deadly, unnecessary, but probably unavoidable duel between the two great empires had left them both fatally vulnerable to a new and unexpected attack from the south, that of the Muhammadan Arabs.

The barbarian successor states

The different barbarian peoples who overthrew the political authority of the western Empire were all faced with a similar problem: how to adapt the customs and traditions of a tribal society that had only just broken camp and trekked – warriors, old men, women, children and animals – over hundreds of miles to a new life among strangers, strangers who lived in a structured, urban, literary and self-consciously civilized society. Except possibly in Britain and in the northernmost parts of Gaul the barbarians were

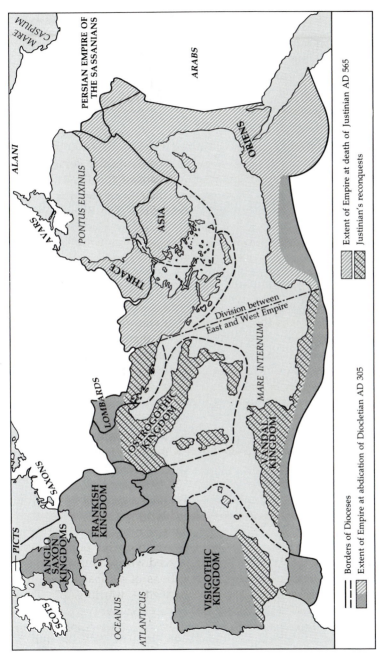

Map 1.2 The sixth-century Byzantine Empire and the western successor states.

PERSIAN EMPIRE OF THE SASSANIANS

ARABS

ORIENS

MARE CASPIUM

ALANI

PONTUS EUXINUS

AVARS

ASIA

THRACE

Division between East and West Empire

LOMBARDS

OSTROGOTHIC KINGDOM

MARE INTERNUM

VANDAL KINGDOM

FRANKISH KINGDOM

SAXONS

PICTS

ANGLO SAXON KINGDOMS

SCOTS

OCEANUS ATLANTICUS

VISIGOTHIC KINGDOM

Borders of Dioceses

Extent of Empire at abdication of Diocletian AD 305

Extent of Empire at death of Justinian AD 565

Justinian's reconquests

always a small minority. In some areas such as the Po valley and the high plateau of central Spain they settled fairly densely, elsewhere much more sparsely. Provided they could survive outside attack – and the Vandals in Africa, the Ostrogoths in Italy and the Suevians in north-western Spain did not – there was still this paradox: the more successfully the Germanic tribes adapted to their new environment, the more they lost their original identity and the more they were absorbed into the Roman society they had conquered. This was a slow process, lasting at least two centuries and producing in the end quite new societies, different from both the late-Roman and the German-tribal societies from which they had originated.

Because our sources for this period, mainly the sixth and seventh centuries, are few and difficult to interpret, this process of the formation of new societies is still rather obscure in detail; and yet it is one of the most important developments in the whole of European history. This becomes clear when the history of western Europe is compared with the history of those parts of the Roman Empire which were conquered by the Arabs in the seventh century. Here too a new society emerged as the result of the conquest of a Hellenized and Romanized society by a relatively primitive people. What emerged was, and has remained into our own times, a very different society from that which developed in the west. The reasons for this difference lie deeply embedded in the very old, pre-Hellenistic and pre-Roman traditions of Egypt and the middle east but also, and vitally, in the different religious histories of the Germans and the Arabs. For those Germanic people who survived, all found that they had to adopt the religion of those they had conquered, Catholic Christianity. The Arabs, by contrast, had their own religion, even though its origins were similar to those of Christianity, and the Arabs imposed their Islam permanently on the majority of those they conquered (see Ch. 2).

The Ostrogoths

The Ostrogoths were not allowed the necessary two centuries to develop a new Gothic-Roman society in Italy. It was not for want of trying.

Theodoric, the king of the Ostrogoths, had been brought up in Constantinople and had married an imperial princess. He set himself to reconcile Goths and Romans. The senate in Rome and the Roman civil service continued to function. Roman law was still administered by Roman courts. Unlike the Vandal nobility in Africa, the Gothic landowners were taxed like their Roman counterparts. Theodoric's court in Ravenna attracted Roman intellectuals and artists. His daughter was educated in Latin and Greek. Classical culture in the west enjoyed a last Indian summer.

But the differences between Romans and barbarians could not be easily and quickly bridged. The vast majority of the Ostrogoths, settled mainly in northern Italy, remained a separate caste of warriors, speaking their own language, obeying their own laws and, perhaps most important of all, believing in a different form of the Christian religion, Arianism. The fate of Boethius, the outstanding mind of the period, reflects the unresolved clash of cultures. Boethius (c. 480–524) was a Roman aristocrat. He was also a philosopher, theologian, poet, mathematician, astronomer and translator and commentator of Aristotle and other Greek authors. He served as a senator and, because he believed in co-operation, also as a minister to King Theodoric. In 523 he was falsely accused of treason and of practising magic. Theodoric had him imprisoned and eventually executed. While in prison, Boethius wrote *The Consolation of Philosophy*, a work alternating verse and prose passages. Philosophy, personified as a woman, appears to Boethius in his deep despair and chases away the muses (the Greek goddesses of the arts), for 'they cannot offer medicine for his sorrows; they will nourish him only with their sweet poison'. Lady Philosophy then consoles him with sweet reason and with the history of Socrates[5] and other philosophers who had suffered for the sake of truth and for the foolishness of aspiring to glory and reputation by taking an active part in affairs of state:

> You have learned from astronomical proofs that the whole circle of our earth is but a point in comparison with the extent of the whole heavens; that is, if it is compared in size with the celestial sphere, it is judged to have no size at all. Of this tiny part of the universe only a quarter, as you know from Ptolemy's proofs,[6] is inhabited by living things known to us. If in your imagination you subtract from that quarter all that is covered by seas and marshes and all the regions which extend in dried-up deserts, only a very narrow portion indeed is left for habitation by men. Now is it in this tightly enclosed and tiny point, that you think of spreading

43

> your reputation, of glorifying your name? What grandeur or magnificence can glory have, contracted within such small and narrow limits?[7]

In the end, God who is all-powerful and all-knowing will reward virtue and punish evil.

It is difficult to overestimate the importance of Boethius for the Middle Ages. His treatises and commentaries became textbooks of medieval university students, and for centuries Aristotle and other Greek authors remained virtually unknown except in Boethius' Latin translations. But most important of all was the *Consolation*, translated as early as the ninth century into Anglo-Saxon and, somewhat later, into other vernacular languages. A humanist Christian philosophy, it appealed to people living in a harsh and hostile world and it helped to keep alive a link with the great achievements of classical Greek philosophy. The personal and cultural tragedy of Boethius remained unresolved. Justinian and Belisarius did not allow the Ostrogoths time to atone for it. Unlike Boethius, the Ostrogoths left nothing to posterity. Only Theodoric's massively elegant funeral monument in Ravenna remains as a symbol of this failed fusion of cultures.

The Visigoths

The Visigoths were luckier. Although the Franks pushed them out of south-western Gaul in the early sixth century, they remained virtually undisturbed in Spain. Neither the Suevian kingdom in the north-west nor the Byzantines in the south-east ever posed a serious threat. In the seventh century both were wiped out.

Like the Ostrogoths in Italy, the Visigoths in Spain took over a functioning Roman administration. In a somewhat simplified form they adapted it to their own purposes, making their own great men the effective military commanders and administrators of towns and provinces. The Visigothic king who had been simply a war-time leader now became an absolute ruler, legislating and imposing taxes like the Roman emperor. Even his court ceremonial came to resemble that of Byzantium. The great nobles might resent particular rulers and, in the sixth century, they tended to murder or depose successive kings. But this did little to alter the kings' essentially Roman position and authority.

44

It is in law that we can see most clearly the adaptation of barbarian customs to Roman traditions. Systematic law and its codification was one of the greatest and most characteristic achievements of the Romans of the later Empire. Practically all the German successor states codified their laws, even the most short-lived, as the Burgundian, and the most barbaric, as the Lombard kingdoms. The very concept of such codification was Roman and, significantly, it seems always to have been carried out by Romans, even when the content of the laws was mainly Germanic custom. With the Visigoths even much of the content was derived from the fifth-century Roman compilations. In some instances, the Visigothic code even goes beyond the Roman and the German traditions. This was so, for instance, in the laws relating to the status and rights of women which was an improvement on both the primitive German traditions and the severe paternalism of Roman law. More often there was a fusion of the two elements, as for instance in the law relating to blood feuds. Blood feuds involve the responsibility of the whole extended family for the acts of one of its members and it is thus a method by which a primitive society, without a strong central authority, copes with the problem of murder or injury done by one person to another. All Germanic law codes tried to restrict the mutual killing involved in feuds by setting monetary fines which were determined both by the nature of the injury done and by the social status of the person who had suffered it. Only the Visigothic code went further and incorporated in the law on blood feuds the Roman law principle that only the individual who commits a crime, and not his whole family, was to be held responsible. These were important restrictions in the murderous practices of a warrior society; but they did not manage to abolish blood feuds altogether. They were to bedevil European society for many more centuries.

For well over a century the Arian Visigoths lived separate from the Catholic Roman-Hispanic population and their laws forbade intermarriage. But in the course of the sixth century these laws broke down and many Visigoths were converted to Catholicism. In 587 King Reccared adopted Catholicism and ordered all Arian books to be burned. Reccared's conversion may or may not have been a matter of conviction, but there is no doubt that it enormously increased the power of the monarchy. The king now had effective control over the Spanish church whose bishops he now appointed, just as he once had appointed the Arian bishops. The kings regularly summoned church councils to Toledo, attended by the great noblemen, as well as the clergy, and presided over by the kings themselves. The model for these councils was clearly Byzantine. No other Germanic king attained such complete control over his Church. From this period dates the characteristically Spanish tradition of the strictest Catholic orthodoxy combined with royal control over the Church and effective autonomy from the pope in Rome. It is in this context, too, that the Spanish monarchy promulgated its first, and very severe, laws against the Jews who had up to that time enjoyed almost complete toleration. Now they came to be disliked and feared as a heterodox and independent element in the state.

In spite of the absolutist claims of the Visigothic monarchy, its contest for power with the great nobles was never fully resolved. By the turn of the seventh and eighth centuries, the monarchy appears to have become once more the object of noble faction fights. Thus when the Muslim Berbers invaded Spain from North Africa, in 711, they were welcomed not only by the Jews and many of the lower classes but even by important sections of the Visigothic nobility who blindly hoped that they could use the Berbers for their own purposes.

The Visigothic successor state, like the Ostrogothic one, failed to maintain itself in the end. But its legacy to Spain, although in many respects still problematical, was undoubtedly much greater than that of the Ostrogoths to Italy.

The Franks

In sharp contrast to the Ostrogothic and Visigothic kingdoms in Italy and Spain the kingdoms of the Franks in Gaul and of the Anglo-Saxons in Britain survived; and it is their survival which had a good deal to do with the slow process, lasting almost a thousand years, by which the economic and political centre of gravity shifted north of the Alps and away from the Mediterranean. But when the Roman Empire fell in the west, none of this was, nor could be, obvious.

The Franks were one of several powerful groups in the chaotic conditions of Gaul in the latter part of the fifth century. They managed to extend their rule over most of Gaul because of their skill as fighters and because of the brilliant leadership by their king, Clovis (482–511). We know of this clever, ruthless and superstitious man mainly from Gregory of Tours' *History of the Franks*, written towards the end of the sixth century. Clovis defeated Syagrius, the last Roman governor of northern Gaul; the Allemanni east of the Rhine; and the Visigoths of Toulouse. His sons extended Frankish rule into Provence and across the Rhine to the lands of the Bavarians and Thuringians.

In all this there was little that distinguished the Franks from other barbarian conquerors. What did distinguish them was Clovis' conversion to Christianity and specifically to Catholicism. Soon the tradition arose that, like a second Constantine, Clovis had called on the Christian God in the crisis of battle and had been granted victory. St Gregory of Tours (538–594), the historian of the Franks, tells the story as it came to be generally accepted:

> Now the queen without ceasing urged the king to confess the true God and forsake his idols; but in no wise could she move him to this belief, until at length he made war upon a time against the Alamanni (AD 496). . . . It befell that when the two hosts joined battle there was grievous slaughter and the army of Clovis was being swept to utter ruin.
>
> When the king saw this he lifted up his eyes to heaven . . . and, moved to tears, cried aloud: 'Jesus Christ, Thou that art proclaimed by Clotild (the queen) Son of the living God, Thou that art said to give aid to those in stress and grant victory to those that hope in thee, I entreat from a devout heart the glory of Thy succour. If Thou grant me victory over these enemies, . . . then I will also believe in Thee and be baptised in Thy name. I have called upon mine own gods, but they have withdrawn themselves from helping me; Wherefore I believe that they have no power, since they come not to the succour of their servants. Thee do I now invoke . . .' And as he said this, lo, the Alamanni turned their backs and began to flee.[8]

It is characteristic of the religious feeling of the period that no one was in the least surprised at this curious deal between Christ and a military leader.

The emperor, glad of a potential ally against the Ostrogoths in Italy, bestowed on Clovis the title of consul. Thus Clovis and his Franks became acceptable to the Gallo-Roman nobility in a way the Arian Goths never could. It was the nobility who provided most of the bishops for the Church in Gaul, and it was for this Church that Clovis and his successors adopted the very accept-

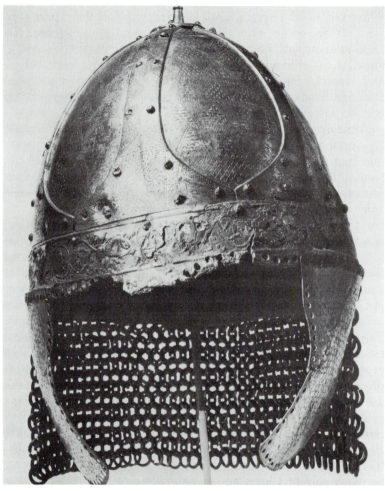

Plate 1.5 Frankish helmet from a burial at Morken, Rhineland,
c. AD **600.**
The object is both functional and elaborately and beautifully decorated,
showing the value a warrior people attached to their armour and the
high level of surviving craft skills in metal work. The man to whom
this helmet belonged was buried with all his armour and other
treasures.

able roles of champions and benefactors. For their part, the Frankish noblemen who took over or shared the estates of the Gallo-Romans saw no reason to change the methods of running these estates or in any way to upset the social relationships which they found. Since there were no laws against inter-racial marriage, Franks and Gallo-Romans fused within a relatively few generations.

While the Franks, like the Goths, took over much of the Roman provincial administration, there was yet a great deal about their rule that was specifically Frankish. Salian law, the law of the Franks, was influenced much less directly by Roman law than that of the Visigoths. Blood feuds remained central to their social order, and the pages of Gregory of Tours' *History* are filled with the gory details of countless murders and carefully planned murderous revenges.

Clovis' success had given a unique prestige to his line, the Merovingians. An aura of divinity came to surround Frankish kingship such as had probably not existed in the earlier history of Germanic peoples. Important as this was, the effective power of the Frankish kings rested nevertheless on more tangible assets. These were: first, the surviving system of Roman taxation, especially the tolls and duties levied on trade; and second, and even more important, the royal treasure and the enormous private estates of the Merovingians. Both treasure and land were used to reward the king's loyal followers. These assets were replenished by gifts from the king's subjects, tribute or diplomatic bribes from other rulers, including even the emperor, but above all from war. Here, rather than in any grand idea of empire, was the motive for the wars of aggression and the extension of Frankish rule of Clovis and his successors even though it was both convenient and morally reassuring to regard such wars as God's battles against pagans or heretics.

How far such motivation was from the Roman idea of empire becomes clear in the custom of the Merovingians of dividing the Frankish kingdom among their sons. For two hundred years after the death of Clovis, the political history of the Frankish kingdom is one of the division and reunification of its different parts, and of the blood feuds and wars between the different branches of the royal family. That the Franks could indulge in these civil wars without suffering the fate of the Vandals or Ostrogoths was due largely to luck, their sheltered geographical position and the weakness of all their near neighbours. The Visigoths, the Ostrogoths and, later, the Lombards, were too much occupied with their own mortal enemies, the Byzantines, to think of attacking the Franks. The small Anglo-Saxon kingdoms of England could never be any danger for the Franks, and the serious attacks of really formidable enemies, Norsemen, Avars and Saracens, did not occur until the middle of the eighth century.

By that time the lands and the treasure of the Merovingians had been spent, and the kings themselves had become personally incapable of ruling. But the kingdom and Gallo-Frankish society had survived in a viable fusion of Germanic and Roman traditions.

The christianization of the Empire

By the year 400 Christianity had become the predominant religion of the Roman world. There were good reasons for this success. In the first place, there was the powerful appeal of a belief which promised eternal life and spiritual peace to all men regardless of their present condition. For life on earth was hard, painful and short for most people; and as if this were not comfortless enough, they also believed themselves beset by evil forces, demons who, it was thought, practised their malicious crafts on people's possessions, on their health and even on their sanity. Such age-old popular beliefs had been strengthened by the direct or indirect influence on the Roman intelligentsia of Persian Zoroastrianism, with its view of the universe as a battlefield between the independent forces of good and evil. The Christian theologians argued fiercely about the origins of evil; but they did not deny the existence and power of the demons. Indeed, they defined the ancient Greek and Roman gods as demons. But they also claimed – and this was their trump card – that through the grace of Jesus Christ they had power to do battle with the demons and to overcome them.

The counterpart of the victory of Christ's spiritual soldiers, the monks, hermits and holy men, over His spiritual enemies was the victory of Christ's military soldiers over His earthly enemies. Since Constantine's victory over a rival emperor at the Milvian Bridge (AD 312) which assured his succession to the Empire and which he ascribed to the Christian God, the military power of the cross came to be accepted with increasing conviction. Old-fashioned pagans protested that the military disasters of the time were signs of the displeasure of the ancient gods at their recent neglect. They were drowned out by the chorus of Christian moralists who, to the contrary, saw these disasters as God's punishment for an insufficiently Christianized world.

Some Christians took a more profound view. St Augustine, bishop of Hippo in Africa, had arrived at his Christian beliefs by way of a long spiritual and intellectual struggle. In his *Confessions* he has left us an account of this struggle. From this personal and spiritual autobiography we know more about the sensibilities of the age, the blending of religious and philosophical thinking, than from any other early Christian source. 'I believe that I may understand,' was St Augustine's own summing up of his position. His penetrating self-perception, including the perception of his own sexuality, was to become a model for later auto-biographical writers, up to our own time.

The sack of Rome by the Visigoths, in 410, left St Augustine as dismayed as most of his contemporaries. His famous book, *The City of God*, was, however, less a reaction to this apparently apocalyptic event than a fundamental attack on the still surviving paganism and a summary and final conclusion to his own thinking about the relation between heaven and earth. The glory of Rome, as it was traditionally seen by both pagans and Christians, was irrelevant to the glory which could be achieved only in the City of God. This was Jerusalem, the spiritual city of all true Christians, both alive and dead, and of God's angels. As against Jerusalem, Babylon was the city of this world. The earthly city which does not live by faith seeks an earthly peace, and the end it proposes in the well-ordered concord of civic obedience and rule, is the combination of men's wills to attain the things which are helpful to this life. The heavenly city, or rather the part of it which sojourns on earth and lives by faith, makes use of this peace only because it must, until 'this mortal condition which necessitates it shall pass away.' In this world the two cities were mixed together, but at the Last Judgement they would be separated.

The profundities and subtleties of Augustine's thought were to nourish a thousand years of Catholic and, eventually, also of Protestant theology. But for political ideas the basic concept came to be Augustine's acknowledgement that worldly, political

51

government and authority were useful, or even necessary, for the pursuit of a Christian life here on earth. In practice this teaching meant a further strengthening of the tradition by which the Christian Church, ever since it had accepted the special favours bestowed on it by the emperor Constantine, had supported secular political authority. With only a few exceptions, the Catholic Church has since remained on the side of established authority; but it could question, and often has questioned, what was legitimate authority.

There was one further element in the development of Christianity which was absolutely necessary for its victory. This was its acceptance and assimilation of the intellectual traditions of the pre-Christian Roman world. Without such an acceptance it is difficult to believe that Christianity would not have simply remained one of the mystery cults of which there were a great number in the Roman Empire. There were those in the early Church who wanted to reject all Roman culture as pagan. They remained in a minority. It simply proved impossible to divorce serious theological thought from the existing traditions and systems of education. From at least as early as the beginning of the third century the great theologians were also learned men, deliberately harnessing pagan rhetoric, science and philosophy to the purposes of Christian thinking and education.

It was not always easy to do this with a good conscience; for was there not vanity in the pursuit of classical learning? St Augustine again shows the conflicts in Christian learning during this period; but characteristically he attempts to overcome these conflicts. Augustine accepted the Neo-Platonists' concept of plenitude, the fullness of the world of all possible types of creation (for God was bound to have created everything that could have been created; otherwise one would have had to suppose that there were limits to God's goodness and creativeness, which was inconceivable). Having accepted this, Augustine also accepted the argument that therefore there must exist an infinite scale of beings, from the angels down to the lowliest worm and to inanimate things. This was the theory of 'the great chain of being'. It was to remain a basic concept in western philosophy and theology until at least the Romantic period of the nineteenth century. In the fifth century, it enabled Augustine to accept the value of classical learning while at the same time severely subordinating it to the higher, religious aims which man should pursue.

Not all Christians managed to handle this problem as tidily as the great St Augustine. Justinian expelled the pagan teachers from the academy of Athens and thus effectively broke a thousand-year tradition of Greek philosophy. But on the whole, the Church, without ever entirely losing its ambivalent feelings about secular culture, came to be the guardian and preserver of the Greek and Roman pagan traditions. Often it was a selective, even capricious guardianship. But the fact of preservation itself was to be of enormous importance to Europe; for it provided a vision of a golden world, glimpsed indeed only from tantalizing fragments, but admired and even venerated, a perennial spur to imitation and emulation. Time and again, during the next thousand years, this vision was to inspire the most creative cultural efforts of European society. The philosophical traditions introduced by St Augustine and other Church fathers into Christianity made necessary at least a certain degree of acceptance of this world. Spirit and flesh, heaven and earth, would war with each other but never be completely separated in the western Christian tradition. It proved to be an uncomfortable but a fruitful heritage.

Heresies

Given the nature of Christian beliefs and the reasons for its spread in the Roman Empire, it is not surprising that it should have been beset by heresies. If personal salvation depended on a specific belief, and if God was to help the believer against both his mortal and his spiritual enemies, then it seemed clear that he had to get his beliefs absolutely right. This conviction would apply at all intellectual levels, from the philosophically trained theologian, worrying about the nature of the Trinity, to the most simple and illiterate peasant praying for divine help against the natural and demonic forces that were constantly threatening him. But what was correct belief? Scripture could be interpreted in different ways – and was by the theologians of the period.

In the eastern part of the Roman Empire, their differences centred on the nature of Christ and the precise nature of his relation to God. If the theologians' arguments were often difficult to understand they were still a matter of the utmost importance to every individual; for on the precise nature of Christ must surely depend one's own salvation. But while the origins of such differing beliefs and even much of their popular appeal were strictly theological, they always became entangled with other, more worldly motivations. The Goths and Vandals accepted the doctrine of the Egyptian Arius, a belief that Christ was not fully equal with God the Father. No doubt, they believed themselves to be theologically correct; but equally they seem to have clung to a doctrine declared heretical by a Roman church council in order to emphasize their difference from the Romans. Armenians, Syrians and Egyptians wanted as much to emphasize their cultural differences from the Greeks as insist on different theological beliefs when they adopted Nestorianism (belief in the basically human nature of Christ) or Monophysitism (belief in Christ's purely divine nature).

The quarrels of the theologians, mixed up as they were with the disputes of the patriarchs of Constantinople, Antioch, Alexandria and of the pope of Rome over pre-eminence in the Christian Church and reinforced by the local loyalties of the urban mobs of the great eastern cities, became a more and more intractable problem for the emperors. In Egypt and Syria the monophysites predominated. They had allies or sympathizers in the capital, among the 'greens' of the circus parties and right up to the court and even to Justinian's empress, Theodora. But the great majority of the Greeks, together with the popes and the westerners, were orthodox, holding fast to the doctrine laid down by the council of Chalcedon in 451, that Christ had a dual nature, both divine and human. The emperors manoeuvred between the parties, generally favouring the orthodox, but unwilling to crush the monophysites completely, for fear of losing Syria and Egypt. They had good grounds for such a fear. The religious tensions between these provinces and Constantinople at least help to explain their unwillingness to defend themselves against the Arabs in the seventh century.

In the west where the theological conflicts centred on the relation between God and man, rather than on the nature of Christ, there was a similar confusion of religious and secular motivation. The most immediately serious schism, or split, in the western Church was the Donatist movement. It had arisen out of a quarrel over the behaviour of African bishops during the persecutions of Diocletian and had effectively led to the establishment of a separatist African Church which could call for support on regional loyalties and social discontent. Its doctrinal differences from orthodox doctrine were slight; but it was one of

St Augustine's major problems and it was not fully resolved until the Vandal conquest of Africa.

Less spectacular at the time, but much more important for the future, was St Augustine's controversy with the Pelagians. Pelagius, a British layman, taught that man could lead a fully virtuous life through his own efforts. It was a doctrine that appealed to many educated persons. In the course of the controversy Augustine argued from a belief in the basic sinfulness of man and denied free will without divine grace. It was an extreme formulation which the Catholic Church never fully elevated into orthodox doctrine. But it remained one pole of a controversy that was to continue into the sixteenth-century Reformation and into the seventeenth-century quarrels between the Jesuits and the Jansenists.

Organization and authority in the Church

Since Christianity had won its great victories through the support of the state, it was inevitable that the Church should involve the state in its religious controversies. The head of the Christian community in each city was the bishop, and it was the bishops who assembled in council and determined matters of doctrine. But it was the emperor who, from the time of Constantine, summoned the councils of the whole Church (ecumenical councils), and it was at his insistence and by his authority that orthodox doctrine was defined and imposed. The first ecumenical council, that of Nicaea (325), condemned Arius and defined the doctrine of the Trinity. The fourth, the council of Chalcedon (451), condemned Nestorius and the Monophysites and confirmed the doctrine of the two distinct natures of Christ, the divine and the human. In the east the emperor never lost his power over the councils and over the declaration of Christian doctrine. The Church, in so far as it remained orthodox, also remained effectively subordinate to his authority. When the Monophysite bishops of Egypt and Syria repudiated the orthodoxy established by virtue of imperial authority, they did not perhaps immediately see that this involved also a political repudiation of the emperor. By the seventh century, however, this too had become clear.

Church and papacy in the west

In the west the development was more complex. As imperial authority declined, or as it was replaced by the barbarian successor states, the bishops often emerged as the sole effective remaining Roman authority. At the same time they had no reason to repudiate the emperor; for the Church in the west had no quarrel with an emperor who was at once blessedly orthodox and happily far away and powerless to interfere unduly with the western bishops.

Few effects of the political collapse of the Roman Empire in the west had such far-reaching consequences as this virtually independent development of the Christian Church in the west. It was to create a dual power structure and a dual focus of loyalty for men, such as had never existed before in the Graeco-Roman world, or in any other civilization. This dualism of Church and state, as so much else that had its origins in this period, was to prove one of the most dynamic elements of European society, a cause of strife and tragedy but also of a peculiarly fruitful and ongoing intellectual and political debate.

Perhaps even then nothing of this would have happened if it had not been for the papacy and for the special political conditions prevailing in Italy. The Visigothic kings of Spain and, to an only slightly lesser extent, the Merovingian kings in Gaul controlled their churches and their bishops almost as effectively as the emperor in Constantinople controlled those of the Eastern Empire. But in Italy there was no such effective political authority. Thus Pope Leo I (440–61) won great renown by his personal encounters with Attila and with the Vandal king, Geiseric; for he was reputed to have persuaded the dreaded Hun not to march on Rome in 452, and the Vandal not to sack the city in 455. In actual fact, Attila had other good reasons for leaving Italy, notably famine and plague in that country. As for Geiseric, he sacked Rome all the same. But such mundane facts were soon forgotten, while the tradition of the saviour-pope lived on to strengthen the reputation of the Papacy.

In 494, when Theodoric the Ostrogoth was ruler of Italy, Pope Gelasius drew a distinction between ecclesiastical and political power. 'There are, Your Majesty,' he wrote to the emperor in Constantinople, 'two things whereby this world is chiefly governed, the sacred authority of bishops and the imperial authority. Of them the burden of the priests is greater, in that they must render account in the divine judgment for the kings of men also.'⁹ There were no immediate reasons to pursue all the implications of Gelasius' doctrine of the two powers or two swords, the spiritual and the temporal, as it was later called. In the chaos of the Gothic and Lombard wars of the sixth century, the popes felt themselves as loyal subjects of the emperor. Yet in practice their relations with the emperor's representative in Italy, the exarch in Ravenna, were often badly strained. As bishops of Rome the popes exercised immediate and effective political control in the city and in large parts of central Italy. Of necessity, they had to manoeuvre between the exarchs and the Lombard kings and dukes in a manner curiously foreshadowing the politics of the Renaissance papacy. At the same time, the bishop of Rome, as direct successor of St Peter, claimed spiritual authority over all bishops, at least in the west, and precedence over the eastern patriarchs at the ecumenical councils. As early as the middle of the fifth century Leo I was speaking of St Peter's princely authority and of the pope's right to 'rule all who are ruled in the first instance by Christ.' One strong-minded pope after another persistently extended such claims.

Gregory the Great (590–604)

The first great climax of this development was reached with Gregory I, known as Gregory the Great. More consistently than any of his predecessors he sought to extend papal authority over the Christian Church in the west. He had greater success in the missionary efforts he encouraged, particularly those of St Augustine of Canterbury in England, than in interfering with well-established churches under strong kings, such as the Church of Spain and the Church of Gaul. But his most lasting work was in Italy itself. It was during his pontificate that the conversion of the Arian Lombards was undertaken in earnest. Finally, it was Gregory, more than any other pope, who transformed the city of Rome and its surroundings into a political and administrative unit – the beginnings of the Papal States.

This development was to give the papacy a territorial interest and a political role that would never be fully divorced from its spiritual role and that often, it was claimed, would get in the way of the spiritual role. In the opinion of the sixteenth-century Protestants, it had actually damaged this spiritual role irreparably. Yet this was not how the problem appeared to Gregory I and his contemporaries: they had to defend Rome from the Lombards. The pope had to provide secure government for Rome's citizens and feed the thousands made destitute by the wars. Moreover, if the pope was to function as the independent head of the Church, he had to preserve his political independence. Otherwise, he would become as dependent on the local political authority as the patriarch of Constantinople or the bishops of Spain and Gaul. Gregory I may not have seen this quite so clearly. The immediate threat to papal independence came from the Lombards, rather than from the emperor. Gregory therefore willingly called on imperial help when it could be had. One hundred and fifty years later it could not, and Gregory's successors had no alternative but to call, unwillingly, on the Franks for protection from the Lombards. The sequel made it clear beyond a doubt that the papacy needed an independent political base if it was to make good its spiritual claims. The history of the next thousand years, not excluding the experience of the Protestant churches after the Reformation, did nothing to show this assumption to have been false. It also did nothing to show that those who pointed to its baleful effects were wrong.

Christianity and intellectual life

The Christian Church had accepted the value of classical culture; but for most Christians the preservation of this culture, however important, was not the main aim of their lives. Even such a dedicated intellectual as St Jerome (c. 347–c. 420), the translator of the bible into Latin, suffered a dream in which Christ rebuked him for reading too much Cicero.[10] But it was not just a matter of attitude and changed intellectual priorities. The barbarian invasions, the wars, the devastations and expropriations largely destroyed the physical basis of the classical tradition, the propertied, urban, leisured class and the schools which it had supported. It was a slow and uneven process. Even during the Indian summer of philosophical and literary activity in Italy during Ostrogothic rule, Cassiodorus (c. 490–c. 585), the friend of Boethius, saw the best opportunities in future for a life of cultivated leisure as being in a well-endowed monastery. He himself founded the monastery of Vivarium to which he then retired. But soon there was little opportunity even in Italy for the pursuit of secular culture. 'What is there left of delight in the world?' asked Gregory the Great, a man who was certainly not hostile to classical learning. 'On all sides we see war, on all sides we hear groans. Our cities destroyed . . . our countryside left desolate.' The wonder is not that much of the classical tradition was lost but that men clung to it so tenaciously in almost desperate conditions and that they preserved so much of it.

It was the same in Spain and Gaul. Their towns had dwindled in size and wealth. Their secular aristocracy, whether Roman or Germanic or of mixed descent, spent their time hunting, feuding and fighting. Those who were literate joined the Church. By the end of the sixth century, the possibility of acquiring secular learning had all but disappeared. St Isidore of Seville (570–636) wrote a history of the Visigoths and a learned chronicle of world history, as well as theological works. But his greatest influence on later generations came from his *Etymologiae*, an immense encyclopaedic collection of classical texts that was specifically intended to make the study of heathen authors unnecessary.

A generation earlier, bishop Gregory of Tours (538–594) had set himself to write the history of the Franks because, he said, 'the culture of the liberal arts was declining or rather actually dying in the cities of Gaul.' Gregory was aware that his style lacked grace but he consoled himself with the thought 'that few people understand a philosophising rhetorician.' What Gregory's style lacked in classical elegance it gained in vigour. His *History of the Franks* is highly readable and it conveys a vivid picture of a society beset by feuds, murders, betrayals and revenge, and dominated in people's minds by supernatural powers, both good and evil. Hermits and other holy persons, both male and female, can control these forces through proper belief and ritual. But perhaps even more useful to the living are the dead, the saints and their relics who unfailingly work miracles. Foremost among them was Gregory's own adored patron saint, St Martin of Tours, to whose shrine thousands came on pilgrimage.

It was also a society which still admired the Roman traditions. But these traditions, except in the form of Christianity, were no longer a living experience but only a splendid memory. Even within the Church the age of the great philosopher-theologians was past and was not to revive until the very different conditions of the twelfth century. For the present, and it was a very long

59

present, there was only one way this society could go: a deter-
mined effort to recover what was thought to have been lost of
Christian antiquity. This was the meaning of the Carolingian
Renaissance of the turn of the eighth and ninth centuries (see
Ch. 2).

The visual arts

The Roman Empire

The remarkable unity of culture of the later Roman Empire is seen
most clearly in its art and architecture. Roman temples and
theatres, Roman baths and aqueducts did not differ greatly from
Spain to Asia Minor. Roman villas with their gay floor mosaics
were almost interchangeable from Britain to Syria. Roman portrait
sculpture was practised with equal attention to a naturalistic
representation of individual character from the banks of the Rhine
to those of the Nile. But well before the fifth century, the classical
style, with its strict rules of perspective and its norm of an idealized naturalism, had begun to be abandoned. Both in unsophis-
ticated provincial workshops and in metropolitan studios serving
the richest classes of society, a new style was being developed,
replacing perspective by a flat, two-dimensional representation of
figures. What was lost in naturalism was gained in the express-
iveness of ideas – the majesty of God or the emperor, the hierarchic order of heaven and of human society. The new style could
become a visual representation of the neo-platonic and Augustinian idea of the great chain of being in a way that the classical
style could not rival. It must therefore not be regarded as a
reversion to primitivism.

For centuries the classical and the new style were practised
side by side, and even in the sixth century we still find examples
of essentially classical art. But the new style proved highly flexible and able to accommodate new techniques and new visual
ideas. Many of these came from Syria, the old intellectual and
artistic crossroads between the Greek and the oriental civilizations. The most striking was perhaps the change in the representation of Christ: from a youthful Apollo he became the grave,
bearded, awe-inspiring figure that he was to remain throughout
western and, even more, Greek Orthodox visual tradition.

Plate 1.6 'New' Byzantine art: transfiguration from the monastic church of St Catherine, Mount Sinai.
The monastery was built in AD 530 in the place where it was thought Moses received the tablets with the Ten Commandments from the Lord. The ceiling mosaic in the apse (the vaulted eastern end of the church) probably dates from 560. The 'new' Byzantine style enabled the artist to present the scene where Moses and Elijah appeared to Jesus and three of his apostles with both great economy and great power. The artist was able to achieve this effect precisely because he did not have to worry about naturalistic representation (see Plate 1.2).

The great climax of the new style was reached in the sixth century and it is justly connected with the name of Justinian. Never before had Christian churches been so magnificent. They had started humbly enough, as basilicas, simple rectangular halls, in conscious contrast to the pagan temples. From the time of Constantine and, even more, from the fifth century onwards, vast sums flowed into Church treasuries from gifts and bequests. The result was not only a huge increase in the number and size of churches, but the adaptation of the most advanced Roman building techniques and artistic styles to the building of churches

61

and to their ornamentation. Nowhere was this more evident than in Constantinople itself. Here, the Hagia Sophia ('Divine Wisdom'), with its huge central dome, its semi-domes and its multi-storied rows of columns became both a symbol for the greatness of the Christian Empire and, for centuries to come, a model for similar, if mostly smaller, churches all over the Christian world.

In many Byzantine churches of this period the pictures and mosaics which adorned their interiors were destroyed during the iconoclasm, the campaign against images, sponsored by the emperors of the middle of the eighth century. They have, however, survived in Ravenna where, in the churches of San Vitale and San Appolinare, they can still be seen in all their brilliance – to contemporaries a testimony of the greatness of Justinian and his empress, Theodora, and their court. To us they also offer testimony of the undiminished creative capacity of the Roman world even after the collapse of the Empire in the west.

The barbarian successor states

There was no way in which the barbarians could have matched the richness, sophistication and variety of the artistic achievements of such an old civilization as that of the Roman Empire. Tribal societies, living on pasturage and primitive agriculture and without fixed settlements for more than two or three generations, could develop neither the resources nor the skill to produce a permanent architecture, not to speak of paintings, mosaics or statues. Their artistic achievements were concentrated on jewelry and on armour. This is what we would logically expect in such societies, and this expectation is confirmed by archaeological finds. Tens of thousands of graves have been discovered – more than 40,000 in France alone – showing men buried with their weapons and women with their brooches, armbands and hairpins. These were evidently their most precious possessions. The styles and decorations of these artifacts are certainly very different from Roman styles. Even so, they appear mostly to have been borrowed originally from central Asian and near Eastern models and then developed according to the Germans' own tastes.

When the Goths, the Franks and the Lombards set up their kingdoms in the provinces of the Roman Empire, they came to rule over a Roman provincial population that maintained its craft skills. In many areas, no doubt, these skills declined both in quality and, perhaps even more important, in the number of persons who still managed to learn them. Yet masons could still build Roman arches, sculptors could still carve in stone, ivory or wood, and painters could still paint icons and decorate the pages of books. This last skill seems to have had an expanding market as, with declining literacy, books became less utilitarian and consequently rarer and more precious.

The invasions, wars and devastations, and the decline of population in the terrible plagues of the sixth century meant that there were now fewer resources for building and the arts and also that much of what still was built or painted has not survived. The relatively small number of craftsmen, however, was open to outside influences, perhaps precisely because there were so few. Jews, Syrians and Greeks travelled in barbarian kingdoms, trading precious fabrics, carved ivories, books and other valuable objects. The prestige of Constantinople remained enormous. The emperor and the barbarian kings exchanged gifts. Thus we find Coptic, Syrian and, above all, Byzantine stylistic influences in the art and architecture of the sixth and seventh centuries, as far north and west as the Rhine and Guadalquivir.

At the same time Germanic tastes in artistic style and decoration began to affect western Roman provincial art in much the same way. In some cases it is clear that the royal courts favoured it. In the recently excavated tomb of the Frankish queen, Arnegunde, of the middle of the sixth century, there was preserved her rich clothing and jewelry, all in essentially Germanic style. This contrasts with the tomb of King Childeric of 482 in which was found, together with some Germanic jewelry, much more that was essentially Roman. Artists, builders and craftsmen, working in a still living Roman tradition, were subject to influence from the whole Mediterranean world, including those of the Germanic tribes who had settled there. Gradually they evolved strong regional variations on the basic Roman style. These variations can be observed as early as the sixth and seventh centuries, as for instance in the use of the horseshoe arch in Spain, well before the Muslim invasions. Their first full flowering, however, was not reached until the eighth and ninth centuries.

Conclusions

Not until our own time have there ever been such far-reaching changes in the structure of European society as there were in the 300 years between AD 400 and 700. A politically unified empire with an urban and literate culture was replaced by a number of separate kingdoms whose culture was provincial, rural and largely non-literate. And yet, the life style of the vast majority of ordinary people, the country-dwellers, had neither changed as much as we might have expected, nor had it greatly deteriorated. Literacy and the Latin language had not disappeared altogether but continued to be cultivated by churchmen. The Christian Church had survived triumphantly and had, moreover, achieved great successes in the conversion of the Germanic tribes.

The head of the Church in the west, the pope in Rome, continued to acknowledge the authority of the emperor in Constantinople. But in practice he was almost completely independent of the emperor. This independence of the papacy – in sharp contrast to the dependence of the Christian patriarchs on the emperor – was to have the most profound consequences for the development of the Christian Church and of Christian civilization in the west.

Among the reasons which historians have proposed for these changes, and especially for the fall of the Roman Empire in the west, those which stress the internal developments of the later Roman Empire, whether religious, moral, racial or social, have been found insufficient; for none of them explains satisfactorily why the eastern half of the Roman Empire survived. The decisive force was the invasion of the Germanic tribes. The fusion of the tribal Germanic and the settled Roman societies took several centuries to accomplish and, since it took place in different ways and at different speeds, it produced a rich variety of new political, social, ethnic and cultural structures and societies. Nevertheless, all these looked back to and often tried to recapture a common Christian and Roman heritage.

Neither trade nor travel and cultural exchange ceased on the Mediterranean and in the lands of the former Roman Empire, though there was a good deal less of both than there had been before the barbarian invasions. In the east the Roman Empire had triumphantly survived both the attacks of the German tribes and those of the great rival empire, Sasanid Persia. Constantinople had become the greatest Christian city and the emperors continued to claim authority over the whole Christian world, even if in Britain, Gaul and most of Spain few people took much notice of this claim. Only in the seventh century was the east Roman Empire to lose its dominion over the Mediterranean and only then was the cultural unity of the Mediterranean world finally broken. Even then, the east Roman Empire survived as Byzantium until the middle of the fifteenth century. But by that time the rest of Christian Europe had been completely transformed and no longer greatly cared what happened to Constantinople.

References and Notes

1. **Sidonius**, *Poems and Letters*, trans. W. B. Anderson. Loeb Classics: Cambridge, Mass. 1936, **vol. 1**, p. 421.
2. Quoted in **Jones, A. M. H.**, *The Decline of the Ancient World*. Longman: London 1966, p. 251.
3. **Thompson, E. A.**, *A History of Attila and the Huns*. Clarendon Press: Oxford 1948, p. 177.
4. **Procopius**, *Buildings*, **Bk I.l**. 28–35, 53–57, trans. H. B. Dewing and Glanville Downey. Loeb Classics: Cambridge, Mass. and London 1961, pp. 17, 25–27.
5. Socrates (*c.* 470–399 BC), Athenian philosopher, generally regarded as one of the founders of philosophy. He was accused of corruption of the young and forced to drink poison.
6. Ptolemy, Alexandrian mathematician, astronomer and geographer of the second century AD whose mathematical model of the universe was widely accepted until the sixteenth century (cf **H. G. Koenigsberger**, *Early Modern Europe, 1500–1789*; History of Europe. Longman: London 1987, Ch. 5).
7. **Boethius**, *The Consolation of Philosophy*, trans. S. J. Tester. Loeb Classics: Cambridge, Mass. 1973, p. 217.
8. **Gregory of Tours**, *The History of the Franks*, **Bk II**. 21, trans. O. M. Dalton. Oxford University Press: Oxford 1927, pp. 68–69.
9. Pope Gelasius on the two powers: **B. Tierney**, *The Crisis of*

Church and State 1050–1300. Prentice Hall: Englewood Cliffs, N. J., 1964, p. 13.

10. Marcus Tullius Cicero (106–43 BC) Roman statesman and philosopher, whose thought and Latin style had immense influence on Europe throughout the Middle Ages.

Chapter 2

The Carolingian Empire and the Invasions of Europe, 700–1000

The climate

For the vast majority of people living in Christian Europe in 700 life was desperately hard, as hard or harder than it had been in the last century of the Roman Empire in the west. As far as we know, even the weather seems to have got worse. The results of the study of deposits in the valleys of the Alps and of pollen analysis in the peaty country of the North European plains are difficult to interpret and the experts are not entirely agreed. But the pattern seems to be this: from AD 200 to 700 Europe north of the Alps got colder and wetter. Not by very much, but probably enough to make a difference to the harvests. From about 800 the climate improved again, until the eleventh century. Mean temperature rose slightly and the summers and autumns were drier.

This pattern of the changes in European climate fits well with the pattern of European agrarian life. In the last centuries of the Roman Empire in the west and up to about AD 700 agrarian life was depressed. Harvests were poor and people struggled desperately to make a living. But after 700, and especially from the tenth century, harvests improved. No doubt, the improved climate was at least partly responsible. Climate and changes in climate, however, are not by themselves enough to explain the course of European economic history.

Population and settlements

If we must largely guess about the climate and its effects, we are in little better condition to assess the number of people who lived in Europe at this time. The plagues of the sixth and seventh centuries had caused great loss of life, although we do not know exactly how great. It is unlikely that, by 700, these losses had been made good. Europe was a very sparsely populated continent. This does not, however, mean that people lived alone or at great distances from each other. In those areas where Roman settlements had been especially thin, roughly north of the river Loire, groups of Germanic families had usually settled together in villages on previously cultivated or easily accessible land. In Gaul the Franks had often merged with the earlier inhabitants. In England the Anglo-Saxons had done this too and they had settled mostly in the lowlands which were suitable for the arable farming to which they were accustomed from their original homes. They left the hills with their lighter soils and a predominantly grazing economy to the Celtic Britons.

The villages or groups of villages, with their fields surrounded by forest, scrub or marsh, were mostly self-contained – small oases of cultivated land in a vast uncultivated continent. Forest, marsh and scrub were neither impenetrable nor economically useless. The great west-central European rivers, from the Loire to the Rhine and the Elbe, together with their countless tributaries, were highways rather than barriers. The forests provided building and heating materials, food for pigs and game for food and sport. But the villages could not easily extend the area of land they cultivated into the forest and scrub. The most obvious reason for this was the attitude of lords who often wanted to keep the forest for hunting. More important still was the sheer physical difficulty of cultivating new land. Iron tools were scarce and expensive. We know from ninth-century inventories that quite large estates in northern France possessed no more than two or three hatchets and no greater number of spades and sickles. What could they achieve against forests of beech and oak? Most farm implements were made of wood. Even the common plough of the period was a wooden stick with a wooden hook, hardened by fire.

These daunting difficulties of attacking the forest were further increased by psychological barriers. Germanic paganism was centred on the worship of trees and thus there was a taboo on destroying forests. The introduction of Christianity did not immediately change people's old beliefs, and for many generations churchmen continued to denounce the persistence of pagan rites associated with holy trees such as the Scandinavian mythological ash tree, Yggdrasil, whose roots were believed to hold heaven and earth together.

Family structure and settlements

Perhaps most important of all were the psychological consequences of the prevailing family structure. The Germans had tended to settle in groups of extended families, with brothers, sisters, cousins and everyone's spouses and children, all staying together with the grandparents. Intermarriage in the adjoining groups of villages had tended to knit these communities even more closely together. Even people's attitude to crime and punishment was based on their conception of kinship. In the Roman Empire, as in our time, crimes such as murder were regarded as offences not only against the victim but also against society as a whole or against the state. In principle, at least, it was the state and its law courts which judged and punished such crimes. This view of crime did not altogether disappear in the barbarian successor states. Powerful kings still maintained law courts and attempted to punish crimes, even if the laws their courts administered were the traditional laws of the particular Germanic peoples (see Ch. 1, p. 45). But in the chaotic conditions of western Europe, where kings were weak, as they were for instance in the early centuries of Anglo-Saxon England, there had to be another, more effective, way of dealing with crime. This was the practice of holding a person's kin responsible for a crime he had committed. It could be done by means of a blood feud when the victim's kin exacted vengeance of the kin of the alleged wrong-doer. These, in their turn, would then be very likely to retaliate in kind. It was a practice which multiplied murder. In different parts of Europe it lasted in various forms well into the later Middle Ages, until governments finally became powerful enough to suppress it. But there existed also a less murderous alternative which was to settle the wrong by a fine paid to the murdered person's family. In England this fine was called *wergeld* and its value varied with the status of the person murdered. The *wergeld* of a nobleman in Kent, for instance, was the huge sum of 300 shillings, of a freeman it was 100 shillings and of a freed slave it might be as low as 40 shillings. The *wergeld* of a woman was at least as high as that of a man of equal social status or it might be even higher. It was not often in this society that women were valued more highly than men and in the case of the *wergeld* it did not mean that they had greater or even equal social rights. The specific values, the methods of payment and the degree of kinship of those who were either required to pay or who received the payment were all fixed by law or custom.

This system of kin responsibility provided a certain degree of security for individuals by its deterrent effect on would-be attackers and also by channelling feelings of outrage and revenge into socially less destructive and more manageable forms than they would otherwise have taken. Undoubtedly, they strengthened kinship ties. At the peasant level this fitted in well with the economic organization of labour. Family and kinship solidarity was more important than the individual, especially when the individual was a woman. Forced marriages, even the sale of girls as wives was common, and this not only in the case of slaves. Yet the system was comfortable and, within the limits set by the harvests, it provided some economic and probably a good deal of emotional security. But it also made it difficult for young men to set up their own households and it offered them little encouragement to undertake the back-breaking labour of clearing new land.

It was again the Church which began to break down the traditional customs and values of this agrarian society. Since Roman times the Church had championed the nuclear family based on the indissoluble marriage of two individuals. There was no doubt an analogy to Roman law in this policy of the Church; but more important was the power which the Church derived from it. For, as the sole dispenser of the sacrament of marriage and the sole judge of its maintenance, it gained a great deal of control over individuals and it gained it at the expense of the kinship groups. In practice it was a long struggle against the ingrained customs and prejudices not only of the peasants but of the highest members of lay society, including the Carolingian kings themselves. Only in 789 did a Frankish church council definitely declare marriage to be an indissoluble sacrament and

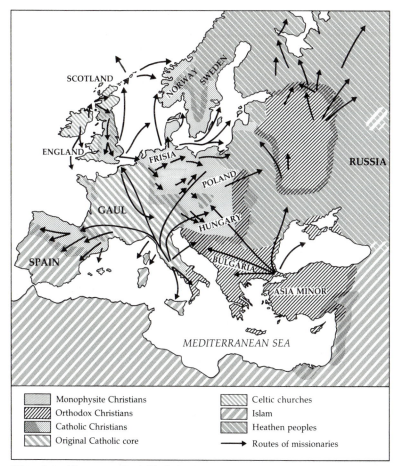

Map 2.1 The spread of Christianity.

condemn concubinage and the easy dissolution of marriages, which usually meant that the divorced wife was sent back to her own family, often followed by open hostility between the two families. At the village level the new attitudes penetrated even more slowly. When they did, they helped to weaken the traditional structure and values of the extended family. The gradual spread of the nuclear family and household introduced a new and dynamic element into the agrarian society of Europe, for young couples would now want to set up on their own. Without such a change in attitude, the rapid growth of cities in the eleventh and twelfth centuries would have been greatly hampered; for the cities recruited the great mass of their citizens from the countryside. As yet, however, these developments lay far in the future.

The introduction of the nuclear family can also be seen as a most important step in the very slow history of the emancipation of women. In the traditional, extended, family the household was, inevitably, dominated by the most senior woman of the family, a matriarch who would tend to set the rules for all other females, whether they were married or not. This was a domination often as harsh and always even more immediate than the dominion of women by men. But in the nuclear family, although of course the subordination of female to male continued, the young wife would at least be immediately mistress of her own household and control the upbringing of her children – an enormous advance in the position of the majority of women.

Agricultural yields and mortality rates

For centuries, within the vast uncultivated areas of the European continent, the actual human settlements tended to be over-populated. Moreover, because there were so few iron implements and so little incentive for individual cultivators, agricultural techniques remained desperately primitive. Such few figures as we have for the yields of Frankish estates show that in cereal cultivation the proportion of harvest to seed was rarely 2:1, and often it was less. The surplus, such as it was, was reserved for the lords, lay and ecclesiastical. The barbarian invasions had led to a diminution of the very heavy tax burden which the Roman Empire had imposed on the rural population. The Germanic successor states did their best to continue to collect Roman taxes. But this best, except in the case of the Ostrogoths in Italy who took over a still largely functioning administration, was not as effective as the imperial system had been. Even the lower taxes remained unpopular. We hear, for instance, that a tax collector of a Frankish king was killed by an angry crowd in Trier in 548, and that there was an uprising against royal taxation in central Gaul in 579. But the tax burden on the country population had undoubtedly decreased since Roman times. In the long run, however, this decrease was compensated for by increasing dues and rents paid to landowners.

For the peasants, therefore, misery and hunger were ever-present realities. From an analysis of Hungarian graves of the tenth and eleventh centuries historians have derived some rough figures of the effects of such conditions: one in every five skeletons was that of a child below the age of 1, two of every five children died before the age of 14, and more than one in five women died before the age of 20. These figures would undoubtedly hold good for other parts of Europe. At least when there was no war or plague, childhood and childbearing were the most dangerous periods of life. Small wonder that in most parts of Europe population did not increase during this period.

Economic structure

Throughout Christian Europe the characteristic unit of agrarian society was the great estate. The estates grew out of Roman origins (see Ch. 1, pp. 20–21) and the barbarians had not found it difficult to take them over, nor to imitate and spread them. Gangs of slaves still worked the demesne, or home farm, the part of the estate which the owner reserved for himself and cultivated either personally or, more usually, through bailiffs. In theory, at least, the demesne was separate from the holdings of the various types of tenants and from the communal forests and meadows. In practice, these distinctions were not always so clear. Slaves were still captured in war and traded between Christian, Muslim and pagan lands. More commonly, however, they were born in their servile status to slave parents or to parents of mixed marriages. A man could also easily become a slave, either as the penalty for a crime he had committed or by voluntary agreement, if he had no other means of livelihood.

Very gradually slavery declined. The Church, without ever condemning the institution outright, favoured the freeing of slaves. More important, work on the land was highly seasonal and owners of estates found it too expensive and too much bother to feed, house and clothe large numbers of slaves all the year round. It was economical and more convenient to give at least some of the slaves small holdings which would feed them and their families, in return for services on the demesne. In consequence, the status of such slaves with holdings tended to approach that of the semi-free serfs. The early ninth-century

73

inventory (*polyptych*) of Abbot Irminon of the abbey of St Germain des Prés, near Paris, tells us of a slave and his free wife (*colona*) who held half a farm from the abbey and who were required to do a certain amount of ploughing and of carting manure but did not have to make any payments. A group of three families, of mixed slave and half-free (*lidus*) status, held a rather larger farm. On top of ploughing, fencing and carting services they also had to pay 'for the army tax 2 muttons, 8 chickens, 30 eggs, 100 planks [of wood] and as many shingles [for roofing], 12 staves, 6 hoops and 12 torches. . . . Each pays a head tax of 4 pennies.'[1] Legally, there was a sharp distinction between the status groups; for the slave could neither plead nor serve as a witness in a court of law. In practice, the distinction was not always easy to determine, either in law or in economic status. Some of the poorest, a begging, thieving, drifting substratum of the population, were not slaves.

But while there was a tendency for the lowest classes of society to be levelled upwards, there was also a tendency for freemen to be depressed into servitude. Individual free farmers had never entirely disappeared in the Roman Empire, and the barbarian settlements had increased their number. But their position in villages belonging to great estates was very vulnerable and it was almost as bad when they were only just neighbours. Economic disasters, such as a succession of bad harvests, or simply harassment frequently forced free men to give up their freedom and their free ownership of their land in return for protection by a great lord. Charlemagne's instructions for the administration of the royal farms, the 'Capitulary De Villis', makes such protection explicit: 'If our serf should seek justice outside our estates, his master should expend every effort to gain justice for him. If the serf is unable to obtain justice in a particular locale, the master should not allow the serf to suffer for this but . . . inform us of this.'[2] At the same time it is also made clear that, on the estate itself, it is the lord or his deputy who controls justice: 'Every steward in his territory (should) hold frequent hearings, dispense justice and see to it that our people live law-abiding lives.'[3] The process of depressing men into servitude continued for centuries, although the class of free peasants never disappeared entirely. There were also important areas of Europe where geographical conditions made serfdom an uneconomic form of social organization. There was simply no way of forcing a coastal fisherman or a mountain shepherd to perform regular labour services.

The economic ethos of an underdeveloped society

The vast majority of men and women had to work on the land and this work was hard and unrewarding. All the more important, in people's minds, were values derived from strictly non-economic activities: booty from war (and this included slaves and ransom for important captives) and gifts. Generosity in presenting gifts was regarded as contributing to a person's status and nobility. King Alfred of Wessex (871–99) was praised as 'the best ring-giver'.

Not peaceful commerce, but peaceful exchange of gifts was the ideal of this period. For it was an exchange. Gift required counter-gift, equal or greater in value, so that the recipient of the gift could hold up his head. Churches and monasteries would offer prayers in return for gifts, and ecclesiastics were not slow in requesting them. Thus the abbot of Fernières, in northern France, wrote to the king of Wessex asking for a gift of lead, for roofing, and arranged for his serfs to collect the metal at the coast.

In this case, and in many others, valuable commodities were transported over long distances without the intervention of merchants and without any idea of commercial profit. Many of the early hoards of English, Byzantine and Arab coins found in Scandinavia and Russia do not at all indicate regular international trade but the proceeds of plunder or of gifts and of the diplomatic subventions which were a regular feature of Byzantine diplomacy. Coins of gold and silver were valued for themselves, just as were gold and silver jewelry; and while the minting of coins was certainly a profitable business and helpful to such trade as there was, its primary importance was often to demonstrate the prestige of the masters of the mint, the kings of the Franks, the English or the Lombards and, of course, of the Byzantine emperors and the caliphs.

At the local level goods had to be exchanged without money, for there were no coins of a value small enough to be used for buying a few loaves of bread. Often the owners of great estates would acquire lands in areas with different climates, so as to produce their own wine or oil. These commodities would then be transported, but not traded, over considerable distances. This society invested little except labour in economic production; for its ethos was conspicuous consumption and even conspicuous waste. This ethos held for all classes of society, from the peasants

Plate 2.1 The Lindau Gospels, *c*. 870.
The upper cover of the binding. The book itself has become a precious object. The many semi-precious stones on the leather binding, no doubt presented by aristocratic lay donors, produce a very sumptuous effect. The beardless, crucified Christ seems a benign figure and shows no sign of human suffering, except perhaps compassion for humanity; but intense personal suffering is expressed by the angels and human figures on the panels.

who wasted their miserable surpluses in gluttonous and drunken wedding and funeral feasts, to the nobility and the kings themselves, with their extravagant and equally drunken festivals and lavish gifts of treasure to their followers. Not for nothing are so many medieval epics (usually originating in this early period) centred on hoards of treasure and above all on gold, the shiny, incorruptible metal that casts its spell over dragons and monsters just as much as over Christian men and women.

The role of the Church was, as so often, ambiguous and in its very ambiguity, dynamic. Monks and nuns took vows of poverty; but the monasteries, convents, churches and cathedrals as institutions, and the bishops and archbishops as persons, were bound by no such vows. For them the glory of the Church consisted in the collection and the display of spendid treasures, of golden chalices and silver crosses, of ivory carvings of crucifixions, of silken banners and vestments. Above all, it consisted in the building of stone churches and cathedrals. Not until the thirteenth and fourteenth centuries was there any persistent criticism of this attitude and when it came the Church reacted violently in defence of its traditions (see Ch. 4).

The pagan barbarians had buried their most precious possessions with their dead. These possessions would vary, from the weapons of ordinary men and the simple bronze or copper jewelry which even poor women owned to the treasures of great warriors and kings, such as those superbly rich objects of Sutton Hoo, in Suffolk, buried about the middle of the seventh century (see below, p. 91). For the archaeologist and historian these objects are magnificent and tangible evidence of the life style of the people of the period. For these people themselves, however, the buried goods were permanently lost and this was a serious loss at all levels of the economy. Churchmen denounced these burials as pagan and tried to persuade people to leave their valuables to the Church. It was a long struggle against old practices and, even in the Church, capital in the form of treasure often lay idle for long periods. But at least this capital was no longer lost and it was often brought back into circulation by ecclesiastical spending on building or on the purchase of wine, incense and precious objects. It has even been argued that confiscation of church treasure and, later, plunder by the Vikings, had the beneficial effect of making treasure available for economic transactions.

Trade in an agrarian society

Those who owned wealth invested it in land, for power and prestige. Yet they, and even the ordinary villagers, had needs which could not be met by the landowners' practice of exchanging the produce of their own estates or of exchanging gifts with their friends. Local surplus was exchanged at local markets, but salt, metals and wine were not usually produced locally, or not all of them, and they had to be bought. It was the same for high quality wool for rich people's clothes, and mostly such wool came from England. Slaves were bought and sold all over Europe. If you wanted to waste goods magnificently, as rich people did, you had to have something to waste. Preferably such things were obtained by war and plunder, but where this was not possible you had to get what you wanted by trade.

This trade was carried on by professional merchants. Often, but certainly not always, they were Jews. They still sailed their ships on the Mediterranean, as they had done in Roman times, or they travelled by boat up and down the great European rivers. Only where boats would not serve they travelled, more expensively and much more uncomfortably, in caravans with pack animals, horses or mules, and only rarely with waggons. Everywhere there were adventurers or marauders, travelling in greater or smaller groups, plundering and stealing where they could, but turning themselves into peaceful merchants when they came to a place that was too strongly defended. Towns were hardly needed for such trade, although there were some ports through which it was most conveniently carried. Where Roman towns survived outside the Mediterranean area they did so mostly not so much as centres of trade but as seats of bishops or as centres of local administration. Compared with the Byzantine Empire and the contemporary Muslim caliphates, western Europe was an isolated and underdeveloped region.

Europe begins to develop a money economy

Nevertheless, the economic isolation of western Europe was not absolute. That essential instrument of trade, money, still functioned on an international level. Around 700 all three areas, Byzantium, the Arab world and the Christian west all issued both gold and silver coins. The gold coins of the Franks, however, were undervalued. Merchants found that they could get more silver for Frankish coins in the eastern Mediterranean markets than in the west. They therefore exported gold from the west in return for silver. After some time, so little gold was left in the west that the Frankish kings had to give up coining gold altogether. But since silver was relatively plentiful, they began to coin a new silver penny (*denarius*). Twelve pennies made a shilling (*solidus*) and 20 shillings, or 240 pennies, a pound (*libra*). There were no actual coins for shillings and pounds, at that time, and these units are therefore called money of account.

The Anglo-Saxon kingdom of Mercia followed the Frankish lead (*c.* 785) and the English currency of pounds, shillings and pence (£ s d) persisted for twelve hundred years until 1971. The unit of the pound with the £ sign (from libra) is still used, even though there are now 100 pennies to the pound.

A further result of the movement of silver from the east in the eighth century was that its value fell. The silver penny, minted also in fractions, therefore became more readily usable for everyday transactions by ordinary people. Gradually, if unevenly, western Europe began to develop a money economy. Weekly markets became common in many places and many lords began to require money payments from their peasants. This change made necessary some rationalization in the management of the great estates. It gave the owners greater control over their estates and their bailiffs and it accounts for the introduction of writing into royal and ecclesiastical administration, a characteristic of the Carolingian period. At the same time, trade became more profitable and gradually regular trade routes began to appear: from the Mediterranean over the western Alpine passes and up the river Rhône into central France; from England to Frisia and to Dorestad, on the estuary of the Rhine; and from Sweden and Hedeby in Denmark to Kiev in Russia, and from there to Byzantium and to Persia. There were also land routes from west and north of the Alps to Frankfurt, Regensburg, Prague and further east. But by far the most important trade routes between east and west were from Constantinople or Alexandria to Venice.

All these routes were precarious and many of them broke down altogether, often for long periods of time. Dorestad and many other towns in western Europe suffered Viking blackmail and plunder in the latter part of the eighth century. In the early ninth century the Magyars blocked the overland routes to the east. On the Mediterranean coast North African pirates gained footholds on the south coast of France and in some of the Alpine passes. Traffic on the coast from the Tiber to the Ebro was virtually blocked altogether. Europe would have to deal with these invaders before its trade could effectively revive. It did so in the course of the later ninth and of the tenth centuries.

Not all the economic effects of the invasions were negative, although those who suffered them certainly did not see it in this way. Churches and monasteries, as well as local magnates, spent money on fortifications and soldiers. The money and treasure which the Vikings plundered or extorted in blackmail was taken to their homes in Scandinavia; but from there it often returned, in the form of Scandinavian coins, back to the Continent and into economic circulation. It may also be that the invasions forced many people to move from their traditional habitations and therefore helped to make migrations and new settlements the dynamic element in European society which they became in the following centuries.

The kingdom of the Franks

The history of the Merovingian kings of Gaul was, as we have seen (Ch. 1), a dismal and gruesome succession of mutual struggles, treachery and civil wars. To fight these wars the kings had to reward their followers. By the beginning of the eighth century they had spent their assets, the royal treasure and the enormous royal estates which Clovis had amassed. Effective power slid into the hands of the mayors of the palace, the family that came to be called the Carolingians. The dispersal of the royal estates had been the Carolingians' gain, for they had acquired a great part of them. Men came to look to the mayors of the palace for advancement and reward for services to the king.

Here were all the elements of political catastrophe for the great Frankish kingdom: divided loyalties and, perhaps, the division of the kingdom or, worse still, conquest by an outside power. Until this time the Franks had been lucky in their geographical situation. None of the other barbarian successor states to the western Roman Empire had been even remotely in a position to threaten them seriously and the Byzantines were much too far away to attempt the reconquest of Gaul as they had attempted the reconquest of Italy. But in the early eighth century the geopolitical situation changed. The Saracens, i.e. the Arabs and the north African Muslims, had conquered Visigothic Spain with ease (see below, pp. 114–17) and soon they crossed the Pyrenees into Gaul. No doubt, they overextended their communications; but at least the conquest of southern Gaul was a distinct possibility. It took a great effort by the Franks, led by the mayor of the palace, Charles Martel (Charles the Hammer) to defeat and turn back the Muslims between Tours and Poitiers, in 732. Twenty years later, Charles Martel's son, Pippin, reconquered Nîmes and in 759 the last Arab garrison in southern Gaul was destroyed.

This defeat of the Muslims, in which the Merovingian kings played no personal part, enormously enhanced the prestige of the Carolingians. In 750 Pippin sent to Rome to ask the pope whether he who had no power should continue to be called a king. The pope replied that he who exercised the power should bear the title. It was a decision which agreed both with the Roman and the Augustinian tradition of the proper order in the great chain of being (see Ch. 1, p. 52) and with Germanic practice.

The Merovingian Childeric III and his son were therefore packed off to a monastery, and Pippin was consecrated king with holy oil by Frankish bishops (751), just as David had been anointed by Samuel to replace Saul. For the Franks, at least, this was an entirely new ceremony, clearly designed to stress the biblical parallel; for were not now the Franks the Chosen People of the Lord?

Early in 754 the sacred Christian and also Roman character of the new kingship and dynasty was confirmed when the pope himself came to the Frankish court, reanointed Pippin and his sons and bestowed on them the imperial title of *patricius*. Pope Stephen II had undertaken this journey, quite possibly with the approval of Constantinople, because he was hard-pressed by the Lombard kings who were extending their authority in Italy at both imperial and papal expense.

The papal-Frankish alliance was most effective. In 755 and in the following year Pippin led Frankish armies into Italy. The Lombards were forced to promise peace and good behaviour, to hand over hostages and great treasures and to give the pope twenty-two cities and castles. These were to form the northern part of the Papal States.

Pippin died in 768, the first Frankish king in centuries to have made a name for himself beyond the borders of his kingdom. In traditional Frankish fashion he divided his kingdom between his two sons, Charles and Carloman. It is difficult to say whether European history would have taken a very different course if both had survived. Certainly it was lucky for the reputation of Charles, known as Charles the Great or Charlemagne, that Carloman died after three years.

Charlemagne (768–814)

There can be no doubt about the historical importance of Charlemagne's personality; for effective leadership, at that time as at others, depended on personality as much as on resources and opportunities. We know a certain amount about the man Charlemagne from his biographer, Einhard, a learned Frankish layman who lived at the king's court and wrote his biography, after his death, in the manner of the Roman biographer Suetonius. Charlemagne was tall, with a thick short neck and a high penetrating voice. In the museum of the Louvre, in Paris, one can now see a ninth-century bronze statuette on a fifteenth-century horse. If, as some historians hold, this statuette represents Charlemagne, then he wore drooping moustaches, rather than the long beard with which he was later commonly pictured. What is absolutely certain is the enormous physical and mental energy of the man and, in terms of his age, his inquiring mind. During his meals, Einhard writes, he had history and accounts of great deeds read to him and, rather more surprisingly for a warrior-king, he had a special liking for St Augustine's *City of God*. He found writing difficult, having started to learn it only late in life, but he knew Latin and even some Greek, and he was particularly interested in astronomy.

Charlemagne's forty-five-year reign was filled with wars and campaigns. Some of these were conducted against rebellious subjects, such as the duke of Bavaria, or against aristocratic

Plate 2.2 Bronze equestrian statuette of Charlemagne, ninth century.
Some authorities think this is a statuette of Charlemagne's grandson, Charles the Bald. The profile, however, and especially the nose look very much like those on Charlemagne's silver pennies. The technical standard of the bronze casting is very high. The pose of the rider is based on classical models.

conspirators, including one of his illegitimate sons. But his most famous campaigns were those conducted outside his kingdom. The hardest and longest was fought to subdue the Saxons, a pagan tribe living between the rivers Weser and Elbe. It started with mutual raids, escalated into punitive expeditions by the Franks and finally led to the incorporation of the Saxon lands into the Frankish kingdom, in 785. The war was fought with great bitterness on both sides. At one point the king had some 4,500 Saxon prisoners slaughtered. For the Franks it was a war for Christianity, and it was through the imposition of Christianity and the destruction of the old pagan centres of worship that the Franks finally subdued the Saxons. Even so, all resistance did not cease until the early years of the ninth century.

Almost as difficult was the campaign in northern Spain and the establishment of a Spanish March, a special frontier province, between the Pyrenees and the river Ebro. Before this could be accomplished, Charlemagne had to retreat with his army and his rearguard was massacred by Christian Basques in the Pyrenees pass of Roncesvalles (Roncevaux). We do not know why the Basques attacked fellow Christians but we may well guess that the Frankish army, like most invading armies, was not very particular about distinguishing between friend and foe. In popular mythology, however, the action at Roncesvalles was soon transformed into a heroic war against the Infidel and the incident became the basis of the great French medieval epic, the *Chanson de Roland*, a characteristic French national myth and, later, also a characteristic piece of crusading propaganda. Here is the passage describing Count Roland's death as a Christian hero:

> The County Roland lay down beneath a pine;
> To land of Spain he's turned him as he lies,
> And many things begins to call to mind;
> All the broad lands he conquered in his time,
> And fairest France, and the men of his line,
> And Charles his lord, who bred him from a child;
> He cannot help but weep for them and sigh.
> Yet of himself he is mindful betimes;
> He beats his breast and on God's mercy cries:
> 'Father most true, in whom there is no lie,
> Who didst from death St. Lazarus make to rise,
> And bring out Daniel safe from the lions' might,
> Save thou my soul from danger and despite

Of all the sins I did in all my life.'
His right-hand glove he's tendered unto Christ,
And from his hand Gabriel accepts the sign.
Straightway his head upon his arm declines;
With folded hands he makes an end and dies.
God sent to him His Angel Cherubine,
And great St. Michael of Peril-by-the-Tide;
St. Gabriel too was with them at his side;
The County's soul they bear to Paradise.[4]

The translation gives only a pale idea of the literary power of the Old French verse but a good deal more of its emotional impact on readers and listeners; and therein lay much of its historical importance.

At the other, eastern, end of his vast dominions Charlemagne moved against the Avars, one of the succession of central Asian peoples who had broken into Europe and established a loose empire over the Slavic peoples along the middle Danube and its tributaries. In 791 the Franks pushed as far east as the river Raab and they continued their campaign in the following year to break the power of the Avars and capture the vast treasure the Avars had robbed from their subject peoples. After their defeat, the Avars, a relatively small tribe, seem to have been rapidly absorbed in the local population. Frankish missionaries, based on Regensburg in Bavaria and on the newly established see of Salzburg, now competed with Greek missionaries, sent from Constantinople, in the task of converting the Danubian Slavs.

The imperial coronation

After Pippin's successful campaigns in Italy, the Lombards' relations with the papacy had, not unnaturally, remained strained. In 773 the newly-elected pope, Hadrian I, alleging breach of faith, broke openly with King Desiderius of the Lombards. When Desiderius moved against papal cities, Hadrian called on the king of the Franks for help, just as Stephen II had done twenty years earlier. For the last time a Frankish army marched against the Lombards. Desiderius appears to have been deserted by his magnates and in 774 he surrendered, accepting Charlemagne's authority as 'king of the Franks and of the Lombards and patrician of the Romans'.

The Frankish-papal alliance had clearly paid enormous dividends for both parties. There was therefore every reason to continue it. As Charlemagne's successes mounted over the next quarter of a century, clerical circles at his court and in Rome, those that is who were educated and knew some history, began to talk of a renewal of the Roman Empire in the west. The opportunity for giving some reality to such sentiments came almost by chance, in the early winter of 800. Charlemagne was in Rome to settle a violent quarrel between Pope Leo III and his political enemies in the city who had maltreated the pope and forced him to flee from the city. For Charlemagne it was essential to restore his own and the pope's authority in Rome. From his point of view, it was a fortuitous circumstance that at this time the Empress Irene, having deposed her son in 797, was ruling in her own name in Constantinople. A near-contemporary chronicle tells the story of what happened in Rome:

> And because the name of the emperor had now ceased to exist in the land of Greeks because they had a woman as emperor, it was seen by both the apostolic Leo himself and all the holy fathers who were present . . . and the rest of the people, that they ought to name as emperor Charles himself, king of the Franks, who now held Rome itself, where the Caesars were always accustomed to have their residence . . . and therefore it seemed to them just that he, with the aid of God and with all the Christian people asking, should not be lacking that title. King Charles did not wish to deny their request, and with all humility, subjecting himself to God and to the petition of the priests and all the Christian people, he received title of emperor through the coronation of the lord pope Leo on the day of the birth of our Lord.[5]

It is possible, as Einhard later claimed, that the pope's action at mass on Christmas Day 800 took Charlemagne by surprise. But it seems at least as likely that Charlemagne knew quite well what he was doing, which was to reinforce his control over the Roman Church. Constantinople, not unnaturally, was deeply offended and, for some time, relations remained tense with even some fighting over the control of Venice and over the lands on the middle Danube. To most Franks the new dignity meant little. It was a personal title of their king and not attached to his kingdoms, and these kingdoms he intended to divide among his sons, in traditional Frankish manner. But when it became clear that the early deaths of two of his three sons left only Louis (later known as the Pious), Charlemagne crowned him as his co-emperor, in traditional Roman fashion. Only gradually it came to be accepted that only the pope could formally bestow the imperial dignity; but Leo III's action in 800 was certainly a most powerful precedent.

After Louis the Pious (813–40) the imperial crown was for several generations worn by men with little power; but the dignity was never again lost to the west. While interpretations and exercise of its power varied greatly in the course of the next thousand years, it was never completely negligible, nor did princes cease to strive for it, not even in the years of its greatest weakness, the early tenth, the fifteenth and the eighteenth centuries. Napoleon, the man who in 1806 effectively forced the dissolution of the Holy Roman Empire, had only a few years previously crowned himself emperor, in the presence of the pope and in deliberate imitation of the old Roman tradition.[6] Nor, in view of this history, is it really surprising that the Habsburg emperors of Austria, having given up the Roman imperial title, never found another effective symbol to attach to themselves the loyalty of their multi-national subjects.[7]

The end of Charlemagne's empire

Louis the Pious was as conscious as his great father of the significance of the imperial title. The churchmen with whom he surrounded himself confirmed him in this attitude. They also confirmed his disapproval of the tolerant sexual morals of his father's court and of Charlemagne's generosity to his great nobles, especially when this generosity had been practised, as it often had been, at the expense of Church property. Louis determined to restore such property to the Church. The great lay lords were naturally offended. This was the more serious since the Frankish empire had reached its strategic limits even before Charlemagne's death. Louis could no longer replenish his family resources with captured treasure and lands acquired by conquest. But since he still had to reward his principal followers, the emperor's resources, and thus his authority, began to run down quite rapidly.

Louis wanted to pass his whole empire and his imperial title to his eldest son, Lothair. But his younger sons were absolutely unwilling to accept such an un-Frankish arrangement. During the last decade of Louis's life and even more after his death in 840 they fought to secure the greatest possible share for themselves.

Map 2.2 The Carolingian Empire and the Treaty of Verdun.

To gain support they had to make lavish gifts of land and treasure to their followers. From this squandering of resources the authority of the Carolingian house never recovered.

In 843, Louis's three surviving sons concluded the Treaty of Verdun by which the youngest, Charles 'the Bald' received the area west of the rivers Scheldt, Meuse and Rhône; Louis 'the German' the area east of the Rhine and north of the Alps; and Lothair the huge middle strip, from Frisia in the north to the old Lombard duchies of Spoleto and Benevento south of Rome, together with the imperial title. They swore the treaty in both west-Frankish (old French) and east-Frankish (old High German). But it was in no sense an attempt to divide the empire along linguistic, or national lines – concepts which were completely alien to the age. It was rather that, in course of time, the political divisions made at Verdun became the basis for the development of national feeling in the two outside kingdoms.

The settlement of the brothers' quarrels at Verdun did not, however, save the Carolingian dynasty from the effects of squandering its resources. In Germany Louis's descendants could do little more than keep the kingdom together. In 911 the family died out and the east Frankish magnates, the richest dukes and counts, elected one of their number, the duke of Franconia, as King Konrad I. In France, Charles the Bald's descendants were even weaker than the eastern Carolingians. Under the attacks of the French magnates and of the Vikings, royal authority and the unity of the kingdom collapsed altogether. By the end of the ninth century the great Frankish monarchy had disintegrated in France. In 987, with Hugh Capet, a new dynasty ascended the throne. But Hugh was no Pippin, legalizing an already predominant position in the kingdom. His authority extended little beyond the Ile de France, the province around Paris. His dynasty survived, but it was to take the Capetians several centuries before they were the effective rulers of the whole of France.

The strategically indefensible middle kingdom collapsed even more rapidly than France. Its broken components became prizes for the French and the Germans to fight over until the end of the Second World War, in 1945.

Britain and England

The post-Roman history of the British Isles was in many crucial ways very different from that of the former Roman provinces on the Continent. In the fifth and sixth centuries Britain was invaded not only by the Angles and Saxons from the east but by Irish peoples from the west. These were Celtic-speaking peoples living

on agriculture and pastoral farming. Their society was tribal, with complex laws and customs, and they were ruled by dynasties of kings or chieftains. So successful were the invasions of northern Britain by the Scots from Ulster that they gave their name to that country, Scotland. Archaeological evidence can trace other invasions further south, in Wales and in Devon and Cornwall, and from there the Celts moved into the Armorican Peninsula and, in their turn, gave it the name of Brittany. We find them even as far south as Galicia, in north-western Spain.

Both Anglo-Saxons and Celts had in common their dislike for cities. Their great men lived in wooden halls; the common people in wooden or mud huts, and the remains of Roman towns became 'the work of giants', unattainable and unwanted achievements. Only the monasteries and monastic churches, spreading in the late sixth and seventh centuries from Ireland to promontories and islands off the Scottish and English coasts, were built of stone. Nevertheless early English lay society was neither completely primitive nor completely cut off from the Continent of Europe. Among the many Anglo-Saxon burial grounds discovered by archaeologists the most fascinating is that at Sutton Hoo, Suffolk, discovered in 1939. It consists of the imprint left by the long-since rotted timbers of an 80-foot (24-metre) long ship on the surrounding sand. From this imprint it is possible to reconstruct the shape of this sturdy and seaworthy rowing boat. It had no mast, although sailing ships certainly existed at the time. It also contained no body; but it did contain much splendid treasure (now in the British Museum, in London): decorated slates of helmets and other weapons, brooches, buckles, the lid of a purse set with garnets, silver spoons, coins and no fewer than forty objects of solid gold. Many of these pieces would have come from the Continent and at least one coin is definitely Byzantine. The burial, or perhaps memorial, was undoubtedly that of a king, and it has been dated as belonging to the first half of the seventh century.

Plate 2.3 Irish stone cross, Durrow Abbey, Offaly.
The monastery at Durrow was founded in the sixth century by St Columba (Columcille), perhaps the most famous of St Patrick's successors. The tenth-century cross is a late and particularly sumptuous example of the preaching crosses so characteristic of early Christian art in Ireland.

According to tradition, St Patrick, a Roman Briton, brought Christianity to Ireland in the middle of the fifth century. It is, however, likely that Patrick already found Christian communities in Ireland. Gradually, Irish monasteries became centres of a highly literate, self-conscious and mission-oriented Christianity with its missions directed both towards England and the Continent.

In England Christianity had almost disappeared in the sixth century. It was revived by the deliberate despatch of the missionary St Augustine from Rome, at the end of the sixth century, and by the founding of the see of Canterbury and other English sees, in 601. From the famous *Ecclesiastical History of England* by the Venerable Bede (*c*. 671–735) we know of the gradual Christianization of England and of the conflict between the Roman and the Celtic inspired parts of the English Church. This conflict was resolved at the Synod of Whitby in 663. There the Roman method of calculating Easter was preferred over the Celtic one. The importance of this decision was that the English Church deliberately linked itself closely to Rome. These links were constantly strengthened by English pilgrimages to Rome, including those of several Anglo-Saxon kings, and by papal appointments to the English bishoprics.

While the English Church was united and strongly papal in its orientation, the country itself remained divided into a number of kingdoms. There had been no English Clovis, a king of the whole country who had adopted Christianity, and hence there was no clear tradition of unity. It is not surprising, therefore, that Bede's *History* is filled with the wars between the different kings and with the periodic attempts of stronger, more energetic or luckier ones to extend their authority over their weaker neighbours. Like the Frankish kingdom, England was lucky in her geographical position and, for some three centuries, was able to work out her own destiny relatively undisturbed. By the end of the eighth century, most of the smaller kingdoms had been absorbed by the bigger ones, and in the Midlands King Offa of Mercia, whose daughters married Charlemagne's sons, claimed with considerable exaggeration to be the Frankish king's equal.

It seems likely that the internal conditions of England, its island position, the absence of great geographical barriers, the ethnic and cultural similarity of its settlers and the unifying influence of the Church, would in any case have led to an eventual

92

political unification – just as the nature of the Frankish kingdom, its enormous extent, the ethnic and cultural differences between its parts and the inherent instability of Frankish kingship were likely to lead to the break-up of Charlemagne's empire. Both processes, in England and in Frankia, were accelerated but not basically diverted by outside pressures: the invasions of the Vikings, the Magyars and the conquests and piracy of the north African Saracens.

The Vikings

The word Viking has never been satisfactorily explained. It was the name given to the Norsemen, the inhabitants of Scandinavia. They were farmers and fishermen. Their life was hard and bleak. They had no stone buildings and no books; but they had adapted the Greek alphabet for their own purposes, mainly the carving of religious and magical texts on stones (see Ch. 1, p. 23). Evidence from hoards shows great numbers of Mediterranean objects, and especially coins, won through trade or robbery. But above all, the Scandinavians were warriors. They had an abundance of iron for their weapons and they worshipped warrior gods, Odin, chief of the gods and master of magic, and Thor, the hammer-thrower and thunderer.

All this would have mattered little to the rest of Europe, had it not been that the Vikings were also superb ship builders and sailors. Some of their ships have been preserved almost complete in Danish bogs. They were long and narrow, with an arching prow, sometimes beautifully carved. They could be rowed or sailed and they were so shallow that they could land on beaches or sail up rivers. From the end of the eighth century these boats had been perfected to such a degree that they could sail on the open ocean. This was the time when improving climate had made the seas just a little less fearful than they had been in earlier centuries.

From this moment the raids began. The first one was the sacking of the monastery of Lindisfarne, on a small island off the coast of Northumbria, in 793. Not until the Portuguese carracks sailed into the Indian Ocean, around 1500, was any European people again to enjoy such overwhelming military advantage from a superiority in naval techniques.[8] The Norwegians, driven by overpopulation and perhaps also wishing to escape from the growing authority of their kings, sailed to and settled on the Shetland and Orkney Islands. From there it was easy to make descents on Ireland and set up strong points from which to plunder the countryside at leisure. From 870 the Vikings settled in Iceland and in the tenth century on some parts of the Greenland coast. They seem to have sailed on, to the coast of the American mainland and of Newfoundland (Vinland); but they did not settle in America and supposed archaeological finds of Viking remains, such as the Kensington Stone in Minnesota, are now generally (although not universally) regarded as modern forgeries. In Iceland, at least, the Norwegians really did escape from the authority of rulers. The free landowners of the island – there were also of course slaves who were mostly Irish – would meet in a great assembly (*althing*) where they would debate matters of general interest and settle feuds and other disputes.

Further south, both in England and on the Continent, the raiders were usually Danes and they came primarily for loot and sometimes for land – very much like the Frankish warriors who followed Charlemagne against the Saxons or Avars. Their ships made them mobile and almost unbeatable; for they could strike with little warning, often deep inland from rivers, and they could retreat easily if they met a superior force. Their immediate targets were monasteries and churches. Many of these were situated conveniently near the coast and all were full of treasures accumulated for centuries and secure from theft by the respect which Christians felt for them. It is no wonder that ecclesiastical writers viewed the pagan Vikings with special horror, and their attitude

Plate 2.4   Oseberg Ship, ninth century.
This Viking ship was excavated from a burial mound by the Oslo Fjord, Norway, in 1903–04, together with a burial chamber with remains of two female skeletons – perhaps a queen and her attendant – and the remains of their clothes and household implements. The ship itself may have been a ceremonial, rather than an ocean-going, ship dating back to *c*. 800. It was 65 ft (*c*. 19.5 m) long and 15.5 ft (*c*. 4.65 m) wide. It was propelled both by oars and one sail. Its elegant lines, almost like a musical instrument, gave it great speed through the water. The style of the decorative carving is clearly related, although it is obviously much cruder, to the Anglo-Celtic book illuminations of the period (cf. Plate 2.9). Here, as so often in human history, men invested some of their highest craft and artistic skills in their weapons and engines of war (cf. Plate 1.5)

has often led historians to exaggerate the numbers of the raiders and the destruction they caused.

Nevertheless, if we now think of the Vikings in their scores and hundreds, rather than their traditional thousands, their raids were real enough. In France they turned men's minds against kings who failed to protect them and transferred their loyalty to those of the magnates who did. In this way the Vikings helped the growth of the territorial principalities. In England they settled, first to gain strong points for further raids, then to own and even farm land. Nearly half of England, from East Anglia through the East Midlands, Yorkshire and Lancashire came under their control. Here we find a proliferation of Danish place names, for instance those ending in *by* and *thorpe*, such as Grimsby and Althorpe, and many Scandinavian words passed into the English language, such as *take, call, window, sky, ugly, happy*. The Danish lords either imposed their own customs or, as often, simply took over the control and profits of the local English courts. While the whole area under their control came to be known as the Danelaw, it is unlikely that the Danish settlers were very numerous.

Moreover, once the Danes were settled, they became vulnerable to counter-attack by land. From the end of the ninth century, King Alfred the Great of Wessex (871–99) and his sons systematically built walled forts for protection and effective counter offensive. Alfred is the only Anglo-Saxon king of whom we have a full-scale biography. It was written by his friend and Latin master, the Welsh monk Asser. Asser paints a portrait of an attractive personality, a brave and skilful ruler and military leader who saw the need to counter the Danes at sea. In an age when education was confined mostly to the clergy, Alfred was an educated man, a prince who, like Charlemagne, delighted in literature and history but who went further than the great Frankish king by encouraging all young freemen of his kingdom to learn to read their own language. He therefore commissioned translations of Latin texts, such as Bede's *Ecclesiastical History*. He even translated himself. Inevitably, Asser and others added to Alfred's *Life* the sort of legends which make a great man both more human and more romantic. Alfred , when fleeing from the Danes, is said to have lived in a peasant hut and, distracted by thinking of matters of state, allowed the cakes to burn which he had been set to watch; or again, Alfred, disguised as a minstrel, entered and spied out a Danish camp. Thus in England Alfred

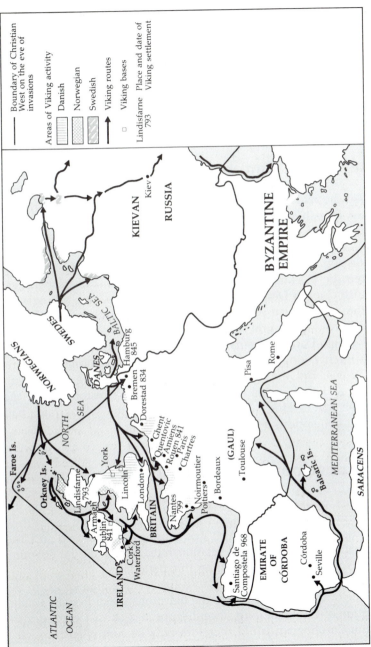

Map 2.3   The Viking invasions.

became a folk hero, rather like, much later, St Louis in France, Frederick the Great (Old Fritz) in Prussia and George Washington in America.

By the middle of the tenth century, the Danes had been thoroughly defeated. The last Scandinavian king of York was deposed in 954 and, for the first time, England became a united kingdom. The Danes were relatively quickly absorbed into the English population.

The Danish Empire

In 980 the raids started again. But this time they were organized by the Danish and Norwegian kings and princes who had become powerful enough to prevent the private initiatives of their subjects. The raids were now on a very much larger and more professional scale than the earlier ones, and they were aimed at systematic blackmail and conquest, rather than private plunder. In 1016 Cnut of Denmark was acknowledged as king of England. In the wars which led to this event, both English and Danish leaders could be found on both sides. In the end, English, Danish and Anglo-Danish magnates were not displeased with the rule of a mighty king who observed the separate customs of all his kingdoms. But the union was too artificial. Cnut's early death (1035) and that of his sons (1042) led to the restoration of the English line of kings. Elsewhere in Europe the Viking raids had ceased generations before.

The development of feudalism

In order to understand the effects of the Viking invasions on the dissolution of the Carolingian Empire it is necessary to go back and discuss the way in which this empire was governed and also the nature of the personal relationships among the landowning classes which developed during this period.

When the Carolingians replaced the Merovingian kings, in the middle of the eighth century, the old professional Roman administration of Gaul had long since disappeared. A vast empire, such as the Carolingian, could therefore only be controlled through a system of relationships between the ruler and powerful men in the kingdom on whom he would have to rely for support and for carrying out his commands.

The Carolingians did this in two ways. They used the old institution of the counts as effective royal governors of the counties into which the kingdom was divided. The counts were appointed for periods of time and could be removed or transferred at the king's will. Charlemagne had between 200 and 300 counts at any one time, and most of them were Frankish noblemen. Secondly, the ruler bound men to himself as vassals (from a Celtic word, latinized as *vassus*) through a special oath of loyalty or fealty. In return he would support them at his table (and this custom persisted, especially in the case of young noble boys brought up in the royal household) and, more and more, through the grant of a *beneficium*, i.e. an honour, an immunity and especially land. This land came to be called a fief. In his turn, the vassal obliged himself to serve his lord, especially in war.

This system could hardly have developed as it did if it had not also rested on much older Germanic traditions of lordship and loyalty. As early as the first century AD the Roman historian Tacitus described this relationship:

> It is in accordance with their most sacred oath of allegiance to defend and protect him (their chief) and to ascribe their bravest deeds to his renown. The chief fights for victory; the men of his retinue for their chief. . . . They look to the liberality of their chief for their war-horse and their deadly and victorious spear.[9]

Loyalty, especially in battle, remained the principal manly virtue, and disloyalty or desertion of one's leaders was the greatest dishonour. More than five hundred years after Tacitus the Anglo-Saxon poem *Beowulf* describes the dishonour of those of Beowulf's men who had run away during the hero's final and fatal battle with a fire-breathing dragon:

> And when the battle was over Beowulf's followers
> Came out of the wood, cowards and traitors,
> Knowing the dragon was dead. Afraid,
> While it spit its fires, to fight in their lord's
> Defence, to throw their javelins and spears,
> They came like shamefaced jackals, their shields
> In their hands, to the place where the prince lay dead,
> And waited for Wiglaf to speak . . .

Then Wiglaf turned and angrily told them
What men without courage must hear . . .

'I say what anyone who speaks the truth
Must say. Your lord gave you gifts,
Swords and the armour you stand in now;
You sat on the mead-hall benches, prince
And followers, and he gave you with open hands,
Helmets and mail shirts, hunted across
The world for the best of weapons. War
Came and you ran like cowards, dropped
Your swords as soon as the danger was real.
Should Beowulf have boasted of your help, rejoiced
In your loyal strength? . . .

. . . Too few of his warriors remembered
To come when our lord faced death, alone.
And now the giving of swords, of golden
Rings and rich estates is over,
Ended for you and everyone who shares
Your blood: when the brave Geats hear
How you bolted and ran, none of your race
Will have anything left but their lives. And death
Would be better for them all, and for you, than the kind
Of life you can lead, branded with disgrace!'[10]

Loyalty between lord and vassal was the psychological cement of early medieval society; but it was a substance frequently flawed by even more basic emotions, by selfishness, greed, ambition and above all, by fear. The converse of loyalty was the lord's liberality, the need to reward his vassals. It was this need which determined much of the political history of the European monarchies.

In the eighth and ninth centuries a formalized relationship between lord and vassal spread through much of Europe, and not only between the kings and their magnates but also between greater and lesser landowners. Unlike the relationship between lord and peasant, it was always one between freemen. The insecurity of the times induced small men to seek the protection of powerful ones and ambition drove these latter to extend their power. It was here that the Viking and Magyar invasions and the civil wars between the later Carolingians played a most important role.

Just as important was a change in military techniques. Charlemagne's armies consisted still, in the main, of foot soldiers who won their victories not least because of the superiority of the Frankish swords and coats of mail. From the middle of the eighth century, however, mailed horsemen became more and more important. Only a considerable landowner could afford to serve as a horseman. Increasingly, social prestige in a society with an essentially military ethos came to be identified with knight service, as it came to be called. About the middle of the ninth century an invention, dating to fifth-century China and possibly to earlier Indian prototypes, began to be regularly used in western Europe. This was the stirrup, and it transformed cavalry warfare. Up to this time, the horseman had been essentially a mobile archer and thrower of spears. Now he became an equestrian battering ram. Heavily mailed, on his equally heavily mailed horse, the horseman could now use the enormous impact of their combined mass through a rigidly held lance, while the stirrups prevented this impact from throwing him out of the saddle. For five hundred years heavily mailed cavalry dominated European battlefields and gave to the knights an unsurpassed social prestige. That of the free warriors on foot, the backbone of the earlier barbarian armies, inevitably declined.

The linking of *beneficium* with vassalage, the practice which came to be called feudalism, was a very effective method of social and political organization and it accounts for much of the success of the early Carolingians. It was not, however, a stable system. Counts and other vassals quite naturally sought to fuse their fiefs with their private property and to make them permanent and hereditary. The later Carolingians were forced to accede to these claims, first in order to buy support and, later, because they no longer had the means to counter them. At the same time, the vassals of the great magnates themselves, seeing the weakness of royal authority and beset by invasions and civil wars, tended to attach themselves more and more closely to their immediate overlords, even while they, too, tried to make their own fiefs hereditary.

They could also become vassals of different lords, for different fiefs, and this practice raised formidable problems about conflicting loyalties. In this new form, in which fiefs were hereditary and could be taken away only in case of a great crime such as rebellion, feudalism became a flexible relationship that varied considerably in detail in different parts of Europe and over periods of time. Its heartland remained the heartland of the

101

Carolingian Empire, between Rhine and Loire. From there it spread in varying forms to England, Italy, Germany and the new Slavonic kingdoms in central eastern Europe. Its hold on Scandinavia and Spain, however, was much more tenuous and even within central and western Europe there were areas, such as Friesland and parts of the Alps where it never appeared at all.

New principalities in the west

The virtual collapse of the Carolingian monarchy in France and in the middle kingdom and the dynamics of feudalism allowed a number of its greatest vassals to establish themselves as quasi-sovereign princes. Counts made themselves hereditary rulers, especially when they managed to combine several counties or marches. This happened, for instance, in Flanders, and the counties of Autun (northern Burgundy) and of the margravate of the Breton March. At the mouth of the Seine the Vikings had settled in the late ninth century and in 911 their leader Rollo (Hrolf) was recognized by the king as duke of Normandy. Aquitaine, always uneasily attached to the Frankish kingdom, became a virtually independent dukedom (*c.* 880). Its ruler still recognized the suzerainty, i.e. formal feudal overlordship, of the king. The rulers of Provence and Italy did not even do that but proclaimed their independence as kings in their own right.

Germany

The Saxon dynasty and the Magyars

In the eastern Frankish kingdom political disintegration proceeded more slowly. The four dukes of Saxony, Franconia, Swabia and Bavaria, originally Carolingian officials, maintained considerable authority in their large dukedoms which roughly coincided with old tribal and dialectal divisions and hence maintained some cohesions.

After Konrad I's death, the German magnates elected the duke of Saxony as Henry I, king of Germany (919–36) or, as contemporaries still thought of it, of the eastern Franks. Gradually, against much opposition, Henry extended his authority, claiming at one time even suzerainty over the west Frankish kingdom. Most important, he organized the first effective defence against the Magyars.

The Magyars were the last of the central Asian nomads during the first millennium of the Christian era who moved into the great Hungarian plain, that westernmost extension of the Asian steppe. They subjugated the Slavs and other peoples living there and destroyed the Greater Moravian principality, in the area of the present Czechoslovakia. Then, from the last quarter of the ninth century, the Magyars raided deep into Italy, Germany and even France, spreading destruction and terror as great as the Vikings.

Henry I countered them by building walled strong points, not unlike those used by the Anglo-Saxons against the Danes. Finally, in 955, Henry's son, Otto I was strong enough to inflict a shattering defeat on the Magyars near the river Lech. It was the end of the Magyar invasions and the end of the movement of whole tribes and peoples from Asia into Europe, until the Mongol invasions of the thirteenth century. Very rapidly, like the Norsemen in Normandy, the Magyars now settled as a landed ruling class in Hungary although, unlike the Norsemen, they kept their own language.

Otto the Great

Unlike his father, Otto I had himself 'elected' king in Aachen, Charlemagne's city, in order to strengthen the Frankish tradition of his kingship (936). For twenty-five years he was busy putting down rebellions of his quarrelsome relatives and other magnates and in extending his authority over the Slavs on the lower Elbe. In Germany he relied, more even than Charlemagne, on the higher clergy, the bishops and abbots to whom he and his sons granted the secular powers formerly exercised by the Carolingian counts. Here was an effective answer to the centrifugal forces of Carolingian feudalism. The bishops looked to the king for support against the lay magnates who were always ready to encroach on ecclesiastical property. They were appointed by the king and were his men or sometimes even his relatives; and because of the celibacy of the higher clergy they could not make their bishoprics hereditary.

It was, in tenth century conditions, a most effective system. Its inherent dangers were to become apparent only in the next

103

century when the papacy began to contest the king's control over the German episcopate and when the prelates came to be faced with an agonizing conflict of loyalties. Nevertheless, it seems possible that Otto had some awareness that his system of government required him to keep some control over the papacy. There were, however, many reasons for his march to Rome. Burgundy, Provence and northern Italy were all politically unstable. It was inevitable that the most powerful king in Christendom should be drawn into their politics, and most of all a king who saw himself as the successor of Charlemagne. Again like his predecessor, he intervened effectively in Roman politics and was crowned emperor (962).

The imperial title, which for some generations had either been assumed by weak Italian kings or had been in abeyance, was now, once again, conferred by the pope on the most powerful ruler of the West, a Saxon but a king of the Franks or, as people gradually came to say, of the Germans. For centuries the destiny of the Germans and the Italians and the papacy would be closely linked. Frenchmen, Englishmen and Spaniards would resent it that the Holy Roman Empire had been 'translated' to or, rather, grabbed by the Germans. But they could not deny the fact.

Otto II and Otto III

Otto I ended his long and successful reign by marrying his son to a Byzantine princess. This son, Otto II (973–83), and his grandson, Otto III (983–1002), both died young and did not have time to work out their policies. Otto II took seven years to pacify the German princes and in southern Italy he suffered a crushing defeat at the hands of the Saracens. But the monarchy was now sufficiently strong to survive the long minority of Otto III. This highly educated half-Greek and half-German ruler used on his seals the legend *Renovatio imperii Romanorum*, the Revival of the Roman Empire. It was, of course, a Christian empire in which, however, the Church and the pope would be the instruments of imperial government. Otto deposed and made popes according to the needs of his imperial politics. In 999 it was the turn of his friend, the French scholar and mathematician Gerbert of Aurillac who took the name of Sylvester II, as a fitting companion to Otto's role as a new Constantine. Pope Sylvester I (314–35) had,

Plate 2.5 Otto III enthroned, *c.* 998.
This illustration, from the Gospel book of the German emperor whose
mother was a Byzantine princess, was painted in the Benedictine
monastery of Reichenau, an island in Lake Constance, Germany. The
emperor, with his imperial insignia – the crown, the staff and the orb
with its cross – and flanked by respectful, almost adoring ecclesiastics
and warriors, is meant to represent the revival of the Roman Empire
in its specifically Christian form. This illumination, monumental even
though only on a book-size page, is a most original blend of the
Carolingian and Byzantine styles. (cf. p. 131)

105

according to a widely believed legend, converted the emperor Constantine the Great (312–37).

Otto III certainly thought in universal terms. He visited Poland whose duke acknowledged his supreme position and he founded a new bishopric in Gnieszno (Gnesen) on the tomb of his Czech friend, St Adalbert of Prague, martyred by the heathen Prussians. Otto set up an archbishopric in Hungary and bestowed a royal crown on its first Christian king, St Stephen. Characteristically, his journey in central Europe ended with a visit to Aachen where he broke open Charlemagne's tomb, took a golden cross from the dead emperor's neck and, as the chronicler tells us, 'the rest was re-interred with great devotion'.

Was it all a misapplication of German resources, a dream that would have been shattered even without the emperor's early death? It is by no means certain. Otto's contemporaries did not think so. National states existed as yet neither in practice nor even as ideas. But the idea of a Christian empire, with its precedent in Charlemagne, was widely believed in and seemed to be an attainable end in practice. What was beginning to become evident was the fragility of a political system which depended so heavily on the personality and physical survival of the ruler, and this at a time when the Italian climate had a notoriously deadly effect on northern armies.

Eastern Europe

To the east of Carolingian Europe and to the north of the Byzantine Empire stretched a huge low-lying plain. In the south it was open grassland, the vast Eurasian steppe, continuing towards the east far into Siberia. This was the ideal ground for the nomads, the horsemen with their herds of cattle and their habit of terrorizing and exploiting more settled communities of farmers. Further north were broad belts of forest land, changing from mixed to coniferous (pine) trees and straggling finally into the desolate open tundra and the permafrost, the lands of perpetually frozen ground, of the northernmost areas of the Eurasian continent. The climate of the whole area was and is harshly continental, with extremes of temperature, like those of the American Middle West, and with only short growing seasons. But it is also an area where the many north- and south-flowing river systems make movement of people and goods relatively easy.

Such were the conditions which determined the character of the history of eastern Europe throughout the Middle Ages. Compared with Mediterranean and western Europe peasant settlements remained small, sparse and self-contained. Trade was carried on by small groups of professional merchants and by adventurers over huge distances, between the Baltic and the Black Sea or the Caspian and on to Constantinople or to Persia. It was a trade in luxuries, and the relatively few permanent trading posts at convenient river crossings or confluences of rivers rarely grew into sizeable towns.

The whole of eastern Europe therefore remained open to invaders who would find it easy to establish loosely controlled empires over vast areas but who would also find it hard to defend their dominions against the next wave of determined invaders. Only when the sedentary peasant populations would manage to organize their own political and military defences, that is their own states, would they be able to get the better of the successive nomad invaders. But this was a process that was to take a thousand years.

The Slavs

These sedentary peasant populations were originally tribes of people speaking different Slavonic languages which all belonged to the group of Indo-European languages. Along the upper Vistula, Oder and Elbe rivers, in central Europe, the western Slavonic languages developed into modern Polish and Czech. In the Balkan Peninsula they developed into Serbo-Croat and Macedonian while further east the languages of the eastern Slavs eventually became Russian.

The first independent Slavonic state was the kingdom of the Bulgars. The Bulgars were originally an Asiatic people who moved from the Volga river into the Byzantine Empire south of the Danube, towards the end of the sixth century. A hundred years later they had become Slavicized by the people whom they dominated and were recognized as an independent state by the Byzantine government. Only in the second half of the ninth century did the Bulgars become Christians, largely through the efforts of the Byzantine missionary brothers, Saints Cyril and Methodius. Cyril and Methodius conducted church services in Slavonic, translated parts of the Bible into that language and

107

Map 2.4 The expansion of the Slavs.

invented the Cyrillic alphabet, a modified form of the Greek alphabet, which is still used in Bulgarian, Serbo-Croat and Russian. The importance of these actions was not only to bring Christianity and literacy to the Slavs, but to link their religions and, hence, much of their cultural life with Byzantium. Only the western Slav principalities of Poland and Bohemia were converted by western Christian missionaries and therefore came to be firmly attached to the Roman Church and its Latin culture.

Kiev, the first Russian state

From the later eighth century small groups of Scandinavian adventurers began to trade and plunder along the great rivers from the Baltic to the Caspian. These Scandinavians were called Rus or Rhos and gave their name to the whole area and its inhabitants, Russia. Being excellent fighters, like their compatriots, the Vikings, the Rus intervened in local wars between Slav princes and they, or their descendants (generally born from Slavonic mothers because the Scandinavians did not take women along on their expeditions), also set up their own principalities and, again like the Vikings and Normans in western Europe, founded ruling dynasties. The most famous of these was the house of the semi-legendary Rurik, which was to rule Novgorod, Kiev and later, Moscow until the end of the sixteenth century.

At first, the Rus principality of Kiev was much the most important. Situated at the confluence of several smaller rivers with the Dnieper, Kiev, developed rapidly as a centre for both the north-south and the east-west trade through Russia. This trade provided the resources for the princes of Kiev to reward their followers and pay for soldiers. They extended their rule northwards over other Rus principalities and eastward over different nomad tribes. These were the wars in which the legends of the great Russian heroes had their origins, just as a hundred years earlier in the west Charlemagne's campaigns were the background for the legends of Roland and the paladins (see above, p. 84).

The success and prosperity of Kiev attracted the attention not only of its neighbouring rulers and their merchants but also of their religious leaders. The Greek Church began to send missionaries and so, rather more hesitantly, did the Latin Church. But there were also Muslims from Persia and the fairly recently converted lands between the Caspian and the Black Seas. Equally important were the Jews. The area north of the Black Sea and as far east as the Volga had for two centuries been dominated by the Khazars a group of Turkish and Iranian tribes. Many of their ruling families had adopted Judaism and there is, at present, a highly controversial theory that the ethnically non-Semitic Khazar Jews were the ancestors of the Ashkenazim, the eastern European and German Jews of medieval and modern history. However that may be, it was the Greek missionaries who won out in Kiev. The

109

princess Olga, ruler for her boy son, was converted secretly in 955 and openly in 957 during a state visit to Byzantium. But it was only in 988 that Olga's grandson, Vladimir (*c.* 980–1015) officially adopted Christianity for his whole kingdom. Vladimir married the sister of the Byzantine emperor and from then on it was Byzantine ritual and Byzantine style of church building and decoration that set the tone for Russian religious life, just as it was the Byzantine concept of rulership which, at least outwardly, came to dominate Russian political ideas.

Islam and the Arab conquests

North of the Mediterranean, successive invaders of the Roman Empire were all, sooner or later, converted to Christianity. For all their ethnic and linguistic differences, they were assimilated, to a greater or lesser extent, to either the Latin or the Greek Christian world. The invasions from the south-east of the Mediterranean had a very different result; for most of the areas which the Arabs conquered were permanently lost to Christianity.

Arabia was an area no one in the Roman Empire had much bothered about. Its deserts and oases, inhabited by semi-nomadic Bedouin tribes, were poor and backward. The Arabs made good soldiers, and both the Byzantines and the Persians used them in their armies, just as they did with the northern barbarians. The towns of Arabia, on or near the eastern shore of the Red Sea, were culturally dominated by Syria, Egypt and Ethiopia, that is by various versions of Christian beliefs and by the Judaism of the diaspora, the Jews settled outside Palestine. There seemed to be nothing here to suggest to any Byzantine or Persian leader that the Arabs would ever become a serious danger to their well-established states.

Plate 2.6 Damascus: the Great Mosque, exterior.
This huge mosque, built 706–15, was intended to represent the greatness of the Umayyad caliphs. Its style is derived directly from Roman models. This is especially evident in the upper row of arches; but the horseshoe arches were also a pre-Islamic invention. The Arabs, however, spread its use and made it a characteristic feature of their architecture. The walls of the mosque were covered with Byzantine mosaics.

In 622, Muhammad, a middle-aged merchant from Mecca, moved to Medina, some way north of Mecca, and began to organize a religious-military movement. It was this move or flight of the prophet, the hijra or hegira, which was later taken as the start of the Muslim era. By the time of Muhammad's death, in 632, his movement had spread throughout Arabia. Muhammad's religion was a strict monotheism, based on Jewish, Christian and local Arab traditions. While recognizing the bible as a holy text, Muhammad claimed that God (Allah) had inspired him, as his prophet, to proclaim the true and final religious belief and that this belief, Islam, was to be spread to all mankind throughout the world, and if necessary by the sword and by conquest. Muhammad's teachings were collected in the Koran (*Qur'ān*).

The prophet's successors, or caliphs, Abu Bakr (632–34) and Omar (634–44), were outstandingly gifted leaders. Their followers were convinced they were fighting for Allah. Within ten years they had conquered Syria, Persia and Egypt. Neither the Byzantine nor the Persian armies could stand up to the fervour of the Arab warriors. 'Have faith in Allah and his apostle and fight for his cause . . .,' the Koran proclaimed. 'He will forgive you your sins and admit you to gardens watered by running streams. He will lodge you in pleasant mansions in the garden of Eden.'[11] No doubt, the enormous booty captured by the rapid campaigns was an equal incentive, both for the riches it provided for the warriors and as a sign that Allah was fulfilling the promises of his prophet.[12]

There was little resistance from the populations of Syria and Egypt, just as there had been little resistance to the pendulum conquests of the Persian and Byzantine armies in earlier years (see Ch. 1, pp. 39–40). Most of the great cities capitulated quite rapidly. There seems to have been little destruction. The secular and ecclesiastical Christian élites and the Jewish populations calmly accepted new rulers who assured them of non-interference with their beliefs. The country population cared little to whom they paid their taxes. From these taxes there was no relief, for the Arabs thoughtfully kept the efficient Byzantine and Persian tax systems intact. Only when the Arabs, far from their original bases, attacked the Greek heartland, Anatolia, the Aegean islands and Constantinople itself, did the populations rally to the resistance.

From the beginning the new Arab empire was based on the

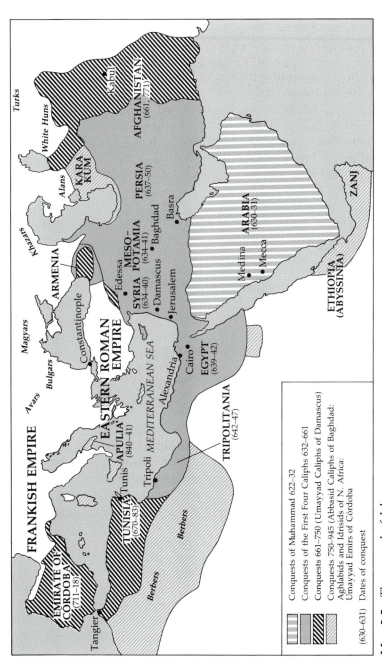

Map 2.5 The spread of Islam.

Conquests of Muhammad 622–32
Conquests of the First Four Caliphs 632–661
Conquests 661–750 (Umayyad Caliphs of Damascus)
Conquests 750–945 (Abbasid Caliphs of Baghdad:
Aghlabids and Idrisids of N. Africa:
Umayyad Emirs of Córdoba)
(630–631) Dates of conquest

great cities – quite unlike the Germanic successor states to the Roman Empire. The Arabs also founded new cities: Basra and Kufa in Mesopotamia and, somewhat later, Baghdad on the Tigris; then Cairo in Egygt and Kairouanne in north Africa (Tunisia). Only slowly, over a period of several centuries, was the majority of the population of the conquered cities converted to Islam. The Jewish communities resisted this conversion almost altogether, just as most of them had, earlier, resisted conversion to Christianity. From the end of the seventh century, Arabic was used as the official language of administration; but it took much longer until it became the current language of the Middle Eastern and north African populations. Arabic never replaced Persian in Iran.

Much of the internal politics of the Islamic empire was concerned with the question of the true succession to the prophet. The quarrels, sects and divisions which arose out of this question seem to have played emotionally a similar role to the great heresies and quarrels about the true nature of Christ in the eastern Roman Empire, even though the formal and intellectual content of these quarrels was very different. In both cases it mattered desperately to people's view of their salvation that they should be absolutely certain of the correct nature and position of the mediator between God and man. For while the caliph, unlike Christ, was never regarded as anything but a man, he was both the spiritual and political leader of Islam. Thus, from a quite early stage, Islamic society tended to splinter. By the middle of the eighth century, the Umayyad caliphs, the great conquerors of the first age of Islamic expansion who had made Damascus in Syria their capital, were displaced by the Abbasids who traced a different line of descent from an uncle of the prophet Muhammad. The principal support of the Abbasids came from northern Persia and Mesopotamia and, in consequence, they fixed their capital in Baghdad. Under different religious colours it was another great Persian-Mesopotamian victory in the millennial struggle for domination of the Near and Middle East.

The Arab conquest of Spain

The caliphs saw themselves as the successors of the shahs of Persia and of the emperors of Rome. Soon they imitated these 'predecessors' in the huge palaces they built for themselves and in the ceremonial they imposed on their courts. It was natural, therefore, that they should wish to rule the whole of the former great empires. They therefore pushed their conquests west, as well as north and east. By 670 they had reached north-west Africa and the Atlantic coast. Their main problem in this area, just as it had been the main problem for the Byzantines, was the fiercely independent Berber tribes. By the end of the seventh century, at least some of these tribes had been converted to Islam. In 711 Muslim Berbers and Arabs crossed the Straits of Gibraltar to Spain. Within seven years they controlled the whole peninsula except for a handful of small Christian principalities in the mountainous north and north-west. The great majority of the Christian and Jewish population of Spain had no more stomach to fight for the Visigothic kingdom than the Syrians and Egyptians had had to fight for the Byzantine Empire. Only when the Arabs crossed the Pyrenees and pushed deep into France did they meet determined resistance. In 732 they were decisively defeated by Charles Martell in the battle of Tours and Poitiers, in central France, and retreated back into Spain (see above, p. 81). It has been suggested that the Arabs were successful only in those regions of the Mediterranean which were geographically and climatically reasonably similar to their own Arabian home.

In Spain itself, the Arabs were never more than a small ruling élite, although the Muslim Berbers who crossed over from north Africa, were rather more numerous. In 756 an Umayyad prince who had escaped the Abbasid massacre of the rest of his family, set up a principality (emirate) in Spain, with its capital in Córdoba. This emir, Abd-al-Rahman I (756–88), formally recognized the Abbasid caliphate in Baghdad; but Muslim Spain, called al-Andalus, was a virtually independent state. Abd-al-Rahman started to build a huge mosque in Córdoba, with a veritable forest of columns, topped by double arches, and deliberately meant to rival that other great Muslim centre, the mosque of Damascus. These mosques were as much a symbol of the greatness of Islam as the Hagia Sophia was a symbol of the greatness of Christianity. It is one of the many ironies of history that, of these three splendid structures, on which their builders expended so much devotion, care and money, only one, the mosque of Damascus, has remained within its own religious faith. Both Córdoba and Constantinople became frontier capitals and eventually fell to

their mortal enemies, Córdoba to the Christian Spaniards and Constantinople to the Muslim Turks.

Highly prosperous and tolerant in religion, al-Andalus remained open to cultural influences from the whole Mediterranean. Its Arabic speaking merchants and scholars could and did travel the whole enormous length of the Islamic world. At the same time contact with the Catholic Latin north was never completely broken. Only much later did Spain again become a front line in the struggle between Christians and Muslims.

Byzantium

From its foundation as an imperial capital, Constantinople had had to serve as a frontier defence post against the barbarian invaders from the north. After the loss of Egypt and Syria it became an outpost also against attacks from the south and the east. No sooner had the Arabs conquered Syria than they organized a Syrian-Arab fleet against Byzantium. They attacked the islands of Cyprus and Rhodes where they broke up the hundred foot tall, but fallen, bronze colossus, one of the Seven Wonders of the World[13], and sold it as scrap metal to a Jewish merchant, in 653. From 674 to 678 and again from 717 to 718 they besieged Constantinople itself. But the great walls of Theodosius II held firm. At sea the Arab fleet was held at bay and finally defeated with the use of Greek fire. This was a petroleum-based compound with sulphur and quick-lime which, terrifyingly, burnt also under water. The Byzantine ships blew it from tubes like flame-throwers. It had a devastating effect against wooden ships. So well did the Byzantines keep the secret of the manufacture of

Plate 2.7 **Córdoba: the Great Mosque (Mezquita), interior.**
The building was started in 786 and extended several times in the following 200 years. The columns, with their Corinthian capitals, are conventionally Roman; but the double arches give the huge structure a light and airy appearance and the 'forest' of the more than 1,000 columns produces a very original visual effect in which the precise outlines and shape of the interior space remain mysterious – very much in contrast to the interiors of the contemporary Byzantine churches in which the interior spaces, even when they are as complex as in Hagia Sophia, always remain entirely clear.

Greek fire that it never leaked to the Arabs, and even now we are not certain of its exact composition.

Important as was the technical superiority of this secret weapon over anything the enemies of Byzantium could command until the days of gunpowder, in the fifteenth century, the restructuring of the social and military organization of the whole state was perhaps even more important for its survival. In Justinian's time the empire had still been an essentially civilian organization, with both the central government and the provincial administration staffed by civilians. The professional, largely mercenary, army had been kept strictly separate. From the end of the sixth century, first in Africa and Italy and then also in the heartland of the Empire, in Greece and Anatolia, the provincial and military administration was combined in districts called *themes* under military governors. The loss of the rich provinces of Syria and Egypt speeded up this development because much of the tax base for the large professional army had now disappeared. Soldiers now came to be rewarded by grants of land. In return they had to serve at least part of the year in the army. The system worked well. For centuries the Byzantine Empire was effectively defended by its free and armed peasants living largely in self-governing villages. They were backed by a core of professional troops, a professional navy with its remarkable fire power, and by an experienced and flexible diplomacy. These organizations were the basis of the continued survival of the east Roman Empire.

The great landowners of late-Roman times had not, however, disappeared. From the end of the ninth century they gradually extended their property and authority again and they did this at the expense of the free peasants. Some emperors, for tactical political reasons, supported these landowners. The full social and military implications of this development became apparent only in the eleventh century.

The loss of Syria and Egypt had meant also the loss of most of the great cities of the Empire. Yet the old Roman bureaucracy continued to function, based, as it had always been, on an educated, urban and non-clerical élite. Nothing like it existed any more in the west, especially not outside Italy. Byzantine administration was no doubt corrupt and its intricacies, together with those of court ceremonial and the convolutions of court politics, became proverbial and made the very word Byzantine a synonym for complexity and deviousness. Yet the Byzantine

Empire was still a more efficiently run state than any of its neighbours and rivals or any of the western successor states of the Roman Empire.

Constantinople, the one big city left in the Empire, was richer and more splendid than ever. Visitors were dazzled by the Hagia Sophia, the sprawling imperial palace overlooking the Bosphorus and the shore of Asia Minor opposite, the hundreds of churches and, above all, the unmatched and seemingly infinite number of Christian relics in these churches. The emperor, with his pearl-encrusted diadem, attired in his bejewelled robes of purple silk which only he and his closest family were permitted to wear – this ruler was held to be God's viceregent on earth, divinely appointed above all other kings and princes. The court ceremonial which surrounded him had a ritual quality, as in divine service. His authority was absolute, both in the state and in the Church; for he made laws, imposed taxes, regulated trade, appointed bishops and patriarchs and even pronounced on matters of doctrine. Yet he was no despot. Roman law always remained in force and Christian orthodoxy was the very condition of his authority. If an emperor was thought to offend against these absolutes, or even if he was simply incompetent or made himself unpopular, court factions or the army would depose or murder him, just as they had done to Roman emperors since the murder of Caligula, in AD 41.

Succession by primogeniture, that is, by the eldest son of the ruler, had never been unequivocally established in the Roman Empire. Significantly, the caliphs, following as so often on Roman tradition, did not have it either. But succession within the imperial family was generally expected. Sometimes, to strengthen their position, emperors elevated members of their family or a successful military commander to the position of co-emperors, just as Diocletian and other Roman emperors had done in past centuries. From 867 to 1056 Byzantium was ruled by the gifted Macedonian dynasty. In the tenth century, in particular, the Macedonian emperors were backed by a series of brilliant military commanders as co-emperors or as effective rulers.

Arab expansion, from the Caucasus to France, had been contained already in the first half of the eighth century. Only in Sicily, captured after 875 from Byzantium, could Islam still win major victories against the Christians. In the ninth century, the great Abbasid empire broke up into a number of virtually inde-

119

pendent states. This was the opportunity for the Byzantines. During the tenth century their armies reconquered Armenia and reached the upper Euphrates. In Syria, Aleppo, Beirut and even Damascus, the former capital of the Umayyads, fell back to the Christians. They were almost within sight of Jerusalem. From the sea the Byzantines landed in Crete and Cyprus and recaptured these islands. Equally important were the successes in the north. By the end of the tenth century the Russian advance on the Black Sea had been contained and the conversion of Russia to Christianity begun. In the Balkan peninsula the Bulgars, now Slavicized and Christianized, had set up a formidable state which more than once had threatened Constantinople itself. Now the Bulgars, too, were decisively defeated by the emperor Basil II, 'the Bulgar Slayer' (976–1025). Once more the imperial frontier ran along the lower Danube. Shortly before his death Basil was planning the reconquest of Sicily; in the end he did not have time, but not since Justinian and Heraclius had the Byzantine Empire been as powerful or its frontiers extended further, and all this after fighting for its very life against Arabs, Avars, Slavs and Bulgars. There could be no more impressive proof of the continued vitality and adaptability of the imperial Roman traditions.

The iconoclast controversy

While the political unity of the Roman Empire had been broken in the fifth century, never to be re-established, the unity of the Christian Church had survived. The Arab conquests, cutting off the quarrelsome and heretical churches of Egypt and Syria, had, if anything, emphasized the religious unity of the Greek and Latin churches. But gradually, and to contemporaries almost imperceptibly, the Greek and Latin churches drifted apart. The first open breach occurred in the eighth century. In 726 the emperor Leo III (717–41), the saviour of Constantinople during the second Arab siege (717–18), ordered an image of Christ to be removed from the door of the imperial palace. Four years later he followed up this act by issuing an edict prohibiting the worship of religious images altogether. Icons of Christ, the Virgin Mary and the saints were very popular, not only as objects of reverence and veneration but of actual worship. They were everywhere, in private houses as well as in churches and civic buildings. They were displayed on the walls of cities, to fend off the enemy, and they were carried into battle to assure the victory of Christ's cause – firmly believed to be the same as the cause of Byzantium. There were even icons which were believed to have a divine, non-human origin. Such, for instance, was the mandylion of Edessa, a piece of fabric with the image of a crucified man. This was held to be Christ's winding sheet. Later it was believed by some to be identical with the 'Turin shroud' which has a similar image but which does not otherwise correspond to what is known of the mandylion and which cannot, in fact, be traced further back than the fourteenth century.

Why then, if images were so popular, did Emperor Leo issue his decree? Historians have much debated this question; for our sources do not give an unequivocal answer. It is at least certain that among Jews and Muslims at that time there was a movement for the strict observance of the second commandment: 'Thou shalt not make unto thee any graven image, or any likeness of any thing that is in heaven above, or that is in the earth beneath . . .' (Exodus 20.4). This movement was finding echoes among many Christians. It seems very likely that these Christians, and emperor Leo himself among them, felt that the disasters which had befallen the Empire were a sign of God's anger, caused by the universal and public disregard of His strict commandment. Image worship was associated particularly with the monasteries. For all the Byzantines' veneration of monks and holy men, there was also much resentment of their ostentatious wealth; and the icons were a symbol of this wealth. And so, icons were removed, painted over or actually destroyed. Few churches escaped the iconoclast (i.e. image breaking) fury. Opponents of the movement were branded as idolaters and persecuted.

In the west there was no such disenchantment with images. That was not to happen until 800 years later.[14] In Rome it was felt that the spiritual independence of the Church was at stake. Pope Gregory II (715–31) protested against the emperor's interference in matters of faith and blocked imperial revenues in Italy. His successor, Gregory III (731–41) convened a Church council in Rome which condemned iconoclasm. The emperor retaliated by imprisoning the papal legate (ambassador) and by removing the Italian bishoprics in Byzantine Italy from the authority of the pope and placing them under that of the patriarch of Constantinople.

The breach between Rome and Constantinople was confirmed

by a council of Greek bishops which reiterated the condemnation of the icons, in 754. It was this breach which virtually forced the popes into their fateful alliance with the Franks, for they had now lost the support of the emperor against the Lombards.

In 780 the widowed empress Irene became guardian and co-emperor for her young son, Constantine VI. Like most ambitious and imperious women in history, Irene has not had a good press from historians. Character traits taken for granted in men have been thought unacceptable in women. Byzantine court politics certainly did not favour gentleness. Irene manoeuvred ruthlessly against equally ruthless attempts, by her son and other men, to get rid of her. In 797 she had her son blinded, a traditional Byzantine way of dealing with opponents, even those in one's nearest family. Irene then declared herself to be emperor – not empress. This declaration gave a legal opening to the pope's action in crowning Charlemagne Roman emperor because, it was argued, that a woman emperor could not exist and that the imperial office was vacant. For her own political reasons and after initial protests, Irene was willing to recognize Charlemagne's title, at least for a while. There was, after all, nothing new or very remarkable in having two emperors, one in Rome and one in Constantinople. Irene needed the support of the west, and for this reason, as well as probably from religious conviction, she had reversed the policy of iconoclasm. In 787 a Church council at Nicaea restored the cult of images. For her initiative in this action Irene was canonized after her death – one of the most unlikely saints, even in the Orthodox Church's generous calendar. Irene's own contemporaries were not quite so forgiving. In 802 she was overthrown and died in exile on the island of Lesbos.

In the ninth century, as the Bulgars extended their dominion in the Balkans and the Byzantines suffered a succession of military reverses, the emperor Leo V once more prohibited the cult of images. Again the western Church condemned this prohibition. Finally, in 843, and again on the initiative of a widowed empress, Theodora, the cult of images was definitely restored. The open breach between the Greek and the Roman Churches was now closed. But the iconoclast controversy had highlighted the different conceptions of the nature of Christian belief in Rome and Constantinople and of the role of the emperor in matters of faith. Feelings remained bitter; but it took another two hundred years before the eastern and western Churches finally broke their communion (see Ch. 3, pp. 181–82).

More important than theological differences, however, was the growing political orientation of the papacy towards the west. The alliance with the Franks had not only freed it from the danger of being overrun by the Lombards and from the restraints of remaining Byzantine authority, but it had given it the chance to put forward political claims that went far beyond anything previously attempted. These were founded on the Donations of Constantine, a document according to which the emperor Constantine had granted Pope Sylvester I the primacy over all other patriarchs, and nothing less than the imperial authority over Rome, Italy and all the western provinces of the Roman Empire.

The actual document was an eighth century forgery but its genuineness was almost universally accepted, probably even by the forgers who saw themselves as only recreating an authentic fact. Here was the theoretical basis of all claims of the medieval popes to judge kings and emperors and even to be the supreme temporal rulers of the West. It was within this tradition that the popes claimed the sole right to crown the western emperors and that they tried to exact ecclesiastical obedience from the whole western Church.

In this aim the popes had the enormous advantage of speaking as the successors of St Peter. At the Synod of Whitby, for instance, the papal view prevailed over the Irish tradition when its spokesman said: 'and even if that Columba of yours . . . was a holy man of mighty words, is he to be preferred to the most blessed chief of the apostles, to whom the Lord said, "Thou art Peter, and upon this rock I will build my Church"?'

For a long time the papacy had to be content with the grants made to it by Pippin and Charlemagne. And these were generous, for they effectively secured to the popes the control over the city of Rome and over central Italy. Within the Frankish kingdom, however, the kings retained authority over their church. Even the Christianization of pagan countries was not controlled by the papacy. St Willibrord, St. Boniface and the other English and Irish missionaries among the Frisians and Saxons, strong papalists to a man, failed to Christianize the mass of these pagan peoples. This was done by Charlemagne and his soldiers who forcibly converted the conquered areas and introduced the

123

Frankish ecclesiastical system and its spiritual sanctions, as much for political as for religious reasons.

With the decline of the Carolingian Empire, the papacy became a pawn in the power politics of the great Roman families. It was Otto the Great and his son and grandson who rescued the popes from this degradation and restored to them the respect of western Christendom. Characteristically, Otto III placed the new ecclesiastical organization of the newly founded kingdoms and eastern principalities of Hungary, Bohemia and Poland under the direct control of the popes, thus by-passing the authority of the old-established Frankish episcopate.

Naturally, the papacy had to pay a price for imperial favours: its virtual dependence on the German emperors. Equally naturally, in time it came to be unwilling to pay this price.

Ecclesiastical organization and monasticism

While the political position of the papacy remained ambiguous during the last three centuries of the first millennium, this was a time when many of the Church's institutions and practices crystallized permanently. The hierarchy of archbishops, bishops and priests and the organization of dioceses and parishes all took permanent form, together with the institution of the tithes, theoretically a tenth of the harvest, as permanent taxes, used especially for the support of the parish clergy. Equally important was the spread of the Benedictine monasteries with their rule of poverty, obedience, chastity and work.

Monasticism is a way of living for those who see life in the everyday world as inadequate, or as too sinful, for their spiritual needs and who therefore shut themselves off, singly or in communities, in order to pursue their religious quest in a more rigorous way than the rest of mankind. It is a phenomenon that has occurred in many of the advanced religions of Europe and Asia, including Judaism, Hinduism and Buddhism. Christianity inherited monasticism quite naturally from its spiritual, intellectual and psychological roots in the Near East. In the fourth century the Greek theologian, St Basil, set down a rule for monastic life that was to become the basis for monasticism in the Christian Church in the east. In the west it was St Benedict of Nursia who, around 540, formulated the rule which became a similar basis for monasticism in the western Catholic Church and which is even now still the rule of the Benedictine order.

Benedict, a patriotic Roman and very much within the Roman tradition of practical organization, turned away from the more visionary life-styles of the Egyptian and Syrian hermits (some of whom, we may remember, had lived in the desert or pursued their quest of holiness on top of a pillar). Much of Benedict's rule is concerned with the organization of monasteries and especially with the position of the abbot who is elected for life by the monks and then governs them autocratically but according to the rule. The poverty of the monks was personal and did not apply to the monastery or to the order as institutions. Obedience was a 'first step of humility' which is the way to 'heavenly glorification'. The monks' days were carefully divided between prayer, manual work and the reading of Scripture and devotional writings. In practice the rule was to be interpreted with some flexibility, according to the age and condition of the individual monks.

The rule of St Benedict has been called, with considerable exaggeration, the first charter for labour in Europe. What it did do was to perpetuate in an often chaotic and savage society a tradition of ordered and regular work together with a tradition of literacy, and this tradition effectively developed into one of learning and the conservation of learning. It stressed humility: yet, like all monasticism everywhere, it was also essentially élitist; for it set off monks and nuns as at least potentially more holy men and women than ordinary people. This ambivalence was no doubt one of the attractions of the monastic life and it was answered by the laity with equally ambivalent feelings towards the monks and nuns. In the later Middle Ages such feelings were often to turn into open hostility or contempt, shown in countless literary caricatures of fat, grasping and cynical monks, and feeding the streams of criticism of the Roman Church which eventually led to the Reformation.[15]

The monasteries were a refuge and opportunity for those in search of God who wished to escape from the pressures of the world. It was also a way of life, and often a very aristocratic one, for men and women with contemplative and sometimes intellectual or artistic tastes. But this alone would hardly have accounted for the willingness of laymen to endow so many monasteries as richly as they did. It was rather that the monks and nuns acted as intermediaries between God and man. Their constant prayers would assure the believer that God would not forget him in the sinful world in which he lived. Only too frequently the bishops and parish priests seemed inadequate for such a task.

The Viking raids destroyed many English, Irish and west Frankish monasteries; but even apart from these calamities, there seems to have been a more general decline in monastic standards during the Carolingian period. The political and social chaos of western Europe in the ninth and tenth centuries made this decline particularly hard to bear. It is therefore not surprising that it was in France that a monastic reform movement started, in the abbey of Cluny, in the tenth century. A splendid liturgy, a devotion to prayer in which the monks would spend six or seven hours, a dignified life-style in which monks would read or copy manuscripts, rather than engage in the more mundane manual labour which St Benedict had prescribed – all this, together with the public display of miraculous relics, would give to prince and peasant the assurance that a true Christian life was possible. Men's religious ideas are inevitably coloured by their own experience. Since the time of the Roman Empire, they had found it more effective to have an influential patron plead their case to higher authority than to do it themselves. The development of feudal relationships had reinforced this practice. What more natural than that men should look for spiritual intercession with God or Christ to the Virgin Mary and the saints and also to other men who showed themselves truly religious, the monks?

Gradually the reforms of Cluny spread. In the eleventh century they reached Rome, with far-reaching results for the relations between the Empire and the papacy.

The Carolingian Renaissance

'Of all kings Charlemagne was the most eager in his search for wise men and in his determination to provide them with living conditions in which they could pursue knowledge in reasonable comfort. In this way Charlemagne was able to offer to the culture-less and, I might say, almost completely unenlightened territory of the realm which God had entrusted to him, a new enthusiasm for all human knowledge.' Thus stated Walahfrid Strabo, abbot of the monastery of Reichenau, Lake Constance, in his mid-ninth-century prologue to Einhard's *Life of Charlemagne*.

Here was the characterization of a 'renaissance', a revival of learning and letters such as was to be repeated in the twelfth and in the fourteenth and fifteenth centuries. Such revivals tried to recapture at least something of a civilization that was recognized as greatly superior. They depended on a certain familiarity with this civilization (even if it was often misinterpreted) and on a tradition which, however tenuous at times, had never completely broken. It is almost impossible to exaggerate the importance of this awareness of classical civilization on the European mind. It spurred men to imitate and emulate the ancients and, in the process, inevitably led them to new achievements. This followed both from the nature of human intellectual endeavour and also, curiously, from the very incompleteness of men's knowledge of the ancients. The Byzantines, with a completely unbroken tradition reaching back to the classical world and with a much more complete corpus of its intellectual achievements readily accessible, felt neither the need for a renaissance nor even the self-confidence to emulate their great predecessors.

It must be admitted that the intellectual achievements of this first renaissance were limited. During the two hundred years before Charlemagne's reign, hardly any of the Roman schools and private centres of intellectual life had survived in transalpine Europe. Outside Italy and Spain, it was in England, especially in the Northumbrian monasteries, that classical learning still flourished, and its finest fruit was Bede's *Ecclesiastical History*.

The English missionaries introduced monastic schools into the newly Christianized areas of the Frankish kingdom and from there they spread back west across the Rhine. The teaching of Latin and of Latin literature, both ecclesiastical and secular, became the central achievement of the Carolingian Renaissance and the deliberate goal of the group of scholars at Charlemagne's court. 'To write sacred books is better than to till the soil for the vine, for the one nourishes the soul, the other only the stomach,' wrote Alcuin of York, the most influential of this circle. The sacred books written at that time are hardly remembered. Much more important are the Latin chronicles, the lives of kings and saints and the formal letters of Alcuin himself and other learned men. But from a modern point of view the real contribution of the age lay in the copies of classical literature which were made in Carolingian monasteries. With few exceptions, they are the oldest manuscripts of the Latin classics that have come down to

us. They were, moreover, written in a beautiful, clear hand which, after it was itself revived in Renaissance Italy, became the model for our modern printed letters.

Einhard tells us that Charlemagne delighted in listening to the Germanic sagas and had these written down. They have not survived, although we know that some of the famous later epics were current already at that time over much of the Germanic speaking world and that, from later in the ninth century, early versions of the *Song of Roland* were current in Romance-speaking countries. What little we do have is of much higher literary value than anything that was written in Latin at the time. The outstanding surviving work is undoubtedly the Old English poem *Beowulf*, which tells of the fight of a barely Christianized Scandinavian hero against various forms of the forces of evil.

Building and architecture

We have seen, in the last chapter, that Roman building skills survived the collapse of the Empire in the west. However, a very poor society, without cities and genuine city life (at least outside Italy and Spain), gave little opportunity to the skilled builder and stonemason. The private houses even of the rich were usually wooden halls. Fortifications were constructed of earthwork topped with wooden palisades. Only some churches were built in stone and not many built before the middle of the eight century have survived.

It was the great Carolingian monasteries which revived monumental church building in stone, although even then the naves often continued to have wooden roofs. Their style was derived from Roman traditions but was open to Byzantine and Syrian influence and was affected by local Germanic, Celtic or Slavonic traditions in building in wood. Most striking and most

Plate 2.8   Aachen: the Palace Chapel, interior.
The chapel was built 790–805 by one of the first transalpine architects known to us by name, Odo of Metz. The columns had to be brought from Rome and Ravenna, and the bronze railings and gratings were also imported from Italy or made by Italian workmen. The clarity of the chapel's interior space (in contrast to the Great Mosque in Córdoba), the great height and the massiveness of the columns all became prototypes for the churches and cathedrals of the Romanesque style in the following centuries.

original, as against Roman practice, was the increasing emphasis on a strong vertical element, i.e. on towers. The most influential example was the monastic church of St Riquier, near Abbeville, a huge structure, some 250 feet long, and dominated by nine towers, the highest of which rose to 180 feet. Here was the prototype for the later fully developed Romanesque style and also for that passion for towers which was to give to medieval European cities their characteristic spiky appearance.

Rather different was a deliberately 'imperial' style practised at Charlemagne's court and by those patrons who shared his imperial ideals. Its most characteristic product is the Palace Chapel at Aachen, with its central octagonal room topped by a dome above three galleries of columns and arches. It was a subtle variation on the Byzantine church of San Vitale in Ravenna. The chapel is relatively small, but it formed part of a big complex of a palace, baths and other buildings. North of the Alps it was a new idea that a kingdom should be administered from a fixed royal residence, even though in practice this could not be done for more than relatively short periods at a time.

Painting and book illumination

Building in stone was always expensive and often the skilled masons and even the stone itself had to be imported. The marble columns for Aachen, for instance, came from Italy. But what are generally, and unjustifiably, called the minor arts could be practised by local craftsmen and usually with local materials. It is a sign both of the inherent creative gifts of human beings and of their quite basic need for artistic expression that, as soon as conditions of life became a little more settled, nearly all parts of Europe produced a large amount of beautifully wrought objects. What is most striking, after the relative uniformity of style of the later Roman Empire, is the sheer richness of variety of the artistic production of Europe, from the seventh to the tenth centuries. This went together with a technical virtuosity in the handling of different artistic forms that far surpassed anything in earlier Barbarian art. It varied from the carved Viking ships, themselves both functional and beautiful, to the big Irish stone crosses and the Irish, Scottish and English altar carvings derived from them. It encompassed the classicizing and monumental stone figures in Lombard and post-Lombard Italian churches, the stone carving of capitals, from Asturias to Bavaria, and the sophisticated ivory and whalebone carving of the Carolingian and Ottonian periods. Everywhere the old Germanic traditions of the forging of splendid swords and helmets and the making of every conceivable type of jewelry became more skilled, more elaborate and often much more costly.

Perhaps the most characteristic art form of this period, however, was book illustration. It is the art form of a society which, while literate, did not take its literacy for granted any more, in the way the educated Romans had done. Books – and they were of course nearly always religious books – had themselves become precious and almost sacred objects, to be cherished, adorned and preserved with elaborate, often very expensive bindings and, happily, to be copied in the most splendid way possible. Nowhere else can we see so clearly how open the different parts of Europe were to artistic influences both of the successive peoples settling in any particular area and to Byzantine, Syrian, Armenian, Arab and even central Asian traditions. In each case such influences were assimilated in the course of several centuries and transformed into distinctive styles differing widely from each other. Except to a skilled analytical art historian, it is not at all easy to see the similarities of these styles; but, fortunately, they reproduce well and it is best to look at them: there is, for instance, the strange monumentality of the Mozarabic illuminations of Beatus of Liebana's *Commentary on the Apocalypse*, a most original pictorial language derived from classical, Visigothic and Islamic sources by the Christians living in Muslim Spain. In startling contrast to these, the Celts and Anglo-Saxons produced an incredibly intricate type of design of whirling curves, dragons and tendrils, best seen in the Scottish-Irish *Book of Kells* and the Northumbrian *Lindisfarne Gospels*.

Frankish book illuminations were quite different again and they were also subject to the most marked changes. In the eighth century, Frankish artists created marvellously gay patterns of brilliantly coloured fishes, birds and animals forming letters of the alphabet or columns, arches and crosses framing letters. With the Carolingian Renaissance there was a deliberate return to classical models and especially to the representation of human figures – Christ, the apostles or the Frankish kings. For the first time royal courts not only patronized artistic production but began to determine both its pictorial content and its style.

131

In the Ottonian period, from the mid-tenth century, the style of book illumination changed again. In Germany artists had assimilated classical models sufficiently to be able to break free from them and create a quite new, highly dramatic representation of biblical scenes and religious symbolism. But this development belongs already to a new artistic period, that of the fully developed Romanesque.

Conclusion

In the 1920s and 1930s the distinguished Belgian historian Henri Pirenne argued that both the general economy and the culture of Europe largely survived the barbarian invasions of the fifth century, and that the cultural and economic unity of the Mediterranean was not broken until the seventh and eighth centuries when the Arabs destroyed the surviving trade of western Europe with the eastern Mediterranean. Then towns and cities dwindled and, from the eighth to the tenth centuries, western Europe was reduced to an agrarian subsistence economy.

This theory has been criticized by historians who have argued that the Arabs did not destroy the Mediterranean trade of Christian Europe, or that they did so for only a short period. The critics also claimed that there was a good deal more trade between Europe and the outside world during the eighth, ninth and tenth centuries than Pirenne had allowed. Both criticisms are justified; more recently, however, historians have looked at the problem somewhat differently. The Arab invasions undoubtedly broke the

Plate 2.9 Lindisfarne Gospel, *c.* 700.
St Aidan, one of the most distinguished of the seventh-century Irish missionaries, founded a church and monastery on the small island of Lindisfarne, or Holy Island, off the coast of Northumbria, north-east England, in 635. The Lindisfarne Gospel shows the Celtic-Saxon style of book illustration. It is an amazingly intricate pattern of elongated dragon-like creatures and geometric patterns. The band-like animal patterns which were used especially in metal work came originally from Iran and central Asia. The illuminators of manuscripts fashioned these traditions into a highly original style and devised for themselves complex rules of symmetry, repetitions, inversions and mirror images, reminiscent of the elaborate patterns of counterpoint in seventeenth- and eighteenth-century music.

cultural unity of the Mediterranean area of the Roman Empire. Even though both the Arab and the Christian cultures derived from Greece and Rome, and even though neither cultural nor commercial contact was ever completely absent between them, the two societies, the Christian and the Muslim, demonstrated an almost total unwillingness to understand each other. The reasons for this deliberate incomprehension were primarily religious. Contact by a handful of merchants (and many of these Jews, whom both sides disliked), and trade in a few luxury goods did nothing to break down the mutual distrust and dislike. Later, from the twelfth century, two great areas of contact, Spain and Syria-Palestine, gave greater opportunities for mutual understanding and for intellectual and technical borrowing. But in the heartlands of the two societies attitudes remained substantially unaffected and unremittingly hostile. Later still, from the sixteenth century, the technical and military superiority of the Christians and their consequent imperialism made any deeper understanding of Islam except by a few specialists appear to be unnecessary.

By contrast with the Islamic world, there was as yet no permanent religious breach between western Europe and Byzantium. But the eastern and western Christian worlds were also drifting apart. The century-long breach over Byzantine iconoclasm was an ominous foretaste of what was to come, and the antagonisms it aroused on both sides were not easily forgotten. Scholars and politicians at the courts of Charlemagne and of the Saxon Ottos admired Byzantium and wanted to transfer its glories to the west. The vast majority of the western population thought little of such ambitions, and the Byzantines looked upon them with deep and not altogether unjustified suspicion. Bilingualism in Latin and Greek, still quite common in Rome and Constantinople at the time of Justinian and even of Gregory the Great, had by the end of this period come to be confined to the border areas of southern Italy, where Byzantine and Lombard or Frankish territory met, or to some individual merchants and scholars. The learned emperor Leo VI (886–912) is said to have given a prize of 30 pounds in gold to an Italian who could read a Latin inscription for him. True or not, the story was thought worth recording.

The old Christian Graeco-Roman world was splitting into three large areas: a Latin Christian area, from central Italy and northern Spain to Scandinavia, Poland and Hungary; a Greek Christian area, from Anatolia to Greece, the Balkans and spreading into Russia; and an Arab-Persian Muslim area, from the central Asian mountain ranges of Afghanistan to Syria, Egypt, north Africa and southern Spain.

References and Notes

1. D. Herlihy (ed.) *Medieval Culture and Society*. Harper Torch Books: New York 1968, p. 53.
2. *Ibid*. pp. 46–7.
3. *Ibid*. p. 49.
4. *The Song of Roland*, stanza 176, trans. Dorothy L. Sayers. Penguin Books: Harmondsworth 1957, pp. 142–3.
5. *Annales Laureshamenses*, trans. R. E. Sullivan (ed.) in *The Coronation of Charlemagne: What did it Signify?* Heath: Boston 1952, pp. 2–3.
6. See A. Briggs, *Modern Europe 1789–1980*; History of Europe. Longman: (not yet published).
7. *Ibid*.
8. See H. G. Koenigsberger, *Early Modern Europe 1500–1789*; History of Europe. Longman: London 1987, Ch. 3.
9. Tacitus, *Germania*, trans A. C. Howland. Quoted in D. Herlihy (ed.) op. cit., p. 27.
10. *Beowulf*, trans. Burton Raffel. Quoted *ibid*., pp. 145–6.
11. *The Koran*, trans. N. J. Dawood, Ch. 61. Penguin Books: Harmondsworth 1956, p. 104.
12. *Ibid*., Ch. 48, p. 269.
13. The Seven Wonders of the World were: the Pyramids of Egypt (3rd millennium BC); the Statue of Zeus at Olympia (*c.* 430 BC); the Temple of Artemis at Ephesus (*c.* 550 BC); the Mausoleum of Halicarnassus (fourth century BC); the Pharos (lighthouse) of Alexandria (*c.* 280 BC); the Hanging Gardens of Babylon (roof gardens and terraces, *c.* 660 BC); and the Colossus of Rhodes (*c.* 292–280 BC).
14. See H. G. Koenigsberger, *Early Modern Europe 1500–1789*; History of Europe. Longman: London 1987, Ch. 3.
15. *Ibid*. Ch. 2.

Chapter 3

The Recovery of the West, the Crusades and the Twelfth-Century Renaissance, 1000–1200

The first Christian millennium

If Christian Europe approached the year AD 1000 in dread of the end of the world it has not left us a great deal of evidence of such anxiety; or, at least, not significantly more than other times. The belief in an imminent Day of Judgement remained common even among highly educated men until at least the end of the seventeenth century. In the eleventh century men were, in any case, more concerned with Christ's death and resurrection than with his birth, and hence the year 1033 seemed to many more crucial than the year 1000. The time was certainly full of portents: comets and eclipses were thought to foretell disasters and upheavals or the overthrow and death of great men. The heavenly bodies seemed to be at war, the devil and his demons fighting the powers of light. In the great chain of being which St Augustine had elaborated (see p. 52) all events in the universe were interconnected. The monks of the eleventh century who chronicled the events of their time were not slow to point to the moral and religious decadence of their own age.

None of this was unusual; but for some chroniclers at least the end of the year 1033 seemed to signal the passing of a cosmic crisis.

> In the thousandth year after the passion of Our Lord [wrote the Burgundian monk, Radulfus Glaber] the rains of the thunderclouds ceased in obedience to divine goodness and mercy. The sky began to smile . . . and by its serenity and peacefulness demonstrated the magnanimity of the Creator. The whole surface of the earth was covered in pleasing verdure and in an abundance of fruits which put famine to flight.[1]

To the modern historian this picture of the dawning of a new and bountiful day may appear as a valid metaphor for the economic and cultural history of Europe after the year 1000.

The climate

It seems as if the climate, which had been improving for some time, continued to get better in the eleventh and twelfth centuries. Historians of climate speak of the 'little optimum' of this period, a rise of temperature, not enough to change the basic distribution of European vegetation but sufficient, for instance, to allow wine growing in southern England. The best of these wines, or so patriotic writers of the time claimed, were as good as French wines. Warmer weather had its disadvantages, too; for we read of locust swarms penetrating into France. Of the effects of the improved climate on the ordinary harvests we know virtually nothing; but it is reasonable to think that shorter winters and longer summers would have made a difference in countries where the growing season was normally dangerously short: in Iceland and Scandinavia, in Scotland and perhaps also on the Castilian central plateau, the meseta.

Population

We know rather more about population trends. Figures, it is true, are hard to come by, for the age was not given to counting heads. But some approximations can be made. Thus it seems fairly certain that the population of England was around one and a half million at the time of the Norman conquest (1066) and had trebled by about 1340, just before the great plague struck. In the rest of Europe population certainly also increased.

The causes of this increase are complex. Europe was more peaceful after the end of the Viking, Magyar and Saracen invasions of the ninth and tenth centuries. But violence remained a part of everyday life and local wars and feuds continued to take their toll of human life. More important for the growth of population was the decline of slavery. Landowners found it more convenient and cheaper to provide their workforce with holdings of land, rather than with food, clothing and shelter all the year round. Holding land, men would marry and raise families. The gradual dissolution of the extended family and its supersession

137

by the nuclear family (see pp. 69–72) had the same effect.

Infant and child mortality, however, remained appallingly high. A rate of 15–20 per cent for mortality in the first year of life has been suggested by historians, with perhaps 30 per cent for the first twenty years of life. Between the ages of twenty and forty women were much more vulnerable than men. Child-bearing was often fatal and still more often it left a legacy of ill health, aggravated by the heavy work in field and home which women were expected to do. Thus women were usually the first to fall prey to tuberculosis and smallpox and, in Mediterranean countries, to the ravages of malaria. So heavy was female mortality that it far outweighed the mortality of young men in warfare. In the age group from twenty to forty there seem to have been, on average, some 20 to 30 per cent more men than women. The high regard which the age had for celibacy and monasticism was undoubtedly religious in origin; but it made sense in a society that was chronically short of marriageable women.

Agricultural expansion

But perhaps the single most important cause of the growth of population was the expansion of agriculture. Most commonly this took the form of cultivating new land near existing settlements. By the latter part of the twelfth century some areas in western Europe, such as Flanders and the Rhineland, ran out of the more easily accessible new land, and men were forced to look further afield. Here was the driving force of the first great movement of population from west to east which Europe had experienced in a thousand years. To the Germans who trekked across the Elbe, the Oder and the Vistula to settle and Christianize land populated only sparsely by apparently backward pagan tribes this movement appeared as a great colonizing and civilizing mission. To the Slavonic peoples who were successfully cultivating much of this land, the Germans appeared as invaders, stealing land and massacring its inhabitants. This movement will be further discussed below.

Technological changes

The great agricultural expansion of the eleventh and twelfth centuries would not have been possible with the tools and implements of the Carolingian era. The most important change was the much greater diffusion of metals. Iron was mined in many parts of Europe and traded to areas which did not mine it. Demand came in the first place from the warriors, for swords, helmets and chainmail. But swordsmiths could also make sickles and scythes, axeheads and saws, hammers and nails. With such tools it became possible to build watermills. Watermills were an old invention, dating back to the first century BC, and evidence for their use in grinding grain has come from as widely dispersed areas as China, Anatolia and Denmark. In the early Middle Ages, however, they remained fairly rare. But in the eleventh century, when metal tools were more easily available, they spread rapidly. In 1086 the Domesday Book (see below, p. 140) recorded nearly 6000 in England. For the first time a machine, driven by a natural mechanical force and not by human or animal power, had entered the common experience of almost everyone in Europe. In practically every village there would now have to be someone with sufficient skill at least to repair such a machine when it broke down. Once the principle of the watermill was widely understood, it could be put to an increasing number of uses, such as the working of hammers and bellows in forges.

In flat country, without swiftly flowing streams to power the watermills, windmills could be built. They had been invented in Persia in the tenth century or earlier. Their appearance in Europe, like that of many other technological inventions, is controversial. But whether they were introduced by the Arabs or invented independently, they can be documented in England and France from about 1180. They spread very quickly throughout Europe and the Middle East. Until the first half of the twentieth century they remained a characteristic and beautiful feature of the European landscape.

Ploughs and field systems

Equally important was the increasing use of iron for farm implements. The heavy wheeled plough with an iron ploughshare had first been used by Slavonic peoples in the early Middle Ages. It was effective in the heavy soils of the broad belt of low-lying land, from Poland through Germany, northern France and the English Midlands. But it was adopted only slowly. Not only did iron have to become relatively cheap, but this plough also needed

139

a team of six or eight oxen to pull it. Ploughing therefore had to be a village rather than a family activity. In order that the team of oxen did not have to turn continually, fields came to be laid out in long, narrow strips, owned individually but worked communally. It was easier to arrange this in newly cultivated land than in older settlements which were traditionally laid out in small, squarish fields, suitable for the cross ploughing of the light, wheelless plough. Very generally speaking, the wheeled plough and the open field system with its long strips became common north of the Alps, while in Mediterranean countries, with their lighter soils and denser settlements, the traditional plough and field systems continued to predominate.

In the early Middle Ages it had been common practice to cultivate a field for one or two seasons and then leave it fallow for several years. With growing population, land came to be cultivated more economically by dividing it into three parts. One would be sown with winter grains, mainly rye and wheat; the second with spring grains, oats, barley and occasionally also beans; and the third would remain fallow. The fields would be used for these purposes in rotation. It took a long time for this 'three field system' to become at all common. Where it did, yields, that is the proportion of grains harvested to grains sown, seem to have improved from 2 : 1 to 3 : 1. By modern standards such yields are still desperately low. At the time, however, it was a remarkable improvement; for it left twice as much from the harvest for consumption than had been common in Carolingian times.

Seigneurie and manor

Some of this increased wealth benefited the peasants, and more were able to survive. But much of it was syphoned off by the owners of estates, the manors and seigneuries. We know most about them in England, from the famous Domesday Book of 1086. This was compiled on the orders of William the Conqueror (1066–1087) by royal commissioners sent into the counties to set down in every village the ownership or tenure of land, the number of tenants, their obligations to their lords and even the ploughteams and farm implements they owned. The information had to be provided for three points of time, the time of Edward the Confessor, Harold's predecessor; secondly, the time when

King William granted the estate; and thirdly, the date of the compilation, i.e. 1086. The purpose of the compilation was not so much that it should serve as a basis of taxation but rather as a legal record of entitlement to land after the chaos of conquest, resistance and take-over of Anglo-Saxon property by the Norman invaders. Domesday Book also established once for all the important principle that all land was held from the king. No such comprehensive source exists for Continental countries; but for the historian the written records of individual estates, especially those of monasteries, go some way to fill this gap.

On many of these estates the peasants were serfs, i.e. they were unfree, could not leave the estate without the owner's permission and often had to work on the owner's home farm. They also had to pay certain dues and fines when they inherited their holdings and on other occasions. Many lords possessed rights of jurisdiction. These frequently extended beyond the actual estate to a whole village or district and they could produce a handsome income from fines and confiscations.

A growing money economy

The expansion of agriculture and the increasing surplus of food-stuffs meant that more people could now pursue other occupations than the production of food. Craftsmen and merchants, monks and nuns, lords and higher clergy would increasingly buy their necessities, even if they themselves owned land. In village markets and country fairs men gave up bartering goods and began to buy and sell for money; for money was now becoming available. Silver was mined, mainly in Germany, and was spread by trade and plunder. The Vikings were able to carry off large sums from England and received even larger sums by blackmail, the famous *danegeld*. Most of this money had come to England in the first place from the export of wool. This trade was to be the principal source of England's monetary wealth throughout the Middle Ages.

Much of this money had its origins in silver mined in the Harz Mountains in central Germany where silver was discovered around 970 and, according to one of our sources, by the emperor Otto I himself. The Harz Mountains remained an important source of silver for a long time and its mines seem to have been the originals of the seven dwarfs of the Snow White tale.

141

Once money had begun to penetrate the countryside, land-owners could demand money rents in place of farm produce or labour services. Here was a development which began to dissolve the organization of the manor and seigneurie as early as the twelfth century. But this dissolution was a slow process, depending as much on local traditions as on the economic development of different areas and on rational calculation of the profitability of either serf labour or free hired labour or of money rents.

Specialization and professionalization

The growth of a money economy was both the result and a cause of another dynamic phenomenon of the period. This was the increasing division of labour, of specialization and professionalization. At the village level, the free farmer-warrior, while he had not completely disappeared everywhere, had been largely replaced by the landowning knight, the professional fighter *par excellence*, and on the other hand by the unfree peasant who had ceased to be a warrior. If he still wanted to fight, he would usually have to give up farming and become a professional soldier. There were many such in the army with which William the Conqueror invaded England in 1066. Even within the peasant class there were now specialists such as smiths and wheelwrights, and there were men who would be part-time farmers but also specialist carpenters or joiners, brickmakers or bricklayers, millers or shoemakers.

But what of more highly developed skills, not usually found at the village level? Take for instance bell founding. After a master founder had cast four or six church bells for a small town – a once-for-all investment which the town would hope never to have to repeat unless its church burnt down or it built a second one – he would have to move on; for there would be no further work for him in this town. In fact, the chances were that he would have to move quite a long way for his next job. It was the same for other specialists: the master builders of the cathedrals, the learned scholars, the forgers of fine weapons and even the wielders of these weapons. The Normans, the most skilled and professional fighters of the eleventh century, were in demand all over Europe, in Byzantium and southern Italy as much as in France, England and Ireland.

Most important of all, there was the clergy. They, too, were specialists and professionals whose skills were required throughout Europe. Most towns and villages could, at best, provide the local parish priest who often had to eke out a bare living by part-time farming. Of necessity, he could perform only the most basic church functions: baptisms, marriages, confessions and burials and, if the villagers were lucky, some very basic pastoral care. For everything beyond that, for church administration, for education, for missions to pagan lands, rarer skills were needed than could be supplied locally. Men who had acquired these skills therefore moved about to where they were needed, and such movement was made easier by the virtual monopoly which these clergy maintained of an international language and its literature, Latin. No one in the eleventh century thought it unusual that William the Conqueror and his son should have appointed two Italians, Lanfranc and Anselm, as archbishops of Canterbury. From its beginnings in the Roman Empire, the Christian Church had been an imperial and, hence, an international institution. Churchmen, and especially the popes, worked consistently to keep it international.

Specialization and the unity of medieval Europe

It was at this level of highly developed skills, and at this level only, that there existed something which may be called the unity of medieval Europe. At every other level, medieval Europe must be seen as a continent of peasant and tribal communities, clinging stubbornly to their age-old customs and their traditional languages, and rarely looking beyond their local horizon. But it was also developing a small group of men with highly advanced and varied skills. These skills which European society wanted and needed could mostly not be afforded on a local level but needed the whole continent to support them. What was true of skills was true of products. Most localities produced most of what they needed themselves. Their small surpluses were likely to be specialized products, not wanted in the neighbouring villages or even regions: flax and wool for clothing, furs both for warmth and as status symbols, hemp for rope, wine for the mass and for ordinary consumption, salt for seasoning and preserving food, and every type of metal for every type of implement and tool or weapon. All such commodities had to be traded, often in remarkably small quantities but over equally remarkable long distances. Some regions began to specialize in the production of certain raw materials: parts of England in sheep farming for wool, Scandinavia, Spain and parts of central Germany in the mining of iron and Germany also in that of silver. Other areas developed skills in manufacturing high quality cloth, as did Flanders and northern Italy. By the twelfth century these two regions had become the economically most advanced parts of Europe, and trade between them became a kind of commercial axis along which much of the economic life of Europe was to evolve. No longer was this a matter of exchanging gifts or of the occasional passage of a caravan of Jewish traders. Rather it was becoming (what it had never entirely ceased to be in the Mediterranean) an organized trade, regularized by a growing body of international treaties and commercial law, and carried on by skilled professional merchants, men who had to be literate and numerate and who had to communicate in an international language. This language was Latin, just as it was for the Church, although in some parts of Europe some other tongue could become a regional *lingua franca*, as for instance German in the Baltic and Norman French in the English Channel.

International trade, fairs and towns

The merchants met and exchanged their goods at international fairs where they engaged in quite complicated monetary and credit transactions. But they also needed permanent homes and warehouses, places where they could live outside the framework of feudal society with its military and labour services attached to ownership of land and with its feudal and customary laws. How could a merchant function if he had to engage in trial by combat every time he was engaged in a dispute over some piece of property? He needed appropriate laws and customs and these he found in towns and cities.

Many of the towns of Europe, especially in Italy and Spain, but also elsewhere in the territory of the old Roman Empire, had been Roman foundations and had continued to exist, even if much reduced in size, through the early Middle Ages. Many more were founded north of the Alps from the eleventh to the thirteenth centuries. Frequently, the founders were princes or bishops for whom towns represented centres of administration and authority,

Plate 3.1   Venice: façade of the Basilica of San Marco.
The city of Venice was a late-comer among Italian cities, since it was
not founded until the sixth century, but it became the longest-lived of
the Italian city republics. Since the middle of the eighth century it was
effectively independent of its political overlord, the Byzantine emperor,
and it never became part of the Holy Roman Empire. Continued trade
with Constantinople made the city wealthy, and its contacts with
Byzantine culture showed itself clearly in its architecture. The Basilica
of St Mark was built 1063–73 to house the tomb of the evangelist Saint
Mark whose body, it was claimed, had been miraculously found in
Alexandria and transferred to Venice. The Byzantine style of the
basilica, a relatively low building with multiple cupolas, like St Sophia,
and with a highly decorated façade, stands in dramatic contrast to the
contemporary Romanesque style of the cathedral of Pisa (Plate 3.10).

military strongpoints and refuges for their subjects, and above all
sources of money. The townspeople, in their turn, wanted authority to make their own laws and to control their own destinies
by taking over the administration of their towns. In return for
services, grants of credit or outright money payments they
obtained charters from their princes. At times they had to fight
for their autonomy. By the year 1200 many of the Italian cities had
become virtually independent political units, and most of the
larger towns north of the Alps had achieved at least some degree

of local self government. The differences depended on the different political constellations in the different countries (see Ch. 6).

It is almost impossible to overestimate the historical importance of this development. Parallel with the spread of the hierarchic and military principles of feudalism and of the elaboration of more effective princely government (see pp. 151–57), there now appeared institutions based on the very different principle of fraternity, the co-operation of free men in at least originally voluntary associations. Neither these associations, nor their guiding principles, were democratic in the modern sense. They did not usually give equal rights to all individual members, but their members together formed a corporation, both in law and in their awareness of privileged separateness from the outside world. This separateness was demonstrated to everyone by the city walls and, more subtly but as importantly, by the differences between feudal and urban law. Thus in 1066 the charter of Huy, in the Netherlands replaced trial by combat with an oath. If you wanted to declare yourself guiltless of a debt you now needed three 'oath-helpers'. Fifty years later the much more important city of Ypres obtained similar privileges and in the course of the twelfth century, so did most other major towns. Equally important for trading cities was the break with the common right of the local lord to seize the property of a merchant who had died on his territory. Compared with feudal law, urban law was written, uniform and rationally calculable. Originally it was usually confined to the free burgesses or citizens, excluding day workers, apprentices and male and female household servants. But in most towns there was a gradual evolution towards equality before the law and this equality came to be extended to unfree persons who settled in towns. 'Town air makes free' became an important principle in medieval law.

These legal differences distinguished the medieval town sharply from that of the ancient world and also from our modern cities, in both of which citizens of town and country live under substantially the same law. The political corporations of the medieval cities were underpinned and imitated in different associations of more limited, non-political types: guilds of merchants or craftsmen, universities for students and their teachers, orders of knighthood for the nobility. Perhaps no other institutions distinguished Latin Europe as much from other civi-

146

lized societies as its ubiquitous corporations and the pervasive corporate spirit which they engendered.

Once established, the towns acted as magnets for the country population of an economically developing continent and, in their turn, became a motor of its economic growth. They provided not only the conditions for the exercise of long distance trade but they also pioneered that most important institution, the permanent market or retail shop. The first shops were those of the artisans, the butchers, bakers, shoemakers or tailors who made or prepared the goods and then sold them from their houses or workshops. Only later were they followed by shops of people who did not actually make the goods but simply sold them by retail. Apart from the complex and specialized activities of the townspeople, their lifestyle also provided them with conviviality, entertainment and the chance of intellectual intercourse. They attracted not only merchants and craftsmen but also great nobles. 'Almost all the bishops, abbots and great men of England are, as it were, citizens of London,' so runs an account of the 1170s; 'they have their fine houses there . . . where they live expensively, when they are called by king or archbishop to councils or come to transact their own business.'

For all their attractions, however, most towns remained small by modern standards. In England, at the time of Domesday Book, a town of 2000 inhabitants was considered large. Only London and Winchester had more than 5000. On the Continent, and especially in Italy, towns were often larger. But no town in Latin Europe could compare remotely in size with Constantinople or with some of the great cities in the Arab world, Damascus, Baghdad or Cairo. In the course of the eleventh and twelfth centuries the political control of the western towns tended to fall into the hands of patriciates, small groups of families who could be of either noble or commoner origin. Usually they were those who engaged in the lucrative but also risky long distance trade and they owned much of the urban land and monopolized the membership of the town councils. It was they who built the characteristic symbols of urban greatness and independence, the town halls with towers that rivalled those of the bishops' cathedrals. But while relations between the local bishop or lay prince and the town council were often strained, basically they needed each other, politically, militarily and economically and, most important of all, they shared the same religious beliefs; for the townspeople thought of themselves as, first and foremost, forming a Christian corporation.

The European kingdoms in the eleventh century

Social attitudes

By the end of the tenth century the political structure of Europe had been shattered by the Vikings and by internal strife. The attempts by the three Ottos to rebuild the Empire on the basis of Germany and Italy had failed. It was to take centuries before a clear political pattern of Europe was to re-emerge – if indeed it can ever be said to have done so. In the meantime, the outstanding characteristic of the political life of Europe was its continuing instability.

Between 1000 and 1200 feudalism reached its widest extent. This meant that European society was dominated by a class of men brought up from boyhood to the profession of arms. As vassals, the knights had sworn allegiance to their feudal lords for their fiefs, i.e. their lands and honours. They respected their lords, the kings, dukes and counts, and even the archbishops and bishops, most when these were effective military leaders. Everywhere they built castles. These were huge and elaborate stone structures, with high walls and higher towers and often in the centre the keep, or donjon, a massive structure serving both as residence and as the last and strongest defence of the castle. These castles were very different from Alfred the Great's earthen-walled forts. The lords of the castles would dominate the surrounding countryside and ride out to fight each other. On the Rhine, one of the great European traffic ways, there were castles every few miles on both sides of the river and their lords blackmailed the river traffic into paying tolls at each castle. So universal and so destructive were the fighting and the robberies of the feudal nobility that the Church, despairing of preventing Christians from fighting each other, tried at least to limit such fighting. Knights were induced to take oaths to keep the 'peace of God'. This meant that they should respect churches and certain holy places, notably regular routes of pilgrimages, and that they should always spare the clergy and the mass of the poor people.

148

Plate 3.2 Framlingham Castle, Suffolk.
This twelfth-century castle belonged to the Anglo-Norman Bigod family, earls of Norfolk. Square or round towers, joined by 'curtain' walls, were typical for many medieval castles, as was a big central tower – the keep or donjon.

Later, the 'peace of God' was supplemented by the 'truce of God' which prohibited fighting on Sundays and Church festivals, or sometimes from Wednesday to Monday morning, out of respect for Christ's passion.

The 'peace of God' and 'truce of God' movements spread gradually from the south of France throughout Europe. They were never fully effective; but to many knights it seemed worth while to give up fighting and plundering on weekends if one could do it for the rest of the time with a better conscience. These attitudes also fitted in well with an increasingly popular view of society as it was supposed to have been created by God, the division of men into three estates, those who prayed (the clergy), those who 'protected' society by fighting (the knights) and those who worked (the great mass of the common people). This model was sufficiently close to actual experience so as not to appear absurd to the educated, and at the same time sufficiently simple to be understood by everyone. The clergy offered a ladder to intelligent and ambitious young men to rise in the world. But a dramatic rise was still a rare occurrence. Basically, the Church reflected the structure of lay society into which, after all, even the most devout churchman was born. Serfs, let alone slaves, were not normally allowed to become priests. As early as the fifth century, Pope Leo the Great had argued that to make slaves priests would be to steal them from their masters and that the soldiers of the Lord had to be free from the claims of other men. Leo's views were echoed throughout the Middle Ages and they were enshrined in canon law, the law of the Church. Bishops and heads of great monasteries functioned as territorial magnates or princes. In the dark days of the invasions of the Vikings and the Magyars they had to defend their bishoprics and monasteries by force of arms. In the brighter days of the crusades (see below, pp. 184–91) they accompanied the Christian counts and princes, not only as spiritual guides and comforters but also as military leaders and organizers. Who else but men from noble families, accustomed to organize men and to command even in war, would therefore be suitable for such high ecclesiastical appointments.

The arguments were not all on one side. It was never completely forgotten that Christ had preached the gospel to the poor and sick. Certain orders, such as the Cluniac Benedictines and the Cistercians, rejected aristocratic privileges, at any rate in their early histories. So did many Christian intellectuals, such as Abelard. Even some princes and great lords with the right to appoint to ecclesiastical benefices preferred to raise their bondmen to such dignities, so as to be doubly sure of the loyalty of their clergy. But practical common sense and ingrained attitudes reinforced each other to preserve the aristocratic bias of the Church in this society of three estates. There were even some convents which would admit only noble women; for, as Abbess Hildegard of Bingen (1098–1179) argued:

> Different classes of people should not be mixed, or they will fall out through conceit and arrogance, and the shame occasioned by their differences. The greatest danger of all is a breakdown in peaceful manners through mutual backbiting and hatred when the upper class pounce on the lower or when the lower is promoted above the higher. God distinguishes people on earth as in heaven; i.e. into angels, archangels, thrones and so on.[2]

Kingship and empires

Kings, we have said, were expected to lead their vassals in war. But there was more to medieval kingship than fighting. On his accession the king was anointed with holy oil, which signified that his office had religious as well as political aspects. Right into the eighteenth century the kings of England would touch people to cure 'the king's evil', scrofula, a disease of the lymphatic glands. It was the king's duty to uphold the law under which his subjects traditionally lived, to respect their rights and privileges and to adjudicate their disputes according to established law. If he did not do this, his subjects might rebel against him; and if he lacked either the personal qualities or the material resources to fulfil his royal functions his subjects might transfer the crown to a different family – as the Franks had done in the case of both the Merovingians and the Carolingians.

There were three ways in which a king could be successful. He could conquer other countries, which would give him both prestige and land to distribute to his followers. He could conclude marriage alliances, which might allow him or his heirs to inherit new dominions Or he could try to strengthen his power in his own kingdom by binding powerful men or families or institutions to himself and by improving the institutions of his government.

When all or most kings pursued such aims, or at least the first two, the result was bound to be international strife. Much would depend on personalities. The eleventh century, in particular, was a period when large international empires were built up quite rapidly by one or two rulers, only to break apart again in the second or third generation. The chances of building such empires or kingdoms were particularly good where a former effective authority had collapsed, as in France during the reigns of the last Carolingians, or in those borderlands where Christians disputed large areas with pagans or Muslims, as in central-eastern Europe and in the Mediterranean countries. The founders of these international empires might well be originally kings or leaders of one ethnic group, but their empires tended to be multi-ethnic. Men were very much aware of their ethnic or tribal origins, and dislike of other groups was strong But such emotions did not determine the politics of the period.

151

France and England

In the year 1000 the kings of France of the new Capetian dynasty controlled little more than the region around Paris. The royal title still gave the Capetians a faint aura of respect, especially among French churchmen; but it was no foregone conclusion that it would be the Capetians who would reunite the West-Frankish kingdom, i.e. France, rather than one of the other great French princes of the period, the duke of Normandy or of Aquitaine, or the count of Flanders or Anjou or Blois. Only fierce competition between them was certain, a struggle for supremacy, fought with shifting alliances, until one after another could be eliminated as a serious contender. It took some 450 years to arrive at the final result, about the middle of the fifteenth century.

There is little doubt that the struggle would have been concluded much earlier if other powers had not also become involved in it. Such involvement was always very likely because rulers could never ignore what happened in neighbouring countries, for fear of being suddenly faced with a new, or a more powerful old, enemy. In the case of France, the most important of the interfering neighbours was England.

In the first half of the eleventh century England was itself a part of a large North Sea empire which included Denmark and Norway. Characteristically, this empire did not outlast its founder, Cnut, and his sons. But the restoration of the English line of kings, in 1042, did not assure the continued independence of England. In 1066 the king of Norway (now also again independent of Denmark) invaded England. Harold, the English king, destroyed the invaders at the battle of Stamford Bridge. It was a decisive victory which put an end to 200 years of Scandinavian invasions of England. But within days King Harold had to meet a new and even more dangerous invader, the duke of Normandy.

William of Normandy had taken three decades to establish his rule in his own duchy. With or without justification, he claimed the English crown as successor of the former, half-Norman, king, Edward the Confessor (1042–66). Both William and Harold maintained that King Edward had designated them as his successor. At the end of September William landed his army on the English south coast and, on 14 October 1066, he defeated Harold at the battle of Hastings.

No other battle of the period is so well known, nor did any

Map 3.1 The Kingdom of France in the eleventh and twelfth centuries.

other have such far-reaching consequences. In the Bayeux Tapestry, a huge stretch of embroidery, commissioned by the Norman bishop of Bayeux but probably of Anglo-Saxon workmanship, we can follow the details of Duke William's campaign

153

Plates 3.3 (a) & (b) The battle of Hastings: scenes from the Bayeux Tapestry.

The scenes here come from the height of the battle between the heavily mailed Norman horsemen, with their spears or lances, and the Anglo-Saxon footmen, also in chain mail but armed with long swords or axes. On the left, the brothers of Harold are cut down: the Latin inscription reads. '[hic ceciceru]nt Levvine et Gyr Fratres Harol[di regis]' (*here fell Leofwine and Gyrth, the brothers of King Harold*). On the right, Bishop Odo of Bayeux rallies his men whilst William raises his visor to show his followers he is still alive. The inscription say '[hic Odo] ep[i]s[copus] baculu[m] tenens confor[tat]: hic est Willel[mus] dux' (*here Bishop Odo, holding a mace cheers* [his men]: *here is Duke William*).

The length of the whole embroidery, probably made for Bishop Odo, William's half-brother, is 231 ft (*c.* 70 m) and its width 19.5 inches (*c.* 50 cm). It is thought that another part, perhaps the crowning of William at Westminster, is missing.

and the history of King Harold, represented with the grandeur, sense of inevitability and absence of romanticism of a Greek tragedy. It took William 'the Conqueror' another four years to crush all resistance. The risings against the Normans and their often brutal repression gave rise to an anti-Norman tradition in England that was at once literary and popular. Later, from the fourteenth century, this tradition merged with other, anti-noble and anti-government, traditions and gave rise to the legends and ballads of Robin Hood, the 'English' outlaw who spent his time

154

robbing the rich to give to the poor and thwarting the sheriff of Nottingham, the agent of the foreign, i.e. Norman, king.

From the conquest the history of England was that of a mixed Anglo-Saxon and Norman-French state. William rewarded his soldiers with large grants of land in England, confiscated from the Anglo-Saxon nobility. William probably commissioned the Domesday Book precisely to show what the position was, about twenty years after the conquest. Not that William or his officials added up their findings. No one in the eleventh century thought as yet in even the most elementary statistical terms. It is modern historians who have calculated from the information in Domesday Book that the Norman royal family owned about a fifth of the land of England, the Church about a quarter, and ten or eleven of the greatest magnates another quarter. Thus some 250 persons owned most of England and nearly all of them came from the Continent. So did the majority of the knights who were substantial but not large landowners. We cannot be certain that on the Continent land, and therefore wealth, was distributed as unequally as in England; but it seems quite likely. What the conquest had done was to give England a new ruling élite, much as the barbarian invasions had done in the provinces of the western Roman Empire, 600 years earlier.

The new ruling élite in England continued to speak French, while the written work of government came to be done in Latin.

155

Map 3.2 France and England in the eleventh and twelfth centuries.

The Norman nobility intermarried with the Anglo-Saxons, but it took more than two centuries for a new English language to develop from the fusion of Anglo-Saxon and French.

Historians are still disputing how far the Norman conquest changed the political and legal institutions of England. There is no doubt, however, that the Normans systematized and adapted for their own purposes the institutions which they found in 1066. William kept for himself enormous tracts of land as a 'royal domain' and he built castles in strategic places to assure his control over the country. The most famous of these castles is the Tower of London. William kept the Anglo-Saxon administrative divisions of counties and also the smaller divisions of groups of villages, the hundreds. The chief royal officer in the county was the sheriff who commanded the military forces of the county and also headed the county court. The office was an Anglo-Saxon institution, parallel to that of the Carolingian count; but unlike the counts the sheriffs did not succeed in making their offices hereditary or the basis of a territorial lordship. Most of the medieval counties have survived, although with some redrawing of boundaries in the twentieth century.

William and his successors developed the system of royal courts and of royal taxation initiated by the Anglo-Saxon and Danish kings of the tenth and eleventh centuries. This allowed them to raise comparatively large revenues, and England acquired the rather misleading reputation of enormous wealth. But until the Normans established themselves in southern Italy and Sicily, no other western ruler was as powerful in his country as the king of England. This powerful king was, at the same time, still duke of Normandy, formally a vassal of the king of France, in practice more powerful than his feudal lord. For the kings of France it was to prove a long and difficult struggle to assert their superiority over such a vassal who would naturally always ally himself to the king's enemies.

Italy and the Normans

The death of the emperor Otto III, in 1002, had left Italy without a central political authority. In the north great noblemen manoeuvred and fought for temporary ascendency. In Rome the papacy became once again the pawn of rival Roman families. In the south Lombard dukes disputed dominion with the now weakening Saracens and the even weaker Byzantines. Here was a situation with splendid possibilities for an ambitious empire builder. The one to come out on top was Robert Guiscard. He and his brothers came to Italy from Normandy and proved themselves to be the most brilliant leaders of Norman knights, and in diplomacy a match even for the Byzantines. Like his compatriot, William the Conqueror, Guiscard was gifted with an unfailing eye for the main chance. Some time before his death, in 1085, he had made himself undisputed ruler of southern Italy and had obtained a ducal title from the pope. His brother Roger, in the meantime, conquered Sicily from the Saracens. It was a hard struggle and it took him thirty years, 1061–91.

The Normans impressed their contemporaries by their combination of apparently contradictory qualities and they naturally aroused mixed feelings. The monastic historian, William of Malmesbury, wrote about them, in about 1125:

> The Normans were – and still are – proudly apparelled and
> delicate about their food, though not excessively. They are a race
> inured to war and scarcely know how to live without it.. . . They
> live in huge houses with moderation. They envy their equals and
> wish to excel their superiors. They plunder their subjects, though
> they defend them from others. They are faithful to their lords,
> though a slight offence makes them perfidious. They measure
> treachery by its chance of success.[3]

In Italy, just as in England, the Normans proved their special genius for adapting existing institutions for their own ends. In the multi-racial and multi-religious society of southern Italy and Sicily they built up highly centralized and well-administered states which soon came to play major roles in Mediterranean politics.

Spain

Spain presented similar opportunities. The decline of Muslim power had allowed the Christian kingdoms to break out of their mountain fastnesses. In central Spain they established the Christian kingdoms of Leon and Castile in the ninth and tenth centuries. The most successful of the Christian kings was Alfonso VI of Castile and Leon (1072–1109) who conquered Toledo from one of the successor states of the once mighty caliphate of Córdoba. Much of this reconquered territory was settled by free Christian peasants, while to the east, in the kingdom of Aragon, Muslims remained much more numerous, especially south of the Ebro. It was, characteristically, on this frontier between Christianity and Islam that an outsider also managed to carve out a kingdom for himself. This was Rodrigo Diaz (*c.* 1043–99), famous in history and literature as the Cid (from the Arabic *as-síd* = lord). An effective fighter and skilful politician, taking service indifferently with Christian and Muslim kings he managed to make himself king of Valencia, in 1094. But unlike Guiscard, he did not manage to found a dynasty; for Valencia was reconquered by the Muslims after his death. In the *Poem of the Cid*, composed about 1140 but probably not written down before the early fourteenth century, the Cid is portrayed not so much as a crusading hero, fighting the infidel like Roland, but as a clever but honest hero fighting treacherous opponents, Christian, Muslim and Jewish.

Central and eastern Europe

The eastern edge of Catholic Europe also offered opportunities for empire building. Hungary, officially a Christian kingdom since the year 1000, became a relatively stable political unit, in spite of bitter family feuds in its ruling house. Further north, however, the political situation remained much more fluid. Boleslav the Brave of Poland (992–1025) managed to extend his rule westward across the river Oder, southward over Bohemia and eastward right up to Kiev. This Polish empire did not survive his death and it then became the turn of the North German, Bohemian and Silesian dukes to build their own, more modest dominions, nearly always on a multi-ethnic basis. The central areas of Poland survived as a separate state. But this state was without natural boundaries and was surrounded by aggressive neighbours. The movement of German settlers into the area between the Elbe and the Oder, and even beyond, to the Vistula, added further disturbing elements. Although this movement was often accompanied by bitter fighting, this was not a racial or ethnic war. There was a great deal of intermarriage between Germans and Slavs, and assimilation of population took place in both directions. Very roughly, west of the river Oder the German language came to predominate and east of it the Polish. It is not surprising, however, that shifting boundaries and periodic fights for the

159

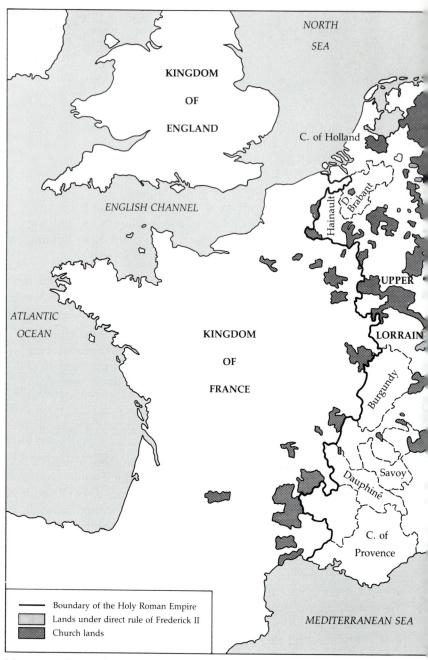

Map 3.3 The medieval German Empire. (K = kingdom; D = dukedom; M = m*

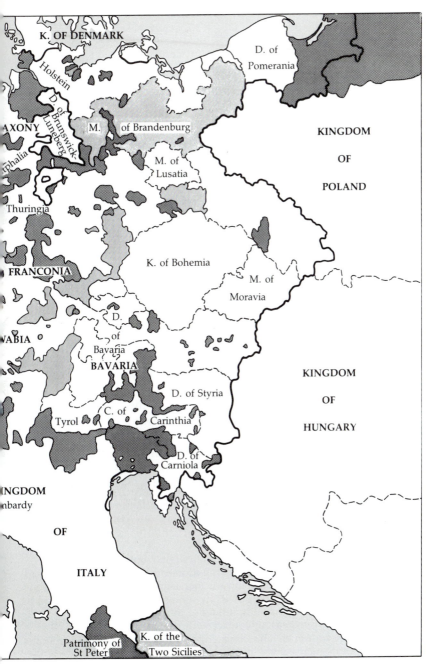

(L = landgravate; C = county).

independence of the state became the leading characteristics of Polish history right into the present century.

Germany and the Holy Roman Empire

In Germany, Otto III's immediate successors very reasonably concentrated at first on reaffirming royal power in Germany itself. So successful were they that Konrad II (1024–39) and his son Henry III (1039–56) could again lead powerful armies to Rome. Like Otto III they made and unmade popes. By the middle of the eleventh century it looked as if the biggest and most powerful of the new empires in Europe would again be the Holy Roman Empire. As it turned out, however, this empire was as vulnerable and unstable as the other political structures of the eleventh century.

Effective imperial authority depended on the private estates of the ruling house, on the loyalty of the great nobles and on imperial control of the Church and its vast properties and influence. The private imperial estates were no longer as extensive as they had been under the Ottos; for with Konrad II a new and much poorer house, the Franconian Salians, had been elected to the German throne. This meant that almost everything now depended on the personality of the ruler. Henry III's early death produced a royal minority which gave the great nobles the opportunity to try to become as independent as the great French princes. The new ruler, Henry IV (1056–1106), managed to restore the situation to some extent when he came of age and defeated his most dangerous opponents, the Saxon nobles. What he could not foresee was that at this very moment he would lose control of the one remaining pillar of royal authority, the Church. To understand how this happened it is necessary first to turn to the history of the Church and, more particularly, of the papacy.

Plate 3.4   Arles: cloisters of the Church of St Trophime, *c.* 1130.
The cloister, or arcaded passage way around a small garden, provided a human and private dimension for monastic churches, in contrast to, but still blending with, the public monumentality of the church and its massive tower. The reforming influence of Cluny was gradually compromised by increasing contact with the outer lay world. This cloister, rich with lively and often grotesque sculptures, is a sumptuous example of its increasingly luxurious spirit – against which a later generation of reformers, the Cistercians, reacted in their turn. Such ornaments were banished from their austere churches.

The Church and the papacy in the eleventh century

A reform of ecclesiastical life and especially of monastic life had begun in the tenth century. Its principal feature was a revival of the spirit of St Benedict, which meant a turning away from the world. From Lorraine and Burgundy, and especially from the great Benedictine monastery of Cluny, the reform spread through France and into England. By the middle of the eleventh century it was also beginning to make headway in Germany and Italy. Its direct influence on the papacy was at first slight.

The reform of the papacy was started in the only way this could successfully be done, by first breaking the control of the Roman aristocracy over papal elections. This was done by the powerful emperor Henry III (1039–56) who deposed three rival popes, in 1046, and appointed a succession of outsiders as popes, of whom the most effective was his own cousin, Leo IX (1049–54).

Leo was imbued with the ideas of the monastic reformers and surrounded himself with like-minded men. But the papacy was no monastery. Inevitably, even if paradoxically, the inward looking spirit of Cluny was turned outward towards the world. The reformers wanted to abolish clerical marriage and simony and to establish the authority of the pope over the whole of Christendom. By simony they meant the sale or purchase of offices in the Church. Only when this very widespread practice had ceased and when priests were celibate, and therefore no longer distracted by family interests, would the Church be truly independent and able to fulfil its spiritual functions. At the same time the problem was not fully under the control of the Church. Bishops, abbots and even parish priests were vassals of feudal lords who had endowed them with their land and other property. It had therefore always been regarded as quite logical and perfectly acceptable that these feudal lords exercised an effective right of appointment to ecclesiastical positions. Naturally, the Church had usually pressed for the appointment of suitable men; but a movement aiming at the complete independence of the Church and of its own control of ecclesiastical appointments was a very different matter. It was bound to affront old-established rights of the laity, and here lay the seeds of conflict.

It was characteristic of the new spirit in Rome that it led very rapidly to a complete breach with the Greek Church, in 1054 (see below, pp. 181–82). But at the time few people took much notice of this breach, and men were more concerned with the implications of the reforms and the new papal policy in the west.

Over the following twenty years a succession of reforming popes greatly strengthened the authority of Rome over the whole Church in the west. Even secular rulers began to acknowledge it, and William the Conqueror was anxious to obtain papal support for his conquest of England. He repaid this support by lavish gifts to the English Church and by appointing men acceptable to the reformers to English bishoprics and abbacies. A mutually advantageous alliance between king and pope was therefore perfectly possible, at least in a country as far from Rome as England.

Henry IV and Gregory VII

It was unlikely to prove so easy nearer home, in Italy and Germany; for here both pope and king would be less willing to compromise. In 1073 the youngest and the most dynamic and intransigent of Leo IX's friends, the Roman Hildebrand, was elected pope as Gregory VII. From his letters and from a list of precepts he wrote out for himself we know his ideals and his aims. They amount to the most far-reaching and uncompromising statements of papal claims up to that time, including the claim that the pope had the right to depose emperors. This was the logical conclusion of the fifth-century doctrine of the two powers, the secular and the priestly, of which the priestly had been held the greater because priests 'must render account in the divine judgment for the kings of men also'. (see Ch. 1, pp. 56–57).

On the other side was an equally forceful personality. Henry IV had just grown out of an unhappy minority and had successfully asserted royal authority over rebel magnates. While not unsympathetic to the moral principles of the ecclesiastical reform movement, he had no intention of giving up royal powers over the appointment of the German and Italian bishops who were his vassals for their vast fiefs and on whose support he had to be able to count in his struggle against the great nobles. But to the pope this position was intolerable, for it negated the independence of the Church.

The quarrel broke out over a disputed election to the archbishopric of Milan, the key to northern Italy and thus of vital importance to both the king and the pope. Soon an increasingly acerbic exchange of letters escalated to direct action. Early in 1076 the king and an assembly of German bishops (all Henry's appointees, of course) declared Gregory VII deposed:

> Henry, king not by usurpation, but by the pious ordination of God, to Hildebrand, now not pope, but false monk: . . . You were emboldened to rise up against the royal power itself, granted us by God . . . Wherefore relinquish the Apostolic See which you have arrogated . . . Descend! Descend![4]

Frankish and German kings and emperors had certainly deposed popes before this; but they had done so in Rome and with an army at their back. When it came to acting at long distance, the pope could do much better than the king. Gregory replied by excommunicating Henry and releasing his subjects from their allegiance to him. The result was shattering. The German princes, happy to grasp such a splendid opportunity to break the power of the king, declared Henry deposed if he did not obtain absolution within a year. Even most of the bishops now deserted him. Henry had no choice but to come to terms with the pope. In January 1077, with only a few followers, he crossed the Alps by the snow-bound Mont-Cenis Pass:

> Straining every nerve, now scrambling on hands and feet . . . now staggering and slipping and falling . . . they just managed to reach the plains. The queen and the other ladies of their company were sat on oxhides and dragged down.

Thus stated an eye witness account. Henry met the pope in the small castle of Canossa, in northern Italy, and 'stripped of his royal robes . . . barefoot, fasting from morning till evening . . .' he waited for three days until Gregory granted him absolution.

It was a terrible humiliation for a successor of Charlemagne and Otto the Great, and it did nothing to resolve the issues between king and pope. But it gained Henry time to rally support in Germany and Italy. The civil war in Germany continued, but Henry gained the upper hand. When Gregory later renewed his excommunication it had little effect. Men had come to distrust the pope's motives. Henry led an army into Italy, set up an anti-pope and was crowned emperor. Gregory had to flee from Rome and ended his life in exile (1085). His great adversary ended little better, with Italy lost again, with many of the Germany princes still in revolt and with his own son making common cause with the rebels (1106).

Once himself king, however, this son, Henry V, continued the struggle with the papacy and, at one point, even kidnapped the pope. In 1122 a formal compromise was finally concluded. The emperor agreed to give up the 'investiture' of bishops and abbots with staff and ring, i.e. with the symbols of their ecclesiastical office; but for all their lands they still had to do homage to the king. This was a position that had been reached in both England and France already some time earlier and without the dramatic struggles of Gregory VII and Henry IV. Somewhat misleadingly, this one, rather formal, aspect of the struggle has given its name to the whole as the 'Investiture Contest'. What remained still undecided was the much more important question of who effectively appointed men to high ecclesiastical office.

The historical significance of the Investiture Contest

For the first time the dualism between Church and state, that dual power structure and dual focus of society which had its origins in the collapse of the Roman Empire in the west, had led to open conflict. It had not happened earlier because of the disproportion between the enormous military power of the emperors and the relative weakness of the popes. But with great tenacity and in the face of many setbacks, the popes had over the centuries extended their authority over the Christian Church in the west. A convergence of several lines of development made this authority quite suddenly much more effective in the middle of the eleventh century. This was the reform movement within the papacy and its alliance with monastic reform, together with the emergence of a number of dynamic personalities prepared both to push papal claims to hitherto undreamt-of lengths and to use realistically favourable political situations, such as the rebellions of the German princes and the political ambitions of the Normans in southern Italy.

At the same time the sudden advance of the claims of the papacy has to be understood in the context of the process of international professionalization (see above, pp. 142–44). The Church as we have seen, represented a highly specialized set of skills that were most effectively performed on an international level. The popes themselves were now often Germans and

Frenchmen and, in the twelfth century, even English. Conditions were therefore favourable for transforming the Church into an international organization effectively controlled from Rome – a very different matter from just insisting that the bishop of Rome had precedence over all other bishops and patriarchs. In this sense, the 'Investiture Contest' was a deliberate attempt by the papacy to professionalize the clergy further by making it independent of lay control. Since in feudal society, however, bishops were not only churchmen owing obedience to the pope, but vassals and subjects owing allegiance to their temporal rulers, conflicts of power and loyalty became inevitable. These conflicts were to dominate the history of the succeeding centuries and were to leave an even longer legacy of political thinking and political traditions.

Western Europe in the twelfth century

The first half of the twelfth century saw the gradual revival of the French monarchy. Patiently and laboriously, Louis VI, the Fat (1108–37) and Louis VII (1137–80) extended the royal domain and, with the domain, their authority. Their greatest success was the marriage of Louis VII to Eleanor of Aquitaine, the richest heiress in France, in 1137. At about the same time England was overtaken by a series of civil wars, fought over the succession to the throne between Henry I's daughter, Mathilda, who had married the count of Anjou, and Henry's nephew, Stephen of Blois. Stephen had the better of this fight, at least in England itself. But because of the paralysis of England during these wars, the real victor of the struggle was the king of France.

Then (to use a typically medieval metaphor) the wheel of fortune turned. In 1152 Louis VII divorced Eleanor of Aquitaine, and she promptly married the son of Mathilda and the count of Anjou. In 1154 this son succeded Stephen as Henry II of England (1154–89). He now ruled not only England but the whole of western France, from Normandy to the Pyrenees. There could be no more dramatic demonstration of the effects of marriage alliance than this sudden appearance of the 'Angevin Empire' in western Europe. The survival of this empire would, however, depend to a large measure on personalities.

To a large measure, but not completely so. The more intelligent

and farsighted of the medieval kings worked hard to institutionalize their power. Few did so more systematically than Henry II
of England, the first Norman-English king who was fully literate.
From his Norman predecessors Henry II had inherited an effective administration of the royal treasury. His chief ministers, the
'barons of the exchequer', would regularly receive the accounts
of the royal taxes locally collected by the sheriffs. They sat around
a table with a chequered cloth which they used as an abacus. It
was an elementary device for adding and subtracting on which
sums of money were indicated in columns representing thousands, hundreds, scores (20s) and single pounds, and also shillings and pence. The sheriffs were given receipts in the form of
tallies, pieces of wood with incisions corresponding to the
columns of the exchequer table. Clerks would also enter the
details of the accounts on pieces of parchment which were then
rolled up as 'pipe rolls'. Many of these have survived and are an
important source for historians. Only the papacy had as advanced
a system of controlling finance as the kings of England.

As early as the mid-twelfth century there was a school of
Roman law in Oxford. The idea of codifying and systematizing
English local customs as common law, administered by royal
courts for the whole kingdom, was essentially a concept derived
by English jurists from an analogy with Roman law. During
Henry II's reign a rudimentary jury procedure was systematized.
The jury of local men were required to denounce local criminals
to the sheriff or royal judge, or they were to declare, from their
own local knowledge, the true owner of a stolen or disputed piece
of property. The jury system, in varying forms, was to become
the keystone of most European legal systems. Immediately more
important, however, was the provision of 1166 by which knights
could appeal from the local courts of the great lords to the royal
courts. Here was at least a potential community of interest
between the monarchy and the numerous class of knights which
might, one day, be directed against the magnates.

Equally important in extending the king's authority and
providing coherence to the kingdom was the development of
royal writs. These were written royal commands, usually
addressed to the sheriff, to see that justice was done on a
complaint or in a dispute. It was now that the form of the writs
was standardized and that they could be obtained, against a
requisite payment, of course, by any freeman in the kingdom.

169

Henry II and Becket

It was to be expected that the extension of royal authority in the judicial field would meet with opposition. The most violent opposition came from the Church. Although since the conquest the kings of England had generally been on good terms with the papacy, the problems of divided authority and divided loyalties existed in England as much as on the Continent. These problems came into the open at the turn of the eleventh century and in terms essentially similar to those of the first Investiture Contest. In 1093 King William Rufus (1087–1100), son and successor of William the Conqueror, appointed the distinguished theologian Anselm as archbishop of Canterbury. Anselm, an Italian nobleman and abbot of the Norman monastery of Bec, was close to the Cluniac and papal reform movement. From the beginning of his archiepiscopate Anselm quarrelled with the king, both over the property of the see which the king had confiscated during the vacancy before Anselm's appointment and over the archbishop's consecration. More fundamentally, Anselm plainly told the king that the pope held the keys of the kingdom of heaven, while no emperor, king or duke held a similar charge. The argument was almost as offensive to the king as Gregory VII's claim that the power of kings and dukes came from the devil. Anselm's relations with Henry I (1100–35) were no improvement on those with William Rufus. Anselm refused both investiture by the king and also the usual act of homage for the lands his see held from the king, on the grounds that a Church council in Rome, in 1099, had prohibited such practices. The breach between king and archbishop, however, did not lead to open conflict because the English Church did not support Anselm. His attempts to reform the morals of the clergy were not popular, especially when he insisted on clerical celibacy. Many parish priests and even some bishops were married and sometimes they passed their clerical offices on to their sons. In England the king also maintained a greater hold on clerical appointments than the emperor managed to do in Germany. Anselm spent years in exile and finally agreed to a compromise, in 1107: the king gave up the right of investiture of bishops with the symbols of their spiritual authority but he continued to exact homage. It was essentially the same compromise which the emperor Henry V was to make with the pope in 1122 (see above, p. 167).

Some sixty years later the dispute between king and Church flared up again. This time it took the form of a quarrel between Henry II (1154–89) and Thomas Becket, archbishop of Canterbury, over the question of excommunication of royal officials, appeals to Rome, the income from vacant sees and, with special acrimony, over the question of the king's claim that he had the right to punish clergymen convicted of crimes in ecclesiastical courts. Becket denied this claim as an invasion of the Church's independence and as an injustice to men who would be punished twice for the same crime. Just as in the case of the emperor Henry IV and Pope Gregory VII, personalities played their part in the quarrel. To Henry II Becket, his former chancellor and his own choice as archbishop, seemed to be breaking his obligations, both of personal and of feudal loyalty. For Becket the need to live down his past as a worldly courtier and to prove his true commitment as a churchman seems to have been almost as important as the issues in the dispute. A series of compromises failed to resolve the conflict. Finally Becket excommunicated several English bishops who had supported the king and Henry showed his anger in public. Four knights took it as an invitation for action and murdered the archbishop in Canterbury cathedral, on 29 December 1170.

The details of the murder have come to us from a letter by Becket's secretary and friend, the historian John of Salisbury.

> The martyr stood in the cathedral, before Christ's altar . . . ready to suffer; the hour of slaughter was at hand. When he heard that he was sought – heard the knights who had come for him shouting in the throng of clerks and monks 'Where is the archbishop?' – he turned to meet them on the steps which he had almost climbed, and said with steady countenance: 'Here am I! What do you want?' One of the knight-assassins flung at him in fury: 'That you die now! That you should live longer is impossible.' No martyr seems ever to have been more steadfast in his agony than he . . . and thus, steadfast in speech as in spirit, he replied: 'And I am prepared to die for my God, to preserve justice and my Church's liberty. If you seek my head, I forbid you on behalf of God Almighty and on pain of anathema to do any hurt to any other man.'. . . He spoke, and saw that the assassins had drawn their swords; and bowed his head like one in prayer.[5]

As a sign of Becket's holiness, John mentioned especially that, after his death, he was found to have worn a hairshirt 'crawling

171

with lice and worms'. It was to be a long time yet before personal cleanliness was held to be a virtue next to godliness.

Intellectually Becket was not remotely the equal of Anselm. The arguments which he and Henry II put forward were entirely conventional and did not reach the level of the controversies between papalists and imperialists on the Continent. Nor was Alexander III prepared to back the archbishop unreservedly. He had no wish to drive the powerful Henry II, ruler of England and of half of France, into a close alliance with the emperor Frederick Barbarossa (see p. 173). But what the Becket affair lacked in intellectual interest and in political significance it made up for in dramatic interest and in its effect on the religious sensibilities of the people of medieval Europe. Becket was immediately acclaimed a martyr. The pope canonized him in 1173, and the tomb of St Thomas became a centre of pilgrimage, not only for England but for the whole of Europe. Only Rome itself and the supposed tomb of the Apostle St James, at Santiago de Compostela in north-western Spain, rivalled Canterbury in popularity. Henry II had to undergo a severe public penance. The immediate points of dispute between the monarchy and the Church were, as usual, settled by compromise. In practice the king's hold over the English Church remained unbroken since he maintained the right to appoint bishops.

Empire and papacy in the twelfth century

The settlement of the Investiture Contest, in 1122, was followed for the papacy by a period of consolidation. The papal court, the curia, now emerged as the most advanced and sophisticated central government in Europe, especially in its writing office, the chancery, and in its financial organization. The college of cardinals became the pope's chief adviser on all spiritual and governmental matters. To the cardinals was reserved the exclusive right to elect the pope.

This right was meant to block lay intervention in papal elections. It did not do this because it did not provide for the case of disputed election when a minority of the cardinals refused to accept the candidate elected by the majority and elected their own candidate instead. Such dual elections had occurred on a number of occasions, the last being in 1130. At that time, owing to the weakness of the emperor, the papacy suffered little damage. It was quite otherwise in 1159. A new emperor, Frederick I of the Swabian house of Hohenstaufen (1152–90), had once more re-established royal authority in Germany, athough at the price of allowing his cousin Henry 'the Lion', duke of both Saxony and Bavaria, virtually a free hand in nearly half the kingdom. Henry used it mainly to expand his power further across the Elbe and it seems as if he wanted to build up another one of the large personal empires of the period. Partly, at least, to compensate for this, Frederick turned his attention to Italy. With some justification he regarded the election of Pope Alexander III (1159–81) as a deliberate challenge; for this man had spoken of the imperial crown as a 'benefice' bestowed by the pope on the German king.

The word benefice was open to differing interpretations. It might mean just a benefit; but many persons, on both the papal and the imperial side, interpreted it in the feudal sense (see p. 99), with the implication that the pope meant that the emperor was his vassal. More clearly even than the attempts of mutual deposition by Henry IV and Gregory VII this raised the quite fundamental problem of the superiority of pope or emperor over each other or, as people were now more and more beginning to think of this problem, of the relations between Church and state. And this problem had now been posed as one of principle, regardless of the worthiness or unworthiness of the individual occupants of the office of pope and emperor.

Nevertheless, the principal protagonists in 1159 still thought in personal terms. Frederick, not surprisingly, supported the 'anti-pope' elected by a minority of cardinals. Alexander III answered by excommunicating the emperor. The struggle lasted for almost twenty years. Alexander was supported by most of the European kings but found his most effective allies in the north-Italian cities. These feared and resented the emperor's attempts to impose on them his officials and to tax them for his own purposes. Frederick I, whom the Italians called Barbarossa or Redbeard, was a man of great ability and charm but capable of acts of truly barbarian brutality. He fought several successful campaigns in Italy, only to find that the resistance of the Italian cities and the deadly Mediterranean malaria, which could destroy whole armies, cheated him of final victory. In the end Frederick and Alexander were officially reconciled in another compromise which settled some of the immediate points at issue but not the

173

fundamental question of Church-state relations. After this it was relatively easier to find another compromise with the Italian cities.

Frederick made up for these partial defeats by destroying his overmighty and insubordinate cousin, Henry the Lion, in Germany. The great duchy of Saxony was broken up once and for all. The principality which later came to be called the dukedom and electorate of Saxony was only a relatively small part, the fairly recently settled south-east, of the old tribal duchy. Frederick's greatest success was, however, not the result of a victorious campaign but, characteristically, of a marriage alliance. His son married the heiress to the Norman kingdom of Sicily which, by this time, included the whole of southern Italy and was, as we have seen, the best organized and one of the richest secular monarchies in Europe. When Henry VI (1190–97) succeeded his father he occupied the most powerful position of any European ruler since Charlemagne. Although without his father's charm and the popularity that made Barbarossa a legendary figure in German history and popular culture, Henry was an immensely able politician. When the western European kings, fearing his great power, combined against him he broke their coalition by ruthlessly blackmailing Richard I of England, the 'Lion-Heart', who had been captured by personal enemies in Germany on his return from the third crusade.

But, like all other medieval empires, the Hohenstaufen empire depended on the person of the ruler. When Henry VI died prematurely, another German victim of the south Italian summer, leaving a two-year-old child as his heir, the empire once more collapsed.

The historical significance of the second Empire-papacy struggle

While the political achievements of Frederick Barbarossa were short-lived, the results of his struggle with Alexander III had more lasting results. But these results were in the realm of ideas and political attitudes, rather than in any lasting settlement of the Church and state conflict which was, in fact, not achieved. The arguments of the Investiture Contest had been largely a matter of the interpretation of Scripture and of the Church Fathers. The arguments of the middle of the twelfth century were more legal-istic, not least because in the meantime the study of Roman law had made great progress. There were papal lawyers who argued that Christ had been rightful lord of the world and that therefore all legitimate political authority came from the pope, Christ's vicar on earth, who had bestowed it on the emperor and therefore could take it away again if the emperor proved unworthy. The royalist lawyers maintained against this argument that emperors had existed before popes and that their authority derived directly from God and from election by the people.

Perhaps the most interesting were the more moderate voices, such as the Italian canon lawyer, Huguccio, who argued that:

> Up until the coming of Christ the imperial and pontifical rights were not separated, for the same man was emperor and pontiff. But the offices and rights of the emperor and the pontiff were separated by Christ and some things, namely temporal affairs, were assigned to the emperor, others, namely spiritual affairs, to the pontiff, and this was done for the sake of preserving humility and avoiding pride. If the emperor or the pontiff held all offices he would easily grow proud, but now since each needs the other and sees that he is not fully self-sufficient he is made humble. . . . Here it can clearly be gathered that each power, the apostolic and imperial, was instituted by God and that neither is derived from the other . . .[6]

Style and language would later change, and the argument would be drained of its religious content; but it would still remain basically the same for all those, right up to the framers of the American constitution, who feared an excessive concentration of authority and saw the safest defence against tyranny in the separation of powers. It was the achievement of the protagonists of the medieval Church-and-state disputes that they initiated this most fateful and vital of western traditions, the quest for a legitimate defence against tyranny and the need to justify all political authority not merely by tradition or the fact of power but also by reason.

Russia

The golden age and the decline of Kiev

The Christianization of Kiev was followed by a period of prosperity and advancing civilization. An early eleventh-century

175

description claimed that the city of Kiev itself had 'more than forty churches, eight market places and countless multitudes of inhabitants.' At its height, Kiev may have numbered something like 20,000 inhabitants, and this made it comparable to the biggest western European cities of the time, although not of course to Constantinople.

Soviet historians write of the period as one of feudalism. But this means no more than there was a class of large landowners, originating both from Scandinavian followers of the princes and from chiefs of the old Slavonic tribes. They came to be known as boyars. But they had not received their lands as fiefs, nor were they bound by the complex legal relationship of vassal to lord that was characteristic of feudalism in western Europe. The peasants, although no doubt often hard pressed by the wealthy land-owners, were largely free, with the right to move where they pleased.

While the grand-princes of Kiev, as they began to call them-selves, had taken over many of the trappings of the Byzantine court, the administration of their vast territory remained, by Byzantine and even by western standards, very primitive. It depended largely on the continued flourishing of the inter-national trade in luxuries down the Dnieper, the ability of the grand-princes to protect their territory from the invasions of Asian nomads and on the willingness of the princely family, the Rurikids, the descendants of Rurik, to operate their complicated rules of succession, from elder to younger brother. After about the middle of the twelfth century, none of these conditions held any longer. Genoese and Venetian merchants diverted much of the Black Sea trade to the Mediterranean. New invaders from the Asian steppe crushingly defeated Russian armies while the princes of the house of Rurik fought each other until the Russian state of Kiev dissolved again into the different principalities to which the rulers of Kiev had given some superficial and tem-porary unity.

The rise of Novgorod

The most important of these principalities was Novgorod. Its princes had extended their authority far to the north-east and north-west and, in the process, Slavic settlers had assimilated the Finnic speaking inhabitants of that area or had pushed them into

Plate 3.5   The city walls of Novgorod.
This view from the Kremlin of Novgorod shows the river Volkhov, on
which the city's original trading prosperity was founded. The
fortifications, largely fifteenth century in their surviving form,
incorporate portions of earlier walls.

a relatively narrow belt along the eastern coast of the Baltic,
Finland and Estonia. The decline of Kiev gave the inhabitants of
the city of Novgorod the opportunity to declare their independence from princely power, in 1136. From then on Novgorod was
effectively a city republic, ruled by an oligarchy, a small group
of boyar and rich merchant families, much like western and
central European towns, but unique in Russia. Novgorod

continued to accept princes but only on its own terms. In the latter part of the twelfth century German merchants from the recently-founded Baltic port of Lübeck made Novgorod the eastern terminal of their growing east-west trade and thus assured the economic prosperity of the Russian city.

The Russian Church

As in Latin Europe, it was the Church which preserved the cultural unity of a large and politically divided region. Kiev itself became the metropolitan bishopric for the whole of Russia and soon some ten further bishoprics were founded. All acknowledged the ultimate authority of the patriarch of Constantinople and, quite naturally, they found themselves on the Greek Orthodox side when the final breach with Rome took place in 1054, (see below, p. 182).

Extreme and rigid orthodoxy became the leading characteristic of the Russian Church. It could hardly have been otherwise. The Russian Church conducted its ritual and, indeed, all of its religious thinking in Slavonic. But only a relatively small number of Christian texts were translated into that language. The vast corpus of Greek and Latin controversial theology and practically all the philosophical works of the Ancients on which that theology was based therefore remained virtually unknown in Russia. A renaissance, the attempted recovery of a superior lost world (see below, pp. 197–204) was therefore unthinkable. Russia, although now Christianized and, in this sense, essentially European, was therefore set to develop a very different intellectual and cultural tradition from that of Latin Europe, with its growing habit of questioning, arguing and rationalizing. In Russia, by contrast, men saw nothing to question in what all came to accept as the true faith and doctrine. Moreover, the Russian Church, through its Byzantine tradition, would accept the absolute authority of its princes even over the Church itself in a way which the Roman Church found itself unable to do.

It is conceivable that growing contact with western Europe might yet have modified these Russian traditions. The experience of the later medieval centuries, however, when Russian energies were taken up first with the life-and-death struggle with the Mongols, and then with survival under Mongol domination, extinguished all such possibilities (see Ch 4).

The Islamic world

The Fatimid caliphate

In the middle of the ninth century the Islamic world still maintained a unity which the Christian world had lost for centuries. In Spain, it is true, the Umayyads were politically independent but they still recognized the religious authority of the Abbasid caliphate in Baghdad. A hundred years later the Abbasid empire had disintegrated. Incompetent caliphs found themselves beset by 'barbarian' Turkish invasions from the north. Turkish tribes settled within the empire and finally 'barbarian' military leaders set up their own secular dynasties in regional kingdoms. Details might vary; but it was all a familiar pattern in the history of Mediterranean and Near-Eastern empires.

In the tenth century an attempt to revive and reunify the Islamic world was undertaken by the Fatimid dynasty – much as Justinian had undertaken it for the Christian world, 400 years earlier. Unlike the Umayyads and Abbasids, the Fatimids, who took their name from Fatima, the daughter of the Prophet, belonged to the Ismaili branch of the Shiite sect, and they started their conquests not from Arabia, nor from Persia or Mesopotamia, but from north Africa. With the help of some of the fierce Berber tribes they conquered Egypt, founded Cairo as a new capital, and there set up a rival, Shiite, caliphate to that of the Sunni caliphate of Baghdad. By the middle of the eleventh century they had pushed their conquests along both the Arabian and Syrian coasts; but they failed to reach Mesopotamia and, more fatefully still, they failed to convert the Sunni majority of their subjects to Shiism. Islamic unity was never re-established.

For the first time since the Roman occupation at the time of Cleopatra, Egypt was independent again, and it was to maintain this independence until the sixteenth century when it was conquered by the Ottoman Turks. For the first time, too, in many centuries, European trade with the eastern Mediterranean was expanding again. While Constantinople remained the greatest centre of east-west trade, many Europeans now found it more convenient to buy their eastern spices and silks in Alexandria. Two to three hundred merchants from Amalfi (southern Italy) alone were counted at one time in Cairo, in the eleventh century. The revived Egyptian trade with Christian Europe had the knock-

179

on effect of inducing Arab traders to sail from India through the Red Sea rather than through the Persian Gulf, as they had done traditionally. Thus the economic centre of gravity of the Islamic world was shifting from Mesopotamia back to the eastern Mediterranean.

For a time, the Fatimid caliphate of Egypt, with its generally tolerant religious policy, its military prestige and the legendary splendour of the caliph's court in Cairo, represented the most vital part of the Islamic world. But the armies on which the caliphs had to rely were outsiders: Berbers from north Africa, Nubians from the Sudan, Arabs, Armenians and, most important and most effective, Seljuq Turks.

The Seljuq Turks were a central Asian nomadic people who had, for a long time, filtered into northern Persia and Armenia in relatively small bands and who had been used by the Abbasid caliphs of Baghdad as soldiers and settlers. In the eleventh century they broke into this area in large units. Using the usual nomad advantages of fighting ability, mobility and complete ruthlessness towards settled peoples, together with a clever use of their political and administrative institutions, they conquered a huge, if loosely controlled, empire, stretching from Tashkent and Bokhara through Persia and Mesopotamia to Syria and as far south as Jerusalem and the Dead Sea. The Abbasid caliph in Baghdad remained the religious head of Sunni Islam, but was left with little political power outside Baghdad and Mesopotamia. Towards the end of the eleventh century it seemed only a matter of time before the great Seljuq-Sunni counter-offensive would also swallow up Fatimid Egypt; for Seljuq generals and soldiers already had a foothold in Cairo. At this point, however, a new and formidable military and political force appeared in the eastern Mediterranean. The crusaders, although hostile to both the Seljuq Turks and the Egyptian Fatimids, effectively blocked the Seljuq advance into Egypt and thus allowed the Fatimid caliphate to survive for almost another century (see below, pp. 184–91).

Byzantium

The great Macedonian line of emperors from Basil I to Basil II (867–1025) had restored Byzantium, if not exactly as a world empire, at least as the greatest organized military power west of

China. This success would not have been possible if it had not been for the internal divisions of the Islamic world. The life-and-death struggle of the seventh and early eighth centuries was succeeded by campaigns for individual provinces or cities, in between long periods of uneasy peace or truce – a classic 'cold war' situation. Nevertheless, the position of the east Roman Empire remained precarious. As always in autocracies, even in those which were as old, venerable and backed by as highly an organized administration as Byzantium, too much depended on the personal qualities of the head of the state, the autocrat. Basil II did not have successors of the same calibre. The Byzantine system had its way of dealing with incompetent emperors. They were either murdered or blinded and banished to monasteries. This was effective enough; but the sequel, also as usual, was not. The throne came to be disputed by imperial princesses and generals. All tried to buy support. The great Anatolian landowning families exploited this situation by breaking down still further what remained of imperial protection for the independent peasantry. The basis of the military power of the Empire was becoming dangerously narrow.

The schism of the eastern and western Churches

It does not seem as if the ruling circles in Constantinople fully understood the implications of these social changes. The situation was the more dangerous as a new and formidable enemy of the Empire had appeared in the middle of the eleventh century. This was Robert Guiscard and the Normans in southern Italy. It was by trying to maintain imperial authority against the attacks of the Normans that Byzantium became involved in a new conflict with the papacy. At first this was no more than a sharpening of the old disputes over the respective authority of the patriarch of Constantinople and the pope of Rome over the south-Italian bishops. With the victory of the reform party in Rome, however, the disputes rapidly escalated into conflicts of principle. The principle at issue was both theological and ecclesiological, i.e. concerning the structure of, and the supreme authority, within the Church. In the original formulations of the doctrine of the Trinity, in the fourth century, the relation of the Holy Spirit to the two other persons, the Father and the Son, had not been elaborated. In the sixth century, Spanish theologians, anxious to

181

reaffirm the doctrine of the divinity of Christ against the beliefs of the Arian Visigoths (see Ch. 1, pp. 53–4), produced a new formulation by which the Holy Ghost was said to 'proceed' from the Father and the Son – *filioque*, in the Latin creed. This *filioque* was felt in Constantinople to be an unwarranted insertion into the creed.

The matter had little importance until, in the eleventh century, Rome started to insist on the Spanish formulation. To an age for which the precise formulation of doctrine seemed essential to personal salvation, the precise wording of the creed was of supreme importance. Soon other differences of opinion surfaced: about the use of unleavened bread in the mass, about the marriage, or the absolute prohibition of marriage of priests . . . the number of points at issue would become endless, once the theologians had set their minds on them. They did so because authority was involved. Who had the right to formulate doctrine? Who, indeed, held the ultimate authority in the Church? By 1054 the dispute had reached such a pitch that Pope Leo IX sent Cardinal Humbert to Constantinople to try to make peace. It was an unfortunate choice. Humbert was an imperious figure, a dedicated Cluniac reformer, a maker of popes in the conclaves and a passionate believer in papal supremacy within the Church. In Constantinople he met the Patriarch Michael Cerularius, a man of similarly imperious temperament. Their meeting ended as meetings of such men so often do, in the hardening of their respective positions, and this even though the emperor, Constantine IX Monomachus, and the patriarch of Antioch worked hard for reconciliation. Humbert publicly deposited a bull of excommunication against Patriarch Michael and his supporters on the principal altar of the Hagia Sophia (16 July 1054). The patriarch answered with a similar blast against the papal legates who had, he said, come to 'the God-guarded city (Constantinople) like a thunder or a tempest or a famine, or rather like wild boars, in order to overthrow the truth'.

No one at the time foresaw that this dramatic event was not a temporary breach, as others before had been, but the beginning of a permanent schism between the Greek and Latin Churches, a schism which has, so far, defied all attempts at permanent reunification. Humbert and Cerularius were no doubt narrow-minded and opinionated theologians. But they embodied the growing distance and mutual incomprehension of the Greek and the Latin Christian worlds.

182

The Turkish offensive

In the second half of the eleventh century, however, the eastern emperors were more worried by the military dangers from the Normans in the west and the Muslims in the east. The Seljuq Turks followed their rapid conquest of the Abbasid empire in Persia and Mesopotamia by incursions into the north-eastern provinces of the Byzantine Empire in Armenia and Anatolia. In 1068 leading circles in Constantinople manoeuvred a successful general onto the throne, precisely in order to deal with this situation. In 1071 Emperor Romanos IV Diogenes' army was annihilated by the Turks at Manzikert, near Lake Van. Tactical mistakes, the superior mobility and fire power of the Turkish mounted archers and treachery within the Byzantine army all played their part in this catastrophe. On his return to Constantinople the emperor was deposed and, later, murdered.

Romanos IV's immediate successors failed to stem the Turkish advance through Anatolia. The old military system based on a free peasantry no longer functioned. The Anatolian peasants, exploited by the great Byzantine lords, either accepted the religiously tolerant rule of the Turks or fled to the fortified coastal towns. The interior of Anatolia now became more and more Turkish as the conquerors took over Byzantine lands.

The Comneni

But, as so often before, the Byzantine Empire still showed remarkable vitality and powers of recovery. A new military emperor, Alexius I Comnenus (1081–1118), restored the military situation on the Greek Adriatic coast against the Normans, on the Balkans front he annihilated the Pechenegs (still another steppe people who had swept across the lower Danube), and in Anatolia he halted the advance of the Turks. The costs were high. The famous Byzantine gold coinage was devalued by two thirds; the Venetians who had helped in the fight against the Normans were given unprecedented trading privileges in Constantinople; taxes were increased everywhere.

Alexius' son John II (1118–43) and his grandson Manuel I (1143–80) continued these successes. The Seljuqs, at war with other Muslim dynasties, were no longer as formidable as they had been in the eleventh century. But a new force had now appeared in the politics of the eastern Mediterranean, the western crusaders. While Byzantine aims were still directed primarily towards the east, the survival of the Empire came to depend more and more on its relations with the Latin Christian powers. From the middle of the twelfth century, the Venetians, the kings of France and the western emperors were beginning to talk of an attack on Byzantium. Nothing could show more clearly the economic and political revival of the west and the enormous increase in its self-confidence as against the age of Justinian or even that of Charlemagne. Constantinople countered this new danger by extending its diplomatic activities, which now included all the major European states as far west as France, with the intention of exploiting their mutual enmities. In this way Byzantium was playing an important role in the development of the modern European state system, even if in the twelfth century only the outlines of such a system were dimly visible.

But Byzantine resources, long-since stretched to the limits, could not in the long run maintain the great power position to which the emperors aspired. The Holy Roman Emperor Frederick Barbarossa talked disparagingly of the 'kingdom of the Greeks'. In 1176 Manuel I's army was annihilated by the Seljuqs of Anatolia. It was an even worse disaster than the battle of Manzikert, a hundred years earlier, especially as Manuel's reign was once more followed by the baleful Byzantine pattern of incompetent or tyrannical emperors, usurpations and imperial assassinations. This time there was to be no rescue from the approaching catastrophe.

The western counter-offensive

Catholic Europe had been on the defensive against outside invaders for more than 500 years. From about the year 1000 there was a change. A rising population and growing wealth, improved political and military organization, and a growing wealth, improved political and military organization, and a growing religious and intellectual self-confidence gave Catholic Europe a distinct advantage over the pagan peoples of the north and east. Scandinavia, Iceland, Poland and Hungary were rapidly Christianized and to a very considerable degree assimilated and integrated into the old Christian society of Catholic Europe. Only in

184

Prussia and Lithuania there still remained pockets of paganism between the Latin Catholic west and the Greek Orthodox east of the now Christianized Russia.

The Muslims, however, were a tougher proposition than the pagans. Culturally they could hold their own against the Christians. Militarily it depended on circumstances. It took the Normans thirty years to conquer Sicily for themselves and Christendom. It took the Spaniards five centuries to reconquer the whole of the Iberian peninsula. Since in this process of reconquest the Muslim and Jewish populations were often left alone or only nominally converted, a curious paradox developed: gradually a society came into being which was multi-racial and multi-religious and which yet prided itself on its Catholic orthodoxy. Historians of Spanish culture and literature have argued fiercely about the extent of Arab and Jewish influence and of the effect of such influences on the Spanish character (if indeed there is such an entity as the Spanish, or any other clearly definable, national character – a proposition which not everyone would accept). But it can hardly be doubted that the Arab and Jewish influence was considerable and that it gave Spain traditions distinctive from those of the rest of Europe.

The crusades

It was in Spain that a Christian version of the idea of a religious or holy war first began to develop; and one may well speculate whether this was not an adaptation of the Muslim concept of the *jihad*, the duty imposed on Muslims by the Koran of spreading Islam by war. The most famous expression of this idea in its Christian version was the *Song of Roland* (see above, Ch. 2), with its Spanish setting of the Christian fight against the infidel. The emphasis was on the fight and on the slaughter of the infidels, rather than on their conversion. Not for nothing was the patron saint of Spain the apostle St James 'the Moor Slayer'. (Of course, slaying one's enemies was regarded as virtuous, whoever they were. Thus the emperor Basil II was approvingly named the 'Bulgar Slayer', even though the Bulgars were Christians [see above, Ch. 2, p. 120. Still, the Bulgars were threatening God's city, Constantinople, and it was generally held to be best to fight non-Christians.)

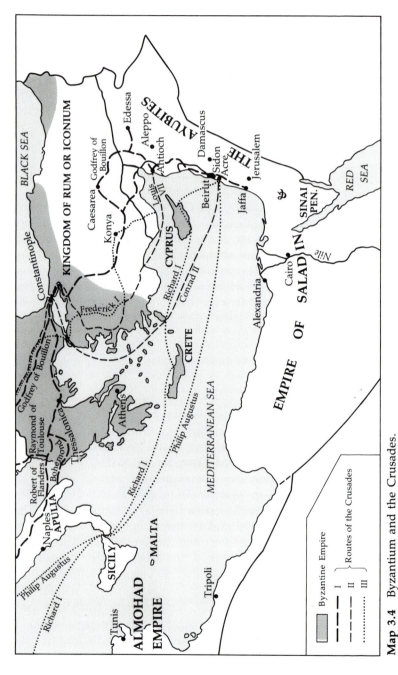

Map 3.4 Byzantium and the Crusades.

Up to the end of the eleventh century the opportunities for emulating the legendary Charlemagne and his paladins were restricted to Spain and southern Italy. All this changed quite suddenly in 1095. The Byzantine emperor Alexius I appealed to Pope Urban II (1088–99) for help against the Seljuq Turks in Asia Minor. In itself, this was not a very remarkable action. Alexius, well-established some fourteen years after seizing the throne, and with a whole string of successful campaigns to his credit, was thinking of offensive rather than defensive action. Evidently, he did not regard the Church schism of 1054 as an obstacle to employing western soldiers, as indeed his predecessors had done for centuries. The pope, however, interpreted the appeal in a very different fashion. Still hard pressed by the emperor Henry IV and by the anti-pope Clement III, Urban saw the Byzantine appeal as a splendid opportunity for regaining the spiritual and political initiative. Help for the eastern emperor was transformed into the need and Christian duty to liberate Jerusalem and the Holy Sepulchre, the tomb in which Christ was buried. 'An accursed race, a race utterly alienated from God' (i.e. the Turks) had conquered the holy places and killed and oppressed the Christians living there, the pope claimed. Christians should now emulate the deeds of Charlemagne against the infidels.

For several hundred years, but especially during the first century after 1095, the preaching of the clergy and the mood of Catholic Europe was unequivocal. The very name of Jerusalem, the centre of the orb of the world, the city of the twelve pearly gates whose streets were pure gold (Revelations 21.21) seemed to promise both heavenly glory and earthly riches. St Bernard (1090–1153), abbot of the great Cistercian monastery of Clairvaux – one of the first and greatest houses of a new monastic order of men who wished to recapture the original spirit of St Benedict by founding their houses in the wilderness, beyond the confines of traditionally settled and cultivated land – St Bernard, the keeper of the conscience of Catholic Europe in the first half of the twelfth century and the most fervent advocate of crusade by other men, had no doubt of its justification:

> How glorious the victors return from the battle! How blessed are the martyrs who die in the battle! Rejoice, stout champion, if you live and conquer in the Lord, but exalt and glory even more if you die and join the Lord.[8]

187

The reality was, inevitably, more sordid. For the clergy had provided the justification for men's traditional inclination for aggression. Adventure, plunder and slaughter could now be pursued with a good conscience. One could make a good beginning even at home by turning on the Jews. The Church granted full indulgence to those who took the crusading oath, i.e. it remitted the temporal penalties of sins forgiven in the sacrament of penance. The precise theology of the doctrine of indulgence took a long time to develop; but to the popular mind it seemed to signify the simple forgiving of sins.

There were also more practical, material advantages to those who took the cross. The Church promised the protection of the families and the property of crusaders. It was an extension of the principle of the truce of God, and the preachers stressed the favour Christian men would gain in the eyes of God by fighting his enemies, rather than each other. In practice it would also mean that crusaders would escape from the claims of creditors or from those who were sueing them in a court of law. The language of religion and of business was intermingled, even by the most austere preachers:

> Are you a shrewd business man, said St Bernard, a man quick to see the profits of this world? If you are, I can offer you a splendid bargain. Do not miss this opportunity. Take the sign of the cross. At once you will have indulgence for all sins which you confess with a contrite heart. It does not cost you much to buy and if you wear it with humility you will find that it is worth the kingdom of heaven.[9]

There were of course many ordinary people who had little to gain and genuinely wanted to free Jerusalem. A certain Peter the Hermit led a huge unorganized mob of such men through the Balkans and across the Bosphorus into Asia Minor, where most of them were soon slaughtered by the Turks – to the great relief of the Byzantines who had understandably been horrifed by this uncalled for invasion (1096).

It was especially the French nobility, those Norman and Lotharingian dukes, counts and knights whose uncles and cousins had made their fortunes with Guiscard in Apulia and with William the Conqueror in England, who grasped the opportunities which the crusades would afford of winning status, titles and perhaps even principalities in the east. We have a brilliant account by Anna Comnena, the daughter of Alexius I, of the

Plate 3.6 *The Capture of Jerusalem.*
This is a thirteenth-century miniature from a copy of William of Tyre's
twelfth-century *History of the Latin Kingdom of Jerusalem.* Jerusalem is
shown on the lower right as an earthly city to be conquered with
stones hurled by catapults, a wheeled wooden tower and scaling
ladders. On the left and the top of the picture it is shown as the
spiritual centre of Christianity, the place of Christ's Passion.

descent of the 'Franks' on Constantinople, in December 1096 and early 1097, and of the impression they made on educated Byzantines. To Anna the 'Franks' appeared as good fighters but, above all, as greedy and treacherous. 'They were all of one mind . . . to all appearances they were on a pilgrimage to Jerusalem; in reality they planned to dethrone Alexius and seize his capital.'[10] Anna's description of one of the principal leaders, Bohemond, is both funny and chilling. Bohemond, the son of Robert Guiscard and an old-standing enemy of Byzantium, was characterized by Anna as a man of low birth and little wealth but enormous ambitions. In Constantinople he tried to impress the emperor. But, being regaled with splendid Byzantine dishes, he feared poison and happily made his companions eat these dishes, while himself was having specially prepared food from raw meat which the emperor, foreseeing Bohemond's suspicions, had thoughtfully provided.

Alexius made the leaders of the crusaders swear allegiance to him for any conquests they might make from the Turks and promise to hand such conquests over to him. The crusaders effortlessly forgot these promises and set up Edessa, in Armenia, and Antioch and Tripolis, on the Syrian coast, as Latin principalities. Bohemond became prince of Antioch.

Once out of Byzantine territory, the crusaders had to fight all the way and they did so with great determination. Even so, it is unlikely that they would have been successful if the Turkish princes who disputed the broken Seljuq empire among themselves had given up fighting each other and been prepared to combine against the crusaders. It took the crusaders two years to reach Jerusalem. They celebrated the fulfilment of their quest with three days of massacre, looting and prayer:

> Entering the city [15 July 1099] our pilgrims pursued and killed Saracens up to the temple of Solomon, in which they had assembled and where they gave battle to us furiously for the whole day, so that their blood flowed throughout the temple. Finally, having overcome the pagans [i.e. non-Christians], our knights seized a great number of men and women, and they killed whom they wished and whom they wished they let live. . . . Soon the crusaders ran throughout the city, seizing gold, silver, horses, mules and houses full of all kinds of goods. Then rejoicing and weeping from extreme joy our men went to worship at the sepulchre of our Saviour Jesus and thus fulfilled their pledge to him . . .[11]

The majority of the crusaders were what they called themselves, pilgrims. Having prayed in Jerusalem they returned home. Those who stayed to settle became a kind of colonial society. They stayed mainly to improve their economic and social status. Some came to farm, but the majority found life in the ancient fortified cities both safer and more attractive. Antioch, for instance, was famous for its pleasant climate, for its 400 towers built by the Byzantines, and for the running water and drains in its houses, comforts which in western Europe had disappeared with the fall of the Roman Empire.

By the end of the twelfth century there were perhaps 100,000 Latins in the Holy Land. They spoke mostly French and they did not mingle much with the native population, although there was some intermarriage with local Christians. In contrast to what happened in Spain and Sicily, there was little fruitful cultural interchange between the Christian and Muslim societies and not very much between the crusaders and the different eastern communities. In the end, the crusades remained an interlude in the complex history of Syria and Palestine. Its most visible modern reminder is a number of spectacular crusader castles, surviving incongruously in an alien landscape.

The military orders

The most permanent legacy of the crusader settlements, apart from the castles, turned out to be the military orders. In the atmosphere of mingled piety and militancy which was so characteristic of the crusades it is not surprising that the idea arose to combine the qualities of the monk with those of the warrior. The first military order was that of the Templars who derived their name from their headquarters in the royal palace in Jerusalem, known as Solomon's Temple. The members took the usual vows of obedience, poverty and chastity and they added a fourth, to offer help and protection to pilgrims going to Jerusalem. The Hospitallers, or Knights of St John of Jerusalem, had as their fourth duty the care of the sick. Both orders soon attracted gifts and bequests of property over much of Europe. The popes, seeing in the orders an instrument to advance their own authority in the Church, granted them extensive ecclesiastical privileges and, in return, claimed sole authority over these orders and made them independent of any local bishop.

191

With so much institutional wealth and with such privileges the Templars and Hospitallers soon attracted many noble recruits and began to spread their activities far beyond Syria and Palestine. They found imitators in more localized and national orders. The Spanish orders of Santiago, Calatrava and Alcántara helped in the reconquest of Spain from the Muslims and they continued as great aristocratic land-owning institutions. In Germany the order of St Mary or order of the Teutonic Knights conquered a large territory on the eastern Baltic from the heathen Prussians, Lithuanians and Livonians, and set up a state which eventually became a dukedom and, later still, the kingdom of Prussia.[12]

The second crusade

It was St Bernard who was the moral force behind the second crusade, 1145–49, and it was his fervour which helped to persuade the two most powerful kings of Latin Europe, Louis VII of France and Konrad III of Germany, to lead the campaigns personally. From the beginning things went wrong. The North German princes decided they would prefer to direct their crusade against the Wends, a pagan Slavonic-speaking people living east of the Elbe. The pope recognized this campaign as a full crusade and granted the participants all the usual crusading privileges. It was an ominous precedent for German aggression eastward, on a broad front along the southern shores of the Baltic Sea.

In the east the crusade foundered because of the westerners' bad relations with Byzantium. The French army was at one moment poised to attack Constantinople but was finally dissuaded by King Louis. More fateful still were the contradictory aims of the crusaders and the native crusader barons of the kingdom of Jerusalem. These barons, anxious to maintain their alliances with local Muslim princes, virtually sabotaged the campaigns of the two kings. The only lasting result which the crusaders achieved was the incidental capture of Lisbon, at the other end of Europe, in 1147. Lisbon became the capital of the Iberian kingdom of Portugal.

In the west people variously blamed the devil, the Turks, the Greeks, the impossibly difficult conditions of the east or Bernard of Clairvaux. In his defence the saint pleaded the pope's commission to preach the crusade and also, going higher still for superior orders, he argued that his critics were really attacking God and not himself.

The third crusade

For a generation after the middle of the twelfth century Christian Europe was too much occupied with its own problems to think of crusades. Its emperors and popes, its princes and knights chose to fight each other rather than the infidel. In Egypt the Fatimid caliphate was clearly dying. In 1169 the most powerful Sunni rulers of Syria sent an army into Egypt. Its leader, a Kurdish officer, Salah ad-Din Yusuf ibn Ayyub, whom the Westerners called Saladin, overthrew the Fatimid caliphate (1171), proclaimed himself sultan and returned Egypt to the Sunni fold. In the following years he extended his authority over Syria. Once again, a brilliant leader had been able to build a huge, though ramshackle empire in the Middle East, stretching from northern Mesopotamia to the Yemen in south Arabia. In practice it was little more than an overlordship over largely autonomous Muslim princes. Saladin deliberately set out to inspire a renewed religious and moral fervour in Islam. For the first time in their history the crusader states had to face a united Muslim enemy. In July 1187 Saladin annihilated their army in the battle of Hattin. One after another the crusader cities and castles fell to the victor. Only Tripolis, Antioch and Tyre held out, but Jerusalem capitulated, in October 1187. Unlike the crusaders of 1099, Saladin spared the inhabitants and although the crosses on the churches were replaced by the crescents of Islam, Christian services were allowed to continue in the church of the Holy Sepulchre.

The fall of Jerusalem rekindled crusading fervour in the west. Once again pope and preachers called for a united effort of Latin Christendom. This time the organization of the crusade was a great deal more professional than it had ever been before. Rulers imposed special taxes, the Saladin tithe. The emperor himself, Frederick Barbarossa, and eventually also the kings of England and France, Richard I Coeur de Lion (the Lionheart) and Philip II Augustus led the main contingents. But the basic problems had not changed: the need for a long and exhausting overland march through the Balkans or expensive and inadequate transport by sea; the not unjustified suspicion and, at times, open hostility of the Byzantines; the high mortality of the western troops in unaccustomed and hostile climates; most of all the inevitable quarrels of the leaders, both among themselves and with the Frankish princes of *outremer*, Palestine and Syria.

Barbarossa, in his high sixties, died in an accident in eastern Anatolia (June 1190). His German army which had marched overland and had already suffered heavy losses in Anatolia disintegrated. The French and the English, travelling by sea, presented Saladin with a much more formidable military problem than any he had encountered before. The Christians recaptured the coastal cities, notably the important port of Acre; but they failed to make any further progress inland, away from the support of their fleets. Fighting was spectacular and both sides sometimes displayed the chivalry which soldiers always hope for, but which seems possible, if at all, only in desert wars where civilians are not involved. But the fighting was intermittent and alternated with hard-headed negotiations. In the end Saladin managed to hold on to Jerusalem but agreed to allow Christian pilgrims to visit it unmolested.

This was the meagre result that the combined might of Latin Christendom was able to achieve. Even the uneasy alliance of the princes could not be maintained. Richard Coeur de Lion's disastrous return journey showed this only too clearly. He was captured and imprisoned by the duke of Austria with whom he had quarrelled in Acre. The duke handed Richard over to the new emperor, Henry VI, who only released him for a huge ransom. Characteristically, Richard's adventures became part of the romantic legend which soon enveloped this king who spent only ten months of his ten-year reign in England (1189–99) and treated all his realms simply as sources of money and soldiers for his own glory. Barbarossa's posthumous legendary fate was even more curious. Confused with his grandson Frederick II, the last effective German emperor of the Middle Ages, Barbarossa was believed to be alive in the Kyffhäuser Mountain, with his flaming red beard grown through the marble table, awaiting the time when he would restore Germany to greatness.

Saladin died in 1193, and almost immediately his empire fell apart. But he, too, became a great romantic figure, both in Islam and in Christendom, as the wise ruler and chivalrous adversary. In the early fourteenth century Dante placed him in limbo with other admirable non-Christian figures:

With those wise men I passed the sevenfold gate into a fresh
green meadow, where we found
Persons with grave and tranquil eyes, and great
Authority in their carriage and attitude,
Who spoke but seldom and in voice sedate.
. . .
I saw Electra, saw with her anon
Hector, Aeneas, many a Trojan peer,
And hawk-eyed Caesar in his habergeon
. . .
I saw great Saladin, aloof, alone.[13]

The effects of the crusades

The final effects of the crusades have remained difficult to assess.
In Syria and Palestine the crusaders left little more than the
remains of their splendid castles and a singularly bad memory.
Those who settled there adopted some of the tastes and habits
of their religious opponents. But they were too few and too much
on the defensive, and they did not have nearly enough time to
change themselves and those they had temporarily conquered
into a new nation, as the Normans did in England and, to some
extent, the Spanish Christians in the conquered parts of Spain.

The effects of the crusaders on Byzantium and on its relations
with the west will be discussed in the next chapter. In Catholic
Europe itself they were contradictory. On the positive side was
the widening of the mental horizons for the peoples of a continent which had for so many centuries turned in upon itself. Some
of the sophisticated tastes and habits of those who had settled in
Syria filtered back into Europe and played their part in the intellectual revival of the twelfth and thirteenth centuries. Yet even
in this field the more fruitful contacts between the Christian and
Muslim civilizations took place in Spain and Sicily, rather than
in the Holy Land.

Much more definitely, the crusades helped to stabilize European society. With so many unruly and quarrelsome young men
expending their energies overseas, the west became more
peaceful. The Peace of God movement became more effective and
the monarchies were more easily able to assert themselves against
their rebellious barons. At the same time, the circulation of
money and the value of trade increased; for the crusaders had to
sell property to equip themselves and to pay for food and shelter

195

Plate 3.7   Palermo: Church of San Giovanni degli Eremiti.
Sicily, like southern Spain, lay at the crossroads of Byzantine, Arab
and Christian cultures and benefited artistically from all of them,
producing in the twelfth century its own, very original, hybrid style.
The cupolas are a bright brick red, the walls a warm amber colour.
The houses in the background show that the building is quite small.
The rest of Europe, if it knew about this style at all, no doubt thought
that such buildings were altogether too 'Moorish' and did not attempt
to imitate this style.

on the way because, in theory at least, they were not allowed to
plunder other Christians. The greatest gainers were the Italian
seaports. The Venetians, the Genoese, the Pisans and others
transported crusaders and pilgrims and supplied the garrisons of
the Syrian ports. Much of the growing prosperity of the city
civilization of Italy was based on this very profitable activity.

Nevertheless, the total cost of the crusades was high. For the
Muslims they were almost wholly destructive, although it is only
fair to say that the Seljuk Turks had been the aggressors against
Byzantium and that they and the Arabs were as much given to
fighting among themselves as were the Europeans. In Christian

Europe the crusades led to the first great pogroms against the Jews since Roman times. Among the Christians, especially in northern France, there were few families which did not have to mourn a husband, son or brother who would never return. Worst of all, the crusades accustomed Christians to find religious justifications for wars of conquest (as those of the German knights in Prussia and Livonia) or for wars of plunder and destruction (as those of the French monarchy against the Albigensian heretics of Languedoc). Characteristically, these bitter fruits of the crusades began to ripen precisely in proportion as the original crusading impulses dried up in the sands of the Palestine desert.

The intellectual Renaissance of the eleventh and twelfth centuries

The creative impulse of the Carolingian Renaissance, limited and narrow as it had been, did not survive the chaos caused by the Viking, Magyar and Saracen invasions of the ninth and tenth centuries. But at least the achievements of the Carolingian age were not lost. Men continued to learn and to teach Latin, to preserve and copy manuscripts and to illuminate and bind books. It would need a new opportunity before men's creative impulses would show themselves again at their highest level.

This opportunity came with the restoration of relative peace, the increasing wealth of Europe which freed more men from the toil of food production, and with the more optimistic spirit of the eleventh century. While the monasteries continued to play their part, the intellectual and literary revival now came to be centred on the courts of kings and of great princes and bishops. Cathedral chapters founded schools of learning. The most famous in the first half of the twelfth century was that of the small cathedral town of Chartres, some fifty miles south-west of Paris. But it was above all in the larger cities that the new schools began to develop; for cities, like monasteries and courts, brought men together and therefore encouraged conversation and intellectual questioning and they brought together men of more varied interests and backgrounds than monks and courtiers. At first it would be one or several distinguished teachers who would attract groups of students; but gradually permanent institutions came into being with systematic teaching in a whole variety of subjects.

197

Usually all the liberal arts subjects were taught in these institutions: grammar, rhetoric and logic (the *trivium*) and geometry, arithmetic, music and astronomy (the *quadrivium*). Different universities would specialize in one or other of the three higher branches of learning, medicine, law and theology. Salerno, in southern Italy, was a centre for medical studies, perhaps from as early as Roman times. Its greatest period was in the eleventh century, when it benefited from the south Italian connection with both Byzantium and the Arab world. Later it lost ground to more diversified universities, notably Montpelier in southern France.

The fame of Bologna as a centre for law studies was more permanent. It was here that the systematic study of Roman law, in the form given it by the Justinian code, was revived in the early eleventh century. Roman law had, of course, never ceased to be studied in Constantinople. The so-called glossators annotated and commented on the text of the code, demonstrating its consistency and its applicability to particular circumstances. The thousands of students who came, over the years, from all over Europe to study law at Bologna were mostly laymen, rather than clerics, and they were usually older than the students in the other faculties; for they were frequently men who already held positions in the administration of secular states or of ecclesiastical institutions. Parallel with the school of Roman law there grew up a school of canon law, with commentaries and teaching carried on in a similarly systematic form. The students, mostly far from home, formed themselves into self-governing 'nations' or 'universities'. They obtained freedom from local jurisdiction and local taxation. They controlled the price of their lodgings and of their books and even the right to determine the curriculum they wanted to study and the fees they would pay their professors. These rights were recognized specifically by the emperor. The professors, in their

Plate 3.8 Chartes Cathedral: detail of south door of Royal Portal.
The Portal dates from 1150–70. The figures symbolize two of the seven liberal arts, probably an allusion to the famous cathedral school at Chartres. Top left is Music with a bell and a psaltery, a kind of harp. Below her is Pythagoras (*c.* 580–*c.* 500 BC), the Greek philosopher and mathematician who developed the theory of musical intervals. Top right is Grammar, teaching two, perhaps not altogether willing, boys. The figure below her is probably the Roman grammarian Donatus (fourth century AD) whose textbooks were used throughout the Middle Ages.

199

turn, formed corporations and, being mostly married residents of Bologna, put themselves under the jurisdiction of the city. At first, the professors were paid by student fees, but eventually the city paid them salaries, so as to keep out outsiders.

Outside Italy, the centres of learning were dominated by ecclesiastics. What Bologna was for the study of law, Paris came to be for the study of theology. Only in the twelfth century did it overtake the cathedral schools of Charters and Rheims, and it did this largely owing to the inspired teaching of Abelard. Throughout the twelfth century, the masters in arts had to fight the bishop of Paris's chancellor for the autonomy of their school. By the beginning of the thirteenth century they had won, and the university obtained from the pope the right to make its own statutes. As in Bologna, the students organized themselves into 'nations'. Many of them lived in halls of residence, and these halls were the origins of the colleges which received endowments, like monasteries and the religious houses. The most famous of the Paris colleges, the Sorbonne, was founded by Robert de Sorbon, a chaplain of Louis IX. The college system spread to most other European universities but has effectively survived only in England.

Most of the university teachers, ecclesiastics or laymen, were professionals. European society was becoming rich enough to afford such professions. But culture was still desperately expensive. The monastery of Reichenau, in one of the richest regions of Germany, had a library of perhaps 1000 volumes. The monastery of Christchurch at Canterbury possessed only some 600, and Cluny itself had even fewer. The life of scholars was hard. 'The condition of philosophers is not like that of rich people,' wrote the philosopher Peter Abelard's mistress, Heloise, when he wanted to marry her, 'and those who seek a great fortune or whose lives are given up to the things of this world rarely devote themselves to the study of Scripture and philosophy.'

From their letters and from Abelard's autobiography we know more about the personalities and private lives of these two people than about any other individuals of this period. Abelard (1080–1142), the outstanding teacher of the age, virtually created the modern discipline of theology, both by his profound scholarship and by a systematic application of logic to the teachings of the Church. In his personal life – his love for his pupil Heloise, his arrogant egoism and obtuseness in his relationships with other scholars – he characterized an already sophisticated and complex society that was beginning to experience the rift between Church and state, and between the learned ecclesiastic and the educated layman. Characteristically, too, this society could exact dreadful penalties from individuals caught in its contradictory demands. Abelard suffered castration at the hands of Heloise's enraged relatives and, later, persecution for alleged lack of orthodoxy by the highminded and pedantic Bernard of Clairvaux.

Perhaps it was the emphasis on reason that was the outstanding achievement of the twelfth century Renaissance. 'We are dwarves perched on the shoulders of giants,' said one of the twelfth-century scholars of Chartres. 'Although we may see more and further than they, it is not because our sight is keener or our stature greater, but because they bear us up and raise us by their own gigantic height.'[14] With all its deference to the ancients, this was the spirit of intellectual optimism; for the modern dwarves did see further than the ancient giants. Since the time of the Ottos, people had talked about a *translatio imperii*, a translation or shift of empire or earthly authority, from the Greeks to the Romans and then to the Germans. In the twelfth century there arose by analogy the notion of a *translatio studii*, a translation or shift of learning, again from east to west, from the Greeks to the Romans, but then not to Germany but to France.

France had come to be the centre of European intellectual life. Yet France in a cultural sense must be understood widely. It included Norman England and the broad stretch of the old Carolingian middle kingdom, from the Netherlands through Lorraine and Burgundy to the Mediterranean; and, with a certain time-lag, its influence stretched into Germany and, through the Normans, into southern Italy. Conversely, France was open to outside influence, especially from Spain and from northern Italy. For intellectual activities were the preserve of a very small group of men in each country who sometimes travelled and frequently knew each other. They spoke and wrote Latin as a living language and they used it in all literary genres: in sermons and treatises, in legal textbooks, biographies and histories, in poetry and even in popular love and drinking songs.

But Latin set the limit of most men's acquaintance with the ancient world. Very few knew Greek. Thus the impact of the Greeks, above all of the works of Aristotle, was through translation. The Norman kingdom of Sicily was the gateway through which much of Greek literature entered the Latin west. Much also came in a more round about way, through Spain and the mediation of Arab scholars. The Englishman Adelard of Bath travelled in the early decades of the twelfth century through the whole length of the Mediterranean, from Spain to Sicily and on to Asia Minor and Syria, to collect the writings of the ancients. His greatest claim to fame is the translation of Euclid's *Elements* from Arabic into Latin. It became the most famous and widely used of all textbooks on elementary mathematics and as a textbook on elementary geometry it was not superseded until the nineteenth century. Often therefore, as Adelard's Euclid showed, Greek works underwent a double translation, first to Arabic and then from Arabic to Latin. No wonder that much of the work of recovery of the ancients remained fragmentary and had to be supplemented and done over again in the fifteenth and sixteenth centuries.

The process of recovery and assimilation of the works of the ancients or of any unfamiliar knowledge was in any case not a straightforward one. Even where such works or knowledge were readily available they were often not appreciated or used until they answered a felt need. This is particularly evident in the extraordinarily long time it took for Arabic numerals to replace the cumbersome Roman numerals. Arabic numerals, which the Arabs brought from India to the Mediterranean, first appear in a Latin manuscript in 976. But it was from the abacus that Europeans learned the principle of number values according to position; yet for the use of the abacus, which became quite widespread in this period, it was not necessary to use Arabic numerals. The English exchequer, one of the pioneers of the abacus, was using Roman numerals as late as the sixteenth century. Most people were not numerate or even number conscious, especially when it came to numbers higher than 100 (Roman C). That most popular of literary genres, the *Lives of Saints*, rarely provided the dates of the birth and death of their subjects. Even Abelard's autobiography shows this shyness of exact numbers. (A modern analogy of the phenomenon is the slowness of the introduction of the metric system for all measurements in Britain and America in the second half of the twentieth century, when most countries of Europe have used it for nearly 200 years).

But numberlessness did not mean irrationality or lack logic. It was also typical of the twelfth century that it was Aristotle's works on logic which were most readily assimilated into western thinking. These works became the foundation stone of university education in general and of the developing discipline of the scholastic method of philosophical and theological studies in particular. Their greatest development, however, came after 1200.

Aristotle's philosophical and scientific works had their greatest impact in the Islamic and Judaic worlds. The Persian Avicenna (980–1037) posited an Aristotelian conception of a universe existing according to unalterable laws. It blended somewhat uneasily with his affirmation of faith in the Allah of the Koran. Avicenna's *Canon of Medicine*, a vast encyclopaedia of medical knowledge, became the most widely used textbook of medicine in both Islamic and Christian medical schools. At the other end of Islamic society, in Córdoba, and a hundred years later, Averroës (1126–98), a jurist and physician like Avicenna, wrote the first systematic commentary on virtually the whole surviving corpus of Aristotle's works.

> I consider [Averroës wrote] that that man was a rule and exemplar which nature devised to show the final perfection of man. . . . The teaching of Aristotle is the supreme truth, because his mind was the final expression of the human mind. Wherefore it has been well said that he was created and given to us by divine providence that we might know all there is to be known. Let us praise God, who sat this man apart from all others in perfection, and made him approach very near to the highest dignity humanity can attain.[15]

Again, like Avicenna, Averroës was acutely aware of the contradiction between his rational philosophy and the dictates of his religion. It was a tension that was to have important parallels in Christian thinking, and not least because of Averroës' direct influence (usually in Latin translation) on the intellectual life of the universities of Paris and Oxford in the thirteenth century.

Only a little younger than Averroës was his Jewish Córdoban compatriot Moses ben Maimon, known as Maimonides (1135–1204). Heir to the same Greek and Arabic tradition, and equally a distinguished jurist and physician, Maimonides faced the same basic contradictions between rational philosophy and revealed religion. In his *Guide for the Perplexed*, written in Arabic, he definitely subordinated philosophy to revealed truths but still attempted to rationalize Judaism as far as possible. Maimonides' work, although attacked by some orthodox Jews, was to become basic for future Jewish thinking. Like the work of Averroës, that of Maimonides was translated into Latin and was assimilated as one strand in the complex development of European thought in the thirteenth century.

The contact with the Greek and Arabic world, limited and distorted as it often was, proved nevertheless enormously stimulating; but it also exacted its price: it ended the old certainties. Catholic Europe was becoming a continent of rationalizing men, capable of splendid intellectual advances but also, and perhaps precisely because of these advances, beginning to question the very basis on which Christian society was thought to rest. It is no accident that heresies began to spread in the latter part of the twelfth century, and that they did so especially in those parts of Europe most closely in contact with other civilizations, i.e. Italy and southern France (cf. below, Ch. 4).

Vernacular literature

Vernacular literature had never entirely disappeared, but it had been mainly popular literature, the old Germanic, Celtic and Slavonic sagas, sung or told and retold by word of mouth. In the court and urban society of the twelfth century a new public for vernacular literature began to appear, a public of educated laymen and also, just as importantly, of educated or at least leisured women. Some types of this literature, especially lyric poetry, developed in parallel with the same genres in Latin. Sometimes an essentially vernacular subject, like the Celtic sagas of King Arthur, was first given a Latin literary form (by the Welshman Geoffrey of Monmouth) and only then turned back into Norman-French versions. But just as often there were no Latin connections. Thus the many *chansons de geste* about Charlemagne and his paladins received their literary form at the end of the eleventh and during the twelfth centuries. Many of them were translated into German, for they accorded as much with German tastes as with French.

These *chansons* remained popular literature. But there was a sophisticated version of tales of chivalry which treated of courtly love, the love of a knight for a lady, usually a married lady, in whose service he performs the most prodigious deeds and whom he worships with a passion that, consciously or unconsciously, parodied the growing cult of the Virgin Mary. Such literary morality inverted actual social customs in which women were effectively subjected to men. Not surprisingly, the literary convention of courtly love gave rise to parodies and, at the turn of the twelfth century, also to works that encompassed a broad spectrum of ambivalence and irony about the social and emotional relationships of its contemporary society (see below, Ch. 4).

Building and architecture

Radulfus Glaber, the monk and chronicler of the 'spring time' of the eleventh century, wrote that the world was now putting on a 'white mantle of churches.' Everywhere in Christian Europe new parish churches were being built; but most conspicuous were the great new cathedrals, the pilgrimage churches and the monasteries of the late eleventh and the twelfth centuries. So startling and sudden was this outburst of building activity that historians have, with some justice, spoken of an 'architectural revolution'. A definite value system, an order of priorities underlay this 'revolution'. A huge part of the still very slender surplus production of this society was invested in the worship of God and in warfare; for the only other type of building at all comparable to church building was the erection of castles. Private squalor was the inevitable counterpart of public splendour. Europe simply could not afford the resources in materials and skilled labour to add elaborate private houses to grandiose public buildings. Heloise again summed up the situation in her argument against marriage with Abelard:

> Is there any man who, when he is meditating the Scriptures or philosophy, can bear the crying of a new-born baby, the singing of the nurse who lulls it to sleep, the coming and going of servants, men and women about the house, and the constant smell and uncleanliness of children? You will say that the rich do it. Yes, no doubt, because they have rooms set aside in their palaces and great houses . . . [16]

The vast majority of men did not have separate rooms in their houses, and even the castles were, by modern standards, appallingly uncomfortable and bitterly cold in winter.

Public building had become a highly professionalized activity; and because no one area could afford to employ the skilled master builders throughout their careers, it was an international activity. The combination of the essentially international master builders and the masons they recruited locally gave the building style of the eleventh and twelfth centuries its character of basic stylistic unity over most of Europe together with fascinating local variations. This was the Romanesque style, which in England is often called Norman. Because of the admiration of the nineteenth-century Romantic movement for the Gothic style, the Romanesque, with its round arches and massive pillars and walls has not been as universally appreciated in our own time. Yet it is a style that grows on the modern viewer if he is only prepared to look. It can be dramatic, as in Durham Cathedral (see Plate opposite), built in the late eleventh century on a steep rock in a sharp S bend of the river Wear, visible far and wide, a symbol of the might of the new Norman monarchy and its Church. It can be majestic, as in the huge cathedrals of Mainz and Worms, in Germany. It can be richly varied and elegant, as in the pilgrimage churches of France on the pilgrimage route to Santiago de Compostela, and in that Spanish cathedral. In the arcaded cloisters of the monastic churches, often surrounding a flower garden and a fountain, the modern visitor can still feel something of the calm and security which attracted so many men and women of that turbulent and violent age to a monastic life.

The stylistic inspiration of the Romanesque style had originally come from Lombardy. Nevertheless, Italian Romanesque developed differently from that of most of the rest of Europe. The availability of marble for facing buildings, the presence in so many places of Roman remains, an almost completely unbroken craft tradition since the late Roman Empire – all this made Italian

Plate 3.9   Durham Cathedral, interior.
Unlike the ceiling of the nave of the cathedral of Pisa (Plate 3.10) which was made of wood, that of Durham is of stone, with ribbed groined vaults, i.e. the ribs accentuate the intersection of the two vaulted surfaces. This method of construction gives both structural stability and a strong visual rhythm. This rhythm is further accentuated by the alternation of bundled columns with huge, geometrically decorated pillars. The round arch, a Roman speciality, became one of the characteristic features of the new Romanesque style of building. The exterior of Durham is shown in the frontispiece.

Romanesque a much more classical style than its French counterpart. But in Italy, too, it was the economic expansion of the
eleventh and twelfth centuries which produced an enormous
increase in the sheer number and size of buildings. The most
famous example of this is the complex of buildings, cathedral,
cemetery and bell tower of Pisa. Like many other towers of the
period the bell tower was built on insufficient foundations and
hence became the famous 'leaning tower of Pisa'.

The popularity of towers gave Italian cities skylines not unlike
that of Manhattan, although of course on a much smaller scale.
Not only did churches, town halls and castles boast tall towers,
as they also did in northern Europe, but the leading families of
Italian cities built themselves towers, both as urban fortresses and
as status symbols. The small city of San Gimignano in Tuscany
is still a startling sight with its thirteen surviving towers. In the
twelfth century it had forty-eight (see Plate 6.1).

The most original style of the period, however, was developed
in Sicily. Here a blend of Norman Romanesque with Byzantine
and Arabic styles produced both the incredibly rich, mosaic-
adorned splendour of the cathedral of Monreale, and the
enchantment of small dome-topped churches, such as San Giovanni degli Eremiti, set in gardens of dark evergreens and blazing
orange trees (see Plate 3.7).

The revival of sculpture

Wall painting and book illustration continued in this age, as they
had done in the Carolingian and Ottonian periods. In Italy, more-

Plate 3.10 Cathedral of Pisa with Leaning Tower and Baptistry.
This huge complex was built largely with the proceeds of successful
raids on Muslim ports – a visual symbol of revival of the Christian
West in the eleventh century. The style of the cathedral (built
1068–1118) is directly derived from Roman models. The marble facing,
white with green horizontal bands, was to become typical for the
churches and cathedrals of Tuscany. Many medieval towers in Italy are
not fully perpendicular, usually because the subsoil has settled
unevenly. The Leaning Tower of Pisa is the most dramatic of these. It
still stands because the mortar used in building it (1174–1350) has
unusual tensile strength. This type of lime mortar was an invention of
the Romans. At the bottom left can be seen a corner of the
Camposanto, the cemetery. After the Black Death, (1347–49) it was
decorated with some of the most powerful representations of the
Triumph of Death (cf. Ch. 5).

over, the Byzantine art of the mosaic was revived, with results worthy of comparison with sixth-century Ravenna (see above, Ch. 1, p. 62). But perhaps even more remarkable was the revival of monumental sculpture in stone, an art that had virtually died with the Roman Empire in the west. The new sculpture was a public art and a religious art, intended to adorn the capitals of columns and the portals and roofs of churches. St Bernard of Clairvaux, like so many puritan churchmen after him, both Catholic and Protestant, condemned this art which led men 'to read in marble rather than in books.' Happily, most churchmen and nearly all the laity rejoiced in this new visual world, a world which included Christ and his apostles, saints and grotesques, angels and devils fighting for men's souls on judgement day, scholars and humble workmen exercising their professions, petrified gardens of leaves and flowers, and even (on the roof of the cathedral of Laon, in northern France) the oxen that had helped to drag the building stones up to the building site.

Such sculpture, like the cathedrals themselves, was not the work of local craftsmen but nearly always of professional artists. Some we know by name, like the sculptor of the cathedral of Autun, in Burgundy, who carved over its portals the bold legend 'Gislebertus hoc fecit' – 'This is Gilbert's work'. If most others have remained anonymous, this is due as much to our ignorance as to their preference.

Conclusion: Europe in 1200

For the vast majority of ordinary people, Europe in the year 1200 was not so very different from Europe in the year 1000. Life, centring on the village and on the service of the local lord, was still desperately hard. Wars, violence and sudden death were every-day events. Yet there were also differences. Many more men and women were free. Most now lived in nuclear, rather than in extended families. Most people used money for at least some transactions. Many went on a pilgrimage at least once in their life to some distant shrine, perhaps half-way across Europe and a minority even went all the way to Jerusalem. Many more were moving into towns and cities and learning specialized skills. Others migrated to different regions within Europe. In the south-west, in Spain, and in the north-east, in northern Germany, Poland and Prussia, they were disputing land with non-Christians and, at least in the north-east, often merging with the native population, once it had been converted to Christianity. There was probably less intermarriage in Spain; but we are not well informed about this subject.

For the upper classes the changes were much greater. The growing wealth of Europe had made possible the development of a small but already richly varied class of specialists. These specialists often functioned internationally because no single region of Europe could afford to keep them throughout their careers, yet all regions required their services. But, equally, the specialists had to take note of the local traditions in which they worked and, at the same time, they remained open to influences from outside Catholic Europe, from Byzantium, from the Arab world, more faintly but still perceptibly from India and China and, not least, from the world of the ancients, a world that was continually being rediscovered and re-interpreted. The effect of all these different currents was to create an enormously stimulating environment in which men came to question many of their own most revered traditions and to seek new solutions to both old and new problems.

References and Notes

1. Radulfus Glaber, *Historiae* Bk 4, V.
2. Quoted in A. Murray, *Reason and Society in the Middle Ages.* Clarendon Press: Oxford 1978, p. 325.
3. Quoted in M. T. Clanchy, *England and its Rulers 1066–1272.* Fontana: Glasgow 1983, pp. 38–39.
4. Quoted in B. Tierney, *The Crisis of Church and State 1050–1300.* Prentice-Hall: Englewood Cliffs, N. J. 1964, pp. 59–60.
5. *The Letters of John of Salisbury*, trans. W. J. Millor and C. N. L. Brooke (eds), Oxford 1979, vol. 2, pp. 730–2.
6. Quoted in Tierney, op. cit., p. 122.
7. Quoted in A. A. Vasiliev, *History of the Byzantine Empire.* Wisconsin University Press: Madison 1952, p. 347.
8. J. Riley Smith, *What were the Crusades?* Macmillan: London 1977, pp. 32–33.

9. Quoted in H. E. Mayer, *The Crusades*, trans. J. Gillingham. Oxford University Press: Oxford 1972, p. 37.
10. *The Alexiad of Anna Comnena*, trans E. R. A. Sewter. Penguin Books: Harmondsworth 1969, p. 319.
11. From *Histoire anonyme de la première croisade*, trans. J. B. Ross in J. Y. B. Ross and M. M. McLaughlin, *The Portable Medieval Reader*. New York, p. 443
12. See H. G. Koenigsberger, *Early Modern Europe 1500–1789*; History of Europe. Longman: London 1987, Ch. 4.
13. Dante, *The Divine Comedy*, trans. Dorothy L. Sayers. Penguin Classic: Harmondsworth 1949, *Hell* canto IV, p. 94.
14. Quoted in *The Flowering of the Middle Ages*. Thames and Hudson: London 1966, p. 180.
15. D. Knowles, *The Evolution of Medieval Thought*. Longman: London 1972, p. 200.
16. Quoted in Philippe Wolff, *The Awakening of Europe*. Pelican History of European Thought. Penguin Books: Harmondsworth 1968, p. 251.

Chapter 4

The High Middle Ages, 1200–1340

The climate

The climatic cycles of the world usually last several centuries, but about the year 1200 Europe entered a cycle that was to run only a century and a half. It saw a distinct fall in its average temperature which was so pronounced that it has been called, 'the little ice age'. This is something of an exaggeration. We know that Alpine and Scandinavian glaciers were slowly creeping down the valleys and that the Arctic ice sheet was moving south, between Iceland and Greenland, and forcing ships to take more southerly routes than they had formerly done. It is at least possible that by the early fourteenth century high land which had been successfully cultivated had to be abandoned because, with a shorter growing season, harvests no longer ripened. But mean temperatures, by which meteorologists measure climate, are not the same thing as the weather; and, for most parts of Europe, it is the weather which determines the harvests. Now apparently the weather, too, was getting worse in the thirteenth and early fourteenth centuries, and there is evidence, at least from England and some other areas, of a great deal of rain. No doubt, the deteriorating weather affected harvests; but, except for a few regions and a few years, we have no idea, as yet, how much.

Population

There is no doubt, however, that the population of Europe continued to grow, as it had done in the eleventh and twelfth

centuries. There is a good deal of evidence for this growth. For the first time we begin to have some reasonably reliable figures, especially for some cities. Many of these were small by modern standards, with only a few thousand inhabitants. In England only London was large, with some 30,000–40,000 in the early fourteenth century. In France Paris was even more outstanding, with 80,000. In Germany, however, there were several cities bigger than 10,000, with Cologne reaching perhaps 30,000. The large cities, however, were mainly in Flanders and Italy. Bruges had 35,000, Ghent over 50,000. Several Italian cities, such as Palermo and Pisa could match this. Florence, according to the chronicler Giovanni Villani, writing in 1336–38, had 90,000, a figure that is now generally accepted. Of Milan a description of 1288 says that it had 12,000 'dwellings with doors giving access to the public streets . . . and in their number are very many in which many families live together with crowds of dependents . . . Let therefore anyone who can count how many persons live in such a city. And . . . he will count about 200,000'.

Perhaps we should halve this figure, which would bring it into line with Venice and Genoa. Clearly, however, these cities showed really large aggregations of people, and they suggest a growing country population. For since hygienic conditions in the cities were usually poor and mortality rates very high, the cities depended for population growth on immigration from the country.

Agricultural expansion

Now the conditions for this continuing growth of population had not changed significantly from those of the previous two cen-

Plate 4.1 Naumburg Cathedral, Germany: *Ekkehard* and *Uta*.
The sculpture of the early Gothic period achieved a classical style of balanced proportions with figures represented in an idealized naturalism. The figures of the somewhat bovine Margrave Ekkehard of Meissen and his delicately featured wife Uta are among a series of idealized portraits of the founders of the cathedral church of Naumburg, central Germany. They were executed by the French-trained 'Naumburg Master', about 1260–70. The models for this style of sculpture were clearly Roman. It seems to have been easier in sculpture to get away from the overpowering Byzantine style than in painting.

turies. Birth and mortality rates were much the same as they had been. Population growth therefore depended largely on an increasing supply of foodstuffs to feed more people. This might be obtained by increasing agricultural efficiency and this did happen to some extent. The three-field system (see p. 140) spread more widely and, at least at first, increased productivity. But it also tended to exhaust the land more rapidly than the older two-field system. It is therefore not entirely surprising that yields did not rise very dramatically. Agricultural historians tell us that they began to do so about the middle of the thirteenth century but, on average, they did not rise to 1:4 until the fourteenth and fifteenth centuries.

Some very fertile areas, it is true, did very much better. It is no accident that most of the big cities developed precisely in such areas, in the Po, the Rhine, the Seine and the Thames valleys. The towns, in their turn, came to influence production in their surrounding countryside. Their citizens demanded more than bread: a great variety of vegetables and fruit, butter and cheese, and regular supplies of meat. Milan, we are told in the description of 1288, had 300 bakeries, which is not surprising, but also 440 butchers, which is. It means (even if we were cautiously to halve this figure again) that not only the rich but also the common people ate meat regularly.

Equally important was growing regional specialization. Burgundy and the Rhineland were famous for their wine and exported it, both for drinking and for use in the mass. South-west France found its English connection highly profitable as the English were beginning to develop their taste for 'claret', the superb light red wine from the region of Bordeaux. Just as widespread was specialization in the production of industrial materials. Flax for the manufacture of linen, hemp for ropes, vegetable dye-stuffs for every kind of cloth were raised where soil and climate allowed; but above all there was sheep farming for the most universally used textile, wool. There were sheep almost everywhere and the great mass of people made do with a coarse wool which they spun and wove locally. But the rich required finer quality clothes and these were provided by the highly skilled cloth workers of Flanders and northern Italy, and they used only the finest type of wool, most of it from England.

Internal and external colonization

Growing specialization, therefore, brought greater wealth to individuals, to groups and sometimes to whole areas. But an increasing number of mouths had to be fed. In the absence of a significant increase in the yield of arable land, this could only be done by expanding the area of land under cultivation. Such expansion had indeed been going on since the eleventh century (see Ch. 3, pp. 138–39) and continued at a greater rate and with more skill in the thirteenth. Forests and brush land were cleared. Heathland and moors began to be ploughed up. In the valleys of the Po and of other great rivers men drained marshes and built dykes against spring floods. In the Netherlands they built dykes against the sea and won precious land for arable and grazing. In Holland and Friesland every village was organized to help in the defence of the dykes against the ever threatening flood tides, and the Hollanders' and Frieslanders' traditional love of freedom has been ascribed, with some justice, to this tradition of co-operation for survival.

But in spite of all these efforts land, or at least reasonably accessible land, began to run short in the thirteenth century. All over western Europe peasant holdings were being more and more divided until they could barely feed a family. Rents rose steadily, which meant that there was a growing demand for land. Here was one of the principal reasons for the increasing migration of country people into towns. It was also the reason for migration into less populated areas.

It happened everywhere. Anglo-Normans began to settle in Scotland and Ireland, but their numbers were relatively small. Far greater numbers of Frenchmen crossed the Pyrenees to help the Christian Spaniards settle the vast areas reconquered from the Moors. At the opposite end of the continent German miners migrated to central Sweden and developed the copper and iron mines of Dalarna. But the most important migrations, by far, were those of Germans and Netherlanders into East Central Europe, into Prussia, Poland and Hungary. Sometimes they came as conquerors, in the armies of German princes: more often they came by invitation of the local princes, German, Polish or Hungarian. For this area was still underpopulated: figures of two to three inhabitants per square mile have been suggested for Poland, with three to four for England but nine to ten for Italy and eleven to twelve for France. Landlords, i.e. the nobility, needed labour for their estates. The migrants, in turn, were granted attractive conditions and, above all, the right to live by their own, German or Flemish, law which was much more favourable to tenants than the old Slavonic customs.

The foundation of the city of Lübeck, in 1143, was typical of this pattern and became the prototype for more than a hundred towns and cities. The chronicler Helmold of Bosau described it:

> Adolf, count of Holstein, began to rebuild the castle of Segeberg and he encircled it with a wall. But because the land was deserted, he sent messengers to all regions, that is Flanders and Holland, Utrecht, Westphalia and Frisia, so that whoever might be in difficult straits because of a shortage of fields should come with their families to accept land which was excellent, spacious, fertile with fruits, abounding in fish and meat, and favourable to pastures.
>
> At this invitation an uncounted multitude arose from the various nations. Taking their families and possessions, they came to the land of the Wagri to Count Adolf, in order to take possession of the land which he had promised them. . . . After this Count Adolf came to a place known as Bucu and he found there the fortifications of a deserted town which Crutu, the tyrant of God (i.e. a heathen), had erected. He also found a wide island surrounded by two rivers. . . . Discerning the suitability of the place for the erection of an excellent port, the industrious man began to build a city. He called it Lübeck. . . . He sent messengers to Niclot, prince of the Obotrites (a Slavonic tribe), to make with him a treaty of friendship. He won over all the nobles with gifts, so that they would rival one another in loyalty to him and in the cultivation of his land. Thus the deserted land of the province of the Wagri began to gain inhabitants and the number of its settlers multiplied.[1]

Not all settlements were made as peacefully, and all too often the new settlers drove out or killed the previous, Slavonic, owners of the land. Lübeck itself received special privileges of self-government from the emperors Frederick Barbarossa (1188) and Frederick II (1226). The building of Lübeck's twin-towered brick cathedral was begun as early as 1173 and finished in the middle of the thirteenth century.

The limits of expansion

In these sparsely populated areas of Europe immigration benefited both the rulers and lords who invited the immigrants and organized the movement and also the peasants who had responded to it. Further west, however, even these relatively large population movements were insufficient to solve the problems of overpopulation. It has been argued that by the end of the thirteenth century the growth of population in large parts of Europe had reached a critical point beyond which it could no longer be supported by a limited land area and a backward and only slowly developing technology. It is difficult to prove or disprove this Malthusian argument (after Thomas Malthus, 1766–1834, a British economist who argued that natural population increase would always tend to outrun food supply – an argument which is by no means dead in our own time).

There are at least some indications that, in the first decades of the fourteenth century, the economy of Europe as a whole was no longer expanding, that the rise in rents and other prices slowed down or ceased, that population may have stopped growing. There were a number of natural disasters, such as a series of failed harvests in north-west Europe which caused a major famine and high mortality from 1415–17. Such disasters may have been connected with the deteriorating climate of the 'little ice age'. Their repercussions seem to have been especially severe where men had been depending on marginal land which now took its revenge on the over-optimistic cultivator.

But did all this mean more than a purely temporary slowing down of the rapid expansion of the previous 300 years? We do not know, for the European economy was not allowed to continue its natural development. In 1346–49 Europe was struck by the bubonic plague with a total loss of life estimated variously as between a quarter and nearly a half of its total population. The severity of this loss may have been increased by 'Malthusian' reasons. But the disease, the 'Black Death', had its origins outside Europe. It will be discussed in the next chapter.

Agrarian organization

Manor and seigneurie had developed, from the tenth to the twelfth centuries, to provide an effective labour force for the

219

owners of land in conditions of a relatively small and stable market for agricultural produce (see Ch. 3, p. 140). Population growth, the expansion of towns and urban markets, rising prices and the possibility of peasant migrations changed these conditions. It would now be profitable for landowners to farm for an expanding market. This could be done in different ways. The owner could expand his home farm and then work it with free, hired labourers who might well be more efficient than serfs. This happened most frequently in the Netherlands and in some parts of France, England and Germany. It lead to a rapid dissolution of the classical seigneurial relationship. Alternatively, the owner could tighten the screws on his serfs and demand more unpaid labour than ever before, and this happened often in the richest parts and economically most advanced areas, such as south-east England. Or, again, the owner might prefer to take advantage of the competition for land and rising rents and lease out his home farm on favourable terms. This development, too, would lead to the rapid dissolution of the seigneurial relationship, for the lord would no longer need servile labour, although he might well hang on to other seigneurial rights, such as the monopoly of local milling or brewing and, above all, rights of lower jurisdiction. An important variation on the practice of farming out land was the introduction of share cropping, a system by which landowner and tenant literally shared each crop. This became a common practice especially in northern Italy and southern France.

In eastern Europe towns were still very small and production for a wider market had hardly begun. At the same time landlords had to offer tenants relatively favourable terms; otherwise they would simply not have been prepared to migrate from their original homes or, if they had already done so, they would move on to another estate. The classical seigneurie therefore never developed at all in this part of Europe.

Social tensions and peasant movements

All these developments took time to work themselves out. But by the end of the thirteenth century, the former relative uniformity of agrarian organization had given way to a rich variety of lordship and peasant tenures. Inevitably, this caused tensions where economic ambitions of the lords clashed with the defence of the age-old customs and of the social and legal status of the peasants. From the last two decades of the century we read of local peasant rebellions. Between 1323–1328 for the first time a whole region, maritime Flanders, exploded in revolt. From then on peasant movements and peasant revolts became a feature of European life until the end of the 'old régime' with the French and Russian Revolutions. They did not occur regularly nor always with similar purposes. But their basic causes remained the same: the effects of changing economic conditions on a peasant society that was conservative by tradition, and therefore disliked change, and which was, at the same time, legally open to exploitation both by the owners of land and capital and by the tax collectors and recruiting officers of the princes. What also remained the same, at least until 1789 in France, 1917 in Russia and 1949 in China was the basic ineffectiveness of these movements. Their successes were at best local and short-lived. The ruling classes, landowners and princes, remained too powerful to be dislodged; for they commanded all the strategic advantages in such struggles: education and religious tradition, respect for the law, the habit of command and the expectation of being obeyed and, in the last resort, the ability to mobilize and pay for professional troops.

Manufactures: the craft guilds

There was no inherent reason why handicraft manufacturing should not be carried on in the countryside and in the villages, as indeed they were. But the growing towns were natural markets for all types of manufactures, for cloth and clothes, for boots and shoes, for leather and metal goods, and above all for the building of houses, city walls, towns and churches. It was therefore equally natural that the towns should attract craftsmen. With the exception of the brick makers, brick layers and a very few others, the craftsmen would work in their own houses, often employing a few apprentices and trained helpers, called journeymen. From the twelfth century or even earlier, men working in the same craft would band together in craft guilds. These were not like modern trade unions, for they included both employers and employed, with the employers, the master craftsmen, always calling the tune. The guilds had statutes and left written records and, in consequence, historians used to overestimate their importance.

Plate 4.2   Orsanmichele, Florence.
This building, part oratory, part granary, was built by the city council of Florence from 1336, and used by the city's guilds, who vied with each other in its decoration. Each commissioned the great Florentine sculptors, from the fourteenth to the sixteenth centuries, to provide figures for the outside niches, which are thus today a treasury of late Gothic and Renaissance art. Such civic projects were characteristic of the medieval guilds at the height of their influence.

In the twelfth and thirteenth centuries, at least, they were often little more than religious fraternities of men with similar economic interests, providing their members with a feeling of security and friendship which they had lost when they left their villages and also with much-needed charity for disabled or elderly members or for their widows and orphans. They were in any case only to be found in some of the larger cities; for in the smaller towns there were simply not enough members of any one craft to form a guild. In a big city such as London there were guilds of very specialized trades. The articles of the spurriers, of 1345, give a good idea of guild regulations and also of the often noisy and sometimes dangerous behaviour of the citizens, and the ever-present fear of fire in medieval towns.

> Be it remembered that on Tuesday, the morrow of St. Peter's Chains in the nineteenth year of the reign of King Edward III, the articles underwritten were read before John Hammond,

mayor, . . . In the first place, that no one of the trade of the spurriers shall work longer than from the beginning of the day until curfew rung out at the Church of St. Sepulchre without Newgate; by reason that no man can work so neatly by night as by day. And many persons of the said trade, who compass how to practise deception in their work, desire to work by night rather than by day; and then they introduce false iron, and iron that has been cracked. And further, many of the said trade are wandering about all day, without working at all at their trade; and then, when they have become drunk and frantic, they take to their work, to the annoyance of the sick and all their neighbourhood, as well as by reason of the broils that arise between them and the strange people who are dwelling among them. And then they blow up their fires so vigorously that their forges begin all at once to blaze, to the great peril of themselves and all the neighbourhood around. . . . Also, that no one of the said trade shall keep a house or shop to carry on his business unless he is free of the city. . . . Also, that no one of the said trade shall receive the apprentice, serving-man or journeyman of an other in the same trade during the term agreed upon between his master and him. . . . Also, that no alien of another country . . . shall follow or use the said trade, unless he is enfranchised before the mayor, alderman and chamberlain . . .[2]

Only very gradually, and by no means universally, did the guilds acquire the rights to regulate terms of apprenticeship, hours of work, the quality of the product and, on occasion, even prices.

Capitalism in manufacture

This system of manufacturing worked well where the source of the raw materials and the market for the manufactured articles was both local, limited and known to everyone concerned. It did not work when raw materials had to be imported for the manufacture of specialized, high quality goods and where these goods were then sold to a wider market. Thus, by the thirteenth century, both the Flemish and the Italian cloth industry were importing high quality wool from England and the local spinners and weavers had to buy their wool from the importers. Since this was expensive they might well have to buy on credit and thus become indebted to, and dependent on, the importing merchant. More often still, however, they would have to take credit from the exporter to whom they sold their cloth; for, in the nature of this trade, they could have no direct contact with the ultimate customer. In their turn, the merchants who alone had the capital and the know-how for the importing and exporting business, found it convenient and profitable to organize the manufacture of cloth to suit current market conditions. By the end of the thirteenth century this had become a highly developed and organized capitalist business with advanced 'vertical integration'.

We know from the account books of one Jehan Boinebroke, of the Flemish city of Douai in the 1280s, that he had agents in England who bought the raw wool. He then gave it out successively to carders, spinners, weavers, fullers and dyers, to perform their work in their own homes, and finally he sold the finished cloth to foreign merchants. Those he employed were not allowed to accept work from any other employers, even if Boinebroke did not have enough work for them. For he also owned their houses and they were, inevitably, in debt to him. At the same time Boinebroke and his fellow employers sat in the town council and made the laws and statutes which gave public sanction to this system of exploitation.

It was much the same in northern Italy. In Florence, for instance, the manufacture of high quality cloth from English wool was controlled by the 'wool guild', the association of capitalist cloth manufacturers who organized not only the labour of the city dwellers but also that of the surrounding countryside. This type of industrial organization has been called the 'putting-out system'. Naturally, the employers were anxious that the workers did not organize in their turn. The statutes of the Florentine wool guild (*arte della lana*) of 1317 enacted this very specifically.

> In order that this guild may prosper and enjoy its freedom, vigour, honour and rights and in order to restrain those who wilfully resist and rebel against this guild, we decree and declare that no guild member or any artificers, men, or persons of the guild, in any way and by any means or legal subtleties, should dare or presume to form, organise or set up . . . any monopoly, compact, sworn conspiracy, conjuration, regulation, rule, society, league, machination, or any such things against the said guild or the manufacturers of the guild or against their honour, jurisdiction, tutelage, power or authority, under the penalty of £200 of small florins. . . . And concerning this matter, secret informants are to be appointed; nevertheless, it is permissible for anyone to accuse and denounce openly or secretly, and in reward to get half the fine, and the denunciations are to be kept secret.[3]

This was anti-trade union legislation with a vengeance. The chronicler Giovanni Villani tells us that in 1338 the Florentine wool manufacturing industry employed some 30,000 persons, many of them women and children, and produced about 80,000 big pieces of cloth a year. In the previous thirty years the value of this production had doubled while the number of manufacturing firms had shrunk from 300 to 200.

Thus Flanders and northern Italy had developed a genuinely capitalist mode of production in which the workers had effectively become wage earners, a proletariat, owning nothing but their labour, even though there were as yet no factories and the workers worked in their homes and even still employed journeymen and apprentices. The employment of these workers was subject to the fluctuations of an international market which they did not understand and over which they had no control. It is not surprising, therefore, that both areas were beginning to experience industrial strife: strikes and urban revolts. When these coincided or joined with peasant revolts they could, at least temporarily, be very formidable.

What happened in the woollen industry also happened in others. Wherever a great deal of fixed capital was needed in the production of goods, as in mining, or where a great deal of working capital was needed as in building and ship building, the capitalist entrepreneur and his capitalist organization inexorably elbowed the small independent master craftsmen out. This was a slow process which did not happen everywhere at the same time and, as yet, touched only some regions of Europe and a relatively small proportion of its total population. But the thirteenth and early fourteenth centuries were the watershed between a traditional society slowly emerging from the fusion of late-Roman skills and barbarian customs and the dynamic, competitive and deeply fissured society of modern times. It was then that there began to appear patterns of economic behaviour and organization, and consequent problems of human relationships, which are still with us today.

Capitalism and new techniques in trade

If this was so in manufacturing industry, it was even more so in trade. Growing population, growing production of goods and

225

wealth, growing towns and increasing specialization, all these caused an enormous expansion of trade. It occurred at all levels, from the village market to the great international fairs for professional merchants, and from the growth of the local urban grocery stores to the great international trading companies. There was no sharp break with the previous centuries of expansion; but where trade had been sporadic it now became organized and regular. The four Champagne fairs came to cover most of the year and allowed regular contacts between Italian and Flemish merchants – until, in the early fourteenth century, they were superseded by annual fleets sailing from Italy through the Straits of Gibraltar to Bruges and Southampton. The Brugeois then gave up travelling and found they could make a good living by staying at home and specializing in warehousing and brokerage between foreign merchants visiting their city.

More and more the Venetians, Genoese and Pisans defeated their non-Italian rivals in the competition for the carrying trade of the Mediterranean. It was the Italians who developed the most sophisticated commercial techniques; different forms of partnership which allowed them to raise the large amounts of working capital needed for the ships, provisions, goods and wages in overseas ventures that might last many months.

Partnerships made it necessary for merchants to keep regular accounts so that each partner could receive his due profits or carry his share of the losses of any particular venture. So it was that double-entry book-keeping was invented. And since dangers from storms and rocks, from pirates and warfare were ever present, merchants also developed marine insurance as a safeguard for their investments. Insurance rates were high, and many merchants, like Shakespeare's Merchant of Venice even in the sixteenth century, did not think it worth while to use insurance. Nearly all of them, however, used credit. The great expansion of trade in the thirteenth century could not possibly have occurred on a cash-and-carry basis. There was simply not enough money in circulation, even though there was a return to a gold coinage in western Europe for the first time in 500 years when Florence issued its gold florin, in 1252 and Venice followed with the gold ducat, in 1284. It was far more convenient and safer to buy and sell on credit and to write promissory notes instead of constantly handing over large sums (and weights!) of silver and gold coins. These notes, known as bills of exchange, could also be used to

Plate 4.3   Venice: façade of the Ducal Palace.
The Palace was the residence of the duke, or Doge, the head of the
Republic of St Mark (i.e. Venice). He was elected for life by the Senate
but had strictly limited powers. The Palace was also the meeting place
of the Senate and its governmental committees, and it was regarded as
the symbol of Venetian independence, wealth and greatness. Its
present form dates from 1309 and later. It is a most effective mixture
of Gothic arches and, on the façade of the upper part, a flat, geometric
pattern, as if a carpet had been hung over it. There are no flying
buttresses and none of three-dimensional rhythms of the façades of
the contemporary Gothic cathedrals (cf. Plate 4.7).

disguise the interest on loans as apparent foreign currency transactions. The Church frowned on interest since its theologians had
accepted the Aristotelian theory that money was nothing but a
medium of exchange and, hence, 'barren', i.e. incapable of
producing wealth. Nevertheless, it proved impossible to prevent
the charging of interest on loans. Often enough, this was done
quite openly, and not least by papal merchants and bankers.

For banking was now also spreading. Its origins were twofold:
the multiplicity of currencies had become so great, and their rates

had come to vary so much against each other, that it soon became necessary to employ professional money changers. At the same time merchants often found it convenient to leave spare cash in safe hands. When the two functions were combined and when it became acceptable that the deposits could be lent out or invested, modern banking was born.

It was in Italy, and especially in Genoa and Tuscany, that these new commercial methods developed. It was in Italy that the first handbooks of commercial practice were written, in the thirteenth and fourteenth centuries. It was in Italy that there first appeared descriptions of foreign ports and trade routes and glossaries of words and phrases in Italian and eastern languages. It was in Italy, too, that young men could learn the elements of commercial techniques, not only as apprentices in established business firms but also in schools and universities; and it was to Italy that, for centuries, the north Europeans came to learn these techniques.

With the development of the new commercial techniques there developed also new attitudes of mind. Rational calculation of economic enterprise, a numerical, mathematical, assessment of possibilities; and rational, mathematical, commercial methods came to be seen as the recipe for success. Villani records that in Florence, around 1345, between 8,000 and 10,000 boys and girls were learning to read, and that in six schools some 1,000 to 1,200 boys (but apparently not girls) were learning the use of the abacus and of arithmetic. But Florence, Venice, Genoa and a few other Italian cities were far in advance of other parts of Europe. The great majority of people, even the majority of merchants, were traditionalists, content to make a reasonable living, as their fathers had done. The new attitudes towards work gained ground only slowly. The long resistance to the common use of Arabic numerals (see Ch. 3, p. 202) shows the basic conservatism even of the highly educated. Yet the turn towards rational commercial methods and organization by the Italian urban patriciate powerfully reinforced trends towards rationality that were making themselves felt in nearly every sphere of intellectual activity and that were to colour and eventually to determine the whole development of European civilization.

Royal government

By 1200 the age of rapid empire-building in Europe was virtually over. There were good reasons for this. The government of the monarchies of western and southern Europe had become more and more institutionalized. A king's council was still the place in which his great lay and ecclesiastical vassals advised him on matters of high policy, or at least those whom he chose to summon to his council. But it had also become an institution which carried on the king's business even when the king was not there. This business touched two political areas, the administration of justice and royal finance: within these areas subdivisions began to appear. As early as the reign of Henry II (1154–1189) England had a handbook describing the work of its treasury, the *Dialogue of the Exchequer*, (see Ch. 3, p. 202). The Court of Common Pleas at Westminster adjudicated private cases; the court of King's Bench dealt with criminal cases and cases involving royal rights and, in the thirteenth century, came to concern itself also with appeals from all other courts. Moreover, the king's judges travelled about the country, co-operated with local juries and gradually superseded the feudal courts of the great nobles.

In France similar developments occurred somewhat later than in England, but then even more rapidly. Thus until 1295 the Order of the Templars administered the French king's treasury. But by 1306 the 'chambers of account' had already more members than the Exchequer in England. About the same time the French supreme court, the *parlement* of Paris, had seven or eight times as many judges as the courts of Common Pleas and King's Bench combined.

The men who carried on the king's government, in his chancery (i.e. secretariat), his treasury and his law courts were now mostly professionals; and while many of them were still clerics, educated laymen were beginning to compete, and compete successfully. In Germany kings and the other great princes, the dukes and bishops, recruited such administrators from a group of men from whom they had traditionally also recruited their household servants and personal retainers, their own unfree tenants. These were called *ministeriales*. They would often be rewarded by grants of land and, like other feudal vassals, they would tend to make both their holdings and sometimes even their

229

offices hereditary. Thus there appeared a new class of minor nobility who were unfree by the legal definitions of the period – a reminder to historians that feudalism was not a tidy 'system' of social relationships but incorporated many contradictory facets. Only very gradually, in the course of the thirteenth and fourteenth centuries, did the German *ministeriales* become assimilated to the free knights.

The decline of internationalism

The growing complexity and professionalism of government and its increasing interaction with local administration enhanced the sense of community and the stability of political structures. Increasing wealth and a wider spread of education allowed smaller regions to develop into viable political units, more than had been possible in the eleventh and twelfth centuries; for it was no longer necessary to go so far afield to find the professional men capable of carrying on the business of government.

Here was a growing regionalization of Europe which ran counter to the internationalism of earlier centuries. It did not as yet supersede this internationalism. It was rather that the opposing forces of internationalism and regionalism came to dominate the development of Europe for the following centuries.

In the thirteenth century, this development had two immediate consequences. In the first place, it became more difficult for aggressive rulers to conquer new territory. When they did manage to do this, it became more difficult to integrate the newly conquered territories with their older possessions. In the second place while government was becoming more centralized and more effective, it was also involving larger and larger sections of the population in the participation of the government of their community. These two problems will be considered in turn.

Conquests

France

Nowhere was the problem of newly conquered territories more evident than in France. We may remember that the king of

England held most of western France, from Normandy south to Aquitaine, as fiefs from the kings of France. In 1202 King Philip Augustus induced his feudal court to sentence the English king, John, to lose all his French fiefs. John received little support from his own vassals in France, for he and his brother Richard the Lion-Heart had exploited them for their own ambitions. Not surprisingly, therefore, John lost the whole of Normandy and Anjou, to his suzerain (1204). Only Guyenne, in the south-west, remained English. In just such a manner had Henry the Lion lost his dominions to his suzerain, Frederick Barbarossa, in 1180. But where Barbarossa had been obliged immediately to parcel out Saxony to Henry's greatest vassals, Philip Augustus was able to incorporate Normandy and Anjou into his own dominions. Nonetheless, these provinces retained many of their own laws and institutions, and the same was true in the case of Languedoc, Poitou, Toulouse and other provinces acquired by the French crown by conquest, inheritance or purchase in the course of the thirteenth and early fourteenth centuries. Right up to the Revolution of 1789, France remained a country of quasi-autonomous provinces with an increasingly elaborate centralizing monarchy superimposed on them.

England and the British Isles

The kings of England found the integration of new regions under the crown even more difficult than the kings of France; for in the British Isles there was no tradition of an overall monarchy such as the Capetian kings had inherited from their Carolingian predecessors. The English kings claimed lordship over Ireland; but this was acknowledged in Ireland itself almost in direct proportion to the failure of the kings to exercise it in practice. Anglo-Norman knights who had seized large tracts of land in Ireland during the reign of Henry II were as disinclined to pay more than lip-service to the authority of the king as were the Gaelic-speaking native Irish chieftains.

Nor was the position very different in Wales, even though that country's church had been much more firmly integrated into the English ecclesiastical structure than the Irish church. Only Edward I (1272–1307), politically the most gifted king of England since Henry II, was able to subdue the Welsh once and for all. He did this both by a series of military victories and by an elaborate system of castle building. Nevertheless, Wales remained in language, culture and administration a largely foreign and unassimilated part of the kingdom.

But what worked in Wales, relatively near to the centre of English royal power, did not work in distant Scotland. Edward's interference in internal Scottish disputes over the succession to the Scottish crown met only with partial success and set the two countries on a course of two and a half centuries of hostility. The hostility was particularly murderous and unrelenting in the border areas, even though there was little ethnic or linguistic difference between the northern English and the Lowland Scots. As often happens, a hostility once started is difficult to compose for it feeds on resentments handed down from generation to generation.

Moreover, this Anglo-Scottish hostility inevitably became involved in the political power struggles of western Europe, and Edward I was the first English king to be faced with the potentially deadly alliance between France and the Scots, an alliance that was to become traditional.

If Edward I must carry a large part of the responsibility for this, it is only fair to add that every strong medieval ruler who had the capacity would have acted similarly, that his contemporaries did not blame him, and that, given the militaristic ethos of medieval society, Edward had good reason to be concerned about the results of a possibly hostile succession to the Scottish crown. What contemporaries would not forgive was lack of success. When Edward's incompetent and feckless son, Edward II (1307–27), suffered the crushing defeat of Bannockburn at the hands of the Scots (1314), a baronial opposition against him began to organize which was eventually to deprive him of his throne and his life (1327).

Governments: law and community

The problem of the increasing involvement of larger sections of the population with the government of their community was only just beginning to appear. It was sometimes determined by the facts of geography, especially in the case of large islands such as England or Sicily, sometimes by common language, but most of all by common political traditions developed from common lordship and the needs and experience of warfare. As kings extended their authority beyond the purely feudal and personal claims of liege-lord over vassal, so for their part the vassals and subjects attempted either to escape from this authority or to limit it by law to make the exercise of royal authority regular and predictable. Nearly everywhere in Europe kings acceded to such demands for the sake of peace at home and support for their foreign wars; or they were made to accede by armed opposition. Everywhere rulers granted charters to cities in their territories, allowing them varying degrees of self-government, and Frederick Barbarossa even had to grant the cities of northern Italy virtual independence from imperial rule (see above, Ch. 3, p. 173). Equally important were charters to the nobility guaranteeing their rights and privileges and requiring the king to obey the law of the land. Such were the ordinances of 1188 which Alfonso VIII of Leon, one of the Spanish kingdoms, had to publish; such were the privileges of 1220 which the emperor Frederick II granted to the ecclesiastical princes of Germany and which his son had to extend in 1231; such was the Golden Bull of the king of Hungary in 1222 and such was the most famous royal charter of all, the English Magna Carta of 1215.

England and Magna Carta

The immediate causes for the issuing of Magna Carta were the heavy demands made by King John (1199–1216) of England for the reconquest of Normandy, lost in 1204. As so often, personalities played an important role. John was intelligent and autocratic and, with some justice, men did not trust him. But in all these respects he was not very different from his father, Henry II, nor from his popular brother Richard the Lion-Heart. But he lost both his war with France and a civil war with his disgruntled barons and, by 1215, he was left without room for manoeuvre and had to sign the charter. Basically, Magna Carta affirmed the rule of law. No doubt, it was an unequal law, benefiting primarily the richest and most privileged sections of the community, the barons and the Church. Yet, more than most Continental charters, it took account also of non-noble classes and it stated quite specifically that the liberties which the king granted to his men they were to grant their own men in turn. The best known of its clauses states: 'No free man shall be taken or imprisoned or disseised [i.e. have his property taken away] or outlawed or exiled or in any way ruined . . . except by the lawful judgement of his peers or by the law of the land'. The principle of judgement by his peers had been widely accepted in Europe for some time; but it was usually confined to the nobility. Here it was taken very widely, to apply to all free men, and it was linked to an affirmation of the supremacy of law. In the next generation an English judge would draw the logical conclusion that 'the king should be under God and the law'.

The true importance of Magna Carta lies in its history after 1215. It was several times re-affirmed by the great barons and ecclesiastics who formed the regency government for the boy-king Henry III after John's early death. In the fourteenth century parliament interpreted the phrase of 'judgment by peers' to mean trial by jury and to apply to all, and not only to free men.

Magna Carta provided for a committee of twenty-five to ensure its observance. It was, however, only parliament which could do this permanently and the institution of parliament was not a direct result of the promulgation of Magna Carta. The history of parliament will be discussed in the next chapter.

Papacy, empire and state

Innocent III

The death of the emperor Henry VI in 1197 left the papacy without a serious political rival in Italy. At just this moment the cardinals had elected the youngest of their number as Pope Innocent III. Among the many remarkable personalities of medieval popes Innocent III (1198–1216) stands out as the most imperious and politically most successful. 'Lower than God but higher than man', he described himself by virtue of his office. Of the relation of the papacy to the state he wrote that 'as the moon derives its light from the sun . . . so too the royal power derives its splendour from the pontifical authority'. With consummate skill he proceeded to exploit every political opportunity to translate this vision of papal power into reality. Sicily, Aragon and Portugal recognized him as their feudal suzerain and so, for a time, did the king of Poland and even King John of England. Innocent forced Philip Augustus of France to take back his queen

234

whom he had repudiated and claimed to adjudicate in his dispute with King John over Normandy. More effectively still the pope intervened repeatedly in the German civil wars where a Hohenstaufen and a Welf candidate, a son of Henry the Lion, disputed the crown. As a result of the fourth crusade, (see below, p. 251–55) even Constantinople returned a papal obedience. When Innocent celebrated a general Church council at the Lateran, in 1215, the medieval papacy appeared to the Christian world to have reached its highest point.

Frederick II

These appearances, however, were deceptive. Circumstances changed and Innocent's successors could not match his brilliance as a politician. This role now fell to the papacy's great enemy, the emperor Frederick II (king of Sicily 1198, of Germany 1212, emperor 1220–1250). The son of Henry VI, he was the most brilliant of that most gifted German dynasty, the Hohenstaufen. Brought up in Sicily with its multi-racial, multi-lingual and multi-religious heritage, he organized a dazzling court of lawyers, writers, artists and scientists, himself taking part in all their activities as well as enjoying a harem of Saracen women and an army of Muslim mercenaries whose loyalty he could rely on in the face of all papal fulminations.

Having organized Sicily into the most efficient state in Europe, Frederick attempted to revive imperial authority in northern Italy. Inevitably he fell foul of both the Italian communes, the independent cities, and the papacy, which feared, once again, the deadly political pressure of a power that controlled both northern and southern Italy. The struggle, essentially an Italian civil war, was fought with varying fortunes until the emperor's sudden death in 1250 led to the irretrievable collapse of the imperial position.

The Empire and Germany

The suddenness of this collapse was itself a sign of how narrow the basis of imperial power had become. For the rivals in the German civil wars of the early thirteenth century had dissipated the major part of imperial property and authority, and Frederick II himself had had to give up most of what remained in order to

buy support for his Italian policy. His death was followed by an inter-regnum during which several foreign princes had themselves elected king by different groups of German magnates but failed to assert any significant authority. Finally, in 1273, the major German princes, the 'electors', came together to elect a minor German count, Rudolf of Habsburg, as king. Their aim was to put an end to the anarchy of the inter-regnum, while deliberately choosing a weak king who could not revive the central authority of the monarchy in Germany.

They were successful in both aims. Rudolf I could still command sufficient support to deal with the worst outrages of the 'robber barons'. Quite logically, however, he saw that his position would ultimately depend on his own possessions and it was he who set the house of Habsburg on its road to greatness by acquiring the duchies of Austria. The electors, however, continued to elect kings from different houses, chosen primarily for their weakness. These too, were sometimes able to use their royal position to increase their family possessions and with these, in turn to increase royal power. Several of them even marched into Italy to be crowned emperor and revive old imperial claims and hopes. But these forays were mere shadows of the great expeditions of the Saxon, Salian and Hohenstaufen emperors. The German electors continued their stranglehold on the German monarchy and thus effectively preserved Italy and the papacy from German interference.

The papacy and the monarchies

Thus the papacy appeared to have won its great three-round and 200-year duel with the Empire. But again appearances were

Plate 4.4 Burg Eltz, lower Moselle.
The Hohenstaufen emperors tried systematically, but in the end unsuccessfully, to consolidate their power base in Germany. This castle commands the strategic area near the confluence of the Moselle and the Rhine. It is much bigger and more elaborate than the relatively small twelfth-century baronial castles, such as Framlingham (Plate 3.2). Its towers and pinnacles make it a kind of secular-military counterpart to the great Gothic cathedrals, but it is more compact and has no flying buttresses which would have been much too vulnerable to medieval siege artillery, still dominated at this time by the stone-throwing catapult.

237

deceptive. In the course of this duel the popes and their spokesmen and supporters had worked out an elaborate theory of papal supremacy both within the Church and with relation to the secular powers, and they had underpinned this theory with the development of canon law. They had also built up an elaborate organization of central control which allowed the popes to interfere in local ecclesiastical administration by encouraging appeals to Rome from ecclesiastical courts, by taxation of the clergy, by appointments to bishoprics and other ecclesiastical offices and by making use of the new monastic orders of the Dominicans and the Franciscans who remained outside the normal control of the local bishops.

The cost of these achievements was very high. The popes who had fought Frederick II, Gregory IX and Innocent IV, had used every weapon in the ecclesiastical armoury; ban, excommunication, interdict, propaganda and personal smear campaigns, for what appeared to be mainly political ends. Even Louis IX of France (1226–70), whose saintliness and loyalty to the Church were beyond reproach and who was duly canonized before the century was out, did not approve of Innocent IV's methods. In southern Italy the popes bestowed the Hohenstaufen kingdom of Sicily on the French prince Charles of Anjou. But in 1282 the Sicilians murdered the hated French during the famous 'Sicilian Vespers', and offered their country to the king of Aragon. All the efforts of the popes and of Charles of Anjou, now effectively king only of Naples, could not win Sicily back. A relatively small power and a vassal of the pope had successfully resisted him. It was unlikely that the great monarchies would be far behind, for they were anxious to control the Church in their own kingdoms and were bound to resent ever increasing papal interference. If a clash was inevitable, it was, as so often, precipitated by strong personalities. Philip IV of France (1285–1314) was determined both to extend royal authority in his kingdom and to extend its boundaries. In 1296, in the course of a war against Edward I of England, Philip imposed taxes on the French Church, just as, indeed, Edward was imposing taxes on the English Church in England. Pope Boniface VIII (1294–1303) denied both kings' right to do this and commanded the clergy in France and England to disobey their kings.

Not since Becket had the problem of conflicting loyalties been posed so clearly in western Europe. Moreover, both the organ-

238

ization and the concept of the sovereign state had by this time evolved so clearly that the pope's claims were regarded as a frontal attack on this concept. Philip forbade the export of all currency and precious metal from France. Within a few months the pope had to give way. The king of France had found a more effective weapon against the papacy than all the armies of the German emperors. In 1301 he provoked another clash by ordering the arrest and trial of a French bishop, contrary to the papacy's claim that bishops could be tried only in Rome. Boniface reacted angrily and both sides escalated their arguments and, on the French side, forgeries of documents. In November 1302 the pope issued the bull *Unam Sanctam* which contained the most advanced claims ever made for papal supremacy. Its argument, joining the doctrine of the two swords with the belief in the hierarchy of the great chain of being, culminated in the ringing phrase: 'Therefore we declare, state, define and pronounce that it is altogether necessary to salvation for every creature to be subject to the Roman Pontiff'.

Again Philip answered by a practical move. One of his ministers, with a handful of French troops, joined with Boniface's Roman enemies, surprised him in his summer residence of Anagni and captured, insulted and humiliated the old man (1303). Within a few weeks he died.

His successors had neither the courage nor the means to continue the quarrel. Within a few years a French pope, Clement V (1305–14), moved to Avignon on the Rhône, a small papal enclave surrounded by French territory. There the papacy remained in its 'Babylonian captivity' until 1376, not perhaps as much under the thumb of the French monarchy as has sometimes been believed, but with its independence gravely compromised in the eyes of Europe.

The historical significance of the third Empire-papacy and the first papacy-state struggles

It is one of the ironies of history that the papacy, having won its great struggle with the Empire, should have succumbed so soon to those powers which had helped it in its struggles – the staff which pierced the hand that held it, as contemporaries said. But more than irony is involved. There was, in the first place, the almost inescapable moral decline in the course of what was

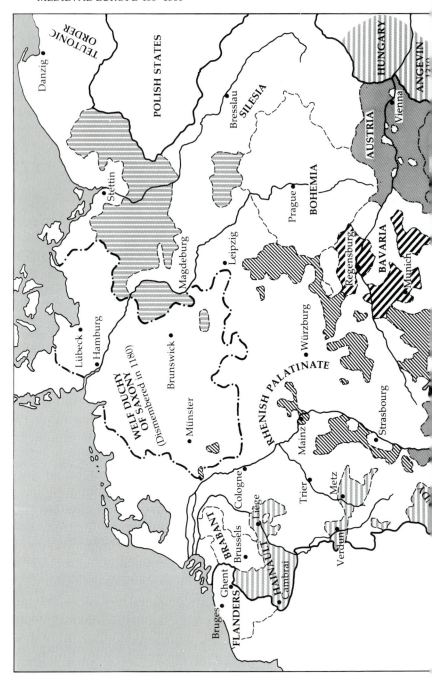

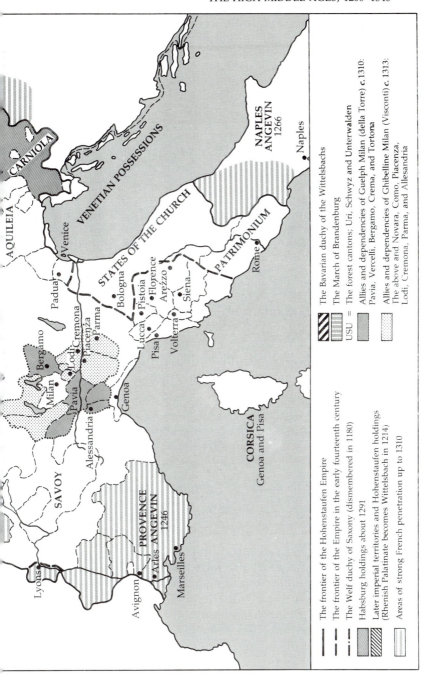

Map 4.1 The Empire and Italy, c. 1300.

The Bavarian duchy of the Wittelsbachs

The March of Brandenburg

USU = The forest cantons; Uri, Schwyz and Unterwalden

Allies and dependencies of Guelph Milan (della Torre) **c.** 1310:
Pavia, Vercelli, Bergamo, Crema, and Tortona

Allies and dependencies of Ghibelline Milan (Visconti) **c.** 1313:
The above and Novara, Como, Piacenza,
Lodi, Cremona, Parma, and Allesandria

The frontier of the Hohenstaufen Empire

The frontier of the Empire in the early fourteenth century

The Welf duchy of Saxony (dismembered in 1180)

Habsburg holdings about 1291

Later imperial territories and Hohenstaufen holdings
(Rhenish Palatinate becomes Wittelsbach in 1214)

Areas of strong French penetration up to 1310

regarded as a life and death struggle; for men would not forgive a pope what they might forgive a king. In the second place the struggle had shifted ground, both politically and intellectually. The emperors had fought on the same grounds as the papacy over the nature of authority, seen still in terms of the old Roman Empire and of a number of biblical texts and their interpretation. But the kingdoms of France or England or Castile were something different. Their kings claimed imperial status but only in the sense of recognizing no earthly superior *within their dominions*, that is, not in terms of a general dominion over the world, which was the way the popes and the medieval emperors had argued (however unjustified this may have been in the emperors' case). In the long run the geographically limited authority of the late-medieval kings, the sovereignty of their states, turned out to be a more effective base from which to challenge the claims of the papacy.

At the same time the arguments of the monarchies received powerful intellectual and emotional support from the rediscovery of Aristotle's *Politics*, in the late twelfth century, and their assimilation into orthodox Christian thought by St Thomas Aquinas in the thirteenth. For Aristotle had posited the origins and ends of the state quite independently of the divine will:

> When several villages are united in a single community, perfect and large enough to be nearly or quite self-sufficing, the state comes into existence, originating in the bare needs of life, and continuing in existence for the sake of the good life. . . . Hence it is evident that the state is a creation of nature, and that man is by nature a political animal. (*A Treatise on Government*, I:2)

Aquinas linked these 'natural' origins of the state to an elaborate theory of natural law. By this he meant the law of the nature of the universe and of man, i.e. without divine revelation. This was not a new idea; but its authoritative formulation by Aquinas set it on a spectacular career in European thought which has lasted into our own times. At the same time, Aquinas accepted from Aristotle the notion of evolution and of a reality that was not the same as an ideal. From this realization it followed that 'the law can rightly be changed because of the changes in man's conditions, according to which different laws are required'. Here was a recognition of the possibility of improving the law and, with it, man's political and social condition. During the Renaissance

242

people would begin to use this possibility for systematic social and political 'engineering'.

It was, of course, perfectly possible to make use of the concept of natural law in religious thought. Aquinas had done just that. For him there was no opposition between nature and divine grace or, as he put it, 'grace does not do away with nature but perfects it'. In the late thirteenth- and early fourteenth-century context of political debate, the concept of natural law and the Aristotelian idea of the state allowed the publicists of Philip IV to undercut the papal position in a way the earlier pro-imperial controversialists had never been able to do. The state now appeared as a rational and moral structure, completely independent of the papacy. The Church, a 'mystical body', the 'congregation of the faithful', could even be regarded as wholly subordinate to the state.

It took time for such ideas to develop, and their more extreme formulations were not immediately very influential. But, for the first time since the reform movement in the eleventh century, the papacy, and indeed the whole Church, had been put intellectually on the defensive.

Religious life

In the opinion of the Byzantines western Christianity had always been rather primitive and crude, suitable no doubt for a backward, still half-barbarian society. It was certainly true that, from the twelfth century on, as western society became richer, more urbanized and more educated, new religious sensibilities began to appear which the Church of feudalized bishops and abbots could not easily satisfy. The Cluniac and Cistercian movements were outlets for those who wished to withdraw from ordinary life, and the extraordinary popularity of pilgrimages and crusades provided outlets for the religious longings of ordinary men and women which the parish priests could not meet. But this was not enough.

Franciscans, Dominicans and Beguines

It was particularly in the growing cities that these feelings took the form of new religious movements. They all had in common

243

the attempt to provide a more personal religious experience. This might be achieved either by the adoption of a truly Christian life-style or, for most ordinary men and women, by the contemplation of and the example afforded by such a life-style and by the opportunity of giving fervent approval to it.

The most famous and most immediately popular of these movements was that of the Franciscans. St Francis of Assisi (1181/2–1226), the son of a wealthy merchant, renounced all property and lived and preached in complete poverty, relying on alms even for his food. His movement, approved by Innocent III over the opposition of the more conservative cardinals, was controversial from the beginning. For the Franciscan friars did not live like other monks in well-endowed monasteries but 'in the world', among the people.

From its foundation, the Franciscan order was highly successful in gaining adherents and popular esteem. For generations people had deplored the worldliness of the Church and the ostentatious living of the higher clergy, including the heads of the great monastic houses. The demand for a return to the poverty, simplicity and spirituality of the early Church had been among the most effective propaganda weapons of the imperialists against the papacy. Here, finally, was a company of men and women (for St Clare, a noble lady of Assisi and a great admirer of St Francis, founded a parallel order for women, the Poor Clares), led by a great saint, who lived just such a Christian life. St Francis himself was reported to have received the stigmata, the wounds inflicted on Christ's hands and feet during the crucifixion. St Bonaventure, general of the order from 1257 to 1274, wrote about this: 'He [St Francis] would be made like to the crucified Christ not by a bodily martyrdom but by conformity in mind and heart'.

Within a very few years of the saint's death, a collection of stories of his and his companions' lives and sayings, *The little Flowers of Saint Francis*, gained wide circulation.

A typical story is that of Brother Bernard.

> Since Saint Francis and his companions were called and chosen by God to bear the cross of Christ within their hearts, to display it in their actions, and to preach it with their tongues, they appeared – and indeed were – men crucified, both in their clothing, the austerity of their lives, and their doings, for they desired to bear insult and shame for the love of Christ, rather than receive worldly honour, respect, or praise from men . . .

244

In the early days of the order Saint Francis sent Brother Bernard to Bologna to bear the fruit of God there. . . . When the children saw him in a ragged, shabby habit, they jeered at him and abused him, thinking him a madman; but Brother Bernard bore all this patiently and gladly for the love of Christ. And in order to receive even worse treatment, he sat down openly in the market-place of the city. As he sat there, a crowd of children and men gathered round him: one tugged at his cowl from in front; one threw dust at him, and another stones; . . .

A wealthy and wise lawyer was so much impressed with Brother Bernard's holiness that he presented him with a house for the order.

When Saint Francis had received a full account of all that God had done through Brother Bernard, he gave thanks to Him who had begun to increase the poor little disciples of the Cross in this manner. And he sent some of his companions to Bologna and into Lombardy, where they established many friaries in various places.[4]

This little story, while it shows the psychology of the spread of the Franciscan movement, also shows the fundamental dilemma of religious movements dedicated to poverty. For here the order was given property. Soon, fierce quarrels arose between the Spirituals, those who demanded absolute poverty, and the Conventuals, who accepted the need for communal property, so that the brothers or friars could more effectively pursue their lives of study and preaching. In the early fourteenth century the popes pronounced against the Spirituals. These men even suffered severe persecution for their beliefs which, their opponents feared with some justice, might serve as justification for popular revolutionary movements.

At about the same time as St Francis of Assisi founded his order, the Spaniard St Dominic (c 1170–1221) founded the Order of Preachers, the Dominicans or black friars. They were mendicants, like the Franciscans, living on alms, and they were even more firmly dedicated to preaching and to fighting heresies; Dominicans – domini canes – the dogs of the Lord, people said. By the middle of the thirteenth century, members of the two mendicant orders, the Franciscans and the Dominicans, occupied many chairs of theology in the universities. The papacy to whom they were directly responsible had gained a very powerful new weapon.

245

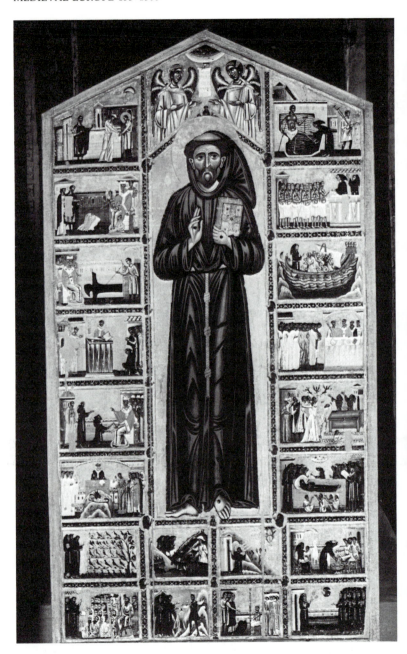

While the Franciscans and some other orders had branches for women, it was in the nature of medieval society and its ethos that life in a regular order could appeal to only a very small number of women, and these mostly of the upper classes (see above, Ch. 3, p. 150). A different style of feminine religious life was needed and this was provided by the Beguines, communities of women who lived in comparative poverty and were dedicated to prayer, without, however, taking vows like nuns. The beguinages were particularly common in the Rhineland and in the Netherlands. A fine example of one of their houses has survived in Bruges (modern Belgium).

Heresies

For all their efforts to provide a deeper spirituality for the Christian laity, these new orders were not wholly successful. The longing for a deeper and more personal religious experience had, from the twelfth century, tended towards heresy. These heresies appeared in different corners of Europe and in many forms. Often enough, they could be coped with by a mixture of persuasion and repression. The Cathars were, however, a more serious matter. Their name, from the Greek, signified 'the pure', and they were sometimes also called Albigenses, after the city of Albi in southern France. They believed in a dualism of good and evil as two independent principles; the material world for them was evil and Jesus was merely an angel. It was a complete denial of the traditional basis of Christian beliefs and of the authority of the Catholic Church. Their life-style was very puritanical and proved highly attractive, especially as the believers were not all required to participate in the extremes of fasting and sexual prohibitions. They were, moreover, favoured by princes and nobles in southern France and northern Italy.

By the early thirteenth century, the movement had grown to

Plate 4.5   Florence, Bardi Chapel in the Church of Santa Croce: *St Francis*.
This painting of *c.* 1250 shows St Francis with his stigmata, the marks of Christ's crucifixion on his hands and feet, in the Byzantine tradition of holy figures. The panels show scenes from his life. On the left, five down, St Francis is being blessed by Pope Innocent III; two below this, he is preaching to the birds; bottom left, he visits the Sultan.

such an alarming extent that Innocent III decided to deal with it. But, what started as an attempt at reconversion was turned, by a series of accidents, by popular fanaticism and by the calculated opportunism of some French noblemen and the French monarchy, into a crusade. The count of Toulouse and other great nobles were dispossessed of their property and lands, several cities were destroyed and thousands were massacred. Catharism was crushed as a significant movement but other heresies were to appear because the social and psychological conditions in which heresies grew continued to exist. Worse still, the 'Albigensian crusade' left an evil heritage of religious fanaticism and a tradition of robber-politics justified by religious motives. These had, of course, been the characteristics of all the crusades; but now they were transferred to the heart of Europe.

The papacy, it is true, attempted to systematize and perhaps even civilize its dealing with heretics. It set up the inquisition, a tribunal which sought to determine whether men held heretical opinions. The Dominican friars, in particular, served as inquisitors, and travelled far and wide to search for heretics and, soon, also for sorcerers and witches. Many inquisitors were dedicated and humane men doing their best to lead those who had 'gone astray' back into the 'bosom of the Church'. But it was a set-up which inevitably attracted the fanatical, the self-righteous, the greedy and the ambitious; and the evil reputation which the institution acquired was only too often well deserved.

The destruction of the Templars

Nowhere, perhaps, is this clearer than in the destruction of the Templars. The Templars, we may recall (Ch. 3, p. 191), were a religious order of knights founded in Jerusalem in the early twelfth century to protect Christian pilgrims and to fight the infidels. Grateful popes and princes granted them wide ecclesiastical privileges and extensive properties. They used these properties to build up an international banking and trade system and they provided credit and financial personnel to the kings of France and other rulers. Naturally, they made enemies. Philip IV of France decided that it would be both popular and profitable to destroy them. On one day in 1307 he had all Templars in France arrested. Then he set the inquisition to work. By the wholesale use of torture the inquisitors extracted confessions of supposed heresies, sexual perversions and ritual murder. A well-organized propaganda campaign, the first such since the persecutions of the Christians in the Roman Empire, convinced the French public of the Templars' supposed guilt. The order was condemned; the French crown confiscated its vast property; and the papacy suffered another set-back as the feeble Clement V failed to protect the order. Needless to say, all the charges were pure fabrications. But Philip IV and the inquisitors had found means to arouse latent anxieties in European society which for centuries were to bear bitter fruits in the persecution of Jews, witches, and heretics and finally in religious civil wars.

The Jews

The Jews were the only religious minority in medieval Europe who were, at least officially, allowed to exercise a non-Christian religion. On this point successive popes and theologians made quite clear pronouncements. In practice, however, the treatment accorded to Jews varied greatly, both in place and time. The barbarian invaders of the Roman Empire had, on the whole, been tolerant; but in the seventh century the Visigothic kings of Spain both legislated against the Jews and set their subjects against them.

The Carolingian period was, on the whole, much better, especially in the Carolingian empire itself. As merchants, financiers and generally educated men the Jews fulfilled useful functions, forming a kind of secondary international élite whose services were generally appreciated. We know very little of their numbers, except that they were certainly small. For England at the end of the twelfth century they have been estimated at about 2,500 or 1 in 1,000 of the population. In southern Italy and Spain their communities were certainly much larger. For fourteenth century Castile, modern estimates vary from 20,000 to 200,000. It was also in southern Europe that their cultural role was most important both for themselves and for the Arabs and Christians, between whom they often acted as intellectual and linguistic intermediaries.

With the economic development of Europe from the twelfth century onwards and with the increasing spread of skills, the functions of the Jews could be taken over by Christians. Inevitably, the Jews now appeared more and more as hated competi-

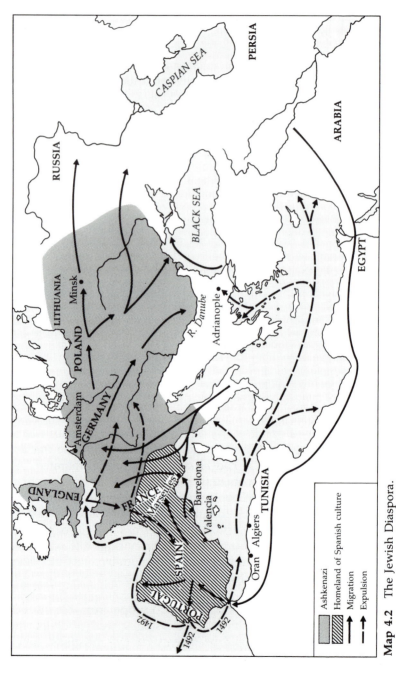

Map 4.2 The Jewish Diaspora.

tors. These feelings coincided with the spread of the new religious sensibilities, and the Jews now came to appear as the enemies of Christ *par excellence*. It was in the twelfth century that the familiar fabrications about ritual murder and other enormities began to circulate against the Jews. At the same time Jews were prohibited from owning land. With rare insight Abelard put into the mouth of a Jew the argument that,

> What remains to us is usury, that we sustain our miserable lives by taking interest from strangers, which makes us most hateful to them. . . . Whoever injures us in any way believes that action to be the highest justice and the greatest sacrifice to his God.

The Christian kings of Europe declared the Jews to be their property and they used, exploited and also protected them. But when popular passions against the Jews became too strong – and the friars in the thirteenth century were particularly zealous in whipping up such passions, for they regarded the existence of the Jews, the 'murderers' of Christ, as an insult to the Christian religion – the kings had no compunction about throwing the Jews to the wolves. Edward I expelled them from England in 1290. The kings of France first expelled them, in 1306, then re-admitted them in 1315 and then expelled them again in 1322.

The fourth crusade and the fall of Byzantium

For the modern historian it is clear that by 1200 the true crusading spirit, however flawed it had always been, had evaporated. At the time, this was not so obvious. Men still went on crusades and fought bravely in the Holy Land for almost another hundred years, and quite serious plans for the reconquest of Jerusalem were made in the middle of the fifteenth century and even later.

It seemed perfectly natural that the papacy at the very height of its power should once more take the initiative in organizing a crusade. To Innocent III the moment seemed especially favourable when, after the death of the emperor Henry VI (1197), all the great kings of western Europe were too busy fighting rivals for the throne or fighting each other to think of taking the lead as they had done at the time of Barbarossa, Louis VII and Richard the Lion-Heart, in the third crusade. The Church, without the kings, had directed the first crusade, and that had, after all, been the most successful one. This time, as a hundred years before, the actual leadership was again undertaken by the French, Netherlands and Italian high nobility. They had now learned that the overland route was too punishing, and they arranged for transport by sea with the Italian sea-ports.

In 1202 the majority of the crusaders, but not all groups, assembled in Venice. There were far fewer than had been estimated, and they were quite unable to pay the full fee on which the republic continued to insist. The old, almost blind, Venetian doge, Enrico Dandolo, therefore suggested that, in lieu of the full fee, the crusaders should help Venice recapture the Dalmatian port of Zara which the king of Hungary had taken from them in 1186. Some of the clergy protested. The king of Hungary was a Catholic and had himself taken the cross. Innocent III hesitated. By the time he forbade the move, on pain of excommunication, Zara had already been taken and the crusading army was now excommunicated.

All might still have been resolved; but at this point the crusaders became entangled with Byzantine politics. From the foundation of the Roman Empire by Augustus the imperial succession had been one of the weakest points in its political structure. Over the centuries, various attempts had been made to overcome this weakness, by establishing hereditary dynasties or by the election of co-emperors during the life-time of the ruler. Every so often these methods broke down (see Ch. 2, p. 119). Manuel I (1143–80) of the originally highly successful dynasty of the Comneni (see Ch. 3, p. 183) was followed by weak emperors, civil wars and usurpations. In 1195 Isaac II Angelos was overthrown by his brother, Alexius III, and, in Byzantine tradition, imprisoned and blinded. While the crusaders were still in Zara, Isaac's son, also Alexius and brother-in-law of the Hohenstaufen king of Germany, Philip of Swabia, appeared in the camp of the crusaders and asked for help against the usurper Alexius III. In return the prince promised the enormous sum of 200,000 marks in silver (the Venetians had demanded 85,000 marks as their fee for transporting the crusaders) and also Byzantine participation in the crusade and the submission of the Greek Church to Rome.

Again, some of the clergy, notably the Cistercians, and also now some of the barons, objected to the diversion of the crusade against a Christian city, and almost half the crusaders preferred to go home. But the others found Alexius' offer irresistible. Historians have long debated whether the diversion of the crusade was a conspiracy, planned well ahead by Prince Alexius with the Venetians and the old Hohenstaufen-Norman enemies of Byzantium, or whether it was the chance result of unforeseen circumstances. Whichever it was, Dandolo and the Venetians acted consistently throughout for the political and commercial interests of their republic. The pope, apparently torn between the glittering prospect of a re-united Church and the horror of a crusader attack on Constantinople, was again too late with his prohibition.

Once the crusaders had arrived outside Constantinople, events unfolded with the inevitability of a classical tragedy. Alexius III fled and blind Isaac II and his son, now Alexius IV, were proclaimed emperor and co-emperor. They were, however, quite unable to pay the huge sums promised to the crusaders or to induce the great majority of the Greek clergy to accept the supremacy of Rome. The Greek archbishop of Corfu was reported by the westerners to have remarked sarcastically that he knew of no other grounds for the primacy of the see of Rome than that it had been Roman soldiers who had crucified Christ. Relations between crusaders and Greeks deteriorated rapidly. The crusaders remembered, or were carefully reminded, that in 1182 the mob of Constantinople had sacked the Italian quarter of the city and, it was claimed, killed 30,000 Latin Christians. In the spring of 1204 open war broke out. On 12 April the crusaders stormed the city. During the night, some soldiers, fearing a Byzantine counter-attack, set fire to some houses. Geoffroy de Villehardouin, one of the leaders of the crusade and its chronicler, tells us:

> The fire began to take hold on the city, which was soon blazing fiercely, and went on burning the whole of that night and all the next day till evening. This was the third fire there had been in Constantinople since the French and Venetians arrived in the land, and more houses had been burnt in that city than there are in any three of the greatest cities in the kingdom of France.

What was not burnt was plundered.

> The rest of the army, scattered throughout the city, also gained much booty; so much, indeed, that no one could estimate its amount or its value. It included gold and silver, table-services and

> precious stones, satin and silk, mantles of squirrel fur, ermine and miniver, and every choicest thing to be found on this earth.
> Geoffroy de Villehardouin here declares that, to his knowledge, so much booty had never been gained in any city since the creation of the world.[5]

The Catholic clergy concentrated on the looting of holy relics. So many were brought back to France, including Christ's crown of thorns, that, to house them suitably, King Louis IX, Saint Louis, was later inspired to build La Sainte Chapelle in Paris. The Venetians, apart from many other prizes, took the famous four horses, which the emperor Augustus had taken from Alexandria to Rome and the emperor Constantine from Rome to Constantinople, and placed them on the portal of St Mark's Basilica.

The Latin Empire of Constantinople

The French set up a Latin Empire of Constantinople; a Venetian became its Catholic patriarch – the papal excommunication of the crusaders and of Venice was lifted in due course – and other western leaders became kings of Thessalonika, dukes of Athens or princes of the Morea (the Peloponnese). All these were little more than robber states, by the grace of and exploited but not altogether controlled by, Venice. The republic reserved for itself Crete (now called Candia) and a string of Aegean islands which secured its communications with Constantinople whose trade they now completely dominated.

What the Germanic invaders had not achieved in the fourth and fifth centuries, and what successive attacks of Persians, Arabs, and Bulgars had never accomplished in the succeeding centuries, the capture and destruction of the Christian city of Constantinople, the Catholic 'Franks' had managed with relative ease. Too late, Innocent III deplored the wilfulness and disobedience of the crusaders and their appalling (but predictable) cruelty and rapacity in the sack of the imperial capital. Rightly, he foresaw that all chances of a genuine reunion of the Latin and Greek Churches were now gone, at least for the foreseeable future. The modern historian can see even more far-reaching implications. The most powerful pope in the history of the Roman Church had started a well-tried and, by then, traditional movement for an overtly religious purpose, the reconquest of Jerusalem and the Holy Sepulchre. Almost from the beginning, the movement had slipped out of his control and into the hands of men who were inspired by a mixture of motives, made up in varying degrees of desire for commercial profit and lust for conquest, and seasoned with the good conscience which comes to those who believe themselves to be acting in the name of their god. Once such motivation was backed by the superior organizing ability of the Venetians and by the superior military techniques of the French, the westerners became unbeatable. For these were the qualities which had made for the success of the fourth crusade, and these were the qualities which were to make for the success of the Europeans in the conquest or domination of the whole globe, from the end of the fifteenth to the middle of the twentieth centuries. But it was the modern European states, and not the papacy or the Church, which controlled, and profited from, this imperialism.

Byzantium revived

None of this could be foreseen in the thirteenth century. Political and commercial organization had not, as yet, come permanently together with military expertise. The new rulers of the feudal principalities in Greece and Thrace fought each other and could not defend their populations from the renewed attacks of the Bulgars. In Epirus (in western Greece) and in Anatolia parts of the Byzantine Empire had survived as separate states. In 1261 one of their armies surprised Constantinople. The Byzantine Empire was re-established under the dynasty of the Palaeologi. The Genoese replaced their rivals, the Venetians, as the most privileged western merchants.

The westerners were not resigned to this outcome, and there were several plans to reconquer Constantinople. The most dangerous for the Byzantines was that of Charles of Anjou, brother of Louis IX, who had defeated the emperor Frederick II's heirs in southern Italy and had received the crown of Naples and Sicily from the pope. Charles's preparations were well advanced when the Sicilians rose against the French occupation. On Easter Monday 1282, to the sound of the vesper bells, they massacred some 2000 French soldiers in Palermo and then offered the crown of Sicily to Peter III of Aragon. Byzantine involvement has never been conclusively established; but it is at least as likely as a premeditated Venetian plan to divert the fourth crusade. Planned or not, the 'Sicilian Vespers' proved to be a most effective Byzantine revenge on the French; for it involved them in nearly 300 years of war with the Spaniards for the dominion in southern Italy. All hope of a move against Constantinople had to be given up.

But Byzantium had ceased to be a great Mediterranean power and, as so often happens in such cases, it could not control the new forces it had called on the scene. In 1311, several thousand Catalan and Aragonese mercenaries, employed by Byzantium, made themselves masters of the dukedom of Athens. Among the old classical temples of the Acropolis, the Propylaeum became the palace of the Spanish duke and the Parthenon became a church of St Mary. The Spaniards were perhaps the most rapacious, and certainly the most firmly established, of the 'Frankish' rulers of late-medieval Greece. Their knights became great landowners and they provided profitable openings for the commerce of the merchants of Genoa and Barcelona. As if to underline the distance from the old crusading spirit, the dukedom of Athens came to the Florentine banking house of the Acciajuoli, in 1388. The alliance of land-grabbing feudal barons and capitalist merchants, which had first demonstrated its power in 1204, continued to be highly effective.

The last crusades

If 1204 marked the triumph of cynicism and of a new military-commercial alliance, not everyone in Europe was caught up in it. Almost half the crusaders of the fourth crusade had, after all, refused to be diverted to Constantinople. Some of them, such as Count Simon de Montfort, had another chance of crusading – against the Albigensians (see above, pp. 247–48). In 1212 the crusading fervour gripped the very young. Thousands of teenagers, mostly from the Rhineland and Lorraine, left their homes to follow youthful prophets. They, the unarmed innocents, they were told, would succeed where the armed adults had failed or had allowed themselves to be diverted. The Church authorities tried to discourage the movement but failed in the face of popular enthusiasm. But no miracle occurred. Thousands of children were lost at sea or sold into slavery. Those who managed to return home were jeered. It was comforting, after the catastrophe, to argue that the children had been misled by the devil.

256

Innocent III was not put off. Not long before his death, in 1216, he organized another crusade (the fifth). It was to be under the close control of a papal legate, so as to prevent another diversion, and it was directed against Damietta, in the Nile delta, on the perfectly sound strategic principle of trying to knock out the most powerful enemy, Egypt. The actual campaign, from 1219–21, had some initial successes but then failed. Contemporaries blamed the excessive interference of the papal legate in military and diplomatic decisions.

From then on the popes lost their central role in the crusades altogether. In 1228 the emperor Frederick II sailed for Palestine while under papal excommunication for having started late. In the following year he made a treaty with the sultan of Egypt for the return of Jerusalem. While still under the interdict, Frederick rode into the holy city and placed the crown of the kingdom of Jerusalem on his own head. What the crusaders had not achieved with much bloodshed and with papal blessing, Frederick II had achieved without fighting and under a papal curse. But for all his studied anti-papal attitudes, Frederick was not the representative of the new age of militant capitalism, as in a sense the doge Dandolo and his French allies were. The emperor rather saw himself as having some sort of divine authority by virtue of his imperial office, and the newly acquired crown of the kingdom of Jerusalem only confirmed him in his beliefs. When he returned to Italy, the local Christian barons soon gained the upper hand again and managed to lose the city in 1244.

The last two major crusades were organized by the king of France. In 1248 Louis IX led a large expedition against Egypt, again in order to strike at the central point of Muslim power. But the French were far from their base. Louis was defeated and taken prisoner (1250). All seemed lost; but at this moment the Mamluks overthrew the sultan of Egypt. They were a professional army of white, mainly Turkish, slaves. As such armies are apt to do, when employed by rulers without other military resources, they made themselves masters of the state. The Mamluks continued to rule Egypt until they were themselves conquered by the Ottoman Turks, in 1517. In fact, their power in Egypt was not finally destroyed until the young general Napoleon Bonaparte defeated them in the battle of the Pyramids, in 1798.[6] In 1250, however, King Louis used the political upheaval to make a bargain to have his army freed. He took it to Palestine and for

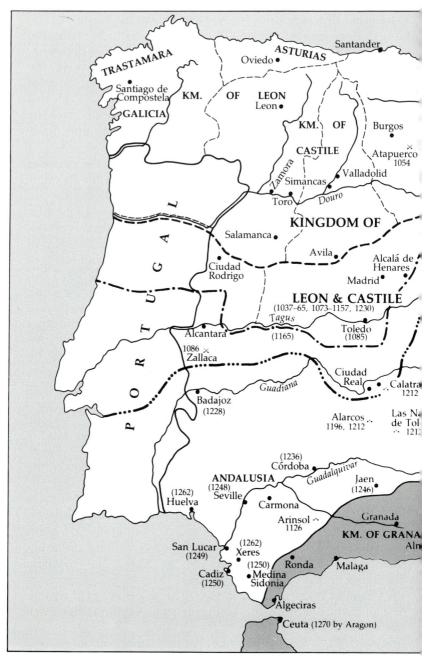

Map 4.3 The reconquest of Spain.

Pamplona
KM. OF
NAVARRE

CTY. OF ROUSSILLON
Perpignan
(1217)

• Urgel
CTY. OF BARCELONA
Gerona •

KM.
Tudela
(1046) OF
• Huesca
(1096) •

Manresa

Lerida
(1149)

ARAGON
(United
1162)
Saragossa
(1118)

Barcelona

Ebro
(1148)
Tortosa

CATALONIA

Tarragona (1091)

1177)
Cuenca

• Teruel
(1170)

ISLANDS

Minorca
(1232)

Jucar

Valencia
(1238)

BALEARIC

Palma

Jativa
(1239)•

Denia
(1245)

(1235)
Ibiza

Majorca
(1229–30)

Formentera

Alicante
(1262)

Murcia •
(1266)

Cartagena
(1263)

— — Northern Limits of Saracen Lands, 1037
•— Northern Limits of Saracen Lands, 1100
•••— Northern Limits of Saracen Lands, 1200
— Frontiers at 1270

Land still held by the Saracens

Dates in brackets show final reconquest, other dates are battles

259

four years he remained there, recapturing most of the old crusader cities and castles, but not Jerusalem itself. In 1254 he returned to France.

Louis IX's crusade was, against all expectations, at least a partial success. The king's last venture, however, turned into pure tragedy. In 1270 he sailed to Tunis, probably at the instance of his brother Charles of Anjou who had recently acquired the kingdom of Sicily. But in Tunis, Louis and a large part of his army succumbed to the plague. In 1291, Acre, the last stronghold of the crusaders, surrendered to the Mamluks of Egypt. Not until the end of the eighteenth century were the Europeans to make their next, and again unsuccessful, attempt to acquire a foothold on the Levant.

Spain

The only front on which the Christians were successful against Islam was in Spain. Here the first half of the thirteenth century saw the greatest Christian advances yet. The kings of Aragon conquered Valencia and the island of Majorca. In the west the Portuguese occupied the Algarve and Portugal attained its modern frontiers. But the greatest advance was made by Castile which conquered the greater part of al-Andalus (Andalusia) the heart of Muslim Spain in the south, right down to the Mediterranean and the Atlantic. Only the kingdom of Granada, a relatively small triangle in the south-east, remained an independent Muslim state (Map 4.3, pp. 258–9).

For Andalusia and its inhabitants the Christian conquest was largely a disaster. It had been a highly urbanized and economically advanced area. Many of its skilled craftsmen and agriculturalists fled or were dispossessed and driven out. The soldiers from the north did not have the skills to continue the sophisticated cultivation of vines, fruits and olives of the former Moorish

Plate 4.6   Granada: The Alhambra. Courtyard of the Lions.
This huge fortress-palace of the Moorish kings of Granada was built on the foothills of the snow-covered Sierra Nevada, in southern Spain, between 1238 and 1358. The richly ornamented interior, the centre of a sophisticated Islamic court culture, dates mainly from the first half of the fourteenth century. The Fountain of the Lions, in this illustration, is an alabaster basin with 12 marble lions.

population. Gradually large areas were turned over to cattle grazing and a few great noblemen and also the military orders of knighthood bought up huge estates. They were to dominate the social and political life of southern Spain right into this century.

There was no such displacement of population in the eastern kingdoms of Aragon and Valencia. Here the Muslims remained, no longer economically or culturally dominant, but largely unassimilated and unassimilable, even when they became nominally Christians. It was a problem that was to bedevil Spanish history for another three and a half centuries and which the Spaniards found as difficult to cope with as we are still finding similar problems of ethnic and religious minorities in our own times.

The Mongol invasions

Christians and Muslims regarded each other as mortal enemies and both hated the Jews. But all three had developed out of similar hellenistic and semitic traditions. They all recognized the bible as a sacred book, prayed to the same god and at least some of their educated élites were willing to learn from each other's ideas and technical achievements. It was very different with the Mongols. Here was a people who had no traditions whatever in common with the Christians, and it is perhaps for this reason that Christendom found it difficult to take them entirely seriously. Except, of course, those who had the misfortune to be in their way.

The Mongols were the last of the central Asian nomad peoples who exploded on the agricultural and urban civilizations of Eurasia, and they did so more effectively and over a larger area than any of their predecessors, from the Huns onwards. In 1200 the Mongols were living between Lake Baikal and the Altai mountains of central Asia. They were a hierarchical society, with a horse- and cattle-owning aristocracy at the top, and slaves or serfs at the bottom. They were illiterate, pagan and, by tradition and force of necessity, excellent fighters. In all this they did not differ greatly from other, similar tribes of the vast inner Asian land mass. From the Huns to the Avars, the Bulgars and the different Turkish tribes, these peoples had, for almost a millennium, shown their capacity to defeat the armies of more advanced societies and to build up very large, loosely controlled empires or dominions – provided always that they did not move too far away from the geographical and climatic conditions of the great Eurasian steppe.

Early in the thirteenth century a leader of genius, Genghis Khan (*c.* 1162–1227), managed to unite all Mongol tribes and then to spread his empire both east and west. There is no evidence that the Mongols were driven by some climatic catastrophe interfering with the grazing conditions of their cattle. What Genghis Khan commanded was a highly organized and disciplined fighting force to which his mounted archers gave matchless mobility and fire-power. He himself contributed great adaptability to strange conditions and a willingness to employ Chinese or Muslim-Turkish engineers in siege warfare. He organized an excellent information service, based largely on his support for merchants of all nationalities and religions. He excelled in the coolly calculated use of both diplomacy and terror. These were the qualities which gave Genghis Khan and his gifted sons, grandsons and their generals victory after victory, over one opponent after another. Peking fell in 1215. It took the Mongols, however, another fifty years to extend their rule over the whole of China. They took much less time to conquer the Islamic states east of the Caspian Sea, with their rich cities of Bokhara and Samarkand (1219–20). Persia had fallen by 1233, about the same time as other Mongol armies conquered Korea, at the other end of Asia. In 1258 they took Baghdad and murdered the last Abbasid caliph. Only the Mamluks managed to defeat a Mongol detachment in Palestine, in 1260, and thus preserved Egypt from Mongol conquest. It was a victory comparable with Charles Martel's over the Arabs at Tours and Poitiers, for it marked the turning point of the invading flood.

Between 1237 and 1241, the Mongols thrust into Europe. Just as in Asia, the offensive was formidable and terrifying. They overran Russia, southern Poland and most of Hungary. At Liegnitz (Legnica) in Silesia, west of the river Oder, they annihilated an army of German knights (1241). Only problems of succession to the Great Khan seem to have induced the leaders of the Mongols to turn east again, after this victory.

Yet the great powers of western Europe, the emperor and the pope, the kings of France and England, were engaged in their own, parochial struggles and they indulged in wishful thinking

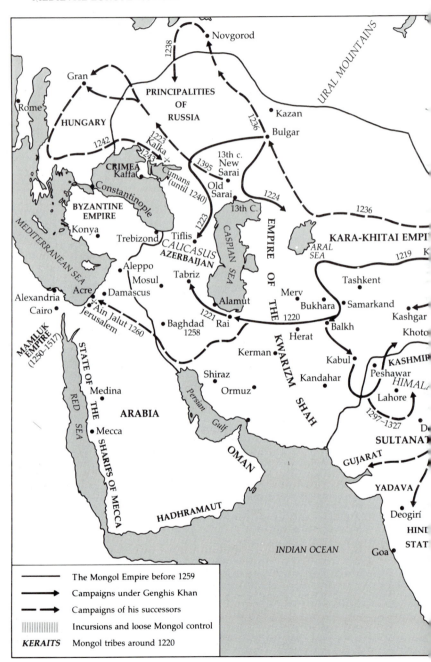

Map 4.4 The Mongol invasions.

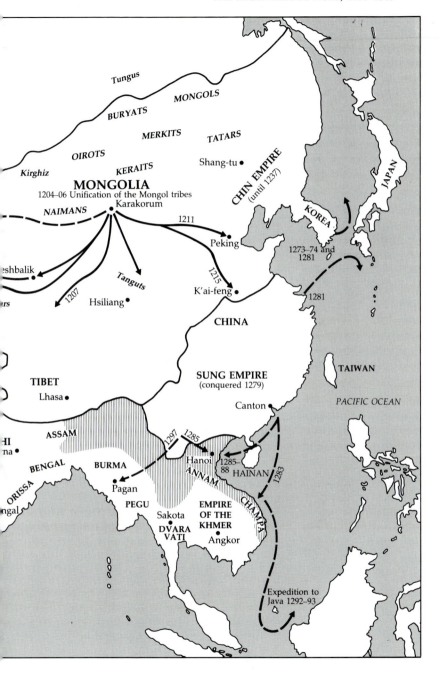

about the identity of the Great Khan with the mythical Christian Prester John or, at least, with the enticing prospect of converting the Khan to Christianity. St Louis even tried to negotiate an alliance with the Mongols against the Muslims in Syria. The Mongols were neither impressed nor greatly interested. In 1245 the Khan said to a papal envoy: 'From the rising of the sun to its setting all the lands have been subjected to me: who could do this contrary to the command of God?'

Was western and southern Europe simply lucky to escape Mongol conquest? Perhaps; for the Russians were clearly not so lucky and had to endure Mongol domination for nearly 300 years. Yet it seems likely that the Mongols had reached the limits of their possible conquests. Their campaigns in the rain forests and jungles of Vietnam and Cambodia did not go well. Their naval forays against Japan and Java were complete failures. Even allowing for their acquisition of an advanced siege technique, could their cavalry armies have prevailed among the hundreds of densely scattered walled cities and castles of western Europe? It seems at least doubtful. The first two generations of Mongol leaders and their followers were motivated by little more than the quest for plunder and the desire to dominate men. But even for this latter purpose elaborate administrative institutions were needed, and such institutions the Mongols, from the very beginning, had to take over from the conquered but more advanced societies, and they had to staff them with experienced Chinese, Persians, Turks and Arabs. The Mongols had no religion of their own which could rival any of the great world religions with which they came into contact: Buddhism, Islam, Judaism and Christianity. Not surprisingly, they tended to keep an open mind about them; and this is why Marco Polo and other western visitors to the court of the Great Khan remarked on the Mongols' tolerance and apparent sympathy for the visitors' religion. But even those modern historians most sympathetic to the Mongols can manage to claim little more justification for their conquests than that the Mongol empire favoured safer east-west caravan trade and that it provided its subjects with a species of *pax mongolica*, a peace following on the elimination of all enemies and potential enemies. In truth, the Mongol conquests resembled those Roman conquests of which a British contemporary had said: 'they make a desert and call it peace'.

In the fourteenth century the Mongol rulers of the different

266

parts of the Mongol empire became Buddhists or Muslims, which meant that they had been effectively conquered by the Chinese, Persian or Arabic cultures in which they lived. With the decline of the great caravan routes in favour of the sea routes, and with the development of the modern military-commercial states, the age of the great continental nomad empires came to an end. They had done nothing directly for mankind and only left a universally bad memory. The indirect results of the successive nomad conquests, however, were immense; for they forced the migration of other, more settled peoples which, in their turn, played havoc with old-established civilizations. Thus it happened with the Germanic tribes in the fourth and fifth centuries who destroyed the western Roman Empire; and thus it happened also to some of the Turkish tribes who finally destroyed what remained of the eastern Roman Empire.

The Mongol rule in Russia

Most of the nomadic tribes which over the centuries had invaded the Russian steppe had looked for land to settle with their herds, and only secondarily for rule over other people. With the Mongols it was the other way round. The Russian monastic chroniclers greatly exaggerated their numbers, just as the western monastic chroniclers had exaggerated the number of Vikings.[7] There were not nearly enough Mongols to settle the vast areas which they conquered. The Mongol armies were the agents of an immense empire, stretching right across Asia and, from the first, they looked for the advantages of dominion over other people. Along the lower Volga and from the northern shores of the Caspian and the Black Sea to ruined Kiev they ruled directly. Beyond this steppe-zone they were content to have their agents at the courts of the local Russian princes, either to collect tribute and taxes or to see that the princes did it for them.

Almost from the beginning of the Mongol conquest, the khan, or emperor, in charge of the western part of the Mongol empire was virtually independent of the great-khan in distant Mongolia or China. He resided in Sarai, on the lower Volga and it was probably his gilded tent or palace which led the Europeans to call these Mongols 'the Golden Horde'. The Russian princes were required to visit Sarai and it was the khan who bestowed the dignity of the grand-prince. The Mongols used the rivalries

267

between the Russian princes to consolidate their power and the princes used the favour of the Mongols to defeat their rivals.

Almost immediately after the Mongol conquest, the Rurikid prince Alexander Nevsky (c. 1220–63) showed how advantageous a policy of co-operation with the Mongols could be. As elected prince of Novgorod he fought German and Swedish invaders of north-western Russia and won a famous victory against the German knights on the ice of Lake Peipus, in 1242. A few years later he denounced his brother, the grand-prince of Vladimir, to the Mongol khan and was rewarded by being made grand-prince himself. He proved himself a loyal ally and put down rebellions against Mongol taxation in Novgorod and elsewhere in north-western Russia – perhaps in order to prevent worse reprisals from the Mongols. Alexander's descendants became the princes of Moscow and eventually rulers of the whole of Russia.

Knowing the history of the reputation of the Cid in Spain (see Ch 3, pp. 158–59), we should perhaps not be surprised that this undoubtedly heroic but also very ambiguous figure should have become one of the great heroes of Russian literature and political mythology and, even going one better than the Cid, that he should have been canonized as a saint (1547). The Russian Church, like Nevsky, supported Mongol rule. The Mongols of the Golden Horde who, later in the thirteenth century, adopted Islam, were in general tolerant towards the Christian religion and rightly saw in the Russian Church a useful ally. By contrast, the papacy was trying at one and the same time to induce the proud and suspicious orthodox Church to accept papal supremacy and to encourage the German knights to attack the Russians in the north-west.

It used to be thought that the Mongol conquest profoundly influenced Russian traditions and transformed Russia from a European into an Asiatic country. But most historians now think that, important as the effects of the Mongol invasion were on the history of Russia, it did little to influence the character of the Russian people and its traditions. These continued to be formed largely by the Russian Church with its traditions of orthodoxy and its hostility towards foreigners, especially towards the hated and feared Latin Christians. What the Mongols could and did teach the Russian princes were those practical pursuits in which they had shown themselves so markedly superior to the Europeans: methods and practices of extracting heavy taxes from all classes of the population, the organization and protection of communications over vast distances and the ability to adapt their opponents' military techniques for their own purposes.

Intellectual life, literature and art

The twelth-century Renaissance did not end in the way the Carolingian Renaissance had ended in the disasters of the ninth and tenth centuries. The men of the thirteenth century revered the ancients as much as their grandfathers had done. They were, in fact, better at emulating them for they were both able to recover more of Greek and Latin writings and they had the experience of the twelfth century to build on. Nor did they despise outside help. It was in the thirteenth century that Maimonides, the Spanish-Jewish philosopher (1135–1204) and Averroes, the Spanish-Muslim philosopher (1126–92) were read in the west. While, understandably, some pedants were horrified by such influence, the finest Christian minds not only appreciated Maimonides and Averroës for their advanced medical works and their commentaries on Aristotle and Plato but had to come to terms, whether positively or negatively, with their discussions of metaphysics and religion.

The universities and scholasticism

Europe was richer and socially and politically more highly organized than it had been. It therefore both needed and could afford to maintain a much larger number of educated men than before. (A few women were educated; but this was still very rare.)

Primary education was provided, as it had been in previous centuries, in local schools or, for the rich, by private tutors. But higher education was now coming to be concentrated in the universities. They received charters from kings or popes and their masters were permitted to form associations which controlled the courses that were taught and the degrees that were given. Only in the famous law school of Bologna did the students organize the university and choose their instructors. By the middle of the fourteenth century there were at least fourteen universities in Italy, eight in France, seven in Spain and Portugal, two in England (Oxford and Cambridge) but as yet only one in central

Europe (Prague). German, Scandinavian and Polish students would go to Bologna or Padua or Paris, and many continued to do so even after universities had been founded in their own countries, in the later fourteenth and fifteenth centuries.

With the exception of Paris and Bologna, most universities were still quite small, owned few buildings and no university library. Books were very expensive and lecturers would dictate passages from a basic authority – the bible or St Augustine or the codex of Justinian – together with the comments of famous authors, much more rarely their own. Problems arising from these texts would be discussed in 'disputations' in which propositions and counter-propositions would be logically confronted, distinctions made and conclusions drawn. This was the scholastic method which gave its name, scholasticism, to the whole of late-medieval philosophy. It was a rational and civilized method of philosophical inquiry and, in the hands of outstanding intellects, a very effective one. In the hands of the second-rate it could, however, become a pedantic and arid exercise in logic chopping. It was this quality which was seized on by the humanists of the fifteenth century who managed to give scholasticism a permanently bad name.

But in the thirteenth century scholasticism and universities were expanding rapidly and provided a small élite with an intellectual life that was richer and more varied than anything that had gone before. Degrees in theology and law were those with the greatest professional value; but every student started with three years in the seven liberal arts: grammar, rhetoric, logic, arithmetic, geometry, music and astronomy, and these, too, had their experts. Thus the English Franciscan Roger Bacon (c. 1220–92) praised mathematics as the only discipline by which truth could be established without fear of error, and he visualized all sorts of inventions which were a kind of science fiction; but, unlike the modern genre which places as yet unmade inventions in the future, Bacon typically credited them to the ancients:

> I shall therefore now describe first of all works of skill and marvels of nature, in order to designate afterwards their causes and characteristics. There is no magic in them, so that all the power of magic seems inferior to these mechanisms and unworthy of them. And first, through the shaping and planning of skill alone. Instruments for sea-faring can be made without rowers, so that the largest ships . . . are steered by one man only in control

(and) at a greater speed than if they were filled with men. Similarly, carts can be made to move without animals at an incalculable velocity, as we think the chariots with scythe blades must have been in which the ancients fought. Similarly, flying machines can be made so that a man sits inside the machine rotating some ingenious contraption by means of which the wings, artfully arranged, beat the air like a bird flying . . . Also instruments can be made for walking in the sea or rivers right down to the bottom without any physical risk. Alexander the Great used such instruments to probe the secrets of the ocean, according to the stories of Ethicus, the astronomer. These things were done in antiquity and in our own day as well, and this is unquestionable; except a flying machine, that I have not seen or known anyone who did.[8]

St Thomas Aquinas

The most outstanding, as well as the most typical, of the thirteenth-century scholastics was Thomas Aquinas (1225–74). This Dominican professor at Naples and Paris attempted nothing less than to harmonize Christian faith with nature and reason in one all-embracing system:

> Arguments from authority is the method most appropriate to this teaching (of the things of faith) in that its premises are held through revelation; . . .
>   All the same, holy teaching uses human reasoning not indeed to prove the faith, for that would take away from the merit of believing, but to make manifest some implications of its message. Since grace does not take away nature but brings it to perfection, so also natural reason should assist faith as the natural loving bent of the will yields to charity. St. Paul speaks of *bringing into captivity every understanding unto the service of Christ*. Hence holy teaching uses the authority of philosophers who have been able to perceive the truth by natural reasoning . . .[9]

Not all of Aquinas' contemporaries were prepared to accept all his conclusions. But they could never be ignored, and though they remained a fruitful source of debate and even controversy, they also represented a further shift of Christian thinking into rationalism, into the acceptance of the natural world and the value of studying it.

271

Literature

While the intellectual debates of the period, all university teaching and most governmental documents were carried on and written in Latin, the vernacular languages were becoming increasingly popular for historical writing and for all types of poetry. The Frenchman William of Tyre (*c*. 1130–85) wrote the finest contemporary account of the crusades of the twelfth century in Latin. Geoffroy de Villehardouin (*c*. 1150–1213) wrote his eye-witness account of the fourth crusade and the conquest of Constantinople in French – the first time anyone had attempted to compose such a work in French prose. It became the model for a long succession of distinguished French chronicles and histories. The most famous during this period was the Seigneur de Joinville's *History of Saint Louis*, finished in 1310. Perhaps the finest passages are those dealing with St Louis' two crusades, on the first of which Joinville accompanied the king. But it is Joinville's description of Louis IX as the ideal champion of medieval kingship that had the most impact:

> In summer, after hearing mass, the king often went to the wood of Vincennes [near Paris], where he would sit down with his back against an oak, and make us all sit around him. Those who had any suit to present could come to speak to him without hindrance from an usher or any other person. The king would address them directly and ask: 'Is there anyone here who has a case to be settled?' Those who had one would stand up. Then he would say: 'Keep silent all of you, and you shall be heard in turn, one after the other'. Then he would call Pierre de Fontaines and Geoffroi de Villette, and say to one or other of them: 'Settle this case for me'. If he saw anything needing correction in what was said by those who spoke on his behalf or on behalf of any other person, he would himself intervene to make the necessary adjustment.[10]

The French monarchy lived for centuries on the mystique of kingship built up by St Louis, but it would hardly have been as effective without the literary skill of the Seigneur de Joinville.

Villehardouin's history has sometimes been called a *chanson de geste* in prose. Many of these *chansons* and many of the old sagas and epics received their final written version, either in verse or in prose during this period. The stories they told were often old, but their treatment was essentially modern, i.e. reflecting the lifestyle and values of European society of the thirteenth century.

Only one can be mentioned here, the *Nibelungenlied*, written about 1200 in Middle High German verse by an unknown Austrian writer. Its subject matter, the deeds of Siegfried the dragon slayer, his murder by Hagen, and Burgundian Gunther's and Hagen's end at the hands of the Huns was based on Germanic sagas and memories going back to the fifth century. Its principal theme is that most highly prized of medieval chivalric virtues, loyalty. But it is no longer the simple and admirable loyalty of Roland to Charlemagne, but the crimes and tragedies to which men are led by divided loyalties – a medieval counterpart, one might think, of the Greek problem of the individual caught between the demands of conflicting laws, presented in its classic form in Sophocles' *Antigone*. If this was a reflection of the experience of thirteenth century society with its divided loyalties between church and state, and also at least an implied criticism of its accepted values, it was also an implied criticism of its treatment of women; for both the murder of Siegfried, and his wife Kriemhild's dreadful revenge on her brothers, were the direct result of the appalling way in which she, as a woman, had been treated, a type of treatment which corresponded only too well to the experience of many women at the time.

Less dramatically, the *troubadours* of southern France had criticized the treatment of women by making them the centre of their love songs. Their stress on the emotions of individual men and women produced the first romantic poetry in European literature:

> Is there a paradise, my dove?
> What is paradise but love?
> 'Tis nothing really, my sweet love.
> Where is paradise, my dove?
> He who sleeps in love's embrace
> Will enter paradise apace.
> Where is paradise, my dove?
> What is paradise but love?[11]

Such poetry was to have enormous influence, first in southern France, northern Italy, Spain, and perhaps even at the Arabic-speaking court of Córdoba, and later throughout Europe.

It is in this context that there appeared one of the most popular French medieval poems, the *Roman de la rose*, written in two parts about 1240 and 1280. It was an extended allegory on courtly love. The later part was interspersed with long digressions on the

supposed hypocrisy of the mendicant friars and other established figures, institutions and values of the time. Such social and moral criticism was becoming one of the most distinctive and creative aspects of European society.

Architecture and art: the Gothic style

Histories of architecture have shown how the Gothic style – the name was not contemporary but appeared only in the Renaissance as a synonym for barbarism – developed logically and step by step from the use of the rib in a new method of dealing with intersections of vaults. When this method was joined with pointed arches it allowed the builder of a church to raise its ceiling; this, in turn, made necessary the use of outside buttresses to receive the thrust of walls and ceilings and it also made possible thinner walls, perforated by large windows. This was the indispensable technical aspect of the style. But the architects who developed it were not only highly trained professional builders with considerable knowledge of mathematics and mechanics, they were also artists who used the new techniques to create one of the most original building styles in world history. In their hands ribs, vaults and columns became means to shape structured interior space. The structural wall-supports became flying buttresses, used deliberately to give rhythmic, three-dimensional patterns to the outside of the building and to emphasize its soaring vertical lines. These were enhanced by a profusion of sculptures, mostly of human figures, rendered now with an almost classical feeling for idealized naturalism. The enlarged windows were filled with painted glass, seen at its finest perhaps in Chartres and Bourges, which gave the interior of the cathedral both a marvellous softly bright light, varying with the sun at different times of day, and a representational world of God,

Plate 4.7   Bourges Cathedral, exterior.
The building of this very big cathedral in central-eastern France was begun about 1195 and the nave was finished by 1265. The flying buttress made possible a very high structure with large windows in the walls. At the same time, the flying buttresses emphasize the upward thrust of the building and give it the appearance of a gigantic three-dimensional sculpture. It presents an interesting contrast to Salisbury Cathedral (see Plate 4.8), which was under construction at the same time.

angels, saints, men, animals and flowers that could rival in its coloured brilliance even the great Byzantine mosaics.

Inevitably, some builders and their patrons were over-ambitious and expected the impossible from the wonderful new techniques. They raised the ceilings of the naves higher and higher, to get the greatest possible effect of space and light. Several ceilings, in different parts of Europe, collapsed. The most spectacular failure was that of the choir of the cathedral of Beauvais, in northern France. Built to a height of 158 feet (48 metres), it collapsed in 1284. It took forty years to restore, and from then on masons were usually more careful. In Cologne Cathedral the vaults were planned to be almost as high, 150 feet, but they were not completed until the nineteenth century.

Some historians have attempted to read an elaborate symbolism into Gothic cathedrals and have seen their style as a parallel or analogy to scholasticism. Now it is certain that many details of buildings, and especially their decorations, were meant to have symbolical meanings. For a whole building and its structure, this is much more difficult to prove; for we do not have detailed contemporary treatises on this subject, as we have them for the buildings of the Renaissance. It is, however, fair to assume that thirteenth-century architects and their ecclesiastical patrons, as educated men, were aware of the predominant philosophy of the day and of its emphasis on the harmony of the universe and of all created things. We even have paintings representing God the creator as an architect with the architect's characteristic instrument, the compasses.

The Gothic style spread rapidly from France to England, Germany and Spain. Only Italy proved to some extent resistant to its attractions. This rapid diffusion was, in the first place, due to the employment everywhere of the best architects and their

Plate 4.8   Salisbury Cathedral.
Perhaps the most elegant of English cathedrals, it was built in a relatively short time, 1220–58. The English version of early Gothic, called the Early English style, emphasizes the horizontal lines, rather than the verticals as in France cathedrals. The flying buttresses are neither as important structurally nor visually as they are, for instance, at Bourges (Plate 4.7). The very high tower and spire (404 ft/123 m) were added in the fourteenth century, in the Decorated Style, an almost entirely English variant of the later Gothic style.

teams, and these were mainly French, and to an international system of apprenticeship which attracted aspiring young builders to the lodges of the great masters, just as young scholars were attracted to the best teachers of the greatest universities. Architects could also learn from drawings, either through handbooks of design which were now beginning to appear or from the detailed designs of actual buildings. So elaborate were these designs that it became possible to complete the unfinished cathedrals of Cologne and Ulm with absolute authenticity as late as the nineteenth century.

But perhaps even more important for the wide diffusion of the Gothic style and for its long life – on the Continent until the middle of the sixteenth century and in England until the eighteenth – was its quite evident aesthetic and religious appeal. In its many varied forms, differing quite sharply in the different European countries and over periods of time, it proved satisfying to generation after generation of Christian worshippers. Only this fact will explain the sheer number and size of the Gothic cathedrals and churches built all over Europe in the thirteenth century and later. For the value system, the order of priorities, of European society had not substantially changed from the eleventh and twelfth centuries: the worship of God and warfare, cathedrals and castles, still consumed the greater part of its surplus production.

Conclusion

The thirteenth and early fourteenth centuries were a period of expansion. There were more people in Europe than there had ever been before and their numbers were growing. Most people were still very poor, but life in the towns and even in the villages was becoming more varied and, for a growing minority at least, richer and more interesting. Men developed new skills, technical, intellectual, even military, and such skills were becoming much more widespread and readily available. This was reflected in the growing richness of local life. While communications improved and people and ideas travelled and interacted more than before, the different regions of Europe were, through this very spread of wealth and diffusion of skills, becoming more self-contained.

Some of the finest literature was now being written in the vernacular languages in Spain and Iceland, in Italy and Germany, and above all in France.

Within the overall Gothic norms, cathedrals and castles were being built in increasingly differentiated regional styles. The papacy pushed its universal claims and international organization to their highest point and defeated the rival universal claims of the Holy Roman Empire, only to be defeated, in its turn, by the regionally based monarchies.

Here was the turning point of internationalism in the Middle Ages. The distinguished philosopher-historian Arnold Toynbee saw it as the point where the history of European society took a tragically wrong turn which would lead, almost inevitably, to the ultimate fall of this society. It seems rather that the turning away from internationalism occurred not because something went wrong in the development of European society but, on the contrary, because this development was proceeding very success- fully. The internationalism of the central Middle Ages which, as has been shown, was the internationalism of only a small educated and skilled classs – this internationalism could have survived only if Europe had become an economically static and intellectually stagnant society. But this would have negated all the dynamic elements of this society deriving ultimately from the merging of the barbarian tribes with the advanced civilization of the late Roman Empire. It was the success of the international sector of medieval society in creating economic and cultural growth which fragmented Europe and undermined this sector itself. This fragmentation, in its turn, was a further dynamic element; for it increased variety and competition and thus forced men to modify traditions through reason and inventiveness. It was these characteristics which, by the end of the fifteenth century, were to give the Europeans their technological, military and political edge over native Americans, Africans and most Asians. They were conquered and sometimes enslaved. But the Europeans, too had to pay a price. They had to come to terms with the collapse, during the Reformation, of their cherished ideal of a unified Christendom and found themselves embarked on a course of apparently inescapable wars between states, all claiming the universality which seemed to have belonged to the Church. The achievements and the tragedies of European and human history cannot be easily separated.

References and Notes

1. Quoted and trans. by D. Herlihy (ed.), *Medieval Culture and Society*. Harper Torch Books: New York 1968, pp. 176–77.
2. *Pennsylvania Translations and Reprints*. Pennsylvania University Press: Philadelphia n.d. vol. 1, 2, no. 1, pp. 21–22.
3. Anna Maria Agnoletti (ed.), *Statuto dell' Arte della Lana di Firenze (1317–1319)*, trans. R. de Roover. Felice le Monnier: Florence 1940–48, pp. 114–15.
4. *The Little Flowers of Saint Francis*, trans. L. Sherley-Price. Penguin Books: Harmondsworth 1959, Ch. 4, pp. 36–38.
5. Villehardouin, *The Conquest of Constantinople* in Joinville and Villehardouin, *Chronicles of the Crusades*, trans. M. R. S. Shaw. Penguin Classics: Harmondsworth 1963, Ch. 12, p. 92.
6. See A. Briggs, *Modern Europe 1789–1980*; History of Europe. Longman: (not yet published).
7. See above, Ch. 2, p. 96.
8. Roger Bacon, *De Secretis Operibus*, trans. and quoted by Harry E. Wedeck in *Putnam's Dark and Middle Ages Reader*. Capricorn Books: New York 1965, pp. 158–59.
9. St Thomas Aquinas, *Summa Theologica*, Ia 1, 8, 2. Trans. Thomas Gilby (slightly modified). Eyre and Spottiswoode: London, n. d.
10. Joinville and Villehardouin, op. cit., p. 177.
11. Anonymous, thirteenth century rondel, trans. and quoted by Harry E. Wedeck, op cit., p. 331.

Chapter 5

The Later Middle Ages: Transalpine Europe, 1340–1500

The Black Death 1348–50

Population

> In the year of grace 1349 . . . a great mortal plague spread through
> the world, starting from the southern and the northern areas, and
> ending with such devastating ruins that scarcely a handful of men
> survived. The towns, once densely populated, were emptied of
> their settlers and so rapidly did the intensity of the plague grow
> that the living could scarcely bury the dead . . . A disease among
> cattle followed closely on the pestilence; then the crops died; then
> the land remained untilled because of the scarcity of farmers, who
> were wiped out. And such misery followed these disasters that
> the world never afterwards had an opportunity of returning to its
> former state.[1]

In such bleakly artless terms a contemporary English chronicler
described the impact of the greatest calamity to befall Europe
since the sixth century. Medieval people were well acquainted
with killer diseases: tuberculosis and leprosy, amoebic dysentery,
malaria and all the many disorders that went by the name of
fever. But this was bubonic plague, spreading west from eastern
Asia along the trade routes of the Mongol empire and reaching
Italy, in Genoese ships from the Black Sea, it was said, in 1347.
It was the final and the most dreadful, though of course unin-
tended, result of the dreadful Mongol conquests. From Italy the
plague spread in the next two years over most of Europe. Its
effects were devastating. Plague is a rodent disease spread by
fleas. Infection was therefore most likely in crowded urban areas
infested by rats, and this was the condition of all medieval towns.

281

Plate 5.1 Bourges Cathedral: late medieval stained glass.
The scene is the adoration of the Magi. The glass is brilliantly coloured
and illuminated from the outside by daylight. The glass painting filled
areas much larger than any other medieval painters, except for the
makers of mosaics, had ever attempted. But since only small panes of
glass could be manufactured, these had to be set in strips of lead
which then became part of the design. The building operations of
cathedrals, with their workshops for stone masons, carpenters, metal
and glass workers were by far the biggest and the most highly
organized economic enterprises in the Middle Ages.

Among those infected the death rate was terrifyingly high and, as the English chronicler noted, there were the secondary effects of the temporary collapse of food production in many areas.

The total mortality of the Black Death has been variously estimated at up to a quarter or more of the population of Europe. Since, however, the toll was uneven, mortality in some areas or towns and villages was very much higher. In Hamburg for instance sixteen of twenty-one city councillors died, eighteen of forty butchers and twelve of thirty-four bakers

Naturally, the psychological effects of such a catastrophe were shattering. Most immediately, there was fear. 'The calamity instilled such terror in the hearts of men and women,' wrote the Florentine writer Giovanni Boccaccio (1313–75), 'that brother abandoned brother, uncle nephew, brother sister, and often wives left their husbands . . . even fathers and mothers shunned their children'.[2] With fear came hysteria. Some indulged in unrestrained drinking and sexual activities. Others sought to placate God's evident anger by the most severe self-punishment. Brotherhoods of flagellants, men and women lacerating themselves with sharp-thonged whips, had appeared already in the thirteenth century. Now they spread rapidly and their dismal processions added to the horror of the times. Inevitably, there was a search for scapegoats, fiends in human form or servants of the devil who had deliberately poisoned the wells. The Jews, as so often, were the first to suffer from such fantasies; but often enough any stranger at all could find himself the object of a sudden deadly manhunt.

Not all were thus affected. The wealthy could retire to the country and, at least, comparative safety and there ride out the storm, like Boccaccio's ladies and gentlemen, who told each other the amusing and racy tales of the *Decameron*. The basic structure and institutions of European society seemed to have survived. Yet the full effects of the Black Death took a long time to work themselves out.

Unhappily, the Black Death was not a unique occurrence. It came again in 1360 when it struck down especially children – probably because many of the adults who had survived the first outbreak were now immune. It came again in 1371. From then on the intervals between outbreaks grew longer, the mortality gradually lower. But plague remained an extravagant killer, right up to the last great European outbreak, in 1664–5, the outbreak described so graphically by Samuel Pepys and by Daniel Defoe. It was these recurring outbreaks which prevented a rapid recovery of population. The gains of the twelfth and thirteenth century were wiped out and only in the latter part of the fifteenth century did a slow recovery begin. In 1340 France had a population of perhaps 21 million; in 1470 it was still only 14 million. For England the estimates for these dates are 4.5 and 3 million and for Germany 14 and 10 million.

It is now thought that this decline of population started already in the half century before the Black Death. By about 1300, the limits of food production had been reached, given the level of agricultural techniques and the difficulties of transporting large quantities of foodstuffs from such areas as still enjoyed a surplus of production to those which suffered famine. Between 1316 and 1319, for instance, large parts of western Europe experienced disastrous harvests and famine prices. On the coasts of the North Sea, unusual spring floods inundated large areas and whole villages. The shape of the Zuyder Zee, the large inland gulf in Holland, was permanently changed – at any rate until the twentieth century when the building of a long dam across its entrance and extensive land reclamation changed the Zuyder Zee to the Ijsselmeer, effectively now an inland lake.

These losses in the early fourteenth century signalled the limits of the expansion of the previous three hundred years; but by themselves they were puny, compared with the catastrophe of the Black Death and the recurring plagues.

Agriculture: the end of serfdom

Throughout the Middle Ages land was by far the most important source of wealth. By the turn of the thirteenth century it had become scarce and, in consequence, very expensive. This meant that both rents and agricultural prices had risen; but labour had become relatively abundant and cheap. After the Black Death this relationship was reversed. Land was easily available; demand for foodstuffs and hence prices had dropped sharply, and labour had become scarce. Indeed it had become doubly scarce; for not only had the plague killed many agricultural labourers but many landless workers or smallholders were now able to move into empty holdings.

The results were far-reaching. In the first place, wages rose; or rather, while agricultural prices declined (after the first period of chaos and famine, following immediately on the plague), many wages did not. The landowners reacted immediately by trying to fix maximum wages. In England for instance parliament passed the Statute of Labourers (1351) specifically for this purpose. But such legislation was not very effective, at least in the long run; for employers could not be prevented from bidding up wages.

In the second place, the owners of land had to adjust to the new circumstances. Those who could still hope to supply an outside market might try to re-impose labour services on their tenants more strictly than ever. But, again in the long run, such a policy proved difficult to maintain. With landlords competing for labour and with holdings vacant, tenants would simply flee from estates which demanded labour services to more attractive holdings in other parts of the country. More and more lords were therefore forced to let out their land for rent, or, in southern Europe, for share cropping. With a depressed market and falling or strongly fluctuating prices, it was better to live on fixed rents and let the tenants cope with the market.

As a result, the old feudal seigneurie and manor which were already beginning to dissolve in the thirteenth and early fourteenth centuries, were now substantially transformed. Lords became rentiers. Labour services disappeared and with them disappeared the status of villeinage or serfdom. The peasants came to hold permanent, inheritable tenures or temporary (though usually long-term) leases. It was an uneven development, too slow for many peasants, and demands for the complete abolition of serfdom now became common in many peasant risings, even when these had other immediate causes, such as that in England in 1381. These were classic examples of what the modern sociologists would call revolts precipitated by disappointment of expectations in a generally improving situation.

The later fourteenth and fifteenth centuries have sometimes been called the golden age of the peasant and the agricultural labourer. This is exaggerated; but it does seem to be true that, in general, the peasants and labourers did well in a situation of relatively plentiful land and scarce labour, and that the lords did correspondingly worse; for their incomes had often declined and they could no longer exploit even temporarily favourable market conditions.

285

The peasants and the state

Nevertheless, the peasants did not reap the full advantage of the reversal of market conditions. These conditions remained depressed, for the cities had become both much smaller and generally poorer. Often it was either not possible or not profitable to re-populate holdings, or, alternatively, owners turned former arable land into pasture; for far fewer hands were needed to look after cattle or sheep than to plough the soil and sow and harvest grain. Thus all over western and central Europe hundreds of villages disappeared altogether. Only fairly recently have historians realized the vast extent of this phenomenon of 'lost villages'. They can often be spotted by aerial photographs which show old field systems and the foundations of houses beneath a new landscape of grass and hedge. Furthermore, the peasants were not the only beneficiaries of the new conditions. They had to share their profits with the state. For the princes, finding that revenue from domain lands had suffered in the same way as that of the individual lords, began to compensate this loss by the systematic imposition of taxes. They did this either by levying export or import duties or by imposing direct taxes. From the time of Edward I (1272–1307) the kings of England imposed taxes on the export of wool. The merchants who exported the wool to the cloth towns of Flanders did not suffer from this; for they were allowed to form a monopoly company, the Company of the Staple, and thus they managed to pass the tax on to the producer by paying him lower prices.

Worse still, because they affected more persons, were direct taxes such as the English poll taxes of 1377 and 1380, i.e. impositions on persons. It was these taxes which precipitated the peasant's revolt of 1381. From both sides of the Thames, from Essex and Kent, men marched on London. There they found allies, and the boy-king, Richard II, and his advisers had to give in to the rebels' demands. Once the peasants dispersed, the authorities broke their agreements and took revenge on the peasant leaders. But the memories and myths of popular revolts remained. The ironical and bitter query of the English peasants of 1381,

> When Adam delved and Eve span
> Who was then the gentleman?

translated easily into similar couplets in other Germanic languages and became the slogan of countless rebellions in the fifteenth century. What was particularly disturbing to the authorities was the religious flavour of such propaganda. Yet how could it have been otherwise? All aspects of men's lives were ordered by religious precepts and every aspect of morality was religious. Obedience to authority was central to all morality, and rebellion was the fruit of the most deadly of the seven deadly sins, pride. (The others were anger, avarice, envy, gluttony, lust and sloth; but it was pride which had caused the archangel Lucifer's rebellion and fall). If taxes, inhumane treatment or plain hunger drove men and women to rebellion, they would assuredly need to find a religious justification for their actions. But the Catholic Church, the ally, defender and, indeed, the very embodiment of established authority could not provide such justification. This role therefore fell either to outright heresies, such as that of the Lollards in England who wanted the Church to give up all its land and return to a state of apostolic poverty, or to fringe movements, sometimes within and sometimes outside the Church. Such for instance were the followers of various prophecies of an impending millennium. They would generally identify the established authorities with the rule of Satan or, at any rate, they would consider them ripe for overthrow so that Christ's thousand-year kingdom of justice could be ushered into the world.

These movements were highly explosive and relatively frequent; but they were usually geographically limited and socially confined to the lower classes of towns and countryside. The established authorities though showing signs of considerable nervousness, had usually little difficulty in putting them down. Only when both larger geographical areas and wider sections of society became involved did these movements become really dangerous to established society. This was to happen in Bohemia in the early fifteenth century and in Germany in the early sixteenth.

The transformation of feudalism

If the Black Death dissolved the old feudal relationship between lord and serf, it also dissolved that between liege lord and vassal. Here, again, it did not so much start a new development as accelerate one that had begun at least a hundred years earlier.

And here, too, the old personal relationship based on land and service – in this case, of course, military service – gave way to one based on money and contract. Ever since the beginnings of feudalism, in the ninth and tenth centuries, women and children holding fiefs had paid money in lieu of military service. Lords now found it more and more convenient to generalize such payments. With the proceeds they could hire professional soldiers or 'retain' knights and other servants on their staff. Land and land-holding still remained important in this relationship; but men would now also contract to serve kings or great lords in return for salaries, fees or more general favours to themselves or their families, regardless of whether they held land from such lords or not.

Some historians have called this new relationship 'bastard feudalism' and have regarded it as a decline from classical feudalism or as a decadent form of feudalism. It certainly allowed great men vast influence and tended to produce much corruption. Even before the Black Death there were, for instance, complaints in England that

> felons and transgressors escape due punishment because they are maintained by magnates and others who retain them in their households and in their pay and livery, because gaol deliveries of such felons take place sometimes before they have been indicted, sometimes by surreptitious means or by dishonest or cowardly juries.

All the same, it is very doubtful whether the administration of justice had been any better in earlier centuries or whether great men had used their power any less corruptly.

In the new system the basic political and social relationship was no longer that of lord and vassal but of patron and client. It was patronage which made the wheels of this society go round. Where the feudal relationship of earlier generations had been largely military, the new patron-client relationship was largely civilian, although it could be, and was, still used for military purposes. Thus it was a highly flexible and adaptable relationship and it continued as a basic structural element in European society until the end of the eighteenth century. It did, of course, tend to produce corrupt practices; for, in a society based on status and privilege, men will naturally make use of their positions for their own advantage and for that of their families and clients. Indeed they will be expected to do so; for otherwise, what would be the point of having status? This was generally accepted. Yet, from the fourteenth century, voices began to be raised questioning these assumptions. At first, as we have seen, these were only the voices of peasants, artisans and heretics and even these were raised only intermittently. In general, men assumed, and with a good deal of experience to back them, that overt corruption was best restrained by a strong ruler. Yet even the strongest rulers needed clients, powerful men who could assure the loyal administration of the country; for no ruler had as yet a trained, obedient and reasonably honest civil service such as modern governments can rely on. Heaven itself was pictured in this way. For what else were the saints, especially the local, familiar, very personal saints, to whom men and women prayed to intercede for them with God Almighty, but patrons who took care of their clients?

But, gradually, the doubts were to spread until, in the French Revolution and its aftermath, they swept away the old society. The history of Europe from the fourteenth to the eighteenth centuries is, at least in one of its most important aspects, a commentary on this development.

Changing conceptions of the nature of property

The dissolution of the old feudal relationship also affected men's view of property. In classical feudalism, property, especially property in land, was viewed in a dual way. It gave rights to its owner but also imposed obligations on him: the obligations of fealty (loyalty) and military service for noble men and the obligations of labour service, and sometimes also of military service, on peasants. With the disappearance of the obligation of military service and the loosening of the bonds of personal loyalty, property came to be regarded as an absolute right, with none but contractual obligations imposed on it. The spread of Roman law reinforced this attitude and, in England, the common law also tended to view property as absolute. This change in attitude was a slow process, but it had important consequences. The head of the state, no longer able to expect military support from his vassals *qua* vassals, had to claim wider powers and prerogatives over his subjects than he had previously needed. Especially important were his claims to be able to impose taxes. Conversely, the subjects were anxious to deny the prince such rights or, at

Plate 5.2   Late medieval Lübeck (fifteenth century).
Here is the typically spiky appearance of the late-medieval city with its
many pointed towers and spires. The high curtain walls, which once
protected only castles, now surround the whole city; but already in the
fifteenth century they began to prove vulnerable to the fire of big siege
guns.
   The body of the city's patron saint, borne by angels to heaven,
signifies that the Lübeckers, like the inhabitants of all other European
cities, saw themselves as, above all, a Christian commune.

least, they were anxious to limit or control them. It is therefore
not surprising that from this period theories about the 'absolute'
powers of princes began to appear and, at the same time, theories
about the need for princes to obtain their subjects' consent to
taxation. This consent would be given through representative
assemblies.

   By the seventeenth century the concept of property as an
absolute right had become so firmly rooted in people's minds,
that they could hardly think of it in any other way, and they
based all their political philosophies on it. Even the socialists of
the nineteenth and twentieth centuries, who attacked the
morality of a society based on private property, mostly retained
the notion of its absolute nature and only tried to shift ownership
from private persons to the state.[3]

290

Towns and trade

The sharp decline of population affected not only agrarian life but also industrial production and trade. Even where we have no actual figures for urban populations we can often see the decline of towns from fifteenth-century maps. Their city walls, which in the thirteenth century had burst at the seams and had repeatedly been enlarged, had now become too wide and enclosed large open spaces.

The total volume of production and, in consequence, of trade also declined. Before the Black Death the Florentine cloth industry produced some 80,000 to 100,000 cloths a year. In 1378, in the course of a lower-class rising, the Florentine weavers demanded a pledge from their employers of a minimum production rate of 24,000. In England exports of wool declined from some 30–35,000 sacks in the early fourteenth century to about 25,000 (raw wool and cloth) a hundred years later. In Ypres, in Flanders, cloth production fell to 15 per cent of what it had been in the early fourteenth century. The exports of wine from Bordeaux dropped to less than half the pre-plague averages. Indeed, wherever we have figures, we nearly always find a similar pattern of decline.

With declining or stagnant volumes of trade and with future prospects evidently unsettled, merchants and manufacturers tended to adopt more defensive attitudes. They formed companies, such as the English wool exporters' Company of the Staple, designed to reduce competition and to exclude outsiders. They induced governments to guarantee their privileges and, if necessary, to uphold them by force against foreign competitors. This the governments were often quite willing to do; for in return they obtained loans from the merchant companies and could levy taxes on their trade. For the first time commercial motives began to play a role in the international relations of the European monarchies, as they had done already for a long time in those of the Italian and German city republics.

Inside the cities the master craftsmen had a ready instrument to hand to reduce competition: the craft guilds. These had existed in some towns since the twelfth century but had usually not been much more than drinking and feasting and benevolent societies, dedicated to a particular local or professional patron saint. Now they came to be used to restrict entry into a craft, to limit the number of masters and prevent competition by regulating prices

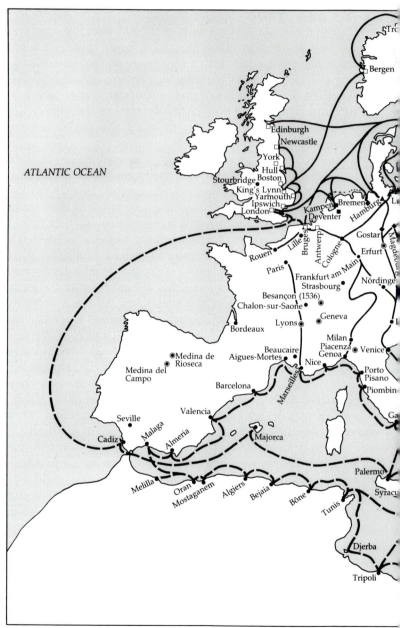

Map 5.1 Late-medieval trade routes.

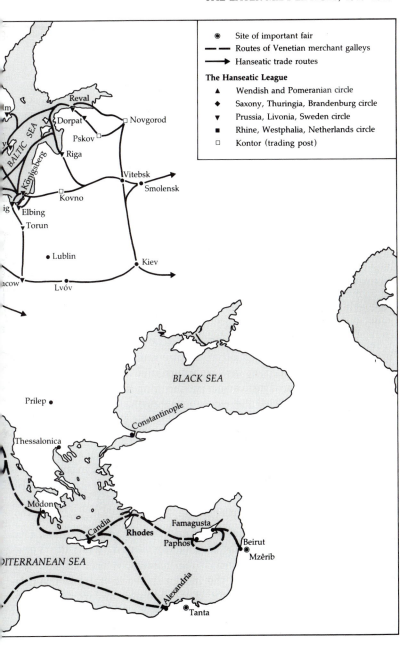

Site of important fair
Routes of Venetian merchant galleys
Hanseatic trade routes

The Hanseatic League

▲ Wendish and Pomeranian circle
◆ Saxony, Thuringia, Brandenburg circle
▼ Prussia, Livonia, Sweden circle
■ Rhine, Westphalia, Netherlands circle
□ Kontor (trading post)

and, sometimes, the quality of the goods produced. One result of their restrictive practices was that some manufacturers began to move out of guild-dominated towns into the countryside.

The result of all these developments was increasing social tension: tension between established masters and journeymen (skilled wage earners) who no longer had any prospect of setting up as masters; tension between capitalist employers, now sometimes in the countryside, and their unorganized workers; tension between town and countryside; and everywhere dislike of increasing government taxation and hatred of the destructive soldiery of kings and princes. Thus in 1358 the peasants of the Ile de France and much of northern France rose in a furious *jacquerie*, a great revolt of the ordinary man ('Jacques') against the marauding, burning and murdering soldiers of both the English and the French kings, and they were joined by citizens of Paris.

Economic transformations

Nevertheless, the later fourteenth and the fifteenth centuries were not a period of unrelieved decline for manufacture and trade, any more than for agriculture. New industries, such as silk, leather, metal and glass-working often compensated for the decline of older industries. Linen, as an alternative to wool, began to become important. The unfree peasants of the Swiss monastery of St Gall had traditionally made linen cloths only for their own use and for the monks, their overlords. In the later fourteenth century they began to supply a wide export market and made their village into a leading centre of the linen industry. The continued vitality of overseas trade showed itself in the development of ship-building. As early as the ninth century, the Byzantines had developed the Arab dhows of the Indian Ocean (themselves probably heavily influenced by the Chinese junks) to build ships with lateen sails that could tack against the wind (see Plate 5.3). These, somewhat further developed, were the Venetian and Genoese two- and three-masters which carried the crusaders to the Levant and the Indian spices to Italy. In the thirteenth century the design of these Mediterranean ships was combined with that of the north-European square-rigged, ocean-going cog. The resulting ship, the carrack, with both lateen and square sails, was the most efficient ship yet built, and the immediate forerunner of the world-conquering Portuguese and

294

Plate 5.3   Mediterranean lateen sail.
Odysseus' ships had single masts and square sails and so, generally,
had Greek and Roman ships, and also the Vikings and the ships with
which William the Conqueror invaded England. All these could sail
only before the wind. Lateen sails allowed ships to tack against the
wind and, hence, greatly increased their manoeuvrability and made
them less dependent on the weather. Technically, when tacking, the
wind does not push the sail, but the airflow on the outside of the
sail's curved surface pulls the sail, and hence the ship, forward. It is
basically the same principle as that by the which the airflow over the
curved wings provides the lift for a modern airplane.

Spanish caravels of Columbus (see Plate 5.4, p. 296) and Vasco
da Gama. With such ships and with the benefit of another
Chinese invention, the magnetic compass, navigation to the ends
of the world now became possible.

In and around Europe itself shipping may well have increased
even during the century of economic contraction, after the Black
Death. Characteristically, the Italians no longer waited for English
wool and Flemish cloth to be brought to Italy, but sent their own
fleets every year to Southampton and Bruges. Equally characteristically, the English did not remain content to ship their raw

W·A·   kraeck.

296

wool to Flanders. From the late fourteenth century they began increasingly to make cloth themselves. Royal taxation on the export of wool, fast-running streams in Yorkshire and the Cotswolds (the hilly country west of Oxford) which powered fulling mills, perhaps the acquisition of technical know-how through Flemish immigrants, but above all the prospects of greater profit – these were the reasons for the growth of the English woollen manufacturing industry. It led English merchants far afield to sell their cloth and, inevitably, into competition and war with commercial rivals. In the first half of the fifteenth century they did well against the Hansards (the merchants of the Hanseatic League of Lübeck and other North German cities) in the Baltic. But in the middle of the century, when support from their government collapsed during the Wars of the Roses, the English were driven out of the Baltic, not to reappear there for nearly a hundred years.

The hundred or hundred and fifty years following the Black Death were a period of overall contraction in the economic life of Europe, but not of stagnation. Technological inventions and improvements continued to be made. Gunpowder (again a Chinese or, for military purposes, an Arab invention) was first used in Europe in the fourteenth century and not only came to change the art of war but induced the growth of new metal and chemical industries. In 1335 the first weight-driven striking clock was erected in Milan, and within a few decades every respectable cathedral tower and town hall displayed this elaborate and sophisticated mechanism. Equally complex mechanisms, cogwheels, gears, suction pumps, were introduced in the mining industry in order to pump water from mine shafts using either horse or water power. Power-driven bellows made it possible, for the first time around 1400, to fully melt iron, and this discovery assured the gradual victory of relatively cheap iron over very expensive bronze. Even so, iron remained scarce and iron prices continued

Plate 5.4   Flemish carrack.
The carrack was a late-medieval, northern, ocean-going ship with a stern rudder and several masts, so that it could combine the advantages of large square sails with smaller lateen sails, as well as carry a considerable cargo. The raised forecastle (fo'c's'le) and sterncastle were used to mount guns and as fighting platforms in sea battles; they were also (wrongly) thought to give ships greater stability in heavy seas.

to rise in the fifteenth century, against the general trend of prices. It has been estimated that even by the end of the century, Europe produced only some 40,000 tons of iron. (In 1964 the United States produced 100 million tons of iron.)

But the three technical advances which were to affect ordinary individuals most closely were the introduction of paper (another Chinese invention) and of eyeglasses in Italy towards the end of the thirteenth century, and that which gave these two its greatest effect, printing. Printing, too, had previously been invented in China, but it turned out that the Latin alphabet of only 26 letters lent itself much more easily to mechanical reproduction than the thousands of Chinese ideographs. The most significant effects of this mid fifteenth-century German invention (or re-invention, for it does not seem as if Chinese printing was known in Germany), were not to be felt until the sixteenth century and later. But then it turned out that the printing press produced the greatest advance in human communications since the invention of writing. It was not only that reading material became much cheaper and therefore more widely available, but equally important was the standardization of texts. Although pirating became an immediate problem for publishers and authors, and although pirated texts were often inaccurate, readers of author-ized books could now, for the first time, feel certain that they read what the author had actually written or, in the case of an ancient author, that they had the text as edited by a modern authority. International dialogue on religious, philosophical, scientific and literary topics underwent a 'quantum leap' in volume and inten-sity. Perhaps the most dramatic effect of this new speed and cheapness of communication was the appearance, in the early sixteenth century, of a vast pamphlet literature on religious and political topics aimed at the 'common man', or at least at the man who could read or who had someone to read for him and do a little explanation. Soon, governments and city authorities used the press to print placards with laws, orders, or information and propaganda which were posted in public places.

Very rapidly, after the establishment of the first press in Mainz in the middle of the fifteenth century, presses were set up in most of the major and in many minor cities of Europe. Most of these were small businesses; but by the middle of the sixteenth century publishing houses had appeared, such as that of Christopher Plantin in Antwerp, who employed scores of skilled workmen and published some 1600 titles. A new technology creating an expanding market for a standardized product, investment of capital, concentration of the workforce under one roof and ambitious entrepreneurship – these characteristics of Plantin's publishing business were the prototype of the way in which the manufacturing industry of Europe was to develop.

Together with technological advance went improvement in commercial methods and organization. There were opportunities for men who knew how to take advantage of changing market conditions, and who were prepared to apply sophisticated commercial and financial skills. The merchants of the small south German city of Ravensburg built up a company with branches in most of the great commercial centres of Europe. But nearly always the most successful were those who could obtain the support of a powerful state. William de la Pole made his fortune in the wool trade and as financier to Edward III, and his son became earl of Suffolk. A hundred years later Jacques Coeur, merchant and banker, did even better as financier to Charles VII of France; but he did not manage to found a noble dynasty, for he became a victim of aristocratic envy and of court intrigues. Marginally safer for the financially ambitious was a career as a papal banker and tax collector or the support of one of the great Italian city states. But here, too, careers were strewn with political pitfalls. At least one family of financiers drew the ultimate conclusion from this situation and made themselves masters of a state. This was the story of the Medici in Florence. It will be discussed in the next chapter.

The European kingdoms

The economic and social developments of the fourteenth and fifteenth centuries had tended to impoverish the nobility and to enrich the monarchies by increasing the possibilities of taxation. At the same time, the upbringing of princes and nobles in the arts of combat and the values of chivalry, instilled into young men in the highly idealized form of romances, chronicles and tournaments, preserved for this society its overwhelmingly military ethos. The two together, the economic and the psychological elements, amounted to an unfailing prescription for war. Princes wished to expand their territory or make good dynastic claims.

They could now tap the wealth of their dominions beyond their domains, and their vassals and subjects were only too willing to serve them for money, positions and honours. Since the most ambitious and pugnacious of them were no longer going on crusades in Syria, Greece or Africa, wars would now take place inside Christian Europe. This was the basis of the political history of the period. Before discussing it, however, it is necessary to look at another phenomenon that became an essential part of European politics and institutions and that set apart the development of European political society from that of all other developed civilizations.

Origins and growth of representative institutions

From the early Middle Ages kings had to rely on the advice and support of their greatest followers or vassals. Frankish and Langobard kings had sometimes also summoned assemblies of free warriors. Where political units remained small, as for instance in Iceland or in some of the Swiss cantons, such assemblies of free, male citizens could persist for centuries, even into our own times. But for the larger kingdoms they proved too clumsy. Their kings preferred more restricted assemblies. A king's more powerful vassals, for their part, came to regard the giving of advice as a useful activity to advance their own interests and they began to turn an obligation of vassalage into a political right. Here lay the origins of the basic ambivalence of the relations between rulers and assemblies; for while the rulers would want the maximum support from their vassals, the vassals might or might not approve of the ruler's policies. They would want rewards for services which went beyond their customary, feudal obligations. Above all, they would want to safeguard their own rights, privileges and properties.

Assemblies of magnates were not, however, representative institutions. The idea of representation had different roots. One was from Roman law, the representation of a client by his attorney in court. In the twelfth century this principle was adopted by ecclesiastical institutions, first in the representation of different houses of an international monastic order, such as the Dominican Order, and then for the Church as a whole. Innocent III summoned the representatives of cathedral chapters and monastic houses to the Fourth Lateran Council, of 1215, and this council was then held to represent the Church as a whole.

From this it was a logical step to extend the idea of representation to secular institutions. It became convenient for rulers to summon not only individual magnates but representatives of rich cities and powerful ecclesiastical corporations. Another Roman law principle, that 'what concerns all must be approved by all', gave a rational basis for representation. It gradually came to take on the colouring of a fundamental political maxim, embodying the notion of a community of interests within a country and, eventually, the need for conscious consent by the community for its government. In this way representative institutions began to be seen in the thirteenth century, and in the fourteenth the idea of representation was given an elaborate theoretical underpinning by Marsiglio of Padua, William of Ockham and other distinguished writers.

A certain feeling of community within a given political structure was an essential element in this development. Where it did not exist, or was not allowed to develop, as in the territories ruled by the Italian city republics, representative institutions also did not develop. It could appear in a country as large as England, and there parliament came to represent the whole kingdom. More usually men's horizons of loyalty were more limited, rarely extending beyond the local county or duchy or province. It was mostly in such units that representative institutions grew in the fourteenth and fifteenth centuries and these institutions, in their turn, helped the growth of the feeling of community. They also helped the growth of the feeling of identity of the different units who were represented. The old model of society of the three estates, clergy, nobility, and commons, was here given palpable form in the estates represented in the assemblies.

It is here that we must seek the reasons for the remarkable diffusion of representative institutions through the length and breadth of Christian Europe. They fulfilled two universal needs, that of strengthening the feeling of community of existing political units, and that of regulating the relations between the ruler of a country and his most powerful subjects, and this in societies where these relations had become much more complex than the simple lord-and-vassal relationship of the ninth and tenth centuries.

The assemblies, the parliaments, the cortes, the landtage or diets, the estates, or whatever their local names, differed in structure according to the social structure of their country and the events of their early histories. In most of France and Spain and in several of the Italian and German principalities they assembled in the three classic estates of prelates, nobility and commons, which meant the city corporations. In others, as in the English parliaments, prelates and barons were grouped together in one house and the representatives of the county nobility and the cities in another. In some countries, in Sweden, the Tyrol and in some French provinces, the free peasants sent representatives; in others, notably in Poland and Hungary, the nobles virtually excluded the towns. In large countries, in France, in Poland, or in countries recently put together from separate parts, such as the Netherlands, there developed both provincial and general assemblies, the latter representing the whole country or at least several political units under one ruler.

None of these assemblies was democratic in the modern sense. Representation rarely meant election, and those who were represented were all privileged, propertied corporations, groups, or areas. Their interests and outlook were often narrow; their representatives were frequently ignorant of wider political matters; not seldom they were corrupt. Yet when they insisted that the ruler observe their privileges they were also defending the rule of law against arbitrary power; when they limited the ruler's demands for taxes they were also protecting the non-privileged; when they insisted on ratifying international treaties and began to criticize their ruler's aggressive policies, they went at least some way towards mitigating the worst aspects of the international anarchy of the times.

While it was the function of representative assemblies to regulate and systematize the relations between rulers and their subjects this does not mean that they could solve all the problems that could arise between them. Rulers found their parliaments useful, but also often a nuisance and, on occasion, a menace. Sometimes they came to prefer ruling without parliaments, and they and their subjects were perfectly clear what this might mean. The French-Netherlandish politician and historian, Philip de Commynes (c. 1447–1511), a man who had served both the duke of Burgundy and the king of France and knew what he was talking about, asked rhetorically: 'Is there a king or other lord who has power to levy even a penny on his subjects without the grant and consent of those who have to pay it, unless it were by tyranny or violence?'[4] His older English contemporary, the Chief Justice Sir John Fortescue (*c.* 1385–1479), had distinguished between *dominium regale*, absolute monarchy, and *dominium politicum et regale*, constitutional government. He meant that the king of France could tax his subjects at will whilst the king of England could not without the consent of parliaments. The French were therefore overtaxed and poor:

> they drinken water, they eaten apples, with bread right browne made of rye; they eaten no flesh but if it be right seldom a little lard, or of the entrails and hides of beasts slain for the nobles and merchants of the land. They wearen no woollens . . . Their wives and children go barefoot . . . For some of them that were wont to pay to his lord for his tenement, which he hireth by the year, a scute, payeth now to the king over that scute 5 scutes. Wherethrough they be arted by necessity so to watch, labour and grub for their sustenance that their nature is wasted . . . They gone crooked and been feeble, not able to fight nor defend the realm . . .

The king of France had to rely for the defence of his country on Scots, Spaniards and Germans.

> Lo, this is the fruit of *ius regale* . . . But blessed be God, this land (England) is ruled under a better law; and therefore the people thereof be not in such penurie, nor thereby hurt in their person, but they be wealthy and have all things necessary to the sustenance of nature. Wherefore they been mighty and able to resist the adversaries of this realm, and to beat other realms that do or would do them wrong. Lo this is the fruit of *ius politicum et regale* under which we live.[5]

Allowing for the Chief Justice's understandable but unjustified patriotic bias – the French had just driven the English out of their country – he had made a valid distinction between two styles of government. His contemporaries agreed with him on this point. Neither Commynes nor Fortescue were saying anything new, but both highlighted the fact that, basically, the relationship between princes and parliaments was one involving political power. In the long run, the history of this relationship would be the story of a struggle for power. From the fourteenth to the seventeenth century this struggle was one of the basic elements in the internal political history of the European states. By the end of the fifteenth century it had been resolved in only a very few cases. For most countries the constitutional crisis was yet to come.

303

France and the Hundred Years War

It was in France that the opportunities for warfare and the attractions of territorial gain and plunder for kings and their nobility were particularly enticing. The kings of France could never accept that the English still held a large part of Aquitaine, south-west France. The kings of England, for their part, had never forgotten or forgiven their loss of Normandy in the early thirteenth century. Open warfare broke out in 1337 and, with many and sometimes quite lengthy intermissions, was to last until 1453. Edward III of England countered Philip VI's attack on Aquitaine by claiming the crown of France by inheritance through his mother; naturally, the French denied this claim. The English won several pitched battles but were never remotely strong enough to conquer the whole of France and enforce Edward III's claim, and it is at least doubtful whether this was ever a serious aim.

The reasons for the considerable partial successes of the English and for the inordinate length of the war lay in the divisions of French political society. Princes of the royal family of Valois held appanages, large dukedoms and counties of which they were virtually independent rulers. These appanages were originally intended to strengthen the royal family and administration. They were meant to provide suitable status and income for a king's younger sons and sometimes also for his daughters. The crown reserved for itself certain rights in the appanages and would re-incorporate them in the royal domain if either the prince became king himself or if his direct line of male heirs died out. In practice, the appanage princes tried to exclude royal influence as much as they could. The most successful was Philip of Burgundy, one of the sons of King John II. In their mutual manoeuvrings one or other of the French princes would ally himself with the English, and at times it looked as if France would break up into quasi-independent principalities, like Germany. At the turn of the fourteenth century the princely houses of Orleans and Burgundy disputed the regency for the mad king Charles VI. The Valois dukes of Burgundy had acquired by marriage the succession to the dukedoms and counties of the Netherlands, the economically most advanced and richest territory of transalpine Europe. Here was a golden opportunity for the English to intervene once more in France, after a generation of uneasy peace. The young and energetic Henry V won the shattering victory of Agincourt (1415) and then, in alliance with Burgundy, conquered all of France north of the Loire, married Charles VI's daughter and was formally recognized by the French king as his heir (1420).

It was the high water mark of English success and it could not be maintained. Henry V died (1422) and, like so many medieval conquerors, left only an infant child as his successor. The French nobility began to rally around the Dauphin, the son of Charles VI. A peasant girl from Lorraine, Joan of Arc, led him to Rheims for his coronation as Charles VII. She claimed to be inspired by voices from heaven and many believed her though others believed, or chose to believe, that she was inspired by the devil. In 1430 she was captured by the English and a year later condemned by a French ecclesiastical court to be burnt as a heretic. Charles VII did nothing to save her; only in 1456 did he instigate a process of rehabilitation which pronounced Joan's orthodoxy. She was canonized in 1920.

More important than the saint's intervention, however, was the reversal of alliances. In 1435 the duke of Burgundy made peace with Charles VII. From then on it was only a matter of time before the superior resources of the French monarchy and the gradually snow-balling defections of the English king's French vassals and allies made the English position untenable, even in Aquitaine. When peace was concluded in 1453 only Calais remained in English hands. The four-hundred-year connection between the English crown and parts of France was at an end.

France and the Netherlands

Nevertheless, the survival of the kingdom of France was still not yet assured. The greatest of the royal princes, the Valois dukes of Burgundy, had built up a formidable power base outside France, in the Netherlands. From there they could both interfere in French politics and further extend their power in the area between France and Germany, the old Carolingian middle kingdom. Charles the Bold (1467–77), 'the Great Duke of the West' tried vainly to obtain a royal crown from the emperor Frederick III but did succeed in betrothing his daughter and heiress, Mary, to the emperor's son, Maximilian. Trying to build a land-bridge between the Netherlands and Burgundy he came up against the Swiss cantons. In three battles in the space of a year the Swiss pikemen defeated Charles the Bold's knights and finally

Map 5.2a   Western Europe: the Hundred Years' War, *c.* 1360

killed him. Louis XI of France seized the opportunity to regain the French duchy (but not the imperial county) of Burgundy, but failed against Flanders. Maximilian of Habsburg, emperor from 1493, and his children held the Netherlands. They now moved

Map 5.2b   Western Europe: the Hundred Years' War, *c.* 1430.

permanently out of the French orbit; but the rivalry between the Habsburg rulers of the Netherlands, kings of Spain from 1516, and the kings of France was to dominate European politics for the next two centuries.

307

Plate 5.5 Joust. Miniature from Froissart's *Chronicles*.
This fifteenth-century illustration shows the most popular of courtly
and chivalrous entertainments. The spectators included ladies, and the
jousting knights often wore their colours. Froissart's story is that at the
St Ingilbert jousts three French knights took on 36 challengers for one
week. Although injuries were fairly common and deaths were not
unknown, jousts were a relatively civilized way for young men to
show off their manliness. Actual warfare, for all that some knights
may have hoped and some chroniclers would have us believe, was a
very different matter from jousting, especially for the civilian
bystanders.

The consequences of the Hundred Years War

For all participants the Hundred Years War was enormously
expensive. Quite early on it became clear that it could not be
fought with only feudal levies. The west European nobility gladly

went to war in pursuit of glory, position, plunder and the fat ransoms which could be extorted from noble prisoners of war. But already in the early years of the fourteenth century, Swiss, Flemish and Scottish pikemen and Welsh bowmen had shown that, in well chosen defensive positions, they could defeat the heavily mailed feudal cavalry. The shattering English victories of Crécy (1346), Poitiers (1356) and Agincourt (1415) emphasized the growing superiority of the despised infantry. The Swiss victories over Charles the Bold clinched it. But this infantry which was becoming more and more professional had to be paid for with cash; and so had artillery which was making its debut in the fourteenth century, both on the battlefield and in sieges. Even the knights were now demanding payment for long campaigns.

Edward III raised funds for the English war effort by taxes on the wool trade. More and more however, he had to turn to parliament, for these and other taxes. Almost imperceptibly, parliament became a regular institution through which the king legislated and raised money and, inevitably, it developed traditions and a will of its own. Quite characteristically, the House of Commons frequently petitioned the king for the maintenance of Magna Carta. The close connection between parliament and the rule of law was evident to all.

When Richard II (1377–99) quarrelled with a powerful group of English magnates it was through parliament that both sides tried to defeat each other and it was by the grace of parliament that the usurper Henry IV (1399–1413) came to rule legally after he had deposed Richard II. Any attempt in the fifteenth century to rule without parliament, as Richard II was accused by his enemies of having wanted to do, was now no longer possible.

Nevertheless, it was not as yet a parliamentary government. In the aftermath of the lost war in France, with the king, Henry VI, suffering from bouts of insanity as his grandfather Charles VI of France had done, central government in England collapsed. Local barons fought out their private quarrels in a loose grouping around the Lancastrian and the Yorkist branches of the ruling house of Plantagenet, who themselves were fighting for the throne and the control of the central government. In this 'War of the Roses' (1453–71) parliament, dominated by the magnates, could play no constructive part. Central government and the rule of law were restored by strong-minded kings, first the Yorkist Edward IV (1461–83) and then the Lancastrian Henry VII, Tudor,

309

(1485–1509). Only then could parliament again play an important role in English politics.

In France, as in England, the kings needed extra taxes to fight the war and, again as in England, they found it easier to levy taxes with the consent of those who wielded local authority, the nobles, prelates and cities. For this purpose the kings used different assemblies of estates: local, provincial, regional, such as those of southern France (Languedoc) and central and northern France (Languedoïl), and even occasionally an Estates General for the whole kingdom. But France was a much larger and more diverse kingdom than England. Feelings of community were strongest in the provinces, and in many of these the assemblies of estates became firmly established. For France as a whole, the feelings of community were centred on the monarchy, the person of the king, rather than on common institutions. For practical convenience, rather than by design, the kings came to prefer provincial assemblies to the meetings of an ill-attended and resentful Estates General. Equally for practical convenience, and to meet the urgent demands of warfare, they came to levy taxes first and ask for approval later, until eventually both the royal lawyers and the public accepted the king's right to tax his subjects for the urgent necessities of the state, even without formal consent.

It is almost inconceivable that this would have happened without the very long war with the English, or if the French monarchy had not won this war. Here was the basis for the distinction which an intelligent observer, such as Sir John Fortescue, could make in the second half of the fifteenth century between the powers of the king of France and the king of England: the former could legislate and impose taxes, if not at will, yet still with considerable freedom; the latter could not. Following Aristotle's method of argumentation, Fortescue generalized these differences in the powers of the French and English kings as two different types of government. It was a differentiation that, in different forms, has been crucial in the political thinking of Europe right into our own time.

Taxation, estates and revolution in the Netherlands

Even more than the kings of England and France, the dukes of Burgundy in the Netherlands were dependent on consent for their military intervention in the French wars; for as rulers they were newcomers in a number of rather different dukedoms and counties, each with its own strong tradition and local patriotism. Only very gradually did a feeling of community of all the Netherlands provinces begin to appear. The dukes' policies of centralizing administration, finance and justice were strongly resented; but even more so were Charles the Bold's demands for taxes for his wars of conquest. When he fell in battle against the Swiss (1477), the States General, led and directed by Ghent, arrested and executed several of his ministers, arranged a treaty with Louis XI ceding some of the dukes' territories to France and forced the young duchess, Mary, to grant a 'great privilege' which left effective control of political authority in the hands of the provincial estates.

It was a real political revolution, and for the first time a representative assembly had actually seized control of the government of a western European country.

It could not last, if for no other reason than that the practical implications of parliamentary government had never yet even been thought about. The members of the assembly of the States General were deputies who, unlike the English members of parliament, had to refer all decisions back to their constituents, the provincial estates, and, beyond these, the town councils. Nobody had as yet worked out how such men could deal effectively with diplomatic or defence or financial policy in rapidly changing situations. In these circumstances, Mary's husband, Maximilian of Austria, managed eventually to restore ducal authority. Even so, it took years of conflict with Flanders and open civil war after the citizens of Bruges and Ghent had, at one point, actually kidnapped Maximilian. The problem of the relationship between ruler and estates in the Netherlands remained and was not resolved until a century later.

Spain

Compared with the dramatic history of north-west Europe in the fourteenth and fifteenth centuries, the political history of the Iberian peninsula remained in a relatively low key. The heroic age of the *reconquista*, the reconquest of Spain from the Moors, was over, although it had not been finished; for the Moors still held Granada. The crown of Aragon (Aragon, Valencia and Catalonia)

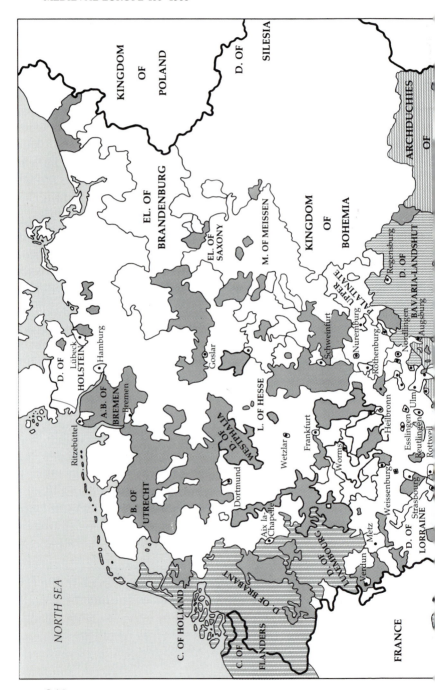

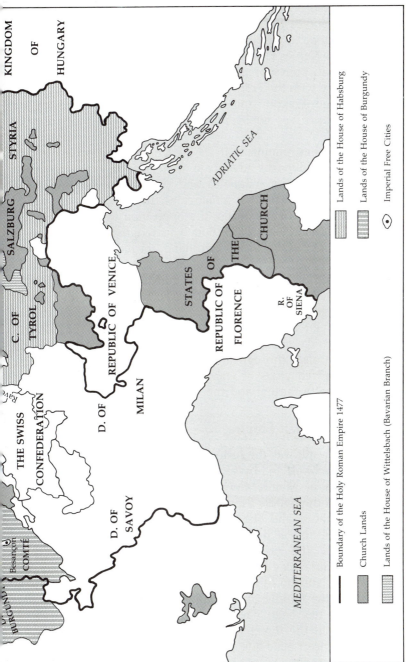

Map 5.3 The Holy Roman Empire in the fourteenth and fifteenth centuries

was interested only in Mediterranean trade and conquests. These were very successful and included Sicily and Sardinia and, for periods of time, a robber dukedom of Athens (1325–88) and the kingdom of Naples (1434–54).

The Italian policy of the house of Aragon was conducted in direct rivalry with the French-Angevin rulers of Naples and therefore involved Aragon itself in permanent hostility to France – a hostility which was fatally inherited by the unified kingdom of Spain.

In the Iberian peninsula itself the Christian kingdoms fought each other for dynastic advantage or engaged in civil wars when powerful factions of magnates and churchmen fought for the control of their respective monarchies. In the course of one of these, in Castile in the 1460s, the opposition to King Henry IV sought to strengthen its position by arranging the marriage of Henry's sister, Isabella, to Ferdinand the son of the king of Aragon (1469). Out of this casual and somewhat fortuitous alliance came the union of the kingdoms of Aragon and Castile which created modern Spain. Ferdinand and Isabella's victory in the last stage of the civil wars forestalled a much more natural union between Castile and Portugal which Henry IV had negotiated for his daughter. Spain was now set on the path for world empire, but also, through its Aragonese traditions, on a course of two hundred years of wars with France – both of immense consequence to Europe and the world.

The Holy Roman Empire

Much tamer still was the history of the Holy Roman Empire. The emperors were elected by seven leading princes of Germany, the archbishops of Mainz, Cologne and Trier, and by the Count Palatine (on the middle Rhine), the duke of Saxony, the margrave of Brandenburg and the king of Bohemia. These seven were called the electors or prince electors. The three prince archbishops were clearly the richest and most influential ecclesiastics in Germany, but it has long been a puzzle why the particular four lay houses, and no others, monopolized the electoral dignity, at least from the middle of the fourteenth century or even earlier. Recently it has been plausibly suggested that their houses all descended in the direct male line from the sisters of Otto the Great, the direct male line of the Saxon emperors themselves, the restorers of the Holy Roman Empire (see Ch. 2), having died out in 1002.[6] None of the emperors of the fourteenth and fifteenth centuries had sufficient power to re-establish an effective central authority. Most of them did not even try and were content to add to the possessions of their houses, Luxembourg, 1346–1437, and Habsburg (Austria), from 1438. In pursuing such policies they did not fundamentally differ from other German princes, so that there was a constant succession of minor wars, divisions, conquests and inheritance of territories. German historians have traditionally lamented this period of their history and the political impotence of Germany compared with the great days of the Salian and Hohenstaufen emperors. But the dynastic wars of the German princes, and even the depredations of the robber barons, probably caused much less devastation and misery to ordinary people than did the Hundred Years' War in France.

Central, eastern and northern Europe

East of the Holy Roman Empire the political situation remained much more fluid. Here were vast, sparsely populated plains of forest and field, intersected by broad, navigable rivers with only the range of the Carpathian mountains providing a natural but far from impassable defence to the north of Hungary. In the thirteenth century the Mongols (Tatars) from the east and the German knights of the Teutonic Order – originally a crusading order not unlike the Templars – conquered large parts of this territory. In the fourteenth century the Tatars were pushed back into southern Russia and in the fifteenth the Teutonic Order was defeated and contained in east Prussia and Livonia.

But more peaceful migrations continued. German peasants moved down the Danube and settled in Hungary and Transylvania. Further north German and Flemish settlers founded towns in Poland with German laws and customs.

In Transylvania and in the more westerly provinces of Poland they settled in sufficiently large groups to maintain their own language and ethnic identity; further east, where there were fewer of them, they tended to be assimilated to the native Slavonic populations.

The Jews, however, never allowed themselves to be fully assimilated. The pogroms which accompanied the Black Death in

315

Map 5.4 Eastern Europe.

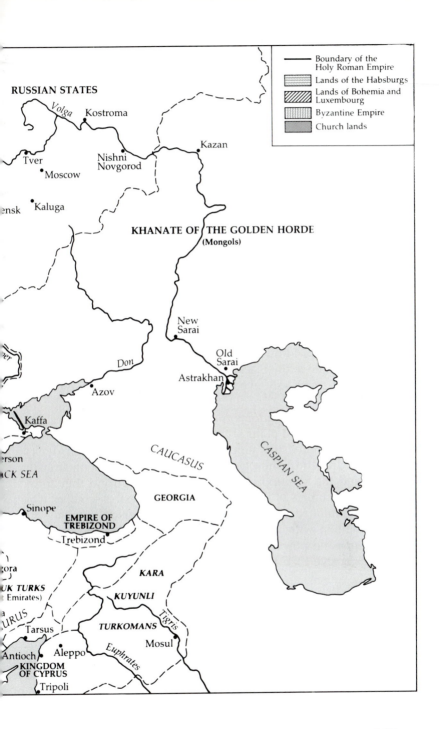

RUSSIAN STATES

Volga
Kostroma

Kazan

Tver
Nishni
Novgorod
Moscow

ensk
Kaluga

KHANATE OF THE GOLDEN HORDE
(Mongols)

New
Sarai

Old
Sarai
Astrakhan

Don

Azov

Kaffa

CAUCASUS

CASPIAN SEA

erson

CK SEA

GEORGIA

Sinope

**EMPIRE OF
TREBIZOND**

Trebizond

KARA

gora

UK TURKS
Emirates)

KUYUNLI

URUS

Tigris

TURKOMANS

Tarsus

Mosul

Antioch
Aleppo

Euphrates

**KINGDOM
OF CYPRUS**

Tripoli

Boundary of the
Holy Roman Empire
Lands of the Habsburgs
Lands of Bohemia and
Luxembourg
Byzantine Empire
Church lands

Germany drove some three hundred Jewish communities east. They took with them their Middle High German speech which was to evolve into Yiddish – just as the Spanish Jews, expelled from Spain in 1492 took with them to Constantinople their medieval Castilian language. In the fourteenth century the German Jews were welcomed in Poland and contributed to the economic and cultural development of that country.

Given these conditions it is not surprising to find not only the formation of the large and composite kingdoms of Bohemia, Hungary and Poland, but also attempts by their ruling houses to unify the crowns of two or, sometimes even all three of them, through marriage alliances and inheritance. Nor is it surprising that even outside powers became involved. The most extraordinary union was that of the crowns of Poland, Hungary and Naples, between 1370 and 1382, under the originally French house of Anjou.

None of these personal unions lasted for more than one or two reigns. The only one which did was that of Poland and the huge grand-duchy of Lithuania (from 1385) which, at times, stretched from the Baltic to the Black Sea and which was ethnically, linguistically and religiously even more heterogeneous than Poland or Hungary.

In all of these kingdoms the landed nobility and higher clergy were the dominant political force. The towns remained small and the rulers needed the support of their nobles for their dynastic policies. In return they had to grant them exemption from taxation and the monopoly of public offices. In Poland they formed the two chambers of the provincial and national assemblies which were summoned at least once a year and which, from the time of the union with Lithuania, insisted on electing the kings. The privileges and powers of the Hungarian nobility were only a little less extensive than those of Poland.

Scandinavia

Unlike the east, the north of Europe was relatively safe from outside attack. But here, too, German merchants and settlers dominated the towns. Here too, the ruling houses strove for the union of crowns and achieved it, for all three kingdoms, Norway, Sweden and Denmark, in the Union of Kalmar (1397). It meant little more than the central European unions. Denmark and

Map 5.5 The Scandinavian Kingdoms in the fourteenth, fifteenth and sixteenth centuries.

Norway, it is true, stayed together, though always as separate kingdoms. The union with Sweden was never really effective and was to lead to bitter civil wars in the sixteenth century. And in Scandinavia, as in central-eastern Europe, the nobility were the main beneficiaries of the dynastic ambitions of the kings.

The rise of Moscow

The Mongol conquest of the Russian steppe had caused large numbers of peasants to flee north and north-east into the thinly populated central forest zone of Russia. The princes of these areas welcomed the newcomers but did not grant them special privileges. At the time this did not seem to matter greatly. There was enough land for everyone. In the long run, however, it left the peasants defenceless against exploitation by the landowners. These landowners were coming to be more and more the special servants of the princes as soldiers or administrators. They developed into a service nobility that was loyal to the prince but had no very strong roots in the locality where they had been granted land. In consequence Russia never developed the strong regional loyalties which bound together the nobles and their vassals in Latin Europe. At the same time, Russian cities remained small and their administration was controlled directly by the princes and the governors they appointed. With the one important exception of Novgorod, the Russian towns never managed to form the autonomous communes with their self-conscious local patriotism which were so characteristic of the rest of Europe. Significantly, Russian houses were not built to face outwards, towards the streets, as in western cities, but inwards, towards their own courtyards, while fences or palisades shut them off from the rest

Plate 5.6 The Kremlin, Moscow.
The Kremlin owes much of its distinctive appearance to the reign of Ivan the Great. The brick fortifications were reconstructed under the direction of Italian architects between 1485 and 1495; and the Cathedral of the Annunciation (partly obscured by the watchtower on the left), built after 1484, and the Cathedral of the Archangel Michael (centre left), built after Ivan's death in 1505, were also designed by imported Italian architects working within the distinctive Russian architectural tradition. Nevertheless, the influence of the Italian Renaissance is clearly to be seen in such details as the graceful shell-shaped gables of the Cathedral of the Archangel Michael.

of the city. Without the community feelings of regions settled for many generations, and without the traditions of autonomous city corporations, the Russians never had the chance to develop representative assemblies which could, as they did in the west, defend regional and class privileges against the growing power of princely rule.

Those central Russian principalities which did not suffer direct Mongol occupation and which were willing to buy off Mongol blackmail by regular payments of tribute and periodic formal acknowledgement of the khan's political superiority, did well enough out of the Mongol rule of southern and eastern Russia, especially when they managed to use Mongol power against their rivals. One such principality was that of Muscovy, or Moscow. Conveniently situated on the river trade routes between the Baltic and the Black and Caspian Seas, with a huge forest hinterland which provided the valuable furs that made up a large part of this trade and sufficiently remote to escape all but a very few of the Mongol raids, Moscow had inherent advantages over other Russian principalities.

Nevertheless, the rise of Moscow was not a foregone conclusion. It required both luck and the clever and persistent policies pursued by a succession of able princes of the Rurikid house. The Muscovite princes managed to obtain the grand-princely title and they further increased their prestige when grand-prince Dmitrij Donskoj for the first time defeated a Mongol army in open battle, in 1380. The Mongols retaliated only two years later by raiding Moscow itself; but their reputation of invincibility was gone for good. During the last four decades of the fourteenth century a Muslim nomad leader of Turkic origins, Timur (Tamerlane) had built up the last of the great nomad empires. From central Asia and his capital, Samarkand, his armies ranged to Mongolia in the east and to the coasts of the Mediterranean in the west. In 1389 and again in 1395 he led devastating expeditions against the Golden Horde in Russia. It left the Mongols permanently weakened, with separate khanates of the Crimea on the Black Sea and of Khazan on the Volga breaking away from Sarai. From that moment the grand-princes of Muscovy were able to play off the now divided Mongol khanates against each other.

Of equal importance to the success of Moscow was the close connection which the church of Moscow maintained with the patriarch of Constantinople, the head of the whole Greek Orthodox Church. From Byzantium the Russian Church took over the idea of harmonious co-operation between Church and state. But the state was by far the stronger partner and the harmony between supposed equals became in practice the domination of the state over the Church. Divided loyalties and struggles between Church and state, which were of such enormous influence on the course of Latin Christian history, were therefore almost completely absent in Russia. At the same time, however, the Russian Church began to assert its independence from Constantinople. It refused to accept the union of the Greek and Latin churches agreed to at the Council of Florence in 1439. In 1459, six years after the fall of Constantinople to the Turks, a synod of Russian bishops meeting in Moscow declared that the metropolitan of Russia in Moscow no longer required the confirmation of his appointment by the patriarch of Constantinople. In practice the Russian Church was now independent of Constantinople, although it was not until 1589 that this independence was formally recognized by the title of patriarch for the metropolitan of Moscow.

Ivan the Great

By the second half of the fifteenth century the leadership of Moscow over most of Christian Russia was beginning to be generally acknowledged. Ivan III (1462–1505), known as the Great, called himself 'by the grace of God, sovereign of all Russia'. When the western emperor, Frederick III, offered to crown him king, Ivan replied: 'We by the grace of God have been sovereigns over our domains from the beginning, from our first ancestors. We pray to God that it may be granted to us and to our children for all time to continue as sovereigns as we are at present; and as in the past we have never needed appointment from anyone so we do not desire it now.' Ivan demanded the title of emperor but this title Frederick would not concede. Ivan forced the other Russian princes to follow his lead in foreign policy. His greatest success was the capture of Novgorod in 1478. Novgorod lost its independence and had to accept a governor appointed by Ivan. Some seventy Novgorod families were deported and given estates far from their homes. For the grand-prince of Moscow the absorption of Novgorod with its rich trade and its large dependent territory represented an enormous increase in power, resources and prestige. It is a more debatable point whether the fall of its only independent city state was a gain for Russia as a whole. The only remaining counterpoise to Muscovite autocracy had now disappeared. This autocracy was not to be seriously challenged until the twentieth century and, in the end, it was replaced by another and even more effective autocracy.[7]

The papacy at Avignon

It was not clear to people in the fourteenth century, as it is to us, that the pontificate of Boniface VIII was both a disaster and a turning point for the medieval papacy. Outwardly, the popes at Avignon were more powerful than ever. They pronounced on matters of faith and doctrine with complete authority. They extended papal taxation of the clergy and perfected their financial control. They appointed bishops and abbots all over Christendom. They called up cases from local ecclesiastical courts to the curia. By exercising the papal 'plenitude of power', the right to bind and loose, which included release from oaths, the popes could and did set aside electoral promises which they had made in conclave before being chosen. Personal absolutism could not go further.

There was, however, a price to be paid for these activities. Both papal taxation of the clergy and papal appointments to benefices needed the co-operation of the local rulers. Kings and princes found such co-operation convenient, for they claimed and got a sizeable cut from the clerical taxes and more and more they told the pope whom to appoint. Naturally the clergy looked to their own princes rather than to the popes for their advancement. By the second half of the fourteenth century a duke of Austria said openly: 'In my land I will be pope,' and other rulers were soon to echo him.

At the very time when the papacy had extended both the international organization of the Church and its central control to its greatest extent, the basis of this organization and control was disappearing. The Church had become an all-embracing international organization in an age when few beside the clergy were literate and when the clergy themselves were few. The papacy, through a succession of brilliant politicians and organizers, had used these conditions, and the relative weakness of the secular states, to impose not only its spiritual but also its political and administrative control over the whole Church. In the course of centuries men came to identify this international organization – a strictly temporal although long-term, phenomenon – with the spiritual unity of Christendom.

But Europe grew richer. It could afford more clergy and even an educated laity. The states of Europe and their rulers no longer needed an internationally organized church. (See Ch. 4, p. 230). They were busily founding universities in their own countries to educate the theologians, lawyers and physicians they needed. No longer did it seem as necessary to look to Rome as once it had done. The local clergy felt papal power to be irksome, and laymen felt it to be remote and out of touch with their spiritual needs. Only a fundamental organizational and spiritual reform would now save the international Church.

Historians have sometimes blamed Boniface VIII or Innocent III or even Gregory VII for steering the Church onto a wrong path. But this is to misunderstand the nature of the religious, moral and political problems these popes faced and the conceivable decisions they could take. Neither they nor any of their contemporaries could foresee that the growth of prosperity, the diffusion of lay education and the increasing powers of the state within its boundaries would erode the economic, cultural and political bases of the splendid edifice they were constructing.

Of course, no one even in the fourteenth century could see the problem in these terms, but the need for reform was widely felt and increasingly articulated. It came to a head in the Great Schism.

The Great Schism and the councils

In 1376 the pope returned to Rome. In the conclave of 1378 the cardinals under pressure from the Roman mob, elected an Italian, Urban VI. Many of the French cardinals who formed the majority of the college were discontented that, for the first time in the fourteenth century, a Frenchman had not been chosen. More basically, however, the problem was constitutional. The college of cardinals was trying to limit the power of the pope and control papal policy. Urban VI was both autocratic and tactless. The reform of the Church, of which everyone was speaking, should, he proposed, start with the college of cardinals. Constitutionally, the cardinals had no way of stopping him. But papal absolutism, so far from being an element of strength, now proved to be a near-fatal weakness. Within a few months of Urban's election, the French cardinals and one or two others declared him deposed and elected a Frenchman, Clement VII, who took up residence at Avignon again.

Europe now divided its allegiance: France and France's allies, Scotland, Naples and some of the Spanish kingdoms, supported the Avignon popes. France's enemies, notably England, the north Italian states and most of the German princes, supported Rome. Some princes, like the duke of Burgundy, changed sides according to circumstances. It was all completely political and with only a few exceptions, such as the university of Paris, the local clergy were content to accept the decisions of their princes. The theologians of the Sorbonne in Paris argued the need for a council, representing the whole Church, which should restore the unity of the Church and reform it 'in head and members'. Here was a constitutional theory which went much further than the constitutional resistance of the college of cardinals to papal autocracy. The rival popes would have none of it; but, as no end of the schism appeared to be in sight, more and more influential churchmen and secular rulers accepted the Parisian arguments. Finally, and largely under French pressure, the cardinals of the two sides decided to act and summoned a general council to Pisa in 1409.

At this point tragedy turned into farce. The council elected a new pope and deposed both the Avignon and the Roman popes. Both refused to accept deposition and Europe now had three popes. Finally a new council was summoned at Constance under the protection of the emperor, Sigismund.

The council of Constance (1414–18) ended the schism. The three popes were all deposed. The famous eighteenth century historian Edward Gibbon described the case against one of them, John XXIII: 'The most scandalous charges were suppressed; the vicar of Christ was only accused of piracy, murder, rape, sodomy and incest; . . .'[8] This time the depositions were made to stick. To prevent the recurrence of a schism or other such scandals the fathers assembled at Constance declared the superiority of the general council over the papacy and provided for regular meetings of such councils. Then they elected a new pope, Martin V.

326

The restored papacy and the universality of the Church

The schism was healed and the universal Church was given the opportunity for both structural and moral reform. Knowing of the Protestant Reformation which broke the unity of western Christendom a hundred years later, we can easily see that it was the Church's last chance. At the time this was not so obvious. A system of regular general councils would have turned the papacy into a kind of constitutional monarchy and it might have revived the interest and concern of the national and local churches and their clergy in the government of the universal Church. Men were aware of the analogy between councils and representative assemblies in secular states. But even those who were thus aware saw conciliarism mainly as a practical means of preventing new scandals such as the schism. Martin V (1417–31) and Eugenius IV (1431–47) for their part saw their role as restorers of papal authority against the new and unprecedented claims of the conciliarists. The history of the new councils, summoned to Basle, Ferrara and Florence (1431–49) was therefore one of a struggle for power with the papacy. But the councils were too disunited. Radical lower clergy attacked conservative prelates. Most delegations were under the thumb of their respective kings and voted in accordance with their power political interests. Some of the best minds of the age, such as Nicholas of Cusa, who had begun as convinced conciliarists, despaired of the narrow-mindedness and factionalism shown in the councils and transferred their allegiance to the absolutist papacy.

By contrast the popes pursued their policy with single-minded skill and were able to score some impressive successes. They and their ally, the emperor, contained and then defeated the Hussites (see below, pp. 331–33). At Florence, in 1439, they re-united the Greek Orthodox Church with Rome and followed this up by reunions with other eastern Christian Churches. In the east, these unions caused more confusion than help and they were soon disowned when it became clear that the west would do little to help them against the Ottoman Turks. But in the west it seemed a great triumph for the papacy.

By the middle of the fifteenth century the papacy had won. But it was a hollow victory. The European kingdoms had not given up the control over their clergy which they had won in the fourteenth century and this clergy now remained only minimally interested in Rome. In the next century most of them would follow their rulers into whatever theological territory they chose to lead them. The popes themselves lost interest in the universal Church and came to act as Italian princes in the interests of their families. The Church, in its fifteenth-century form of a universal institution headed by an autocratic papacy, had outlived its usefulness.

Up to a point, men saw this clearly enough, but only up to a point; kings and their advisers saw little harm in ignoring or even opposing the pope. They did not think that such action would break the unity of the Church. A thousand years of history had conditioned Christians to think of the universal Church as an eternal institution. The idea that, at least in its familiar form, it was a historical phenomenon, could hardly enter their minds. It did not even enter the minds of the Protestants in the sixteenth century. What continued to agitate men's minds, as it had done for a long time, was the problem of moral reform of the clergy and the pastoral activities of the Church. But here, too, the papacy and the Church as a universal institution proved inadequate.

New forms of religious life

It is impossible to say definitely whether it was the growing prosperity of Europe and the spread of education which produced new religious sensibilities. But it seems at least likely. The contrast between the riches of the Church, the life-style of its prelates and the life-style of ordinary men had been acceptable in a relatively primitive agrarian society. It was no longer so in the sophisticated urban society of the later Middle Ages. Precisely as life was becoming a little easier many people began to reject the quest for money. They began looking for a more personal

Plate 5.7 *Dance of Death*: **fifteenth-century German engraving.**
This German engraving of the second half of the fifteenth century presents several of the most popular medieval allegories. Blind Fortune turns her wheel on which men rise – only to fall eventually into the grave. On the right, the Tree of Life is shown in its earthly frailty, for rats gnaw its roots and Death shoots men and women of the three estates indifferently with his arrow. Yet both Life and Death are providentially under the eye of Christ, top left.

spirituality, and demanded a more austere life, if not always from themselves then at least from their spiritual leaders. Already in the twelfth and thirteenth centuries the Cathar and Albigensian heresy had spread precisely in the economically most advanced and urbanized parts of Europe, northern Italy and southern France (see Ch. 4, p. 247). St Francis' movement had been accepted within the Church only against strong conservative opposition in the Church hierarchy. Those of the Franciscan Order, the Spirituals, who proclaimed their belief in the need for absolute poverty, were condemned for heresy. (see Ch. 4, pp. 245–47). Yet much of Christian Europe sympathized at least with their attack on the property of the Church. The letters of two very different women, the aristocratic Bridget of Sweden and the artisan's daughter, Catherine of Siena, show the prevalence in all classes of society of criticism of the riches and worldliness of the Church. Against the outward rules of the Church St Catherine stressed a personal, inward piety. Thus, characteristically, she wrote to the wife of a tailor of her acquaintance:

> If you can make time for prayer, then I beg you to do so. Love in charity all rational creatures. Further I beg you, do not fast except on days prescribed by the Holy Church – if you can. But if you do not feel able to fast, leave it alone. . . . When the heat (of summer) is past, you may fast also on days dedicated to the Virgin, if you can manage it, but not more often. . . . Try to increase your holy longings, but leave other exercises alone.[9]

Both Bridget and Catherine remained strictly orthodox and were later canonized. But the papacy found it more and more difficult to accept such criticism. At best it tended to remain aloof from the new and popular religious movements with their emphasis not on the grandeur of the Church but on personal salvation. These movements took many forms. They would emphasize man's inescapable death, a fate reserved for the mighty and the lowly alike, and hence the need to die a 'good' Christian death. A vast new literature on the 'art of dying' became immensely popular in the generations that experienced the Black Death and its sequels. In scores of cathedrals and country churches walls were decorated with Dances of Death: Death represented as a leering skeleton leading a procession of pope and emperor, through the orders of society, to peasant and beggar.

Woodcuts (another Chinese invention which became popular

in Europe around 1400) proved to be a favourite method of prop-
agating the picture of the Dance of Death and its chilling
message. But equally popular were the handbooks on the pursuit
of a Christian life by the individual in the sense of a personal and
inner piety rather than the observation of the Church's rituals.
Such a life-style also had a special appeal to women; for it
emphasized the importance of the individual for that half of
mankind which had been relegated by the Church to a largely
passive role in spiritual matters.

Wycliffe and Huss

The conservatives in the Church hierarchy and among its theologians who looked sourly on these religious movements were
not, however, unjustified in their fears and suspicions. From the
year 1378 the Oxford theologian John Wycliffe (c. 1330–84)
published books proposing the transformation of the Church
hierarchy into a community of believers and, on the theological
level, denying the doctrine of transubstantiation. The two views
were clearly related, as they were to be in most later Protestant
teaching. Transubstantiation is the doctrine of the true transformation of the bread and wine in communion into the body and
blood of Christ through the special spiritual powers which Christ
had granted to the Church and through the sacrament of holy
orders to the priest. Belief in this sacrament is central to belief in
salvation. Deny the reality of the transformation and you under-
mine the very basis of the spiritual position of the Church and
the priesthood as the sole guardians of the keys to the kingdom
of heaven. This was heresy. To the conservatives in the Church
such heresy followed almost inevitably from the new religious
movements even when these were, strictly speaking, perfectly
orthodox.

What made it even worse was the social and political resonance
of the heresies. Wycliffe's views were picked up by the rebellious
peasants of 1381; and although the peasants were defeated and
Wycliffe's teachings were condemned, his views persisted in
some parts of England until the Reformation. More important,
however, was their diffusion on the Continent and especially in
Bohemia. Here they merged with social and national aspirations
against the Germans who dominated the Bohemian towns as they
dominated the economic and civic life of most central and

331

northern European towns. This was an old story, voiced very neatly in an anonymous Czech pamphlet of 1325:

> Oh, my God, the foreigner is favoured; the native is trampled upon. The normal and proper thing is for the bear to stay in his forest, the wolf in his cave, the fish in the sea, and the German in Germany. In that way the world would have some peace.[10]

The leader of the movement was John Huss (1369–1415), the principal of the university of Prague. He was sympathetic to some of Wycliffe's teachings, especially his attacks on the worldliness of the Church and on the position of the papacy; but he differed from the English theologian in his interpretation of transubstantiation where he remained orthodox. Recently Catholic historians have doubted whether any of his views were really heretical. But in 1415 the council of Constance, to which he had been summoned with a safe conduct from the emperor Sigismund, condemned him as a heretic. No doubt the fathers at the council, having just deposed three popes, were anxious to demonstrate their orthodoxy and also, no doubt, they were frightened by the growing hostility to the established Church. They induced Sigismund to break his word to Huss on the grounds that faith did not have to be kept with heretics, i.e. those who had already broken faith with God. Huss was burnt at the stake.

This was the signal for the Bohemians to rebel. Five times imperial and papal 'crusading' armies invaded the country and five times they were beaten off. The Bohemians, in their turn, took the offensive, and their dreaded waggon fortresses rolled through Germany and Poland, spreading terror and destruction in their wake. But the Bohemians were not united. The nobility and the conservative Hussites who wanted political control of their own country and communion in both kinds for the laity (in Catholic tradition only the priest drank the wine) quarrelled more and more violently with the radical and popular wing of the Hussites who wanted to set up Christ's millennium on earth, with equal political rights for everyone and with common property. Finally, the conservatives came to terms with the council of Basle and the emperor Sigismund and then defeated the radicals in open battle (1434). The descendants of the radical Hussites, in one of those transformations which were to become common in the centuries after the Reformation, were the Moravian Brethren who were to play a highly respectable role in Germany and in

America in the eighteenth and nineteenth centuries. But in the fifteenth century it was the bitterness of the mutual cruelties of Hussites and Catholics that persisted – a deadly foretaste of the wars of religion of the sixteenth and seventeenth centuries. In Bohemia itself it also spelt the end of effective co-operation between the different classes of the population and thus, in the long run, doomed the cause of independence and of resistance to the absolutism of the later Habsburg kings.

Catholic Europe and the outside world

Not since the tenth century had Catholic Europe been so completely on the defensive against the outside world as it was in the last two centuries of the Middle Ages. The crusades and the Spanish reconquest had come to an end. Conversion of northern and eastern Europe was virtually complete. For most people this seems to have been a perfectly acceptable state of affairs. For the educated, however, it did not mean a lack of interest in the outside world. This was, on the contrary, perhaps greater than ever before.

It is a curious and still widespread myth that people in the later Middle Ages believed the earth was flat. From the early Middle Ages, it is true, we have some representations of the earth as a flat wagon wheel, with Jerusalem at the centre. But the Greek view of the earth as a sphere was never completely lost. Aristotle knew that the earth was a sphere and he gave at least a correct order of magnitude for its size. This size had been calculated, even before Aristotle's day, by observing the angles at which well-known stars appeared when travelling north and south. One of the difficulties of transmitting such knowledge accurately was the variations in the units of measurement which people used, difficulties compounded by the problem of translation from Greek or Persian into Arabic and then Latin. As early as 813 the works of the second-century Greek astronomer Ptolemy were translated into Arabic and by the thirteenth century they were completely accepted in the Latin west. Dante, for instance, in his poem *The Divine Comedy*, descends with the Roman poet Virgil to the centre of the spherical earth which, in his poem, is also the utmost pit of hell where they find Satan constantly devouring the two most wicked traitors in history, Brutus and Judas Iscariot.

333

La figur
et la disposicion
du monde le
nombre & ordre
des elemens &
les mouvemes
des corps du ciel apptiement a sa
voir a tout home qui est de franche
condicion et de nobble engin. Et est
bele chose et delectable profitable
& honeste et aveucq ce est neccessaire

pour savoir plus et p especial p̄
astrologie. Et pres afin que le engin
humain peüst plus legierement
tele chose comprendre les sages
anciens composerent ent les autres
un instrument qui est appellé
esper materiel ou artificiel se q̄l
on peut regarder tout en tour m̄
ouvoir et tourner et y considerer
en ptie la disposicion & le mouve
ment du monde & du ciel aussi

More important to medieval Europeans were some of the implications of a spherical earth. Could one travel to or in the southern hemisphere at all? Some influential fathers of the Church thought not. Lactantius, in the early fourth century, argued:

> Can anyone possibly be so stupid as to believe that there are men who walk with their feet up and their heads down? Or that there (on the opposite side of the globe) all that with us lies on the ground is upside down? That crops and trees grow downwards? That rain, snow and hail fall upward to the earth?[11]

St Augustine, as one would expect, was more circumspect. He certainly believed in a spherical earth but thought that it was not necessary to believe in the existence of the antipodes (people living in the southern hemisphere), since the bible made no mention of them. There was no readily accessible experience of ventures to the southern hemisphere. With few exceptions, the Europeans did not get beyond the shores of the Mediterranean and the Black Sea. The existence of the river Niger, in western Africa, was known, though it was held to be an arm of the Nile. In practice, the Arabs had a monopoly of the caravan routes across the Sahara and it was they who supplied the Europeans with black slaves. By the fifteenth century they had an equal monopoly of the trade of the Indian Ocean with Europe, through the Persian Gulf and the Red Sea.

Yet some Europeans penetrated into Asia and their accounts were avidly read at home. The most famous was that of the Venetian Marco Polo who spent the years 1271 to 1295 in the Far East and whose book of his travels became an immediate 'best seller' in Europe. He was evidently a fine observer and an assiduous

Plate 5.8   The spherical earth: Oresme and his armillary sphere.
Nicole d'Oresme (c. 1325–82) was the outstanding mathematician and economist of the fourteenth century. He was master of the Collège de Navarre in the university of Paris and, later, bishop of Lisieux. Charles V of France employed him as his chaplain and as a consultant on the coinage. Oresme translated Aristotle's *Ethics, Politics and Economics* from Latin into French but he did not accept the Aristotelian theory of the movement of the heavens around a stationary earth. He could not, however, provide the mathematical model which Copernicus worked out for the movement of the earth around the sun, 150 years later. The armillary sphere was a device, going back to the second century AD, of teaching the nature of the heavens.

listener; and if he was sometimes credulous and if some of his stories were fantastical and raised the eyebrows of the more sceptical, the majority of his readers were delighted with his tales. They also kept alive the comforting belief that the rulers of the east might become Christians. 'On the Great Khan's own showing', Marco Polo wrote, 'he regards as truest and best the faith of the Christians, because he declares that it commands nothing that is not full of all goodness and holiness.' But Kublai Khan would not actually become a Christian and explained it like this:

> You see that the Christians who live in these parts are so ignorant that they accomplish nothing and are powerless. And you see that these idolaters do whatever they will; and when I sit at table the cups in the middle of the hall come to me full of wine or other beverages without anyone touching them, and I drink from them. They banish bad weather in any direction they choose and perform many marvels. And, as you know, their idols speak and give them such predictions as they ask. But, if I am converted to the faith of Christ . . ., then my barons and others who do not embrace the faith of Christ will say to me: 'What has induced you to undergo baptism and adopt the faith of Christ? What virtues or what miracles have you seen to his credit?' For these idolaters declare that what they do they do by their holiness and by virtue of their idols. Then I should not know what to answer, which would be a grave error in their eyes.[12]

The mixture of rational argument and the magic of the east was irresistible.

In England, Sir John Mandeville in the middle of the fourteenth century had a similar success with his even more fantastical *Travels*. But Mandeville did believe in a spherical earth. While most Europeans were perfectly comfortable in their self-satisfied isolation from the outside world, they were at least willing to look out of the window and expected to see something more interesting than the everyday world around them. Nor is this surprising. Polo and Mandeville still make excellent reading.

Byzantium and the Ottoman Turks

There was one important exception to the generally peaceful relations between Christians and Muslims in this period. This was

336

the steady conquest of the provinces of the Byzantine Empire (centred again in Constantinople after its reconquest from the Latins in 1261) by the Ottoman Turks. They derived their name from their leader Osman (1288–1326) but did not otherwise differ greatly from the Turks in the other principalities who, by the end of the thirteenth century, had conquered virtually the whole of Asia Minor. They were all Muslims and they were *gazis*, fighters for Allah and for themselves. The Ottomans, however, had the most gifted leaders and showed the greatest ability to underpin their military states with stable, city-based administrations, borrowed from Byzantium and from the great central Asian Turkish empires.

By the middle of the fourteenth century they had gained a foot-hold on the European side of the Dardanelles and from there advanced steadily into Greece and the Balkans. They defeated the Bulgars and the Serbs and annihilated an army of west European volunteers at Nicopolis in 1396. It was the most serious attempt by Catholic Christendom to come to the aid of the eastern Christians, but its abject failure did nothing to persuade the west to make greater efforts.

With the conquest of Christian countries, the power-base of the Ottoman state gradually began to change. The Ottoman Turks were tolerant of the religious beliefs of their subjects. Once the initial horrors of conquest and plunder were past, their rule was often less oppressive than the highly developed tax administration of Byzantium. Just as in the first century of Arab-Muslim conquests, so now, in the fourteenth and fifteenth centuries, many Christians chose not to fight the Turks or even to fight with them. The Ottoman sultans – the caliph of Baghdad granted them this title after the victory of Nicopolis – encouraged and developed this tendency. They began systematically to recruit young Christian boys for service either in the administration or in a professional army corps, called the Janissaries. This practice, called *devshirme*, gave the sultans a loyal fighting force which was a political counterbalance to the power of the Turkish notables. Moreover, the *devshirme* stimulated the need for further conquests of Christian lands and therefore the aggressive policies of the Ottomans.

In the long run, Byzantium was unable to resist this new and formidable expansive force. Imperial politics continued to be dominated by faction fights at court and civil wars between

337

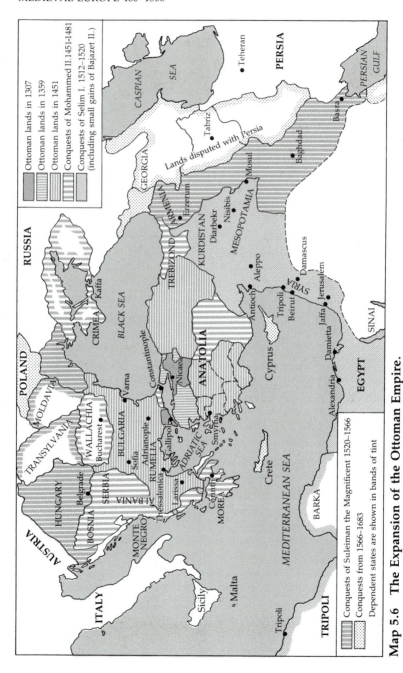

Map 5.6   The Expansion of the Ottoman Empire.

different claimants to the throne. Imperial princes made themselves virtually independent rulers of different parts of Greece. The Genoese and the Venetians continued to tighten their hold on the commerce and on their strategic footholds in the Empire. Worse still, they involved the emperors in their own rivalries and deflected the waning resources of the Empire from defence against the Turks. Four times, in the fourteenth and fifteenth centuries, Byzantine emperors travelled to the west to ask for help in the defence of Christendom. Manuel II (1391–1425) even reached Paris and London. But there was little they could offer in return. Promises to lead the eastern Church back to union with Rome were always immediately repudiated by the Greek clergy. After the disaster of Nicopolis, it seemed as if the fall of Constantinople was imminent.

But the Turks had their own problems. Sultan Bayazid had expanded his dominions not only in Europe but also in eastern Anatolia. Turkish princes whom he had dispossessed fled to Timur's court. The great Mongol-Turkish conqueror decided to deal with the dangerous new power on his western flank. In 1402, at Ankara in central Anatolia (and now the capital of modern Turkey) Timur's army crushed Bayazid. The sultan had been deserted by his own Muslim lords and ironically had had to rely on his Christian troops.

Although Timur did little to exploit his victory, preferring to turn again to the conquest of northern India, he had in fact saved Byzantium for another fifty years. But a genuine revival of the old eastern Roman Empire was no longer possible. Political horizons and religious passions had become too narrow and self-indulgent. When a number of the Greek intellectual élite negotiated a reunion of the Christian churches with the popes in the councils of Ferrara and Florence, in 1439, they were again repudiated in Constantinople.

The fall of Constantinople

In the meantime the Turks had conquered most of the Balkan peninsula up to the Danube. Where formerly they had been content to leave the Christian rulers of the Serbs and Bulgars in position as vassals of the sultan, they now annexed Serbia and Bulgaria outright. A final western 'crusade' reached Varna on the Black Sea in 1444. The Serbians, however, refused to fight their

Turkish overlords and the Venetians, on whose fleet the crusaders were relying, preferred to keep their good relations with the Turks in order to safeguard their commerce.

In 1453 a new and energetic young sultan, Mehmed II, moved against Constantinople itself. The huge walls which over the centuries had resisted so many invaders, crumbled before the sultan's big guns. On 29 May 1453 Constantinople fell to the Turks. The last emperor, Constantine IX, died fighting, and the history of the great Roman Empire finally came to an end, a thousand years after the fall of Rome itself.

Unlike the causes of the collapse of the western part of the Roman Empire, in the fifth century, those of the collapse of Byzantium, in the fifteenth, are not controversial. The fourth crusade and continued western interference in and exploitation of the Byzantine Empire fatally weakened its power base. The fundamental hostility and aggressiveness of the Slavonic states of the Balkan peninsula never allowed the emperors to concentrate on the Muslims for more than short periods of time. Finally, the instability of the imperial political system, the excessively privileged position of the Church and the tendency for the land, and with land wealth and political power, to fall more and more into the hands of a small group of families – all this reduced the powerful and efficiently administered Byzantine Empire to little more than a Mediterranean city state, without the commercial vitality of Venice or Florence. All such city states, even the Italian ones and the autonomous Flemish communes, were vulnerable to determined attacks by great territorial states with large professional armies. They all suffered defeat and, most of them, capture, in the second half of the fifteenth and the beginning of the sixteenth centuries.[13] The fall of Constantinople was, however, more than the fall of a city state and of the last survivor of a great empire. It meant that, at the very moment when Catholic Europe was embarking on its great expansion overseas, it found itself in an inglorious and most dangerous defensive position in its very heartland.

Conclusion

The Black Death put an end to more than three centuries of population growth, of economic expansion, of the founding of cities and of the ploughing up of forest and heathland such as had not been experienced since the barbarians broke into the Roman Empire. Yet plague destroyed neither the wealth of the land nor men's skills. For those who survived, life often became easier, food and clothing more plentiful. Serfdom gradually disappeared in western and southern Europe. But progress was uneven and men's and women's hold on life remained precarious, for the plagues recurred; and if it was not the wrath of God which people had to suffer, then it was only too often the pride of princes, their pitiless tax gatherers and their marauding and murderous soldiers. Against these and other injustices men now began to rebel and often they sought their justification in new and heretical beliefs.

Just as feudalism disintegrated at the level of the manor and the seigneurie with the gradual disappearance of serfdom, so it was transformed at the level of lordship with the gradual disappearance of the military obligations of vassalage. At both levels a more varied and flexible relationship, in which money payments came to play an increasingly important role, superseded the rigidities of feudalism. At the same time, increasing wealth, the spread of education and the growing power of princes undermined the need for an internationally organized church – a church which was caught in attitudes that had earlier led to its greatest triumphs but which now prevented it from changing with changing circumstances. This was an age of violence and sudden death, an age when life became both richer and more precarious, more varied and more uncertain, an age when Europe, between the end of the crusades and the beginnings of overseas expansion, turned its energies in on itself. But the most dynamic part of this society, the cities, will be discussed in the next chapter.

References and Notes

1. Thomas Walsingham, *Historia Anglicana*, trans. Harry E. Wedeck in *Putnam's Dark and Middle Ages Reader*. Capricorn Books: New York 1965, pp. 84–85.
2. Giovanni Boccaccio, *Il Decameron*, trans. D. & P. Herlihy, quoted in D. Herlihy (ed.) *Medieval Culture and Society*. Harper Torch Books: New York 1968, p. 355.

3. See A. Briggs, *Modern Europe 1789–1980*; History of Europe. Longman: (not yet published).
4. P. de Commynes, *Les Mémoires*, Bk 5, Ch. 19.
5. Sir John Fortescue, in *The Governance of England*, C. Plummer (ed.) Oxford 1885, pp. 114–15.
6. Armin Wolf, 'Les deux Lorraines et l'origine des princes électeurs du Saint-Empire', *Francia* 1983 (1984), **11**, pp. 241–56.
7. See A. Briggs, *Modern Europe 1789–1980*; History of Europe. Longman: (not yet published).
8. E. Gibbon, *The Decline and Fall of the Roman Empire*. Methuen: London 1906, Vol. 7, Ch. 70, p. 19.
9. From Louise Gnädinger (ed.) *Caterina von Siena*. Olten und Freiburg 1980, p. 96.
10. Quoted in S. Harrison Thompson, *Czechoslovakia in European History*. Frank Cass: London, 1965, p. 137.
11. Quoted in E. G. R. Taylor, *Ideas on the Shape, Size and Movements of the Earth*. Historical Association Pamphlet.
12. *The Travels of Marco Polo*, trans. Ronald Latham. Penguin Books: Harmondsworth 1982, pp. 119–20.
13. See H. G. Koenigsberger, *Early Modern Europe 1500–1789*; History of Europe. Longman: London 1987, Ch. 2.

Chapter **6**

Medieval City Culture: Central Europe, Italy and the Renaissance, 1300–1500

The cities of the Later Middle Ages

European society in the Later Middle Ages was still an essentially agrarian society. Not more than 10 or, at most, 15 per cent of its population lived in cities, and most of these were small (see Ch. 4, pp. 213–15). In this respect, European society was no different from that of Islamic, Indian or Chinese society during the same period or of Graeco-Roman society of a thousand years before. The importance of cities however, was much greater than a mere count of their populations would suggest; and this, too, was a world-wide phenomenon.

There are good reasons for this importance. Cities, as we have seen (see Ch. 3, pp. 144–48) had been founded or had grown both as military strong points and refuges under the walls of a castle and also as centres of trade, of manufacturing and of consumption. The building of their walls and towers, their houses and town halls, their parish churches and cathedrals, gave employment to scores and sometimes hundreds of carpenters, masons and stone carvers. Their schools and their universities were superseding the monasteries as centres of learning and of intellectual debate. Their city councils and law courts provided careers for men who had acquired a secular education.

The city therefore acted as a magnet and as an internal frontier to the ambitious and to those who could no longer make their living in the country. In popular medieval literature the young man setting out to make his fortune was a recurring theme; but in real life hidden treasures, magic rings and princesses to be rescued from evil demons were disappointingly rare; this left

343

young men without connections only such prosaic careers as soldiering, settling new land on the hostile eastern frontiers of Christendom or moving into a city. Many immigrants into cities were men of some substance who had sold their land because they thought that the city presented opportunities for bettering themselves. Such a one, for instance, was Hans Fugger, a weaver and small-scale merchant who moved to Augsburg in 1367 and founded the dynasty of millionnaire merchants, mine owners and bankers whose financial support would decide an imperial election in the early sixteenth century[1] and who were to acquire the titles of imperial counts and princes. But the majority of immigrants were poor men from areas where population growth had outrun available land. Facing abject poverty, underemployment and even slow starvation, men moved to cities for the opportunities these could offer. In either case, that of the propertied or the destitute countryman, it would be the young, the most active and the most ambitious who would move into the cities.

Few would realize their ambitions, at least in the first generation. In Coventry, in the early sixteenth century, nearly fifty per cent of the inhabitants could not pay the minimum rate of four pence of the taxes. On the continent conditions were similar, especially in some of the older textile towns, like Ypres in Flanders, which had been hit by the slump following the Black Death. The larger cities, such as Paris and London, already had slums that were as dark, damp, evil-smelling and unhealthy as the more famous slums of the industrial revolution of the early nineteenth century. Sanitation was primitive, water supply through fountains often inadequate, and the regular removal of garbage and the cleaning of streets only began to be organized by some Italian and Netherlands towns in the sixteenth century.

In the sixteenth century a Londoner described the city's poorer quarters as 'dark dens for adulterers, thieves, murderers and every mischief worker'. It is therefore no great wonder that urban

Plate 6.1 San Gimignano.
Italian towns had even more towers than transalpine towns (see the picture of Lübeck, Plate 5.2) although mostly flat-topped. Many were built as urban fortresses and status symbols by the local nobility who brought their families' feuds from the country into the city. In San Gimignano, however, only two noble families came from the country. In 1352 the city accepted Florentine dominion (cf. also Ch. 3).

politics could easily become explosive. In Italian and other Mediterranean cities, in particular, the considerable number of domestic slaves – Slavs, Circassians, Berbers and black Africans – added a further element of discontented humanity who, with an understandable lack of any civic feeling, would happily join in riots or lootings. For local riots in times of scarcity and unemployment were common, and political agitators or popular preachers could give such movements political or religious overtones which made them doubly formidable to the established order.

All this was equally true for the great cities of other societies, for Constantinople, for medieval Córdoba and Cairo, for Baghdad and Samarkand or for Delhi or Peking. But the medieval European city differed from all these in one vital characteristic: its citizens had developed a separate body of law and a concept of citizenship which differed from the various forms of the feudal lord-and-vassal or lord-and-serf relationship of the time (see Ch. 3, p. 144). They had had to do this precisely so that they could properly fulfil their economic functions in an agrarian and feudal world. Passing through the gates of the medieval city one therefore literally passed from one world into another in a sense which happened neither in the ancient nor in our modern industrial city. To achieve this, the citizens of the medieval city had had to fight for autonomy or independence, the right to make and administer their own laws. The high town walls with their massive towers, the church and cathedral spires, and the lordly town halls on the market square represented at once the means of carrying on and protecting the life of the Christian commune and the visual symbols of its autonomy and separateness. Hamburg and Bremen reinforced this symbolism by erecting giant statues of the legendary Roland in front of their town halls. Florence set up a whole series of symbols of liberty in front of its Palazzo Vecchio, of which Donatello's *Marzocco*, the lion of Florence, and his *Judith*, the biblical tyrant slayer, are the most famous.

The politics of the city states

From central Italy, just north of Rome, through Germany to the coasts of the North Sea and the Baltic there was, by 1300, a broad belt of virtually independent city states. This independence had not been achieved without a struggle. The Italian cities had fought the great Frederick Barbarossa to a standstill in the twelfth century and in the thirteenth they had defeated his grandson, Frederick II, and assured the victory of the papacy. In Germany the struggle had been fought directly not so much against the emperor as against the German princes and especially the local prince bishops. Nevertheless, it was the victory of the princes over the emperor which gave the cities, like the princes themselves, their opportunity to achieve virtual independence. In Italy the central monarchy disappeared altogether. In Germany it remained too weak to reassert any effective authority over the larger cities. The independence of the Italian and German city states was therefore a function of the absence or weakness of the central monarchy and of the territorial states. When this condition no longer held, the Italian and German city state would be in immediate danger.

Italy: city imperialism

In Italy this was not the only danger. In the early thirteenth century there were some 200 or 300 independent communes. But very soon the larger ones began to swallow up their smaller neighbours. The process was inevitable. Cities were anxious to control their surrounding countryside in order to assure regular food supplies for their citizens and cheap labour for their entrepreneurs. But subject cities and subject territories also provided additional sources of tax revenue and of soldiers and, hence, power. Even if a city council were not aggressively inclined it would still have to prevent its more powerful and aggressive rivals from adding to their strength by adding to their territories. There was only one effective way of doing this: by doing it oneself. Just such a pattern had appeared among the princes of feudal France already in the eleventh and twelfth centuries, and the mechanism for aggrandisement was the same: the need for each political unit to extend its power in order to prevent its rivals from extending theirs (see Ch. 3, p. 152).

The result, in both cases, was constant wars of aggression for territorial expansion or, at best, alliances and vassalage agreements concluded under the threat of aggression. By the end of the fourteenth century the number of independent communes had been sharply reduced. The most populous, the richest and

347

the strategically most favourably situated cities naturally tended to come out on top. Genoa obtained control of most of the Ligurian coast; Florence extended its rule over a large part of Tuscany; the lords of Milan conquered an extensive state in Lombardy and were beginning to direct their boundless ambitions into central Italy; Venice, which already controlled a large overseas empire of coastal strong points on the Adriatic and in the Levant, was half, but only half, reluctantly countering Milanese aggression by a territorial expansion of its own in the lower Po valley. In between, the marquises (later dukes) of Mantua, the dukes of Ferrara and other princes managed to maintain smaller states by superior military skills, by the ownership of virtually impregnable fortress-cities (e.g. Mantua) and by skilful diplomacy.

By the middle of the fifteenth century the Italian states had reached a certain equilibrium, and the 'big five' (the king of Naples, the pope, the duke of Milan, and the republics of Venice and Florence) agreed on the maintenance of this equilibrium. It was then that the concept and metaphor of a balance of power was first used by politicians. It provided some safeguard for the now relatively few surviving smaller city states. But, as it was to do frequently afterwards in European and, eventually, world politics, it could also be interpreted in terms of spheres of influence (in the fifteenth century in the form of alliances) and in terms of a tacit agreement that further successful aggrandisement by any one of the great powers would give the others the right to a compensating aggrandisement.

Diplomacy

It was in such circumstances that the Italians invented the methods and practices of modern diplomacy. Embassies were as old as power politics; but they were sent for special occasions; to conclude an alliance, a peace treaty, or perhaps a princely marriage. But the power-political relationships of the fifteenth-century Italian states were so complex, the need for accurate and quick information of the often rapidly changing circumstances and policies of one's neighbours was so urgent that states began to accredit permanent ambassadors with their neighbours. Just so had the great banking and trading firms of the period established their 'factors' in foreign cities in order both to obtain a constant flow of information and to have agents at hand to carry out commercial instructions from headquarters.

The new 'permanent' diplomacy took time to establish itself. It was expensive and many governments were at first reluctant to admit so near to their centre of power a foreigner whom they often rightly suspected of being both a spy and an intriguer. But, once invented, the new diplomacy proved too useful to neglect. First the Italian states and then, from the turn of the fifteenth century, all the great powers of western Europe established permanent embassies in the more important capitals. With a time-lag of some fifty to a hundred years the powers of eastern Europe followed suit. It was an essential condition for the widening of Italian-style power politics, with its system of multiple alliances, to the whole of Europe and, in our present century, to the whole world. So effective has been this system that, apart from the technical means of communication between ambassadors and their governments, it has changed remarkably little over the last 500 years, not excluding the early habit of embassy staffs of engaging in spying and meddling in the politics of their host country. Seen historically, modern diplomacy was a remarkable advance in the rationalization of politics, a 'continuation of war by other means', (to reverse the famous aphorism of the nineteenth-century military writer, Clausewitz). To the modern historian it has proved a godsend. Where up to the fifteenth century he has to rely mainly on chronicles, the new diplomatic correspondence has provided him with an enormously rich source of information not only on the international politics of European governments and on the basis of their decision-making but also on the internal economic and political life of the different European countries as observed by foreign ambassadors.

Internal conflicts

Inside the cities, power was in the hands of a greater or smaller group of property owners. Originally they were a mixed group consisting of both successful merchants and feudal nobility, who came to form a patriciate, or privileged ruling class. Although they engaged in commerce or banking, they considered themselves aristocrats rather than bourgeois. There was no split between landed and commercial wealth. Those who had done well in foreign trade always tended to invest at least a part, and

349

sometimes the whole, of their capital in land. For land was much safer than ships or merchandise and it provided both added social status and a regular income for the successful merchant. Politically, the patricians operated in extended family groups or clans, and their feuds and vendettas dominated city politics, just as their fortified palaces and the square towers which they built, both for defence and for prestige, dominated the city scapes.

Frequently the patricians were opposed by the 'popular' party, also always considerable property owners who did not, however, belong to the privileged families. Sometimes the craft guilds gained a foothold in city councils, but only rarely did the common people become directly involved in politics, and then usually as the result of definite popular revolts, such as that of 1378 in Florence.

So bitter were the feuds and faction fights, so terrible in the eyes of civic patriots was banishment, the common penalty for losing such fights, that in city after city men came to accept as a lesser evil the rule of a *signore*, a despot. These despots were usually the aristocratic and military leaders of one of the factions. Once established, they sought to fortify their position by obtaining recognition and, eventually, princely titles from the emperor or the pope. By the turn of the fourteenth century the majority of the surviving city states had changed from republican to princely regimes.

Florence: republican liberty and the Medici

Not everyone, however, was content to lose his political liberty, even if it was only the liberty of an oligarchy. Around 1400 the republic of Florence found itself fighting almost alone, against the aggression of the dukes of Milan. The advantages of easy submission were considerable, and many favoured it. It was then that a number of Florentine intellectuals, some of them occupying high offices in the republic, formulated a theoretical defence of civic freedom and postulated the need for scholars to leave their ivory towers and take an active part in civic life in the defence of political freedom. This was something quite new. On a scholarly level it meant, for the first time, an appreciation of the Roman Republic (and not only of the Roman Empire) and in particular a revaluation of the writings and politics of Cicero. Only a generation earlier the poet and scholar Petrarch (1304–74), on discovering Cicero's political letters, had voiced a typically medieval regret:

> Why didst thou desire so much effort and forsake the calm so becoming to thy age, thy position and thy destiny? What vain splendour of renown drove thee . . . to a death unworthy of a sage? . . . . . Oh, how much more suitable would it have been if thou, philosopher as thou wast, hadst grown old in rural surroundings, and there hadst meditated upon eternal life and not upon this trifling existence here below![2]

Now, however, Cicero's defence of the Roman Republic was extolled, together with Brutus whom, a hundred years earlier, Dante had consigned into the very jaws of Satan. The learned chancellor of Florence, Coluccio Salutati (1331–1406), wrote of republics:

> The hope of winning public honours is the same for all, provided they possess industry and natural gifts, and lead a serious-minded and respected way of life . . . it is marvellous to see how powerful this access to public office, once it is offered to a free people, proves to be in awakening the talents of the citizen. For when men are given the hope of attaining honour in the state, they take courage and raise themselves to a higher plane; when they are deprived of that hope, they grow idle and lose their strength.[3]

Another fifteenth-century Florentine made the same point even more succinctly: 'That philosophy seems to me always ripe and superior which dwells in cities and shuns solitude.'

The precise significance of such writings of the 'civic humanists', as they have come to be called, has been a matter of recent controversy. But the esteem in which the civic humanists of Renaissance Florence were held by their contemporaries and by succeeding generations suggests that their defence of the active political life, this worldly slant of their thinking, was finding strong echoes among the educated élite of the fifteenth century and was one more sign of the turning away from the other-worldly ideals of the medieval Church.

Florence managed to fight off the Milanese menace, only to find her internal liberty compromised. First one then another leading family came to dominate her politics. From 1434 onwards it was the house of Medici, the richest banking and merchant house of the city. Over a period of sixty years, first Cosimo de Medici and then his grandson, Lorenzo the Magnificent, consoli-

Plate 6.2 *Marzocco* **(above), and** *Judith* **by Donatello (opposite).**
Donatello's *Judith* was placed by the Medici in their own Medici-
Ricardi Palace with the republican and anti-princely motto: 'Kingdoms
fall through luxury; cities rise through virtue. Behold the proud neck
felled by the arm of the humble.' When the Florentines temporarily
overthrew Medici rule of their city, in 1494, they placed the *Judith* in
front of their town hall, the Palazzo Vecchio, next to the lion *Marzocco*,
the city's symbol of liberty and its heraldic device of the fleur-de-lis on
the lion's shield. 'Marzocco' probably comes from Martocus, little
Mars. The god was held to be first patron of Florence.

dated their political power until it was little different from that of other Italian despots. Machiavelli, in his *History of Florence*, described their methods unflatteringly but realistically:

> When Cosimo had returned [from exile to which his opponents had driven him], those who had brought him back and many injured citizens designed . . . to make sure of their state. And the Signoria [the ruling council] which attained authority in November and December (1434), not content with what its predecessor had done for the (Medici) party, extended the imprisonment of many and imprisoned many others . . . in some cases blood was spilt (for one person was immediately executed and the Venetians were persuaded to extradite four others for execution). This gave the party a great reputation and inspired enormous terror in its enemies, seeing that such a powerful republic (as Venice) should have sold its liberty to the Florentines.
>
> [In fact, Machiavelli thought the Venetians did it to deepen the divisions in Florence.] When the city had been rid of their enemies or those who were suspect to the state, the Medici rewarded new people, in order to encourage their party . . . all the nobility except a very few were reduced to the order of commoners; the property of rebels was divided up. Apart from these measures, they strengthened their position with laws and new ordinances and they prearranged new elections by excluding from the lists their enemies and filling them up with their friends . . . and they saw to it that magistrates who had capital jurisdiction should always be among the principal members of their party . . . and if any word, any sign (cenno) or any usage of those who governed was in any way criticised, this was most severely punished.[4]

Yet so strong were the republican traditions of Florence that Cosimo and Lorenzo had to run the state in the guise of private citizens and with the republican institutions apparently intact. Few were deceived.

Great power intervention in Italy and the end of the Florentine republic

Throughout the fifteenth century one or other of the Italian states had toyed with the idea of upsetting the balance of power by inviting the intervention of one of the great non-Italian powers. For a long time Italy was saved from such intervention by the weakness of her neighbours and their preoccupation with their own problems. But in the last decade of the fifteenth century, this

Smaller independent states
Republic of Venice
Papal states

Map 6.1 Italy in the fifteenth century.

situation changed. The French monarchy had defeated the English and successfully asserted itself against the dukes of Burgundy and other overmighty vassals. The Spanish monarchy, created by the union of the crowns of Aragon and Castile, had conquered Granada, the last Moorish stronghold in the peninsula (1492). The Swiss, riding on the crest of the wave of military success after their dramatic defeat of the duke of Burgundy (1476–77) began to harbour ambitions in Lombardy; and the emperor, Maximilian I, baffled by strong opposition in the Netherlands and in Germany, turned his restless and ill-supported energies to the possibility of achieving fame and conquests on the Adriatic coast. For all their dislike of the outside 'barbarians', the

355

divided Italian states were politically and psychologically incapable of uniting against the foreigners. From this time onwards the internal history of the Italian states became inextricably confused with the power politics of the European states, and more and more the Italians lost control over their own destinies.

This became immediately apparent in Florence when, in 1494, Charles VIII of France marched his army through Italy to revive the old Angevin claim to the kingdom of Naples. The Medici made the mistake of first opposing and then grovelling to Charles VIII and the popular party and the republicans promptly overthrew and exiled the Medici. From this moment the republicans were bound to rely on French support and the Medici on the support of the enemies of France.

For a few years Florence foreshadowed Geneva in accepting the moral and political domination of a preacher, the Dominican friar Girolamo Savonarola. But this 'prophet unarmed', as Machiavelli was to call him, built up no political party or military power to institutionalize his rule. Through the hostility of the pope whose morals he had attacked, he was overthrown and burnt at the stake (1498) – a foretaste, in the most civilized city of Europe, of a passion that was to sweep Europe in the following century.

For a decade and a half the Florentine republic manoeuvred uneasily between the great powers, hamstrung by a financially ruinous and ideologically indefensible war against rebellious Pisa. In 1512 the Medici marched into Florence at the head of a papal and Spanish army. Once more they were expelled, in 1527, when a Medici pope, Clement VII, was a prisoner of the emperor Charles V.[5] But the last Florentine republic was doomed as soon as Clement VII and the emperor were reconciled. Once more, and this time for good, papal and Spanish arms restored Medici rule in a city torn more cruelly than ever by internal factions and class struggles (1530). Within a few years the Medici felt strong enough to break with their old tradition and acquire titles, first of dukes of Florence and, later, of grand-dukes of Tuscany.

Machiavelli and Italian political thought

Florence, the epicentre of the Renaissance, provided also the most brilliant intellectual analysis of its dramatic political history. In letters, treatises, political dialogues and histories, Florentine intellectuals discussed the problems of their city and the reasons for the failure of the republic. Their most brilliant exponent was Niccolò Machiavelli (1469–1527), one time high civil servant and leader of diplomatic missions for the republic before the first return of the Medici in 1512. In his most famous treatise, *The Prince* (1513), Machiavelli analysed the conditions and courses of action that would make a prince successful in acquiring and holding a state. Its theme is the necessity for unsentimental and even completely amoral realism. Savonarola's fall had made a profound impression on Machiavelli and he concluded that

> Many men have imagined states and principalities such as no one ever saw or knew in the real world; the manner in which we live and that in which we ought to live are so widely different, that he who leaves what is done to pursue that which should be done learns rather how to ruin than to save himself.

Hence, a prince 'should hold to what is right when he can, but must know how to do evil when he must.'[6]

It is not surprising that both Machiavelli's contemporaries and later generations found his advice profoundly shocking. Breach of faith, deceit and cruelty were of course nothing new in politics. But they had always been held to be breaches of the Christian virtues to which all men, including princes, were required to aspire. Machiavelli not only let the cat of common political practice out of the bag, he set it over the Christian lamb by declaring that this was how successful politics *should* be conducted. This was unforgivable, but it could not be ignored. In his later writings Machiavelli himself had some doubts about the effects of the rule of a truly 'Machiavellian' prince. At least Machiavelli was a republican and an admirer of the Roman Republic.

From about the middle of the sixteenth century Italian writers on politics developed the theory of reason of state by which Machiavellian precepts were tamed and legitimized by linking them firmly to the good of the state. These writers stressed the rationality of statecraft and divorced the moral precepts which applied to private individuals from those which applied to the state. There was a significant shift of vocabulary to such comfortably familiar concepts as duty and the common weal. By the end of the sixteenth and in the seventeenth century the theory of reason of state had taken on a distinctly religious and moralistic flavour.

'If people are unreasonable,' so runs an anonymous English pamphlet of the period, 'then must the prince bow for a time and little by little bring them to his purpose by some craft or by some holy pretence.'[7]

For about two decades after the fall of the last Florentine republic the Florentine historians and political theorists continued their passionate discussion of the reasons for the failure of the republic. Most were agreed in blaming the relentless social and party strife. But the generation of writers who had themselves lived through this crisis found no successors. The Medici dukes, like most Italian princes of the sixteenth century introduced a rigid and formal court life on the Spanish model. Their politics became increasingly absolutist, and so the inspiration and challenge to acute political thinking which the free republic had promoted disappeared. In place of the clash of parties and principles there were now court intrigues, and in place of the defence of a free republic against foreign despotisms there were the manoeuvrings of a Spanish satellite pretending to a spurious independence. Historical and political writing in Florence, centred no longer on free and informal discussions in private patrician houses and gardens but on a stuffy ducal academy, deteriorated to the dull encomium of the Christian virtues of the Medici dukes.

The German cities

While the victory of the German princes over the emperor in the thirteenth century had given the German cities their chance of autonomy it had also kept them from expanding their territories as the Italian cities had done. For Augsburg, Nuremberg or Strasbourg there were no smaller neighbouring city states to swallow up. Militarily, the German cities remained on the defensive against their princely neighbours. In the fourteenth century they formed leagues for defence and for a time it looked as if the Swabian and Rhenish Leagues would emerge as major political forces in Germany. They might have done if the emperors had consistently supported them. But the Luxembourg and Habsburg emperors of the period were themselves first and foremost territorial princes. The cities were for them useful sources of money, even acceptable allies against this or that rival. But a permanent imperial-urban alliance directed against the princes and aimed at re-establishing an effective monarchy in Germany (as has been suggested by some German historians) was beyond the emperors' political horizon; nor does imperial experience in Italy suggest that it would have worked very well. The Swabian and Rhenish Leagues were therefore defeated and dissolved, although a considerable number of German cities managed to maintain their virtual independence.

The Hanseatic League

Characteristically, it was in northern Germany, far from the centres of what was left of imperial power, that the cities were politically more successful. Here an alliance of cities, headed by Lübeck and called the Hanseatic League, defended itself successfully against the attacks of local German princes and of the kings of Denmark. The League controlled the grain, fur and timber exports from the Baltic to western Europe and the reverse trade of salt, textiles and spices into northern and eastern Europe. Their merchants had privileged settlements from London to Novgorod; they dominated and exploited the economic life of Norway and Sweden and at times their warships controlled the Sound, the sea passage between Denmark and southern Sweden. For two centuries, until the early sixteenth century, they managed to contain the most formidable threat to their prosperity, the attempts of the Dutch and the English to break their monopoly of the Baltic carrying trade.

Since most of the German cities had kept the feudal nobility outside their walls they were at least spared the feuds and, hence also, the slide into one-man rule of the Italian cities. The German princes tried to incorporate neighbouring free cities into their own territories. They did not need to become princes of city states. But, inevitably, the German cities had their share of social and factional conflict. In some cities the guilds gained footholds in the city councils. Everywhere, those outside the tight circle of patricians were jealous of their power. In some cities, such as Nuremberg, the patricians always kept the guilds out of the town council. In many others they gained at least a foothold, but only rarely did they come to control the policies of the cities, as on occasion they did in the Flemish city of Ghent (see Ch. 5, pp. 310–11, & Ch. 6, p. 361).

In contrast to what happened in Renaissance Florence, the civic struggles of the German cities gave rise to no far-reaching intellectual discussions. Or rather, such discussions in the sixteenth century took a religious form, because the civil struggles, and even the defence of city autonomy, became inextricably linked with the conflicts arising from the Reformation. They will be discussed in the volume *Early Modern Europe 1500–1789*.[8]

The Swiss Confederation

Only in the mountain valleys of the Alps have medieval republican institutions survived until the present day. As early as 1291 the three peasant, or forest, cantons of Schwyz, Uri and Unterwalden had formed an Everlasting League for the maintenance of law and for mutual defence against the counts of Habsburg. (In 1273 Count Rudolf IV had been elected king of Germany as Rudolf I, the first of the Habsburg kings and emperors. He had died in 1291.) In the following two centuries the cantons made alliances and federations with Zürich, a city dominated by guilds of artisans, and with Berne, a city ruled by a military patriciate. Gradually up to ten cantons joined in a complex multi-tiered system of confederation. It took a long time for a sense of nationality to develop in this ethnically and linguistically varied area.

Its boundaries remained fluid, and many neighbouring towns and areas were at varying times willing to join the confederation. Its great strength lay in its strategic situation astride the St Gotthard and other passes on the trade routes from Italy to Germany. But, even more important, it provided the Swiss with what the Italian and German city states never had: a native and patriotic army recruited from the highly trained and savage pikemen of the overpopulated mountain villages. In the fourteenth and early fifteenth centuries they beat off a series of Habsburg attempts to subdue them. In 1476 and 1477 they crushed the Burgundian duke Charles the Bold's feudal armies and in 1499 they fought off the emperor Maximilian I. After that, none of the great powers would risk again attacking the Swiss until the wars of the French Revolution. The story of the Swiss national hero William Tell, the marksman who was forced by an Austrian governor to shoot an apple from his son's head, appeared as early as the 14th century.

The cities of western and eastern Europe

Both east and west of the broad belt of German and Italian city states, the European towns never gained full independence; but they often achieved considerable administrative autonomy. From the fifteenth century, the princes began to attack this autonomy. They were most quickly successful in eastern Europe where the cities were relatively small and powerless compared with the alliance of territorial princes and great landowners. In the west it took longer. In England, it is true, the monarchy found little resistance. London, overawed by the royal fortress of the Tower and economically linked with the court at Westminster, had little opportunity or, indeed, desire to play an independent role. The other English cities were too small to have such ambitions. The rulers of the Netherlands, the dukes of Burgundy, had greater problems. Flanders, the richest and most populous of the provinces, was dominated by the three great cities of Ghent, Bruges and Ypres. Like other towns which had flourished in the twelfth and thirteenth centuries, these cities had suffered from loss of population and from the economic contraction of the fourteenth and fifteenth centuries. But Ghent and Bruges were still larger and richer than any other city north of the Alps except Paris. They had won a great degree of self-government from the counts of Flanders and they virtually controlled the assemblies of the Flemish estates which would often meet several times a year. Inside the cities, the guilds had won seats on the town councils. Twice, in the fourteenth century, the weavers' guild spearheaded revolutionary movements in Ghent, although the leaders of the revolutionary regimes which they set up were patricians, well-to-do members of the traditional urban ruling families. The popular movements failed to establish themselves for more than a short time, but the revolutionary traditions of the great Flemish cities lived on and erupted in periodic clashes between the Flemish towns and the Burgundian dukes. Only gradually were the dukes able to increase their control over the cities, and one aspect of the revolt of the Netherlands against Philip II of Spain[9] was an attempt by the towns to reverse this trend and regain some of their former liberties.

The pattern was similar in France. 'The general government and administration of the kingdom . . . and also of our good towns and cities . . . belongs to us alone', declared Louis XI

(1461–83); but fully effective royal control had to wait until the development of the system of intendants in the seventeenth century.[10]

The Renaissance: intellectual life

The memories of the lost world of the ancients, the over-whelmingly powerful feeling of the need to recover at least some of its splendours, these had been among the most persistent forces in European society from the very moment of the collapse of the Roman Empire in the west. They had led to repeated 'renaissances', and the quest for immitation had spurred men to new achievements (see Ch. 2, pp. 126–27). The curiously paradoxical but dynamic nature of this quest had been recognized in the twelfth century in the metaphor of the contemporary dwarfs on the shoulders of the ancient giants (see Ch. 3, p. 201).

In the Italian Renaissance of the fourteenth and fifteenth centuries a new concept was added to this appreciation of the world of antiquity. This was a sense of history and of historical development. To Petrarch, Rome was still the ideal: 'What else then, is all history, if not the praise of Rome?' But the Roman Empire had been impaired, debilitated and almost consumed at the hands of the barbarians. What had followed was a dark age, not even worth writing about. This lamentable condition had not yet changed; but Petrarch was not without hope for the future and he believed that 'Rome would rise again if she but began to know herself. . . . This sleep of forgetfulness will not last for ever. When the darkness has been dispersed, our descendants can come again in the former pure radiance.'

For Petrarch's contemporary, Boccaccio, the light had already begun to break with Dante: ''Twas he who may be truly said to have brought back dead poesy to life.' By the fifteenth century there was a clearly defined idea of a long dark age following on the fall of Rome from which the present was actually emerging by a self-conscious return to the precepts and values of the ancients, and this was happening thanks to the efforts of a few great men: the poet Dante, the painter Giotto and, not least, Petrarch himself. Men saw themselves as living in a new age, and the excitement which even now, after another five hundred years, we can still feel about the civilization of the Renaissance in Italy owes much to this vision.

Plate 6.3 Padua: Arena Chapel – *Lamentation*, by Giotto.
Giotto was the first painter who systematically translated the
naturalistic figures and gestures of Gothic sculpture into pictorial
space, here a fresco wall-painting. The figures look solid and three-
dimensional. Their emotions are recognizably human grief in which
even the weightlessly swirling angels join. As in many later works of
the Renaissance, there is a great deal of symbolic meaning in this
painting. Thus the tree, on the right, recalls the Tree of Knowledge
which withered with Adam's Fall but is restored by the death of
Christ. Giotto's source for this symbol may have been a passage about
the Tree in Dante's *Divine Comedy*. The two great Florentines knew
and admired each other.

Burckhardt and the origins of the Renaissance

This view of the re-awakening or rebirth of the values of the
ancient world became the classical view of the Renaissance,

especially as it was formulated in mid-nineteenth century by the French historian Jules Michelet and the Swiss Jacob Burckhardt. For Burckhardt the Renaissance meant the revival of antiquity, the 'discovery' by man of the world around him and of himself as an individual, and it also meant an interpretation of the Italian Renaissance state 'as a work of art'. Much of this general interpretation of the Renaissance is still accepted by modern historians in the enormous amount they have written on the subject in the last hundred years. What is no longer accepted is the view of the Middle Ages in Petrarchian terms as a dark age. It is not just that we now appreciate more clearly the cultural achievements of the Middle Ages – and in the preceding chapters we have tried to explain and emphasize them – we also see more clearly how the Renaissance developed without a clear break within the late-medieval Italian city civilization.

Where transalpine Europe was feudal, courtly and ecclesiastical, the Italian cities were commercial, republican and secular. The urban businessman's need for secular education, his habit of calculating his business chances, his concern in the running of his city – all this led him to create rational institutions for his activities. At the same time his rational, outward looking life-style began to colour all other activities, and even religious attitudes. 'Without doubt you, fleeing from the world, can fall from heaven to earth,' wrote Coluccio Salutati to a friend who was praising the traditional religious life, 'While I, remaining in the world, can raise my heart to heaven.'

Even the courts of the despots maintained much of the urbanity of the city republics. Precisely because they lacked the legitimacy of the old-established monarchies, the despots were anxious to show off their own and their cities' greatness by displaying the talents of their citizens and of all who could be attracted to their courts in scholarship, literature and the arts. They were imitated by other rich and powerful citizens or city corporations. It may even be that the fact of economic contraction in the later fourteenth and in the fifteenth century inclined men to invest in building and the patronage of artists rather than in business ventures.

If these were the social and psychological conditions for the great flowering of creative activities of the Italian Renaissance – and they have rarely been as favourable in European history – yet the shape of such activities can only partly be derived from these conditions. Equally important were the already existing traditions of these activities, their own inherent logic, and the influence of their most distinguished and original protagonists; in other words, the impact of genius on thinking and on art. By the second quarter of the fifteenth century these developments had gone so far that, without a clearly definable break, they were beginning to produce a new kind of civilization, the civilization which can truly be called the Renaissance.

The humanists

Humanist was the name given to those who studied and taught the humanities and more specifically, classical literature. There was nothing new about this. But Petrarch, Salutati and their followers and students were better latinists than most of their predecessors. Their superior methods of linguistic and literary criticism, coupled with their enormous enthusiasm for the writings of the Romans, enabled them both to publish hitherto unknown classical works and do so in far more accurate editions than the Middle Ages had known. Salutati used his position as chancellor to collect a splendid library of classical authors and he set the tone for many others in a position to do the same. The invention of printing and its rapid spread in Italy in the last quarter of the fifteenth century gave an enormous impetus to these activities. For the first time scholars could read the best editions of the classics in their own cities and correspond with other scholars about the same text.

Equally important was the recovery of Greek literature. There had always been some men in medieval western Europe who knew Greek. But most scholars had read the Greek classics in translation and often in translations from the Arabic. In the fifteenth century, however, knowledge of Greek began to spread and the major universities established chairs of Greek. A whole new world of thought was being opened up by the humanists.

The effects of the work of the humanists were far-reaching and diverse. They created a new form of education, which was to remain influential, both in Europe and America, until well into the present century. In contrast to the medieval tradition of imposing a strict discipline of behaviour and learning on the child, the humanists sought to develop his personality and self-reliance. They used the Greek and Roman classics, as well as the

365

teachings of the Church, to define the values with which they wished to imbue their charges.

In humanist education were exemplified at least two of Burckhardt's concepts, the revival of antiquity and the discovery of the individual. But the same was true for all their activities. In Florence they met at the villa of Marsilio Ficino (1433–99), the translator of Plato, and they called themselves, in the classical manner, an academy. Ficino's academy, patronized by Lorenzo de Medici (himself a considerable latinist and poet), was as yet largely unstructured and unsystematized, but it was to be the model of countless academies founded all over Europe in the following centuries as centres for different types of learning.

Another of Burckhardt's characterizations of the civilization of the Renaissance, the discovery of the world around man, was not one of the humanists' primary aims. Yet, in their quest for the writings of antiquity, they also discovered the large corpus of the scientific work of the ancients and this they also proceeded to publish. The results were unexpected. Differences of opinion among the ancient philosophers and theologians were well known ever since Abelard had deliberately pointed to them (see Ch. 3, pp. 200–01). Men had tried to cope with such differences according to their own philosophical inclinations. Not so with natural science in which Aristotle, Galen and the other relatively few ancient writers who were known in the Middle Ages had been regarded as unquestioned authorities. Now, with greater knowledge of the ancients, it became apparent that they, too, often contradicted each other. There was only one way around this problem: to find out for oneself. This was mostly done in order to prove one or other of the ancient schools of thought correct against the others. The effect was to provide a strong stimulus for original scientific work; and the best minds engaged in it sometimes found that none of the theories of the ancients had been correct and that completely new ones had to be devised. Perhaps the most striking example of this process occurred outside Italy: Copernicus' discovery of the motion of the earth around the sun.[11]

It was at this point that the efforts of the humanists became involved with the work of the late-medieval scholastic philosophers. These dominated the universities and continued to do so until the seventeenth century. The humanists usually attacked them for their rigid methods and the aridity of much of their

366

philosophical discussions. It was they who smeared the scholastic philosophers with the story that they liked to argue about how many angels could dance on the point of a needle. (This problem had indeed, once been set, but as a deliberately humorous exercise in scholastic method for undergraduate student) In fact, scholastic philosophers, from Roger Bacon onwards, had made considerable advances in mathematical and physical thinking. When these were combined with humanist learning and criticism, the results could be very original.

Nicholas of Cusa

This intermingling of various cultural streams is particularly evident in the life and work of Nicholas of Cusa (1401–64). Cusa combined German mysticism, Italian university life and an active church career as a bishop, cardinal and church reformer with, first, conciliar and, later, papal leanings. His personal devotion he had learned from the 'brothers of the common life', a typically late-medieval devotional association of laymen in the Netherlands. He studied theology at Heidelberg and Cologne and was deeply affected by the mystical teachings of the early fourteenth-century Dominican, Meister Eckhart. Unlike oriental mystics, Eckhart had used the limitations of language as a focal point for understanding that God is beyond all description. Cusa, in his turn, used this Eckhartian appreciation of God in conjunction with Italian mathematical and artistic ideas to argue that God was absolutely infinite and that the universe was only limited by God. Therefore there was no end to the universe, except in God. On this basis Cusa proposed, in his theological work *Of Learned Ignorance* (1440), the stunningly original view that the universe was of infinite size and that it was homogeneous and not, as had always been held, made of different types of substance ascending from the impurity of earth through the celestial spheres to the ultimate purity of heaven. For Cusa, other stellar areas were 'each like the world we live in, a particular area of one universe which contains as many such areas as there are uncountable stars'. In *The Idiot* (1450), dialogues on the mind and on wisdom, Cusa replaced the traditional innate Platonic ideas of the human mind with an innate knowing power. This power had to seek its knowledge directly from nature and experience. Thus Cusa advanced a highly worldly form of Neo-Platonism, a view which eroded the Aristotelian hierarchical view of reality and which, at the same time, turned men towards the study of the natural universe.

For Nicholas of Cusa, and indeed for his contemporaries, such philosophical and theological speculations had practical implications. Cusa argued that, since God was both immanent in the universe and transcended it, no religion could exist outside God. Christianity was an all embracing truth, but it included within itself the partial truths of all other religions. In a book on the Koran, written in 1461, he viewed Islam in this light – not, as had been normal among Christians, as the work of the devil. Cusa's friend, Pope Pius II (1458–64), actually thought of negotiating with the Sultan in these terms, to persuade him to become a Christian by pointing out to him the religious and cultural superiority of Christianity, as he saw it. In return he would offer Mehmed the title of emperor. Not surprisingly, neither the conqueror of Constantinople nor the vast majority of the learned pope's fellow Christians would have anything to do with such negotiations. Nor was the pope himself sufficiently optimistic to leave off his own grandiose, but in the end unsuccessful, attempts to organize a crusade against the Turks.

Literature

In Italy vernacular literature developed later than in France and Germany. When it did, from the turn of the thirteenth and fourteenth century, it did so in close conjunction with, and often in imitation of, Latin literature. Dante, Petrarch and Boccaccio, its first great exponents, all wrote in Latin as well as in Italian. Dante's greatest work, the *Divine Comedy*, was clearly based on classical models and especially on the Roman poet Virgil whom Dante actually casts as his guide in his journey through the infernal regions. Dante's poem is a kind of Christian epic with the true character of the epic of encompassing a whole world, the Italy of his own time. With Petrarch, Italian reaches its first great height in lyric poetry and especially in that strict but immensely flexible poetic form, the sonnet. Both the sonnet and the tale, or short story, as Boccaccio told it in the racy prose of his *Decameron*, were to have a triumphantly popular career in the literature not only of Italy but of every European country, right into the present century.

368

So impressed were the Italians with the achievements of Dante, Petrarch and Boccaccio that the Tuscan dialect in which they wrote became the literary language *par excellence* of the whole of Italy. It was in the courts of the despots and princes that the poets of the Renaissance found their most ready audience and, indeed, their own most convenient livelihood. It was at the courts that they developed the characteristic Renaissance cross between the epic and the romance of chivalry, a genre that could be elegant, witty and even moving but which had lost the elemental and dramatic impact of the earlier medieval epics such as the *Chanson de Roland* or the *Nibelungenlied*. Even the first lines of Ariosto's poem *Orlando Furioso* signal this change. Where the *Nibelungenlied* began: 'In olden times we heard much of heroes and their labours' (a rather similar beginning to Virgil's 'Of arms and the man I sing'), Ariosto immediately softens, widens and so to speak civilizes his poetic intent:

> Of ladies and cavaliers, of arms and loves,
> Of courtliness and daring adventures I sing.[12]

Art and architecture

If the Italian humanists and literati of the fifteenth and sixteenth centuries saw the period from Dante and Petrarch as one of rebirth, so did the artists and architects. In Giotto (1266/7–1337) they saw the first artist to attempt a faithful representation of nature, the world around man. The sixteenth-century Florentine painter and historian of the art of the Renaissance, Vasari, put this view in its classic form:

> In my opinion painters owe to Giotto, the Florentine painter, exactly the same debt they owe to nature, which constantly serves them as a model and whose finest and most beautiful aspects they are always striving to imitate and reproduce. For after the many years during which the methods and outlines of good painting had been buried under the ruins caused by war it was Giotto alone who, by God's favour, rescued and restored the art, even though he was born among incompetent artists.

Giotto, a poor farm boy, was spotted by the painter Cimabue and taken by him to Florence.

> After he had gone to live there, helped by his natural talent and instructed by Cimabue, in a very short space of time Giotto not

369

only captured his master's own style but also began to draw so ably from life that he made a decisive break with the crude traditional Byzantine style and brought to life the great art of painting as we know it today, introducing the technique of drawing accurately from life, which had been neglected for more than two hundred years.[13]

Vasari's passage shows the Renaissance view of Byzantine art – a misconception from which uneducated opinion has never entirely recovered – and also the enormous importance of the master artist's workshop as a training ground for gifted boys and young men in Renaissance Italy. It was, however, only in the fifteenth century that Masaccio (1401–28), now with a complete command of the techniques of perspective, was able to carry the imitation of nature to perfection. Relatively few paintings of antiquity were known, but the remains of ancient architecture were there for everyone to see, and especially so in Rome itself. In architecture it was therefore a self-conscious revival of antiquity that was the dominant theme and it found its first great practioner in Filippo Brunelleschi (1377–1446), the architect of numerous churches and of the cupola of the cathedral in Florence. In sculpture the two streams, the imitations of nature and of antiquity, were more evenly balanced, especially in the sculptures of Donatello (1386–1466). The excavation of a number of now famous classical figures, the Apollo Belvedere and the Laocoön group among them, provided artists with the sculptural ideals they wished to emulate.

Soon the theory and practice of art was taken a step further. For Leone Battista Alberti (1404–72), architect, theoretician and admirer of Nicholas of Cusa, both classical and naturalistic representation depended on the principle of harmony. This was the harmony of the universe, the macrocosm, which was mirrored (among many other things) in the proportions of the human figure. It was apprehended, following the philosophy of

Plate 6.4   Florence: Duomo with Brunelleschi's dome.
The dome was to span the largest area yet attempted. A series of architects gave up the attempt, until Brunelleschi solved the technical problem by using a chain of huge oak beams to prevent the weight of the dome from pushing the walls of its base outward. At the same time he designed the most elegant dome in Italy. The campanile, the big, marble-faced bell tower, on the left, was designed by Giotto.

371

Plate 6.5   Equestrian statue of 'Gattamelata' by Donatello, Padua.
Erected in 1453, coincidentally the year of the fall of Constantinople,
Donatello's equestrian monument to the general Erasmo da Narni
(whose nickname means honeycat) was the first large, free-standing
equestrian bronze statue to be cast successfully since Roman times.
Donatello was inspired by antique statues like that of Marcus Aurelius
(see Plate 1.1) whose classical nobility he both rivals and recaptures in
this masterpiece of the early Renaissance.

Nicholas of Cusa, by the knowing power of the human mind. The
proportions of classical art and architecture followed the 'natural'
proportions of the human body, and these proportions were now
to be reflected in both art and in buildings. The discovery of
nature, of man, and of antiquity were here joined in a deliberate
programme; and such a programme was undoubtedly accepted
by the majority of Italian artists in the fifteenth and early
sixteenth centuries. Here, too, was the basis for the phenomenon
of the *uomo universale*, the universal man of the Renaissance.
Cusa, Alberti, Leonardo da Vinci and Michelangelo were
universal men, not because they happened to be performers of
genius in a great many different fields, but because they saw all
their activities as participating in the knowledge of the universal

harmony which God had embodied in the cosmos. In the sense that the artist's mind held the vision of a whole and all its parts, his mental capacity was a reflection of the divine mind. In the sense that the artist's creation presented the visual reality of a whole and its parts, his work presented an image of the divine creation, nature.

It was above all in the use and perfection of perspective that Renaissance artists saw themselves as both imitating nature and as creating a visual world. For through perspective the artist actually 'creates' space, or rather, the illusion of three-dimensional space. In this space, objects are not shown as they are and as they are known to be, but as they appear to the observer from one quite definite point. Thus objects nearer this point appear larger than those further away. The artist constructs space geometrically. It is therefore homogeneous, no one part of space being different from any other. In this respect, the artist's space is not at all like that of Aristotle's universe where space varied according to whether it was on earth or in the spheres of the heavens. It is rather like Nicholas of Cusa's conception of space which remains the same throughout an infinite universe. In truth, of course, Cusa got the inspiration for his view from his artist friends.

The status of the Renaissance artist

In this Pythagorean way of thinking (after the Greek philosopher Pythagoras, fifth century BC) everything in nature could be reduced to a mathematical essence, and this, as we shall see, appeared to be born out by music (see p. 379). Artist, mathematician and philosopher were therefore held to be on the same exalted level. From the time of Alberti, the great artists of the Italian Renaissance no longer regarded themselves as only craftsmen in the medieval sense but as thinkers and creators. Their contemporaries accepted this evaluation and treated them accordingly. To outsiders it was a startling experience. 'Here I am a gentleman,' wrote the German painter Dürer from Venice in 1506, 'at home I am a parasite.' Dürer (1471–1528) was happy to conform to the new role ascribed to the creative artist. His self-portrait looks remarkably like the traditional representation of Christ, Leonardo's resembled God the Father. Michelangelo, with his broken nose, could not compete in this respect, although one

Plates 6.6 and 6.7 Leonardo: *Self-portrait*; Dürer: *Self-portrait*.
If Leonardo in this self-portrait in his old age seems – rather startlingly
– to imitate the traditional representation of God the Father as a wise
old man with a beard, he did not actually think of himself as a god.
But he did think of himself as a creator and he wrote this idealized
description: 'The painter sits in front of his work at perfect ease. He is
well dressed and wields a very light brush dipped in delicate ￧colours.
He adorns himself with the clothes he fancies; his home is clean and
filled with delightful pictures and he is often accompanied by music or
by the reading of various beautiful workes.' (Quoted in M. Kemp,
Leonardo da Vinci. J. M. Dent: London 1981, pp. 177–79).

Dürer's more elaborate self-portrait in oils of the artist aged 28 is
also not meant to suggest that he is God. But the beautiful, long-
haired, serious-looking and mature young man was precisely the

374

image which was usually given to Jesus Christ. Both Leonardo and Dürer, like other contemporary artists, thought of their role as creators after the Creator.

could speculate about his *Moses*; but his contemporaries referred to him as *il divino*, the divine – an epithet derived from the Neoplatonic notion of divine, creative frenzy. The other side of the coin was that the less successful artist tended to become Bohemian.

375

Urban and court culture in the North

The precepts and ideals of the Italian Renaissance were slow to penetrate beyond the Alps. Only in the sixteenth century they became the predominant influence on the intellectual, literary and artistic life of transalpine Europe, and at that time they were almost immediately modified by new cultural sensibilities which derived from the religious and emotional upheaval of the Reformation and the Counter-Reformation.[14] It was not that northern Europe, and especially its educated classes, remained entirely ignorant of what was happening in Italy. On occasion, Italian influence was both evident and fruitful, as in Geoffrey Chaucer's *Canterbury Tales* (*c.* 1390) whose form clearly owed much to Boccaccio as well as to French models, but which, in both their subject matter and in the social and religious values they assume, are essentially English and medieval.

Basically, this society was feudal and courtly and so was its pattern of literary and artistic values. This is very clear with the French chroniclers of the fourteenth and fifteenth centuries who accepted a romantic view of chivalry and in these terms recorded the battles of the Hundred Years' War. Courage and knightly conduct were held to be more important than tactics. The chronicler Froissart tells how, in the battle of Crécy, a great English victory over the French in the early stages of the Hundred Years' War, some Cornish and Welsh men on foot, i.e. the despised peasants, killed many French

> earls, barons, knights and squires . . . at which the king of England was exasperated. . . . The king of Bohemia said to his attendants: 'Gentlemen, you are all my people, my friends and breathren at arms this day; therefore, as I am blind, I request you to lead me into the engagement that I may strike one stroke with my sword.' The knights consented, and in order that they might not lose him in the crowd, fastened all the reins of their horses together, placing the king at their head. . . . He and his companions fought most valiantly, however, they advanced so far that they were all slain, and on the morrow they were found on the ground with all their horses tied together.[15]

The Burgundian Court

The aristocratic ethos was even clearer at the greatest centre of literacy and artistic patronage north of the Alps, the court of the

Burgundian rulers of the Netherlands. Here chivalry, with elaborate tournaments (see Plate 5.5), literary and musical competitions and gluttonous feasts became a deliberate life-style that was imitated by European courts until well into the sixteenth century. Clerical moralists inveighed against the luxury and waste of such festivities at the time, and modern historians have often described them with raised eyebrows and puritan condescension. Yet these festivals fulfilled an important function in an aristocratic and military society. Apart from hunting, they were the only alternative to war that was acceptable to young noblemen who had been brought up to see in fighting the justification for their existence. At the same time, by the important role assigned to ladies in these festivals and by the shifting of at least part of the competition into the fields of poetry and music, they had a generally civilizing influence on the European nobility. They were, of course, as the moralists never ceased to preach, very expensive and wasteful; but they were much less so than real war, and infinitely less destructive. The Flemish cities whose taxes largely paid for this princely extravagance and who were never slow to criticize princely politics, hardly ever raised objections to the great festivals. In the *joyeuses entrées*, the ceremonial entries of a new prince in the cities, at which he swore to uphold their privileges, the city councils vied with the court in staging elaborate and expensive entertainments.

Painting

Not all of this culture, however, was make-believe. A strong streak of realism broke through, on occasion, even in the chronicles. It was most prominent in the Netherlands school of painting. Jan van Eyck (*c.* 1395–1441), Roger van der Weyden (*c.* 1400–64), Hans Memling (*c.* 1430/35–94) and the other great artists of the period were patronized by the court and the great ecclesiastical institutions, but they worked mainly in Bruges and Antwerp and not at court. They cultivated the exact representation of nature as much as the Italians, their use of perspective was almost as accomplished and they antedated the Italians in the practice of portraiture. In the very different cultural traditions of western Europe we therefore find, in the late Middle Ages, aspects of the 'discovery of the world' and the 'discovery of the

Plate 6.8 Jan van Eyck: *The Chanoine van der Paele,* **1434–36.**
This very realistic portrait of the old canon, with his book and eye
glasses, is typically a detail of a painting of the Madonna with saints
and the donor (i.e. the person who paid for the painting), the canon.
Van Eyck was one of the earliest and greatest masters of oil painting,
although it is no longer thought that he invented the technique.

individual' which Burckhardt had seen as the distinctive qualities
of the Italian Renaissance.

What we do not find in the north is the self-conscious imitation
of classical models or the acceptance of classical proportions in
painting and sculpture. Not only were there no classical models
to imitate, as there were in Rome, but the traditions of the
splendid Gothic art of the thirteenth and fourteenth centuries
could not be as easily discarded as in Italy where they had never
been as strong as north of the Alps.

There was, no doubt, some mutual influence between the
artists of Italy and the Netherlands – the Italians learned the technique of oil painting from the Netherlands – but, until the end
of the fifteenth century, artistic developments in Italy and in the
north were parallel, rather than dependent on each other. The
realism of Netherlands art was a realism of detail, rather than a

conception of a whole work of art as an act of recreation of the real nature of the world around us.

Basically, Netherlands art remained within the late-Gothic style of most of the rest of Europe. This does not mean, of course, that artistically the paintings of van Eyck or Memling were inferior to those of their Italian contemporaries, any more than Byzantine art as such was inferior to Italian Renaissance art, even though the Italians themselves thought so.

Music from the Middle Ages to the Renaissance

Music and dance are as old as the human race and as basic as speech. It is surprising, therefore, how little notice most general historians have taken of these very human activities. Yet for every one person, in historical times, who read a book there were a hundred who listened to music, who sang and who danced. Most religions have quite naturally used music and dance in their rituals, and both arts have therefore always had ritualistic and sacral, as well as popular and pleasurable, characteristics. This duality set up tensions which became particularly important in the history of music in Christian Europe.

These tensions were, however, pre-Christian. Plato had spoken of good and bad or, rather moral and immoral music; for Plato, like everyone else, was convinced of the enormous psychic powers of music. The early Church fathers took over this classical belief in the powers of music which, for them, was reinforced by specific biblical examples such as David's playing the harp and calming Saul's madness. St John Chrysostom – he who around AD 400 had taken such an optimistic view of the Roman Empire – voiced a common opinion:

> Nothing elevates the soul, nor gives it wings, nor liberates it from earthly things, as much as a divine chant, in which rhythm and melody form a real symphony [literally, sounding together].

A hundred years later, Boëthius transmitted to the Christian church another classical belief. This was Pythagoras' theory, developed by Plato, that musical harmony was of the same nature or, at least, that it reflected the mathematical harmony of the universe. This was a belief which had arisen quite naturally when stringed instruments fell into the hands of a mathematician. For

379

the halving of a given length of string produces the octave of the original tone. The division of the string in the ratio of 2/3 gives the musical interval of the fifth and a division of 3/4 the fourth. These intervals are basic to human musical perception and in fact appear in the music of nearly all cultures. A more striking demonstration of the (apparent or real) mathematical structure of natural phenomena could hardly be imagined.

These three beliefs, the psychic powers of music, the existence of moral and immoral music, and the mathematical relationship of music to the structure of the universe continued in varying degrees to dominate men's attitude towards music at least until the Romantic movement of the nineteenth century. The last belief, the mathematical relationship of music to the structure of the universe, is found also in the records of Chinese music. There was certainly no direct influence in either direction. It seems more likely that a sophisticated analysis of musical intervals is likely to reveal their mathematical relationship.

Early Church music

For the early Church, the most immediate problem was the second, the distinction of moral and immoral music. It found itself surrounded by music which it could only regard as pagan. 'It must be banned,' cried Clement of Alexandria (d. 215), 'this artificial music which injures souls and draws them into feelings snivelling, impure and sensual, and even a Bacchic frenzy and madness.'

But it was not just pagan music; it was music itself which, through its powers over the mind, could be dangerous. 'When it happens to me to be more moved by the singing than by what is sung,' St Augustine wrote in his *Confessions*, 'I confess myself to have sinned criminally, and then I would rather not have heard the singing.'

Yet Augustine and the other church fathers did not condemn music outright. They were content to banish musical instruments from church services since they were too reminiscent of pagan practices. References to instruments in the bible and especially in the psalms they were constrained to explain away as allegories.

After the fall of the Roman Empire in the west, the problem of pagan or secular music seems to have become less urgent. Secular music certainly continued to exist although little is known about it. All more elaborate musical development occurred within the Church. Most important was the development of Gregorian chant, or plain song. It was represented iconographically as a dove sitting on Gregory the Great's shoulder and whispering melodies to him which he then dictated to a scribe. We now know that the origins of Gregorian chant go back to Greek and Hebrew sources, long before the great pope, but that Gregorian chant as it has come down to us through a living tradition came mainly from the heartland of the Frankish kingdom, north-east France, and dates from the eighth and ninth centuries. It is indeed, best seen as a part of the Carolingian Renaissance.

By this time, the old puritanism had broken down to a considerable extent. The composers of Gregorian chant were introducing tropes (singular: tropus) or musical additions and interpolations, with elaborate ornamentation and complex rhythms. Musical instruments reappeared in the churches, and especially organs – originally a Hellenistic invention of the third century BC. Soon no major church would be without an organ. From the tenth century we read of an instrument in Winchester cathedral with two manuals and, supposedly, 400 pipes needing two players and 70 blowers.

The troubadours

It was inevitable that, with the growing wealth and sophistication of secular society, there should also be a revival of sophisticated secular music. Its centre was the court-life of southern France in the twelfth century, its agents the troubadours (perhaps from *trouver*, to find or invent; or, possibly, from tropus). These were poet-composers, usually of good and sometimes even of high social standing who sang alone or in small groups and always with instrumental accompaniment.

The Provençal-speaking troubadours did not survive the destruction of their courtly patrons in the Albigensian 'crusades' of the early thirteenth century. But their music and their influence survived for another century, in northern France and in Germany in the trouvères and the Minnesingers (*Minne* = love). They represented the musical aspect of the cult of chivalry At the same time, they re-established secular music as what it had been for the early fathers, a serious competitor and one which had an insidious tendency to influence church music.

381

Perhaps even more alarming was the influence of popular music. There was no time when villagers had not danced to the sound of instruments, whether played by a gifted neighbour or by travelling minstrels who were professional musicians, often doubling as acrobats, jugglers, clowns and animal tamers. Such traditions of popular entertainment, which have survived in the circuses of our own day, went back to Roman times and beyond. The Church always looked on them sourly but did not usually condemn them outright. Popular dances were taken up by court society and refined into elegant court dances. Popular tunes found their way into church music.

The theologians had come to regard music as the handmaiden of the Church. But, as will happen with handmaidens, music liked to show herself at her most attractive, with ornaments borrowed from the secular world, and thus her attractions tended to compete with those of her mistress. St Bernard, as one would expect, sounded an early alarm: 'Let chant be full of gravity; let it be neither worldly nor too rude and poor . . . let it be sweet yet without levity. . . . For it is no slight loss of spiritual grace to be distracted from the profit of the sense by the beauty of the chant. . . .' St Bernard's last point, that music had a distressing capacity to make the hearer forget about the words, was to be repeated by countless theologians until well into the sixteenth century.

Music in the later Middle Ages

While such revivals of religious puritanism in music were relatively frequent, their effect was usually limited and rarely lasted for long periods of time. Church musicians were not usually theologians. They and their congregations generally preferred the finest and most elaborate music for the praise of God. And so, popular, courtly and church music came more and more to influence each other, to the benefit of music generally. The philosophical status of music remained assured. With the rise of the universities, music was habitually taught together with geometry, arithmetic and astronomy, as the *quadrivinium* in the liberal arts course.

The two most important developments in music were polyphony and musical notation. Polyphony is the sounding of two or more lines of melody at the same time. Gradually composers introduced varied rhythms in these lines of melody and greater and greater freedom in the use of intervals and, therefore, of harmony. So novel did this advance seem that the musicians of the fourteenth century spoke of their music as the *ars nova*, the new art, which they contrasted, perhaps rather too dramatically, with the *ars antiqua* of the twelfth and thirteenth centuries.

Some form of musical notation was used already in Roman times and transmitted to the early Middle Ages; but it did little more than indicate ups and downs in pitch, in the way the classical teachers of rhetoric had done, together with the use of letters of the alphabet for certain notes. But from the ninth and tenth century, Italian and French musicians began to introduce symbols for note values, for time signatures and, through the use of parallel lines and clefs, for the fixing of exact pitch. It took several centuries to perfect the system as we now know it. Its importance was enormous. Not only could composers now indicate with a great degree of exactitude what they wanted performers to do, they could now also write pieces of a length and of a harmonic and rhythmic subtlety and complexity that had previously been unthinkable.

Music in the Renaissance

By the fifteenth century, the musical life of Europe had become splendidly rich and varied. The bigger cities had their town musicians, usually small bands of brass players, royal and ducal courts vied with each other in their patronage of professional singers and instrumentalists, while leisured ladies and gentlemen sang to the accompaniment of lute (originally an Arabic instrument and word) and keyboard instruments. Perhaps most important of all was still church music. England, northern France and the Netherlands, the latter country with its rich cities and magnificent Burgundian court, became the centres of schools of music from which professional musicians travelled all over Europe. They perfected the medieval polyphonic tradition and their masses and motets, their vespers and magnificats have rightly been seen as the musical counterpart to the classical harmonies of High Renaissance painting, while their virtuoso handling of the mathematical intricacies of counterpoint may be seen as analogous to the Renaissance painters' pride in mastering the geometry of perspective. The non-professional can best study

and enjoy this music and that of the Middle Ages, from Gregorian chant to the troubadours and the *ars nova*, in the authentic performances that are available on gramophone records.

Conclusion

The Carolingian Renaissance and the Renaissance of the twelfth century had been confined to monasteries and the princely courts and to the church schools and universities. The Italian Renaissance of the fifteenth and early sixteenth centuries had a much wider basis: the educated laymen of the cities. The Church, the courts, and sometimes the universities were still important. The citizens of the towns regarded themselves as good Christians and their cities as Christian communes. But their basic view of life was secular. As they had built their cities, amassed their wealth in trade and organized their own forms of government, so they looked on nature and the world around them as something that it was not only legitimate but necessary to investigate and control. To Salutati, the humanist chancellor of Florence, it seemed that a philosopher should no longer lead a purely contemplative life but should plunge himself into the secular affairs of the state, just as Cicero had done. Here was a link with the ancients, a 'renaissance', which an Abelard in the twelfth century could not have conceived of. To the painters and sculptors it meant the investigation of nature through the study of anatomy and, in an artistic sense, the control of nature through its correct representation in perspective. Leonardo da Vinci and others went further and attempted to invent machines for the control of natural forces.[16]

Plate 6.9   Raphael: *School of Athens*, 1509–11.
This fresco in the Vatican is one of the great climaxes of the tradition of which Giotto had been one of the first exponents. All technical problems of perspective representation had now been solved. Raphael created a marvellously harmonious universe, both visually and in the content of this painting. There is a group of philosophers with Plato (left) and Aristotle in the centre, Archimedes, the Syracusan mathematician of the third century BC drawing geometrical figures, Raphael himself and other contemporary artists and architects at the sides, and Michelangelo sitting by himself in the foreground. Every figure is complete in itself, yet all are joined in a grandiose pictorial composition.

Even the Church and the princely courts could not escape this urban atmosphere. Nicholas of Cusa, the philosopher, theologian and church reformer, saw the soul's road to God not only in withdrawn, monastic contemplation but also in the study of God's creation, the world and the universe, and he advised his followers to go into the market place and to learn from craftsmen. The papal court itself became a centre of the new learning and the new art and it was emulated by the courts of the secular princes.

By contrast, the Spanish kingdoms, France and England remained still essentially agrarian, feudal and clerical. Their cities never achieved political independence and, in consequence, never developed an urban aristocratic lay ethic. Chivalry, clerical education, scholastic philosophy, mystical piety and the now traditional Gothic style in architecture and art continued to dominate western European life. It was an end, a brilliant end, of a long tradition, rather than a beginning.

Nevertheless, transalpine Europe, too, was changing. The quasi-autonomous cities of the Netherlands and the fully independent cities of Germany developed cultural traditions which had some similarities to the Italian Renaissance, especially in the visual arts.

Educated men read and learnt from the Italian humanists. Characteristically, however, they turned their skills to biblical and theological studies, and it was against the background of these studies that Luther and Zwingli were to launch their attacks against the Catholic Church.

Only gradually, in the course of the sixteenth and early seventeenth centuries, were the cultural traditions of the Italian Renaissance fully assimilated by the rest of Europe. But, by this time, they had already become mingled with and subject to new social forces and ideas which had their origins outside Italy.

References and Notes

1. See H. G. Koenigsberger, *Early Modern Europe. 1500–1789*; History of Europe, Longman: London 1987, Ch. 2.
2. Quoted in H. Baron, *Cicero and the Roman Civic Spirit in the Middle Ages and the early Renaissance*. University Press: Manchester 1938, p. 17.

3. Quoted in A. Murray, *Reason and Society*. University Press: Oxford 1978, pp. 20–21.
4. N. Machiavelli, *Istorie fiorentine*, Bk 5. IV.
5. See H. G. Koenigsberger, *Early Modern Europe 1500–1789*; History of Europe. Longman: London 1987, Ch. 2.
6. N. Machiavelli, *The Prince*, Ch. 15.
7. Quoted in G. L. Mosse, *The Holy Pretence*. Basil Blackwell Press: Oxford 1957.
8. See H. G. Koenigsberger, *Early Modern Europe 1500–1789*; History of Europe. Longman: London, 1987, Ch. 2.
9. Op. cit. Ch. 2.
10. See Ch. 5.
11. See Ch. 4.
12. L. Ariosto, *Orlando Furioso*, Canto I, 1.
13. G. Vasari, *The Lives of The Artists*, trans. George Bull. Penguin Books: Harmondsworth 1965, pp. 57–58.
14. See H. G. Koenigsberger, *Early Modern Europe 1500–1789*; History of Europe. Longman: London 1987, Chs 1 and 2.
15. Jean Froissart, *Chronicles of England, France, Spain*, trans. T. Johnes, New York 1901; quoted in D. Herlihy (ed.) *Medieval Culture and Society*. Harper Torch Books: New York 1965, p. 390.
16. See H. G. Koenigsberger, *Early Modern Europe 1500–1789*; History of Europe. Longman: London 1987, Ch. 5.

Index